LOOK NOW

The World in Facts, Stats, and Graphics

London, New York,
Melbourne, Munich, and Delhi

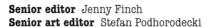

Senior editor Jenny Finch
Senior art editor Stefan Podhorodecki

Editors Steven Carton, Niki Foreman,
Ashwin Khurana, and James Mitchem
Designers Sheila Collins, Mik Gates, Jim Green,
Katie Knutton, Philip Letsu, and Hoa Luc

Managing editor Linda Esposito
Managing art editor Diane Thistlethwaite

Category Publisher Laura Buller

Picture researcher Nic Dean
Production editor Andy Hilliard
Senior production controller Angela Graef
Jacket design Smiljka Surla
Jacket editor Matilda Gollon
Design development manager Sophia Tampakopoulos

Additional consultants Keith Lye,
Professor Denise Cush, John Woodward
and Dr. Adrian Campbell

First published in the United States in 2010 by
DK Publishing, 375 Hudson Street
New York, New York 10014

Copyright © 2010 Dorling Kindersley Limited

10 11 12 13 14 10 9 8 7 6 5 4 3 2 1
175776 – 04/10

DK books are available at special discounts when purchased in bulk for sales promotions,
premiums, fundraising, or educational use. For details, contact:
DK Publishing Special Markets, 375 Hudson Street, New York, New York 10014
SpecialSales@dk.com

A catalog record for this book is available from the Library of Congress

ISBN: 978-0-7566-6286-8

Hi-res work flow proofed by MDP, U.K.
Printed and bound by Hung Hing, China

Discover more at
www.dk.com

LOOK NOW

The World in Facts, Stats, and Graphics

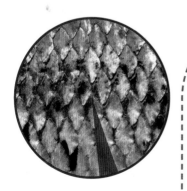

Written by Joe Fullman, Ian Graham, Sally Regan, and Isabel Thomas

Consultant Dr. Stephen Scoffham

Contents

Earth

Our world is a 4.5-billion-year-old ball of rock, orbiting the Sun at a distance of 93 million miles (149.6 million km). Earth is a living planet—not only is it home to around 1.7 million known species of plants and animals, but the planet itself is constantly changing. Over millions of years, its surface has been shaped into the continents and oceans that we see today—the crust is constantly shifting, mountains are forged, and rock is being recycled.

Earth in Space

Compared to the vastness of the cosmos, our planet is almost infinitesimally small. Earth forms just a minute part of the solar system, which is itself just a tiny speck in the Milky Way galaxy. According to scientists, the Milky Way is just one of more than 100 billion galaxies making up the universe, each containing billions of stars.

Bigger and bigger

As big as it is now, the universe is getting bigger all the time. It was formed about 13.7 billion years ago in a giant explosion known as the Big Bang and continues to expand outward in all directions.

5. Our supercluster

Even the Local Group is dwarfed by our supercluster, a massive structure around 150 million light-years across. At its center is the Virgo cluster, a group of galaxies surrounding a giant black hole. The universe is thought to be made up of many superclusters, separated by great voids.

4. The Local Group

The Milky Way is part of an even larger structure, the Local Group, which contains around 30 galaxies. These galaxies come in three main types: spiral, elliptical, and irregular. The Andromeda Galaxy, a spiral galaxy, is the closest major galaxy to the Milky Way.

3. Our galactic realm

The Sun and its neighboring stars slowly revolve around the center of our spiral-shaped Milky Way galaxy. The Milky Way is surrounded by a number of smaller satellite galaxies, the closest being the Sagitarrius Dwarf. The nearby Small and Large Magellanic Clouds are visible only from Earth's Southern Hemisphere.

2 million light-years away

1 million

Ursa Minor

Milky Way

NGC 68222

NGC 185

Fornax

Andromeda (M31)

DDO 210

Triangulum (M33)

Pheonix

Pegasus

250,000 light-years away

200,000

150,000

100,000

Sagitarrius Dwarf

Small Magellanic Cloud

Milky Way

Large Magellanic Cloud

Sculptor

Ursa Minor

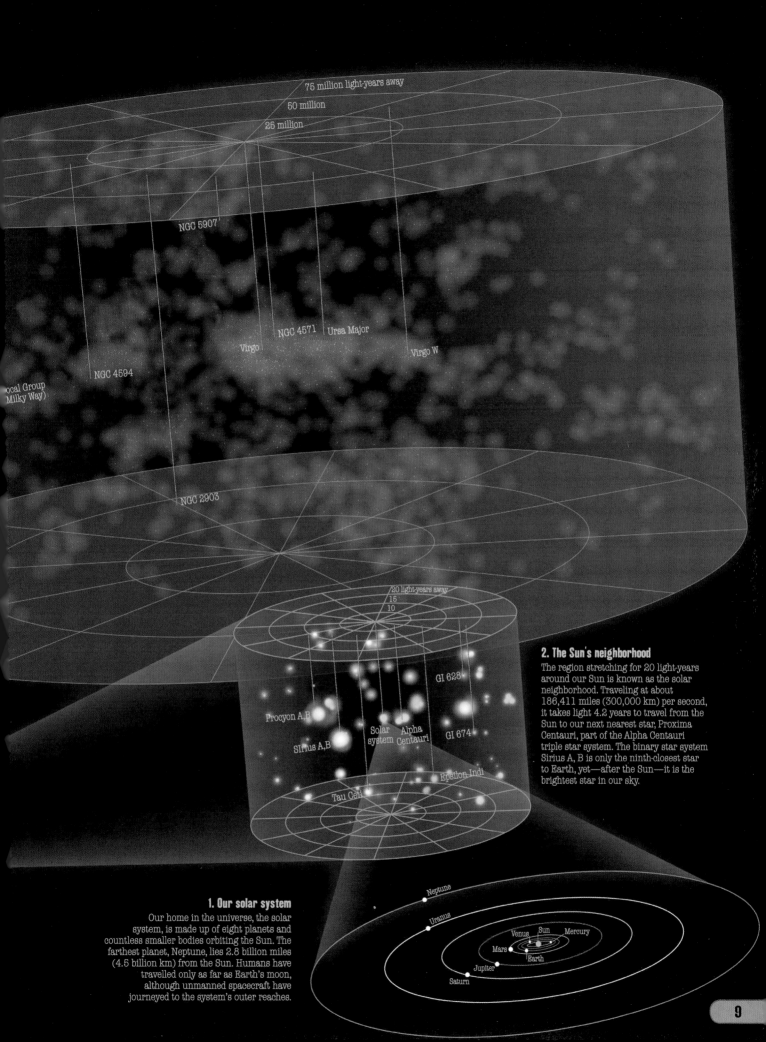

75 million light-years away

50 million

25 million

NGC 5907

NGC 4571   Ursa Major

Virgo

Virgo W

NGC 4594

Local Group
(Milky Way)

NGC 2903

20 light-years away
15
10

GI 628

Procyon A,B

Solar   Alpha
system   Centauri

GI 674

Sirius A,B

Epsilon Indi

Tau Ceti

2. The Sun's neighborhood

The region stretching for 20 light-years around our Sun is known as the solar neighborhood. Traveling at about 186,411 miles (300,000 km) per second, it takes light 4.2 years to travel from the Sun to our next nearest star, Proxima Centauri, part of the Alpha Centauri triple star system. The binary star system Sirius A, B is only the ninth-closest star to Earth, yet—after the Sun—it is the brightest star in our sky.

Neptune

Uranus

Venus   Sun   Mercury

Mars

Earth

Jupiter

Saturn

1. Our solar system

Our home in the universe, the solar system, is made up of eight planets and countless smaller bodies orbiting the Sun. The farthest planet, Neptune, lies 2.8 billion miles (4.5 billion km) from the Sun. Humans have travelled only as far as Earth's moon, although unmanned spacecraft have journeyed to the system's outer reaches.

Story of Earth

Earth evolves

As this time line shows, for much of its existence Earth was almost completely empty of life. The lush, green planet that we know today only began to take shape after life from the oceans colonized the land 475 MYA—nearly 4 billion years after the birth of the planet.

In the long story of Earth, human life doesn't start until the last few chapters. The planet formed along with the rest of the solar system 4.6 BYA (billion years ago), and the first life-forms appeared around 3.8 BYA. However, complex life evolved only 600 MYA (million years ago), while the first humans did not arrive until 200,000 years ago. If you imagine all of Earth's history as a single year, modern humans would not appear until 20 minutes before midnight on December 31.

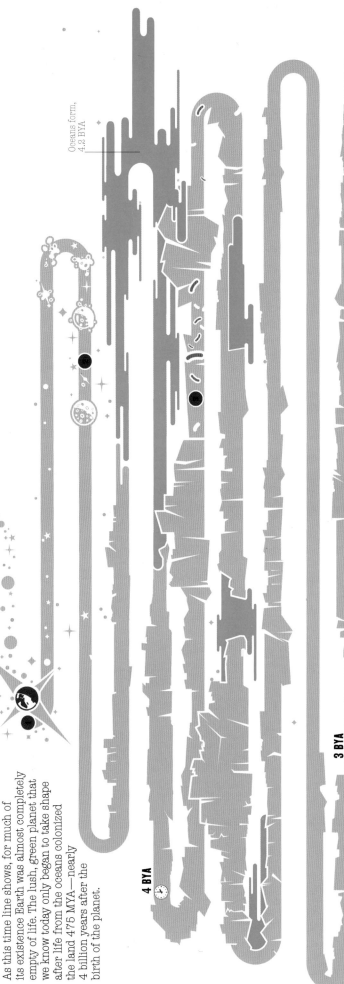

Oceans form, 4.2 BYA

4 BYA

3 BYA

2 BYA

First insects, 400 MYA

Amphibians appear, 360 MYA

First reptiles, 300 MYA

Flowering plants appear, 135 MYA

First birds, 150 MYA

1 BYA

Modern humans

Homo sapiens, the species that would come to dominate the planet, first evolved in Africa around 200,000 years ago.

1. Formation of Earth 4.6 BYA

A giant cloud of gas and dust clumps together to form Earth. The planet's surface is molten, but gradually cools.

2. Formation of the Moon 4.5 BYA

A planet-size object collides with Earth, sending matter out into space, where it comes together to form the Moon.

3. First life 3.8 BYA

The first single-cell life-forms appear in the oceans. Life remains microscopic for more than 3 billion years.

4. Photosynthesis begins 2.5 BYA

Cyanobacteria, a type of algae, start using the Sun's energy to feed on the hydrogen in water, releasing oxygen.

5. First multicellular fossils 1.2 BYA

Single-cell organisms grow more advanced. Multicellular—but still microscopic—life evolves.

6. First known animals 570 MYA

The first large soft-bodied animals were the Ediacarans. They lived in the sea and looked similar to modern jellyfish.

7. First life on land 475 MYA

Plants and fungi begin to grow at the water's edge. Arthropods are the first animals to colonize the land.

8. Carboniferous period begins 360 MYA

For 70 million years, plants take over more and more land, forming great swamp forests that became today's coal.

9. Mass extinction 251 MYA

Earth's history is punctuated with mass extinctions. This one wiped out more than 90% of all species.

10. First dinosaurs 230 MYA

Reptiles dominate the world for the next 165 million years, becoming the largest land animals of all time.

11. First mammals 210 MYA

Early mammals were small, nocturnal creatures. They begin to thrive—and get larger—after the fall of the dinosaurs.

12. Extinction of the dinosaurs 65 MYA

An asteroid impact destroys around 75% of the world's species, ending the dinosaurs' reign.

13. Earliest human ancestors 7 MYA

Humans and modern apes are thought to have evolved from a common ancestor around this time.

14. First footprints 3.5 MYA

Fossilized footprints suggest that early human ancestors start walking on two legs around 3.5 MYA.

15. Out of Africa 100,000 years ago

Modern humans begin to migrate from Africa to other continents, kick-starting the human colonization of Earth.

11

Planet Earth

Our home planet is a ball of rock 7,916 miles (12,740 km) in diameter. At its center is an iron core, surrounded by a large mass of moving rock known as the mantle. Above this is the thin, rocky crust that supports all of the planet's life. If planet Earth were the size of a peach, the part that humans inhabit would only be the thickness of the fruit's skin.

Inside Earth

This cutaway diagram shows the layers that make up Earth's internal structure. The blue ring represents the narrow blanket of gases held in place by Earth's gravitational pull that protects the planet from extremes of temperature.

Earth's atmosphere

Although the atmosphere technically extends thousands of miles up, around three-quarters of the gases it contains are within a thin layer next to the surface called the troposphere. Relatively speaking, you don't have to go very far to get into outer space—NASA considers anyone who travels above 50 miles (80 km) an astronaut.

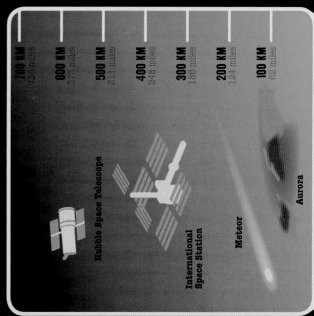

700 KM
435 miles

600 KM
373 miles

500 KM
311 miles

400 KM
248 miles

300 KM
186 miles

200 KM
124 miles

100 KM
62 miles

Hubble Space Telescope

International Space Station

Meteor

Aurora

8,000 KM
4,971 miles

7,500 KM
4,660 miles

7,000 KM
4,350 miles

6,500 KM
4,039 miles

6,000 KM
3,728 miles

5,500 KM
3,417 miles

5,000 KM
3,107 miles

4,500 KM
2,796 miles

4,000 KM
2,485 miles

3,500 KM
2,175 miles

3,000 KM
1,864 miles

2,500 KM
1,553 miles

2,000 KM
1,243 miles

1,500 KM
932 miles

Troposphere

The lowest layer of the atmosphere is the troposphere, and it rises to around 10.5 miles (17 km) from the surface. It is where most weather occurs and is the only part of the atmosphere that supports human life. Above the troposphere, the ozone layer protects Earth from the Sun's harmful ultraviolet radiation.

15 KM
9.3 miles

10 KM
6.2 miles

5 KM
3.1 miles

0 KM
0 miles

5 KM
3.1 miles

Commercial airliner

Cirrus clouds

Migrating birds

Cumulus clouds

Hot-air balloon

Birds

OCEAN

CONTINENTAL CRUST

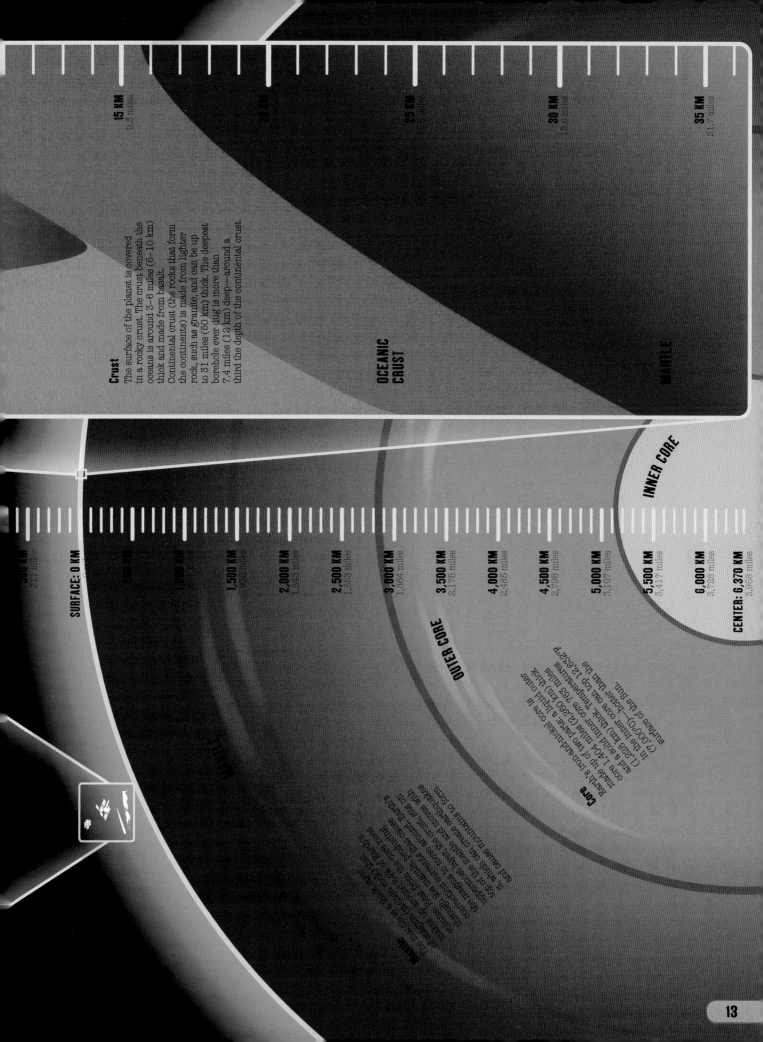

15 KM
9.3 miles

20 KM
12.4 miles

25 KM
15.5 miles

30 KM
18.6 miles

35 KM
21.7 miles

Crust

The surface of the planet is covered in a rocky crust. The crust beneath the oceans is around 3–6 miles (5–10 km) thick and made from basalt. Continental crust (the rocks that form the continents) is made from lighter rock, such as granite, and can be up to 31 miles (50 km) thick. The deepest borehole ever dug is more than 7.4 miles (12 km) deep—around a third of the depth of the continental crust.

OCEANIC CRUST

MANTLE

INNER CORE

OUTER CORE

500 KM
311 miles

SURFACE: 0 KM

1,000 KM
621 miles

1,500 KM
932 miles

2,000 KM
1,243 miles

2,500 KM
1,553 miles

3,000 KM
1,864 miles

3,500 KM
2,175 miles

4,000 KM
2,485 miles

4,500 KM
2,796 miles

5,000 KM
3,107 miles

5,500 KM
3,417 miles

6,000 KM
3,728 miles

CENTER: 6,370 KM
3,958 miles

MANTLE

Core

Earth's iron-and-nickel core is made up of two parts: a liquid outer core 1,404 miles (2,260 km) thick and a solid inner core 765 miles (1,228 km) thick. The inner core temperatures can top 13,632°F (7,000°C)—hotter than the surface of the Sun.

Mantle

This planet is a thick layer of rock. The upper section is a little over 248 miles (400 km) thick. It is made up of molten rock that moves through convection, like water in a boiling pan. The upper section of the mantle is the top of the mantle is connected to the crust, and moves with it, which can create earthquakes and cause mountains to form.

13

Plate Tectonics

We tend to think of the continents as permanent and immovable, but nothing could be further from the truth. Earth's hard outer crust is divided into a number of large pieces called tectonic plates, which constantly move on top of a layer of softer molten rock, known as the mantle. Carried along these moving plates are the seven main continents we know today: Asia, Africa, Europe, Australia, Antarctica, North America, and South America.

Transform boundary

The San Andreas Fault is part of a transform boundary that slices across California's coastal region. A transform boundary is where plates move sideways past each other. Occasionally, the plates get stuck, creating an immense amount of stress. The longer the plates remain stuck, the more energy builds up, eventually to be released as an earthquake when the plates finally pull free.

A giant jigsaw

Earth's tectonic plates fit together like the pieces of a giant rock jigsaw puzzle . Geological events, such as earthquakes, volcanoes, and mountain formation, may occur on the plate boundaries, depending on whether they are coming together, pulling apart, or slipping past one another.

NORTH AMERICAN PLATE

PACIFIC PLATE

COCOS PLATE

CARIBBEAN PLATE

ANTARCTIC PLATE

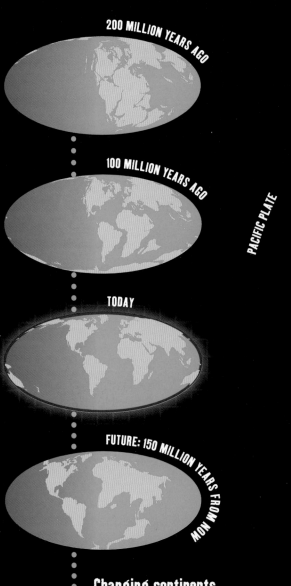

200 MILLION YEARS AGO

100 MILLION YEARS AGO

TODAY

FUTURE: 150 MILLION YEARS FROM NOW

Changing continents

Around 200 million years ago, Earth's continents were fused together in a giant supercontinent known as Pangaea. Since that time, they have gradually drifted apart and will continue drifting to new positions in the future.

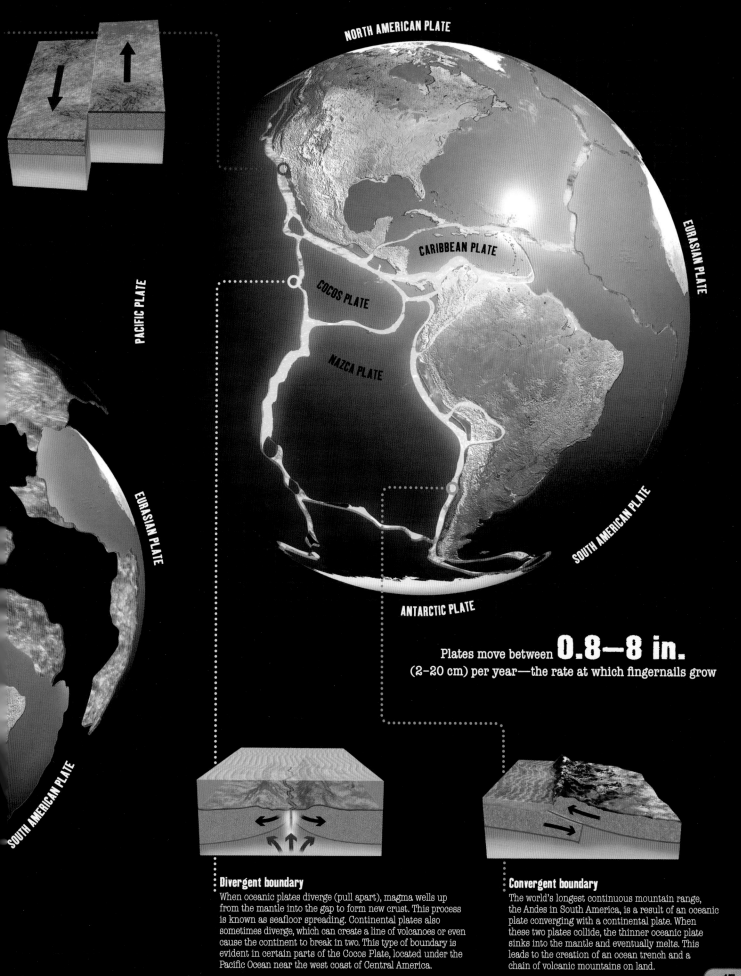

NORTH AMERICAN PLATE

EURASIAN PLATE

CARIBBEAN PLATE

PACIFIC PLATE

COCOS PLATE

NAZCA PLATE

EURASIAN PLATE

SOUTH AMERICAN PLATE

SOUTH AMERICAN PLATE

ANTARCTIC PLATE

Plates move between **0.8–8 in.**
(2–20 cm) per year—the rate at which fingernails grow

Divergent boundary

When oceanic plates diverge (pull apart), magma wells up from the mantle into the gap to form new crust. This process is known as seafloor spreading. Continental plates also sometimes diverge, which can create a line of volcanoes or even cause the continent to break in two. This type of boundary is evident in certain parts of the Cocos Plate, located under the Pacific Ocean near the west coast of Central America.

Convergent boundary

The world's longest continuous mountain range, the Andes in South America, is a result of an oceanic plate converging with a continental plate. When these two plates collide, the thinner oceanic plate sinks into the mantle and eventually melts. This leads to the creation of an ocean trench and a chain of volcanic mountains on land.

Mountains

A mountain is formed by slow but extremely powerful movements of Earth's crust, which gradually push rocks up above the surrounding landscape. Though definitions vary across the world, peaks above around 2,000 ft (600 m) are usually considered mountains, while those below that are hills. Asia has the world's highest mountains, while Australia is the flattest and lowest continent.

Highest mountains

Here, you can see the highest mountains on each one of the seven continents. The 10 highest mountains in the world are all in the Himalayas and are all still growing at a rate of around 2.5 in. (6 cm) a year, as the Indian tectonic plate continues to push into the Eurasian plate.

First ascent

In 1953, New Zealander Edmund Hillary and Nepalese Tenzing Norgay became the first people to set foot on the summit of Mount Everest.

From the top of Mount Everest, you can see for more than **100 miles** (160 km), and you can even see the curvature of Earth's surface

10,000 M	32,800 ft	
9,500 M	31,170 ft	
9,000 M	29,550 ft	
8,500 M	27,890 ft	
8,000 M	26,250 ft	
7,500 M	24,600 ft	
7,000 M	22,960 ft	
6,500 M	21,320 ft	
6,000 M	19,680 ft	
5,500 M	18,040 ft	

Airplane

Most commercial airplanes cruise at altitudes of between 29,850 ft and 39,700 ft (9,100 m and 12,100 m). Air at that altitude is thinner, allowing the planes to fly faster while using less fuel.

Geese

Bar-headed geese are among the world's highest-flying birds. Every year they migrate right over the top of Mount Everest.

Mount Everest 29,035 FT (8,850 M) ASIA

Death zone

Above 23,000 ft (7,000 m), there is too little oxygen to sustain human life. Climbers must bring their own oxygen supply if they venture up this high.

Spiders

The tiny jumping spider has been found up to 22,000 ft (6,700 m) above sea level on the slopes of the Himalayas, making it one of the world's highest-living creatures.

Aconcagua 22,841 FT (6,962 M) SOUTH AMERICA

Mount McKinley 20,321 FT (6,194 M) NORTH AMERICA

Kilimanjaro 19,331 FT (5,892 M) AFRICA

Elbrus 18,510 FT (5,642 M) EUROPE

16

5,000
16,400 ft

4,500 M
14,760 ft

4,000 M
13,120 ft

3,500 M
11,480 ft

3,000 M
9,840 ft

2,500 M
8,200 ft

2,000 M
6,560 ft

1,500 M
4,920 ft

1,000 M
3,280 ft

500 M
1,640 ft

0
SEA LEVEL

Mountain goat
Mountain goats live high above the reach of most predators, using specially adapted hooves to help keep their footing on the rocky terrain.

Iced tea
It's difficult to enjoy a cup of tea on a mountain. Water boils at a lower temperature the higher you get, so the farther up the mountain you are, the colder your tea will be.

Vinson Massif
16,050 FT (4,892 M) ANTARCTICA

Unseen summit
Much smaller than the world's tallest mountains, the Vinson Massif—located in the frozen heart of Antarctica—wasn't discovered until 1958. Its summit was first scaled in 1966 by a U.S. team.

At a length of almost **10,000 miles** (16,000 km), the world's longest mountain range is the mid-Atlantic ridge, which runs below the Atlantic Ocean

Kosciuszko
7,310 FT (2,228 M) AUSTRALIA

Scenic convenience
Situated just below the summit of Mount Kosciuszko, one of the world's highest flushable toilets serves some of the mountain's 30,000 visitors every year.

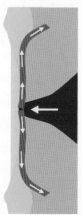

Tallest tower
The tallest structure ever built is dwarfed by even the smallest mountains. The Burj Khalifa in the United Arab Emirates is 2,717 ft (828 m) tall and has 160 floors.

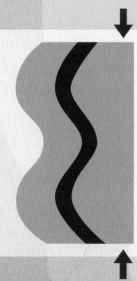

TYPES OF MOUNTAINS

Fold mountains
The most common type of mountain is formed when two tectonic plates collide, pushing the rocks along their borders up into a series of high folds.

Block mountains
Sometimes tectonic plates pull apart, creating giant cracks in Earth's crust and splitting rock into giant blocks, some of which are pushed up to form new mountains.

Volcanoes
Volcanoes occur in places where molten rock rises to the surface, most commonly on the borders between tectonic plates. Over time, the lava may build up to form a cone-shaped mountain or, at sea, a volcanic island.

UNDERSEA GIANT
Everest is the tallest mountain on dry land, but the biggest mountain on Earth is Mauna Kea, which rises to around 33,500 ft (10,205 m) from the floor of the Pacific Ocean. Just 13,796 ft (4,205 m) pokes above the ocean's surface. This diagram shows how the two would compare if they were lined up.

MOUNT EVEREST

MAUNA KEA

Quakes and Shakes

Earthquakes are sudden, unpredictable shocks to Earth's surface. They can range from tiny, barely noticeable vibrations to enormous rolling ground waves that crack roads, flatten buildings, and break bridges in half. Most are caused by the movements of Earth's tectonic plates. Where two plates move past one another, parts sometimes get stuck. The pressure then builds up until the plates finally break free, creating a ground tremor.

Earthquake-resistant architecture
Most deaths following earthquakes are caused by falling buildings. Scientists can predict where but not when a quake will strike. People can protect themselves against harm by constructing buildings that can withstand the tremors. The 49-story Transamerica Building in San Francisco, California, a well-known earthquake zone, is designed to sway by up to 12 in. (30 cm) either side. In 1989, its design allowed it to survive, unscathed, a 7.1-magnitude earthquake.

Richter scale
The magnitude (size) of an earthquake can be calculated using a number of different methods. The best known is the Richter scale, which measures the amount of ground motion caused by a quake using an increasing number scale, with 1 as the weakest. The top of the scale is currently 9.5, but stronger earthquakes in the future could push the scale into double figures.

Seismographs
The instrument that measures the magnitude of earthquakes is called a seismograph. It records an earthquake's strength in the form of a wavy line: the more the line wiggles up and down, the stronger the earthquake.

Measuring the shakes
A seismograph consists of a base, which shakes during a quake, and a weight, which does not. Measuring the contrast between the two gives the quake's magnitude.

Aftershocks
Earthquakes are usually short-lived. Even the largest ones typically last less than a minute, although they are often followed by smaller quakes known as aftershocks.

1

1.0
These tiny tremors take place deep underground. They can be detected by seismographs, but not usually by people.

2

2.0
You might just about be able to feel a 2.0 earthquake if you were sitting still, upstairs in a house.

3

3.0
Though hardly serious, a 3.0 quake is certainly noticeable, with enough force to make hanging objects swing.

4

4.0
You might easily mistake a 4.0 quake for a large truck passing by your house, causing trees to sway and windows to rattle.

5

5.0
A size-5.0 quake may cause liquids to spill from glasses, windows to break, doors to swing open, and (some) people to fall over.

Tsunamis

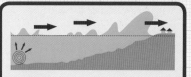

A really big quake on the seabed can cause a series of large waves to form, known as a tsunami. These waves can travel at speeds of up to 435 mph (700 km/h), causing huge levels of destruction when they hit land.

Top 10 earthquakes

The earthquakes listed are the biggest to occur since records began. Larger quakes probably took place in the past, but went unrecorded by science. The largest quakes are not necessarily the most destructive, however, as this depends on how built-up the area is and how prepared for an earthquake it is.

1	Chile	9.5	05/22/1960
2	Price William Sound, Alaska	9.2	03/28/1964
3	West Coast of Northern Sumatra	9.1	12/26/2004
4	Kamchatka	9.0	11/01/1952
5	Off the coast of Equador	8.8	01/31/1906
6	Rat Islands, Alaska	8.7	02/04/1965
7	Northern Sumatra, Indonesia	8.6	03/28/2005
8	Assam Tibet	8.6	08/15/1950
9	Andreanof Islands, Alaska	8.6	03/09/1957
10	Southern Sumatra, Indonesia	8.5	09/12/2007

Predicting earthquakes

Although scientists can measure the size of earthquakes and identify the regions most likely to suffer from future quakes, they cannot predict exactly when an earthquake will strike.

Great Chilean Earthquake—9.5

The biggest earthquake since detailed records began struck Chile in 1960. It triggered landslides, tsunamis, and caused a volcano to erupt, killing thousands.

6

6.0
It can be difficult to stand up during a 6.0 earthquake. The walls in some buildings may crack and tiles may fall from roofs.

7

7.0
A size-7.0 earthquake can cause a great deal of damage, cracking roads and moving houses on their foundations.

8

8.0
Typical damage from an 8.0 quake can include twisted railroad lines, broken roads and bridges, burst pipes, and collapsed buildings.

9

9.0
These intense quakes send out undulating waves across the surface, which unleash total destruction and cause large-scale loss of life.

Earthquake frequency

Although we tend to think of earthquakes as rare events, an estimated 2,500 happen every day—which is nearly 1 million a year. Most, however, are too weak to be felt.

MAGNITUDE	ESTIMATED NUMBER EACH YEAR
2.5 or less	900,000
2.5–5.4	30,000
5.5–6.0	500
6.1–6.9	100
7.0–7.9	20
8 or greater	One every 5 to 10 years

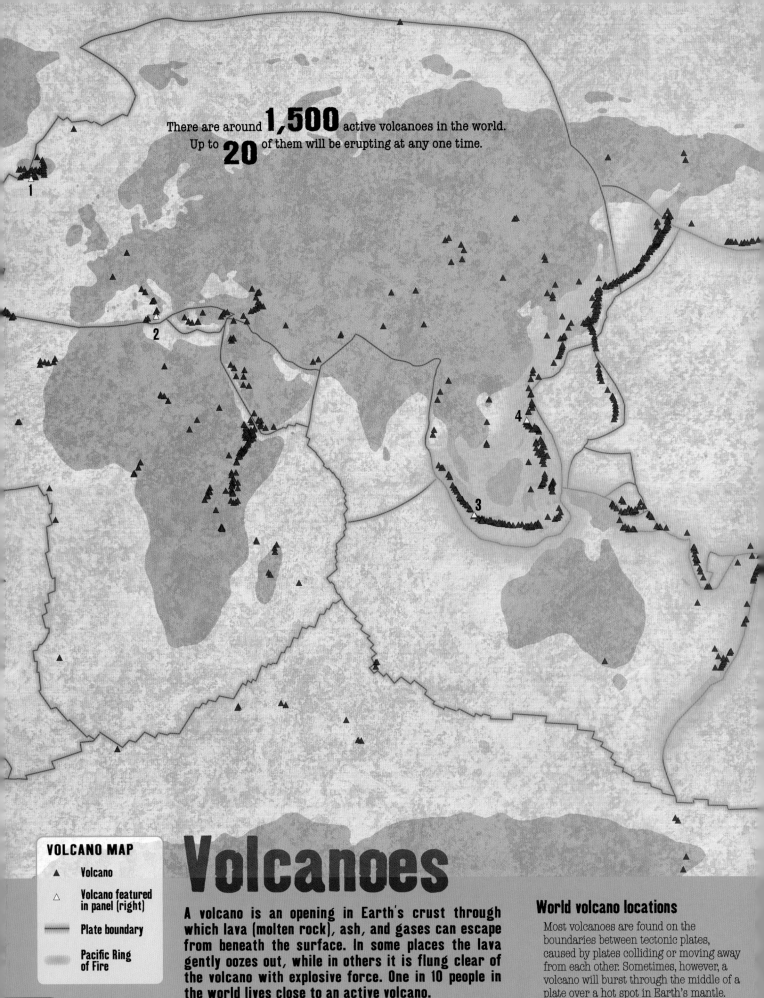

There are around **1,500** active volcanoes in the world. Up to **20** of them will be erupting at any one time.

VOLCANO MAP

▲ Volcano

△ Volcano featured in panel (right)

━ Plate boundary

　 Pacific Ring of Fire

Volcanoes

A volcano is an opening in Earth's crust through which lava (molten rock), ash, and gases can escape from beneath the surface. In some places the lava gently oozes out, while in others it is flung clear of the volcano with explosive force. One in 10 people in the world lives close to an active volcano.

World volcano locations

Most volcanoes are found on the boundaries between tectonic plates, caused by plates colliding or moving away from each other. Sometimes, however, a volcano will burst through the middle of a plate over a hot spot in Earth's mantle.

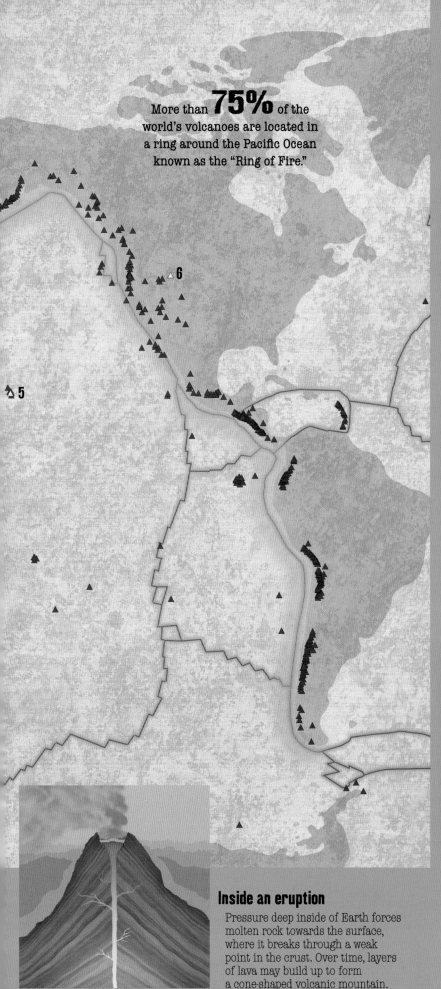

More than **75%** of the world's volcanoes are located in a ring around the Pacific Ocean known as the "Ring of Fire."

6

△ 5

Inside an eruption

Pressure deep inside of Earth forces molten rock towards the surface, where it breaks through a weak point in the crust. Over time, layers of lava may build up to form a cone-shaped volcanic mountain.

1. Surtsey, Iceland

In 1962, the island of Surtsey didn't exist. It was formed by a volcanic eruption on the seabed, 426 ft (130 m) below the surface, which built layers of lava that emerged above the waves in November 1963. The eruption ended in 1967.

2. Etna, Italy

Etna is continental Europe's largest volcano and one of its most active, sending out great plumes of ash, which make the surrounding soils extremely fertile. Despite the risk of lava flows, farms and villages cover its lower slopes.

3. Krakatoa, Indonesia

Heard more than 3,100 miles (5,000 km) away, the 1883 eruption of Krakatoa killed more than 35,000 people. The blast demolished the old volcano, but since then a new one—Anak Krakatoa, or "child of Krakatoa"—has emerged.

4. Pinatubo, Philippines

Mount Pinatubo's 1991 eruption was one of the most explosive of the 20th century. It destroyed nearly 5,000 homes and sent a thick cloud of ash and gas into the air that lowered global temperatures by 0.9°F (0.5°C.)

5. Kilauea, Hawaii

The Hawaiian island chain was formed from lava bubbling up through a hot spot in the ocean floor. Kilauea lies on the south side of Hawaii's Big Island and is one of the most active volcanoes on Earth.

6. Yellowstone, U.S.A

Though its forested landscape looks serene, Yellowstone National Park is the site of a huge network of ancient volcanoes. A giant cauldron of magma 40 miles (60 km) across heats the park's many geysers.

Surface rocks

Most surface rocks are just visitors. They will eventually be worn away by the weather or dragged down into the bowels of Earth by tectonic plate movements. Replacement rocks are brought to the surface through the processes of uplift and volcanic eruptions.

Igneous intrusion

Magma doesn't always break the surface. Sometimes it collects in an underground reservoir, or magma chamber. Here, it will gradually cool and harden to form a mass of solid rock known as an igneous intrusion. Uplift may then bring this intrusion to the surface.

Subduction

When two tectonic plates come together, one may get pushed down (or subducted) beneath the other into Earth. As the plate is dragged deeper, and the temperature and pressure increase, it will begin to melt.

Igneous extrusion

In some places, rising magma will escape through a volcano on to Earth's surface—when it becomes known as lava. Sometimes this lava contains gases that make it erupt with explosive force. Surface rocks formed from cooled lava are known as extrusive igneous rocks.

The oldest rocks on Earth's surface are thought to be more than

3.8 billion years old

UPLIFT

Magma

Magma is molten rock that forms deep below Earth's surface. It can reach temperatures of 2,372 °F (1,300°C). As magma rises and cools it solidifies to form igneous rock.

Melted rocks

Rock that has been pushed deep into Earth at a subduction zone may melt, forming magma. This happens to all three types of rock—igneous, sedimentary, or metamorphic—although different rocks melt at different temperatures.

Metamorphic rocks

Both sedimentary and igneous rocks can transform into metamorphic rocks. Tectonic plate movements may drive these rocks deep underground where they melt, or push them up to the surface via uplift.

Weathering

The rocks on Earth's surface are gradually broken down into smaller pieces by a number of processes. These include the action of rain and ice, extreme temperature changes, and the growth of tree roots.

Transportation and deposition

Small, weathered pieces of rock are transported away by wind, ice, and water. Rivers carry rock particles all the way to the sea where they are dropped, forming layers of sediment on the seabed. This is known as deposition.

Rock Cycle

About **75%** of Earth's surface rocks are sedimentary

Although you wouldn't know it to look at them, Earth's rocks are very slowly but constantly changing. On the surface, weathering breaks large rocks into little pieces, which may be compacted together to form new rocks. Underground, the movement of tectonic plates draws rocks deep into Earth, where they melt, and this also pushes new rocks on to the surface— where the cycle begins again.

Compaction and cementation

As an increasing amount of sediment is deposited, the layers on the seabed get packed more and more tightly. Pressure compacts the particles together, squeezing out any water. The rock grains are then cemented together by minerals, forming new sedimentary rock.

Uplift

Just as tectonic plates can drive rocks down into Earth, they can also push them up to the surface, where they will begin to weather and erode. This process is known as uplift.

Sedimentary rocks

There are several different types of sedimentary rock. Some, such as sandstone, are made of eroded rock particles, while others, such as chalk, are formed from the compacted remains of tiny sea creatures.

Transformation

Deep beneath the surface of Earth, rocks are subjected to intense heat and pressure. Below a certain temperature, this can change the texture and mineral composition of the rock, transforming it from one type of rock into another via a process called metamorphism.

Rock melts

Above a certain temperature, sedimentary rocks can no longer transform into metamorphic rocks, but instead melt, turning into magma.

Water Cycle

Constantly on the move, water falls from clouds and flows along in rivers to oceans, before the Sun's rays evaporate it back into clouds. The journey that water goes on as it circulates between the atmosphere, land, rivers, and oceans is known as the water cycle. It may move around a lot, but the amount of water in the world remains exactly the same and has since the planet was formed.

Precipitation

The water that falls from the air as rain, snow, sleet, or hail is called precipitation. It happens when small, light water droplets in clouds gather together to become larger, heavier ones, which then drop down to Earth under the force of gravity.

Ice and snow

Just 3% of Earth's water is fresh, of which two-thirds is frozen in the form of ice and snow, found in glaciers and ice caps. The remaining 97% is held in the oceans. This water is salty and therefore not suitable for humans to drink.

On the ground

A proportion of the water that falls on the ground soaks into the soil. If the underlying rock is permeable, it will become saturated. Water stored in this way emerges on the surface in marshes and springs. Springs are common at the point where a layer of permeable rock meets a lower layer of impermeable rock.

Water is the **only** substance found naturally on Earth as a solid, liquid, and gas

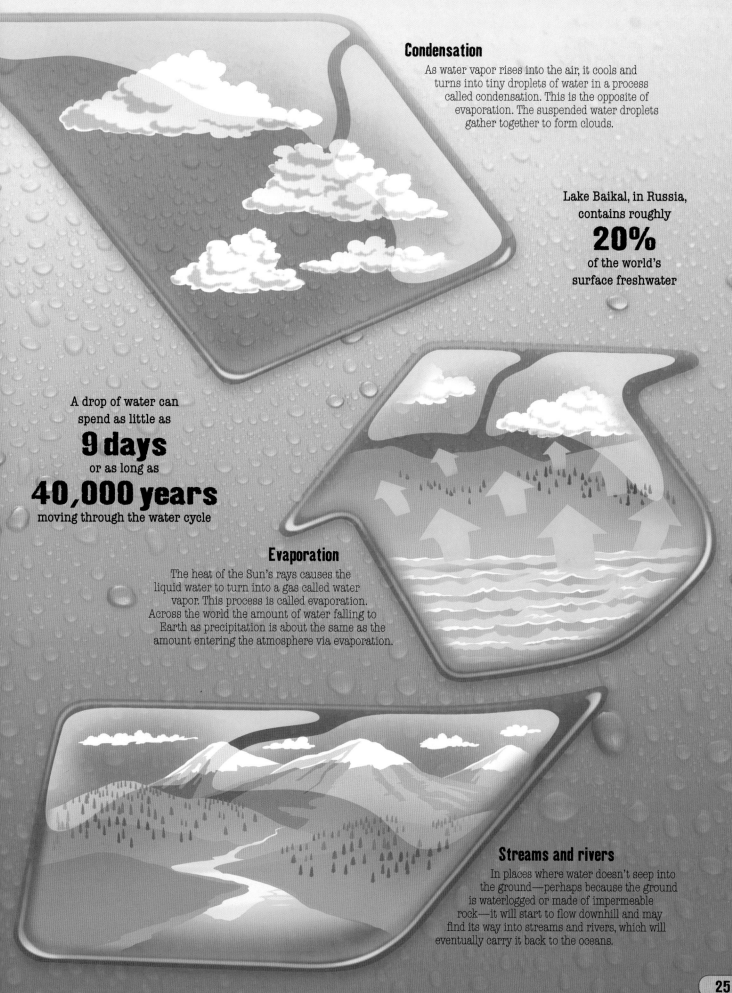

Condensation

As water vapor rises into the air, it cools and turns into tiny droplets of water in a process called condensation. This is the opposite of evaporation. The suspended water droplets gather together to form clouds.

Lake Baikal, in Russia, contains roughly

20%

of the world's surface freshwater

A drop of water can spend as little as

9 days

or as long as

40,000 years

moving through the water cycle

Evaporation

The heat of the Sun's rays causes the liquid water to turn into a gas called water vapor. This process is called evaporation. Across the world the amount of water falling to Earth as precipitation is about the same as the amount entering the atmosphere via evaporation.

Streams and rivers

In places where water doesn't seep into the ground—perhaps because the ground is waterlogged or made of impermeable rock—it will start to flow downhill and may find its way into streams and rivers, which will eventually carry it back to the oceans.

Rivers

Earth has more than one million rivers. They can be found on every continent, except for frozen Antarctica. There are more than 150 rivers that are greater than 620 miles (1,000 km) long. Of the world's five longest rivers, shown below, two—the Yenisey-Angara and the Yangtze—are found in Asia, while the Mississippi-Missouri is in North America, the Amazon is in South America, and the longest river of all, the Nile, flows through Africa.

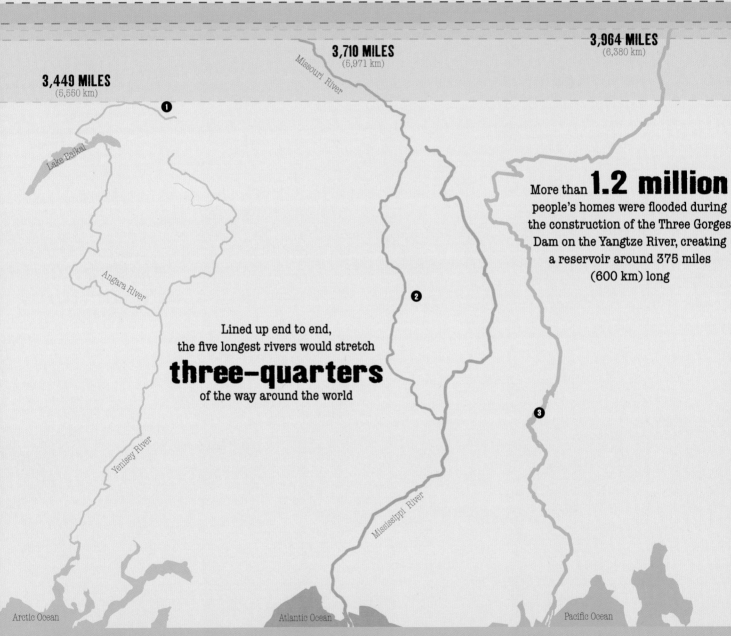

3,449 MILES (5,550 km)

3,710 MILES (5,971 km)

3,964 MILES (6,380 km)

Missouri River

Lake Baikal

Angara River

Yenisey River

Mississippi River

More than **1.2 million** people's homes were flooded during the construction of the Three Gorges Dam on the Yangtze River, creating a reservoir around 375 miles (600 km) long

Lined up end to end, the five longest rivers would stretch **three-quarters** of the way around the world

Arctic Ocean

Atlantic Ocean

Pacific Ocean

Yenisey-Angara

Beginning as a trickle in Mongolia, the Yenisey-Angara enters Russia, where it flows through Lake Baikal— the world's largest freshwater lake. It then heads north through Siberia to the Arctic Ocean.

Mississippi-Missouri

On its journey from the northwest to the southeast of the U.S.A., the mighty Mississippi-Missouri River is crossed by more than 170 bridges. Its drainage basin—the total area drained by the river and its tributaries—encompasses some 1.23 million sq. miles (3.2 million sq. km).

Yangtze

Around 350 million people live near this great Chinese river, which flows through more than 30 cities. The Yangtze deposits 6 billion ft³ (170 million m³) of fertile silt every year onto the Jiangsu Plain, one of the world's major centers of rice production.

BIGGEST RIVERS

[sq. ft (sq. m) per second]

The Nile may be the longest river, but the Amazon is by far the largest in the world, carrying more water than the next four longest rivers combined and holding around 20% of the planet's flowing fresh water. The volume of water that each river carries is measured by how much they discharge into the oceans every second.

54,896 (5,100)	174,375 (16,200)	204,514 (19,000)	333,681 (31,000)	2,357,296 (219,000)
Nile	Mississippi-Missouri	Yenisey-Angara	Yangtze	Amazon

4,161 MILES
(6,696 km)

4,008 MILES
(6,450 km)

The Amazon is by far the widest river on Earth—in the wet season its lower stretches can be up to

25 miles
(40 km) wide

Mediterranean Sea

Atlantic Ocean

❶ Yenisey tributaries

A river usually begins as a thin stream flowing quickly over steep ground. It slows as it reaches flatter terrain and gradually grows in volume as it is joined by smaller streams and rivers, known as tributaries.

❷ Lake Carter

In its middle course a river will often flow in giant loops, known as meanders. Occasionally, the river may change its course, leaving behind a C-shaped body of water known as an oxbow lake.

❸ Three Gorges Dam

Around the world people build dams across rivers, creating huge artificial lakes that can be used to generate electricity. The Three Gorges Dam in China is the world's largest electricity-generating plant.

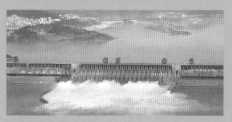

❹ Amazon floodplains

Many rivers flood as part of their natural annual cycle. Every wet season the Amazon River rises by more than 30 ft (9 m), deluging the surrounding area and depositing valuable nutrients back into the ground.

❺ Nile Delta

A river carries huge amounts of sediment, which help it gouge out its course across the land. When the river meets the sea, this material is dropped and may form a low, triangular-shaped area of land known as a delta.

Amazon

This massive river drains water from 40% of the South American continent and has thousands of tributaries feeding into it. It is home to 2,500 different species of fish—more than are found in the entire Atlantic Ocean.

Nile

Passing through 10 African countries, the Nile is a thin ribbon of water for much of its great length, carving its way through the dry Sahara Desert. In Egypt, where the Nile reaches the sea, most people rely on its water and live near the river's banks.

Ocean Depths

From the surface to the seabed, the ocean can be divided into four zones, each one colder than the last. The inky black waters of the ocean's lowest reaches are largely unexplored by people. It is often said that we know more about the surface of the Moon than we do about the ocean depths.

Ocean sizes

Water covers 71% of Earth's surface. Most of it can be found in five interlinked oceans. The Pacific is by far the biggest, covering 69 million sq. miles (180 million sq. km) or around one-third of Earth's entire surface area. This diagram shows how much of the world's total ocean cover is taken up by each body of water.

CONTINENTAL SHELF

200 M
656 ft

CONTINENTAL SLOPE

1,000 M
3,281 ft

SUBMARINE RIDGES

Black smokers

Blue shark

Sting rays

Dolphins

Sperm whale

Elephant seal

Hatchetfish

Plankton

Sea lions

Great white shark

Flying fish

King penguins

Anchovies

Bluefin tuna

Comb jelly

Johnson Sealink submarine

Scuba diver

VOLCANIC ISLAND

Jellyfish

Man o' war

Sea turtles

Nuclear submarine

Anglerfish

Leatherback turtle

Deepsea squid

Around **90%** of all the ocean's water is contained in the midnight zone

Sunlit zone
At the top layer of the ocean, plants and microscopic organisms use the abundant sunlight for photosynthesis. The energy that they create forms the basis of an intricate food chain involving a variety of wildlife, including plankton, fish, crustaceans, marine mammals, and aquatic birds. Around 90% of marine life can be found in this zone.

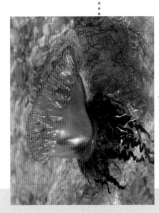

THE VENOMOUS MAN O' WAR JELLYFISH HAS 30-FT (10-M) LONG TENTACLES

Twilight zone
The murky blue waters of the twilight zone receive some faint sunlight, but not enough for photosynthesis. No plants can live at these depths, but plenty of animals do. Many boast special adaptations to cope with the darkness. Some use a process called bioluminescence to produce their own ghostly light to lure prey, attract mates, or distract predators.

ANGLERFISH EMIT A BRIGHT GLOW

Sea cucumber

Trieste

Shinkai submersible

ABYSSAL PLAIN

OCEANIC TRENCH

Alvin submersible

Midnight zone

Not even a glimmer of light filters down to the midnight zone. Although much of this zone is barren, thriving ecosystems are found living around hydrothermal vents, known as black smokers. These vents spew forth superheated water rich in minerals, providing sustenance to a whole array of creatures, including giant worms, clams, crabs, and shrimp.

THE WATER FROM A BLACK SMOKER CAN REACH 570°F (300°C)

Hadal zone

Creatures in the hadal zone eke out an existence as best as they can amid the darkness, cold, and crushing pressure. Many are scavengers, feasting upon the bodies of dead animals that float down from above. People have visited the Mariana Trench, the deepest point in the ocean, just once, in 1960, aboard the submersible Trieste.

TRIESTE CARRIED A CREW OF TWO PEOPLE TO A DEPTH OF ALMOST 6.8 MILES (11 KM)

29

island Formation

An island is an area of land smaller than a continent that is completely surrounded by water. Earth is home to more than 100,000 islands, ranging from tiny patches of sand to giant, almost continent-size landmasses. It is estimated that one in every 10 people lives on an island. The majority of islands are formed either by volcanic activity, changes to continental plates, or the growth of coral.

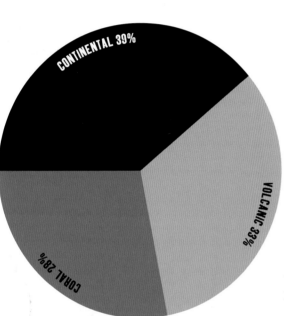

CONTINENTAL 39%

VOLCANIC 33%

CORAL 28%

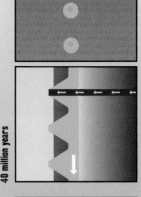

Greenland: 822,700 sq. miles (2,131,000 sq. km)

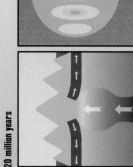

New Guinea: 303,100 sq. miles (785,000 sq. km)

Madagascar: 289,670 sq. miles (748,170 sq. km)

Borneo: 27,000 sq. miles (597,700 sq. km)

Baffin Island, Canada: 194,000 sq. miles (504,000 sq. km)

Giant Greenland

Despite its massive size, the cold climate of the world's largest island, Greenland, means that it is home to just 55,000 people. The next three largest islands — New Guinea, Borneo, and Madagascar — could all fit inside it with room to spare.

Island types

There are three main types of islands. Continental islands fringe the world's major landmasses, volcanic islands are formed by molten rock welling up from beneath Earth's crust, and coral islands are slowly built up by tiny creatures living in warm tropical waters.

Hot spot

Some oceanic islands, such as the Hawaiian Islands, are formed when a plume of molten rock, known as a hot spot, erupts through the center of a tectonic plate. The plate moves over time, but the hot spot stays in the same place. Periodic eruptions gradually form a chain of islands.

VOLCANIC

TIME LINE 0

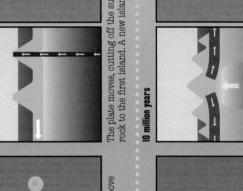

Molten rock from the hot spot slowly rises up above the waves, forming a volcanic island.

20 million years

The plate moves, cutting off the supply of molten rock to the first island. A new island forms.

40 million years

The hot spot may form a whole chain of islands as the process continues.

Ocean rift

Iceland is an example of a type of volcanic island that sometimes forms on the boundary between divergent tectonic plates. As the plates pull apart, molten rock rises up to fill the gap, creating islands. Unlike hot spot islands, these islands stay above their lava source and usually remain volcanically active.

TIME LINE 0

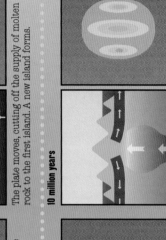

Molten rock wells up in the gap created by two tectonic plates pulling apart.

10 million years

The molten rock continues to rise up, eventually breaking the water's surface.

20 million years

As the plates pull apart, the island grows and spreads. It may have several active volcanoes on its surface.

Shifting plates

When a divergent plate boundary runs through a continent, the gradual separation of the plates may force a portion of the landmass to break off. In time, this will form a new island known as a microcontinent. Madagascar, off the east coast of Africa, is an example of this.

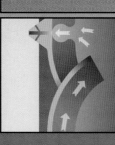

1 million years

2 million years

A continent sits above the boundary between two tectonic plates.

The plates slowly pull apart, eventually dividing the landmass in two.

The sea fills the gap left by the landmass dividing, forming the island.

Oceanic convergance

Where oceanic plates come together, one may get drawn beneath the other in a process called subduction. As the lower plate is pulled under, it melts, sending molten rock breaking through the upper plate to form a lava island. Islands may emerge all along the plate boundary, creating an island arc known as an archipelago, such as Japan.

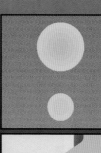

100,000 years

200,000 years

One tectonic plate is gradually drawn down beneath the other into the mantle.

The molten rock pushes through the top plate and gradually builds up to form an island.

The island continues to grow and may have several active volcanoes, fueled by the molten rock below.

Rising sea levels

Many of the world's largest islands, including Great Britain, were formed by rising seas. During the last Ice Age, much of the world's water was frozen and sea levels were much lower than today. When the ice melted as the climate grew warmer, water levels rose and separated land that was previously connected.

5,000 years

10,000 years

Two mountains, one slightly higher than the other, stand amid the frozen Ice Age landscape.

As the ice begins to melt, flooding in low-lying areas of land creates two islands.

The seas continue to rise, covering the smaller island, leaving only one.

Atoll

Coral reefs are limestone structures created by tiny marine creatures called polyps. When a reef breaks the surface of the water, sand may begin to accumulate upon it, turning it into an island. An atoll is a type of coral island that forms around a volcanic island.

10,000 years

20,000 years

A coral reef grows around the outside of a volcanic island.

The island begins to sink, but the reef continues to grow upward around it, breaking the surface of the water. Sand gathers on the top of the exposed reef.

The volcanic island subsides beneath the waves, leaving behind the coral atoll ring. The water inside is called a lagoon.

Weather

The word "weather" is used to describe the day-to-day variations in a number of things, including temperature, wind speed, cloud cover, and sunshine. Climate, on the other hand, is the typical weather in a place over a long period of time. The driving force of weather is the Sun's heat, which powers the constant movement of air and water vapor in the atmosphere.

Water vapor and clouds

Clouds form when rising water vapor condenses into water droplets or ice. If the air already holds a lot of vapor, this happens at low altitudes and forms low-level clouds. At high altitudes, where the air temperature is below freezing, the vapor condenses into ice crystals.

Cirrus clouds

The highest clouds are made up of ice crystals. Cirrus look like tufts of white hair, cirrocumulus resemble small, puffy grains, while cirrostratus clouds form thin, hazy sheets.

Alto clouds

These are the mid-level clouds. Altocumulus can be white or gray and tend to clump together. Altostratus are less distinct, forming sheets of cloud that fill the sky and often produce drizzle.

Stratus clouds

All stratus clouds are thick and featureless and stretch across the sky (stratus means "sheet"). Nimbostratus clouds can produce rain that lasts for days, while stratocumulus produce very little moisture.

Cumulus clouds

Closest to the ground, cumulus clouds look like white cotton tufts Sometimes they gather into giant anvil-shaped clouds known as cumulonimbus, which reach far up into the sky. These can produce heavy rain, hail, and thunder and lightning.

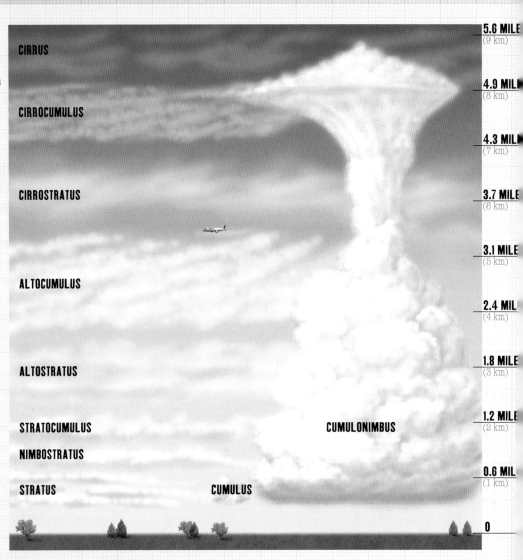

Diagram labels (from top to bottom): CIRRUS, CIRROCUMULUS, CIRROSTRATUS, ALTOCUMULUS, ALTOSTRATUS, STRATOCUMULUS, NIMBOSTRATUS, STRATUS, CUMULUS, CUMULONIMBUS

Altitude scale:
- 5.6 MILE (9 km)
- 4.9 MILE (8 km)
- 4.3 MILE (7 km)
- 3.7 MILE (6 km)
- 3.1 MILE (5 km)
- 2.4 MIL (4 km)
- 1.8 MILE (3 km)
- 1.2 MILE (2 km)
- 0.6 MIL (1 km)
- 0

The coldest temperature on record is **−128°F** (-89°C), and was recorded in Antarctica— the hottest is **136°F** (57.8°F), recorded in El Azizia, Libya

THE BEAUFORT SCALE

BEAUFORT NUMBER	0	1	2	3	4	5	6
DESCRIPTION	Calm	Light air	Light breeze	Gentle breeze	Moderate breeze	Fresh breeze	Strong breeze
EFFECTS ON LAND	Air is still and calm. Smoke rises vertically from chimneys.	Smoke drifts gently in the wind, but weathervanes do not move.	Wind can be felt on the skin. Weathervanes move slightly.	Light flags extend. Leaves and small twigs are in constant motion.	Wind raises dust, fallen leaves, and loose paper. Small branches move.	Branches of medium-sized trees move, and small trees sway.	Branches of large trees move. Umbrella use is difficult.

Falling down

Precipitation is water in the atmosphere, falling from clouds to Earth under the pull of gravity. Depending on the air temperature and wind, this can take the form of rain, snow, sleet, or hail. Raindrops fall at approximately 31 ft (6.5 m) per second.

SNOW

RAIN

— **1.8 MILES** (3 km)

— **1.2 MILES** (2 km)

— **0.6 MILES** (1 km)

| BELOW FREEZING | 32°F (0°C) | ABOVE FREEZING |

Rain formation
Air currents move tiny water droplets around in clouds where they collide and merge with each other, forming larger drops. This is known as coalescence. When the drops become too large for the cloud to hold, they will fall to the ground as rain. Coalescence usually only happens at temperatures above 32°F (0°C). The droplets may start off as snow if the temperature is cold enough, before melting if the air below is warmer.

SNOW

SNOW

— **1.8 MILES** (3 km)

— **1.2 MILES** (2 km)

— **0.6 MILES** (1 km)

| BELOW FREEZING | 32°F (0°C) | ABOVE FREEZING |

Snow formation
At subzero temperatures, ice crystals in clouds collide and clump together to form snowflakes. As long as the air temperature between the cloud and the ground is below 32°F (0°C), these flakes will fall as snow. If the air is warm, however, they will melt and turn into rain. All snow crystals have six sides.

SNOW

PARTIALLY MELTED SNOW

SLEET

— **1.8 MILES** (3 km)

— **1.2 MILES** (2 km)

— **0.6 MILES** (1 km)

| BELOW FREEZING | 32°F (0°C) | ABOVE FREEZING |

Sleet formation
When falling snow reaches a layer of warmer air that partially melts the flakes, sleet forms. The flakes then continue downward into a layer of colder air, which partially refreezes them, forming soft, ice pellets. These are different from hailstones, which are ice crystals that become encased in layers of ice as they are moved around inside clouds by air currents.

36,020°F (20,000°C),
A lightning bolt can heat the air around it to
which is more than three times hotter than the surface of the Sun

Stormy weather

The Sun doesn't warm Earth's surface evenly, which creates areas of warm air and areas of cold air. Where two masses of air with different temperatures meet, high winds and thick clouds develop, creating thunderstorms.

Lightning
A lightning strike occurs when thunderclouds become electrically charged. A negative charge at the bottom of the cloud jumps toward a positive one on the ground, traveling at a staggering 130,000 mph (209,200 km/h) and generating around 300,000 volts of static electricity.

7	8	9	10	11	12
Moderate gale	Fresh gale	Strong gale	Whole gale	Storm	Hurricane force
Large trees sway. It is difficult to walk against the wind.	Twigs and small branches break off. Moving cars veer on the road.	Small trees blown over. Tiles are blown from the tops of roofs.	Medium-size trees broken and uprooted. Damage caused to some buildings.	Large trees broken and uprooted. Widespread damage to property.	Severe damage to property and land. Rarely experienced on land.

Measuring wind speed
Wind is the movement of air from areas of high pressure (where the air is cold) to areas of low pressure (where the air is warm). The bigger the difference in pressure, the stronger the wind will be. Wind speed is measured by the Beaufort scale.

Fiery mountain

Volcanoes erupt in several different ways. Some gently ooze lava, while others send it spurting out like a fiery river. Some of the deadliest volcanoes shoot out a vast cloud of superheated gas and rock, known as a pyroclastic flow, along with volcanic ash. When Mount Tambora, Indonesia, erupted in 1815, the ash sent into the atmosphere blotted out the Sun for several days.

Lava flows can reach temperatures of 1,832°F (1,000°C)

Hurricane

These violent storms (also known as typhoons) are fueled by warm sea water. The water evaporates into the air, forming dense clouds that begin to spin around with tremendous force, capable of causing great damage if they reach land. In 2005, Hurricane Katrina became the most expensive hurricane on record, causing an estimated $181 billion worth of damage to the south coast of the U.S.A..

Drought

Not all natural disasters are sudden events. Droughts usually take hold gradually as the available water in an area slowly runs out. However, the impact of a severe drought can be catastrophic and may be felt for a long time. In China, more than 25 million people are estimated to have died in the 20th century as a result of droughts.

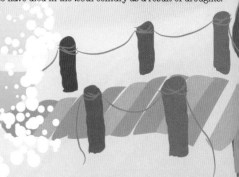

Natural Disasters

The natural world can be a dangerous place. Every year, around 75,000 people die and some $65 billion of property and land is destroyed as a result of natural disasters. According to the United Nations, around 75% of the world's population live in areas that have recently been affected by earthquakes, hurricanes, flooding, or droughts. Often striking without warning, the effects of these catastrophes can last for years.

Shocking shakes

When Earth's tectonic plates collide with each other, it can lead to an earthquake. A really bad one, such as the 2010 Haiti quake, can lead to widespread destruction, ripping apart roads and bridges, collapsing buildings, and causing hundreds of thousands of deaths. In Haiti, the effects were particularly devastating because many buildings were not secure and the emergency services were not equipped to deal with the crisis.

Giant wave

When a giant earthquake takes place on the seabed, it can create a series of huge waves known as a tsunami. These waves spread out in all directions like giant ripples, traveling at speeds of up to 435 mph (700 km/h). Where they hit land, the waves can inflict immense devastation. The deadliest tsunami in recorded history swept across the Indian Ocean in 2004, killing more than 225,000 people in 11 countries and leaving millions homeless.

Tsunami waves can be 98 ft (30 m) high by the time they hit the coast

Twisting times

Tornadoes are giant columns of rapidly spinning air that occasionally form over land during thunderstorms. When a tornado touches the ground, the consequences can be lethal. They can rip the roofs off of houses and toss cars into the air like toys. The U.S.A. experiences around 1,000 tornadoes per year, more than any other country. Most form in a central region locally known as "Tornado Alley."

Tornado winds have been clocked at speeds of up to

311 mph
(500 km/h)

Wildfire

These fast-spreading natural hazards occur wherever there are expanses of dry vegetation, such as grasslands and forests. Most are started naturally by lightning strikes, but some are the result of human carelessness. In 1997–1998, the largest wildfire in recorded history laid waste to more than 23,200 sq. miles (60,000 sq. km) of Indonesian forest.

Air temperatures of
1,470°F
(800°F) are possible during a wildfire

Avalanche

Snow can come loose and slide down a mountainside at any time. Avalanches usually occur on steep slopes where thick snow has become unstable. In 1970, an earthquake off the shore of Peru sent a 0.6-mile- (900-m-) wide mass of ice, snow, and rock from Mount Huascarán crashing onto the nearby village of Yungay, killing more than 17,000 people.

Flood

Of all the natural disasters to afflict Earth, flooding is by far the most common. The most severe floods deluge huge areas of land, forcing people from their homes, ruining crops, and spreading diseases. Around the world people build defenses alongside rivers and coasts in an attempt to hold back the rising waters.

An estimated **4 million** people were killed when China's Huang He flooded in 1931

There are around **500,000** earthquakes per year, but only **100** cause damage

Life on the Land

Regions that share the same climate and support similar types of plants and animals are known as biomes. Earth's land can be divided into 10 major biomes, ranging from almost barren deserts to fertile rain forests teeming with all manner of life.

Water world

The land biomes shown on this page make up just 29% of Earth's surface. The other 71% of the globe is water, which has its own wide variety of different biomes.

71%

29%

Earth's terrestrial biomes

The pie chart on the right shows the percentage of land covered by each biome. The type of biome in an area is not fixed but can change over time due to climate change or human activities.

Boreal forest: 8.5%
Also known as taiga, boreal forest is a cold environment with long, harsh winters and short summers. The landscape is dominated by conifer trees, such as firs and pines.

Cultivated land: 9.5%
The only biome created by people, this environment is made up of areas that have been adapted to grow crops or rear animals. Prior to their cultivation, these areas would have formed parts of other biomes.

Savanna: 10%
Remaining warm throughout the year, these great rolling grasslands support huge herds of grazing animals—and their predators. They experience only two seasons: a dry season and a very wet one.

Ice: 11%
The ice caps of the North and South poles, along with the world's snow-capped mountain peaks, make up the coldest biome. Ice is also one of the most barren environments, supporting few plants or animals.

Tropical rain forest: 17%
These rain-soaked jungles are the world's most fertile biome. They enjoy warm temperatures all year round and support more species of animals and plants than any other environment. The plants here produce most of Earth's oxygen.

Where in the world?

This map shows how 9 of the 10 major terrestrial biomes are distributed across the planet in a series of giant bands sharing the same climate and conditions. Since cultivated land takes up parts of other biomes, it has not been shown here.

Temperate forest: 7%
Unlike rain forests, which thrive all year round, temperate (or deciduous) forests have distinct seasons—the trees lose their leaves in the fall and regrow them in the spring.

Temperate grasslands: 6%
Cooler than the savanna, these great seas of grass are home to burrowing animals, grazing animals, and animals that prey on both. They have hot summers and cool winters.

Mediterranean: 6%
Also known as chaparral, this is a coastal biome that has extremely hot summers and cool, rainy winters. The landscape tends to be dry and parched, with vegetation made up mainly of shrubs.

Tundra: 5.5%
Despite its inhospitable appearance— it consists mainly of frozen, treeless plains—tundra provides homes to a wealth of wildlife adapted to the extreme conditions, including foxes, hares, caribou, and polar bears.

Desert: 19.5%
Any portion of Earth's land that receives less than 10 in. (25 cm) of rain a year is considered desert. Here, plants and animals are few and usually small in size. The Sahara in Africa is the world's biggest desert.

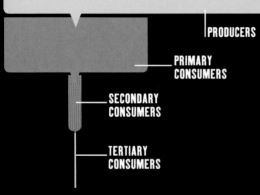

PRODUCERS

PRIMARY
CONSUMERS

SECONDARY
CONSUMERS

TERTIARY
CONSUMERS

Trophic pyramid

A trophic level is the position that an organism occupies in a food web. Each time an organism is eaten, it only passes on around 10% of its energy to the organism eating it. This is why the number of organisms in each trophic level is smaller than the one before it—giving it a pyramid shape—as there is less energy passed on from level to level.

Food Webs

From the tiniest bacterium to the biggest elephant, every organism needs energy in order to survive. The way energy is passed from organism to organism in an environment is known as the food web. Plants (producers) get their energy from the Sun. Part of this is then passed on to plant-eating animals (primary consumers), who in turn pass part of their energy on to carnivorous animals (secondary and tertiary consumers). Eventually, all these organisms will be broken down by decomposers, and the process will start again.

African savanna food web

Organisms often have several different food sources, which means that food webs can be very complicated. The diagram to the right shows how organisms living in the African savanna combine to form an intricate ecosystem. The arrows show the direction energy travels, and the colors show each organism's role in the web.

Decomposer
When an organism dies, those parts that aren't eaten by animals are broken down by decomposers, such as bacteria and fungi. They return the organism's nutrients to the soil—ready to be reused by producers.

Secondary consumer
Next in the web are the animals that eat herbivores, known as secondary consumers. All species of dogs and cats are secondary consumers, with some also being tertiary consumers, depending on the environment.

Producer
All plants, like grass and acacia trees here, are producers and form the basis of most food webs. Producers make their own food using energy from the Sun and nutrients from the ground (or from the water in marine environments).

Tertiary consumer
Some carnivores eat other carnivores as well as herbivores. These are tertiary consumers. A carnivore that has no natural enemies, such as a lion, is known as a "top predator" as it is not hunted by any organism.

Primary consumer
Gazelles, giraffes, and termites are known as primary consumers (or herbivores) as they eat producers. Animals that eat both plants and animals are omnivores. The vast majority of the world's animals are herbivores.

Scavenger
Animals that eat only animals that have already died are called scavengers. They can be primary, secondary, or tertiary consumers. Anything they don't consume will be recycled by decomposers.

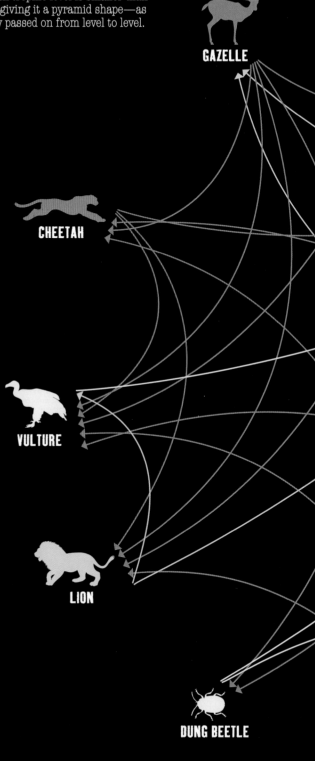

GAZELLE

CHEETAH

VULTURE

LION

DUNG BEETLE

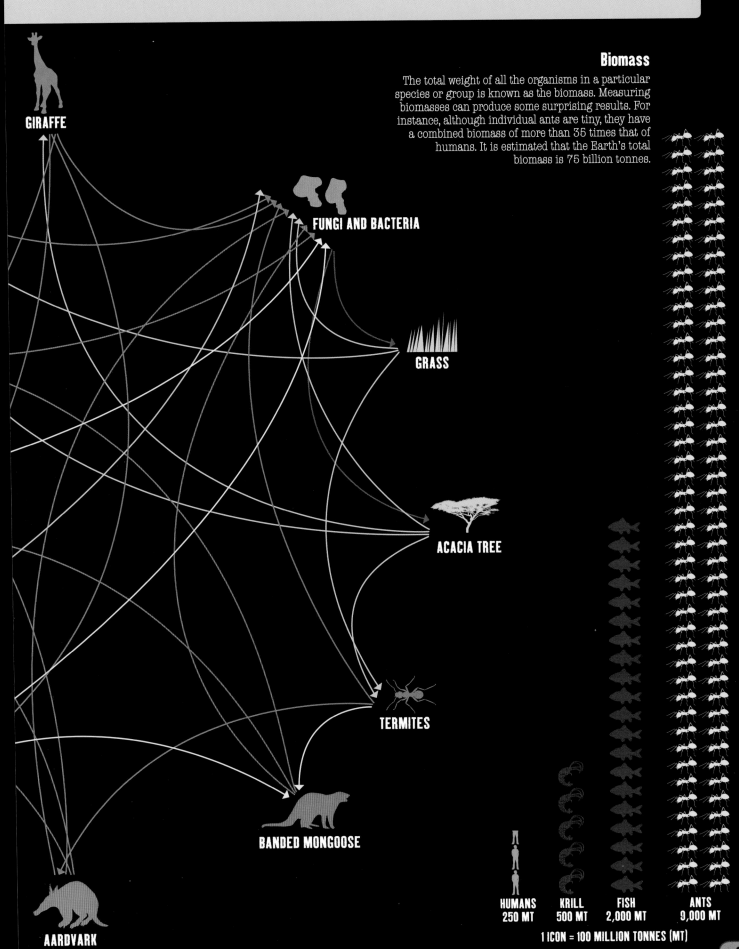

Biomass

The total weight of all the organisms in a particular species or group is known as the biomass. Measuring biomasses can produce some surprising results. For instance, although individual ants are tiny, they have a combined biomass of more than 35 times that of humans. It is estimated that the Earth's total biomass is 75 billion tonnes.

GIRAFFE

FUNGI AND BACTERIA

GRASS

ACACIA TREE

TERMITES

BANDED MONGOOSE

AARDVARK

HUMANS
250 MT

KRILL
500 MT

FISH
2,000 MT

ANTS
9,000 MT

1 ICON = 100 MILLION TONNES (MT)

HEIGHT

| 115 M / 377 ft |
| 110 M / 361 ft |
| 105 M / 344 ft |
| 100 M / 328 ft |
| 95 M / 312 ft |
| 90 M / 295 ft |
| 85 M / 279 ft |
| 80 M / 262 ft |
| 75 M / 246 ft |
| 70 M / 230 ft |
| 65 M / 213 ft |
| 60 M / 196 ft |

Box jellyfish
This jellyfish's stinging tentacles have killed more than 5,000 people in the past 60 years.

King cobra
The deadly 0.4 in. (1.25 cm) fangs deliver venom capable of killing 20–40 humans.

Marbled cone snail
The snail uses a harpoonlike appendage to inject a toxin, strong enough to kill 20 humans.

Blue-ringed octopus
Although its bite is painless, the octopus carries enough venom to kill 25 humans within minutes.

Fastest and slowest

Below, an imaginary race is taking place between the fastest and slowest members of the animal kingdom. Capable of a top speed of around 27 mph (44 km/h), even the swiftest human would quickly be left behind by the speed merchants of the wild.

FASTEST

PEREGRINE FALCON (When diving) 273 MPH (440 KM/H)

SPINE-TAILED SWIFT (Straight-line flight) 106 MPH (171 KM/H)

CHEETAH (Fastest land animal) 70 MPH (113 KM/H)

SAILFISH (Fastest sea animal) 68 MPH (110 KM/H)

PRONGHORN ANTELOPE (Fastest herbivore) 61 MPH (98 KM/H)

SLOWEST

AMERICAN WOODCOCK (Slowest bird) 5 MPH (8 KM/H)

GIANT TORTOISE (Slow-moving reptile) 0.17 MPH (0.27 KM/H)

THREE-TOED SLOTH (Slowest mammal) 0.01 MPH (0.16 KM/H)

SEAHORSE (Slowest sea animal) 0.01 MPH (0.016 KM/H)

GARDEN SNAIL (Slowest animal) 0.002 MPH (0.003 KM/H)

Life spans long and short

From the humble mayfly to the ancient bristlecone pine, this scale shows the planet's longest—and shortest—living organisms. Above, the red arrows identify record-breaking feats of longevity, while below are the average life spans of the shortest-living creatures.

Bristlecone pine 5,000 years

Ocean quahog 410 years

Koi fish 226 years

Bowhead whale 210 years

Giant tortoise 188 years

Geoduck clam 160 years

Human 122 years

| 450 YEARS |
| 400 YEARS |
| 350 YEARS |
| 300 YEARS |
| 250 YEARS |
| 200 YEARS |
| 150 YEARS |
| 100 YEARS |

55 M 180 ft
50 M 164 ft
45 M 147 ft
40 M 131 ft
35 M 116 ft
30 M 98 ft
25 M 82 ft
20 M 66 ft
15 M 49 ft
10 M 32 ft
5 M 16 ft
0

Record Breakers

Life comes in every shape and size imaginable, from bacteria so small that more than one million could fit on to the head of a pin, to giant trees weighing thousands of tonnes. Some creatures have lived for more than 200 years, while others buzz through their entire life within a single day.

Blue whale vs. jumbo jet

The mighty blue whale is the largest-ever animal—and weighing in at 150–170 tonnes, it is as heavy as a Boeing 747. These enormous creatures have hearts the size of cars and blood vessels so wide that a person could swim along them.

Dangerous creatures

There are two types of animals that kill through the use of powerful toxins. Poisonous ones cause harm only if they are touched or eaten, while venomous ones inject their prey by biting, stabbing, or stinging. Both can be deadly.

Inland taipan
The venom from a single bite by the "most poisonous snake in the world" can kill 100 humans.

Poison-arrow frog
The frog secretes its toxin from skin glands. Just 1 milligram is enough to kill 10 humans.

Biggest and tallest

Below, you can compare some of the giants of the living world—past and present. To the right, and towering above them all, is the mighty redwood, the largest known living organism. The biggest specimens can weigh in excess of 1,800 tonnes.

Titan flower Height: 10 ft (3 m)

Ostrich Height: 10 ft (3 m)

African elephant Height: 11 ft (3.3 m)

Giraffe Height: 17 ft (5.2 m)

Blue whale Length: 108 ft (33 m)

Argentinosaurus Length: 115 ft (35 m)

Giant redwood Height: 379 ft (115.5 m)

Dragonfly 4 months

Bees and flies 1 month

Drone ants 3 weeks

Gastrotrich 3 days

Mayfly 0.5–24 hours

16 WEEKS
15 WEEKS
14 WEEKS
13 WEEKS
12 WEEKS
11 WEEKS
10 WEEKS
9 WEEKS
8 WEEKS
7 WEEKS
6 WEEKS
5 WEEKS
4 WEEKS
3 WEEKS
2 WEEKS
1 WEEK

There are around **200 million** insects for every human

INSECTS
1,000,000 SPECIES

PLANTS
372,775

MOLLUSKS
85,000

FISH
31,300

BIRDS
9,998

REPTILES
9,084

MAMMALS
5,490

AMPHIBIANS
6,493

Bursting with life

Scientists still don't know the total number of species that there are in the world. To date, around 1.7 million plant and animal species have been identified—the majority of which are shown here—but there may be twice that many still awaiting discovery. What is certain is that insects are the most abundant life-forms, accounting for more than two-thirds of Earth's species.

Under Threat

Extinctions have always been part of the cycle of life on Earth. It is estimated that more than 99% of all the species that have ever lived are now extinct. Most of these were killed by natural causes, such as volcanic eruptions, asteroid impacts, and changes in climate. Today, however, thousands of species are endangered as a result of human interference, through hunting, fishing, and the destruction of natural habitats.

Lonesome George

George is believed to be the last surviving Pinto Island tortoise. Discovered in 1971, long after the rest of his kind had succumbed to hunting and habitat depletion, his unique status has led to him being called the rarest creature in the world.

AMPHIBIANS 32% With nearly one-third of species classified as endangered, amphibians are under the greatest threat.

MAMMALS 21% More than one-fifth of mammals are on the red list, and almost half of these have declining populations.

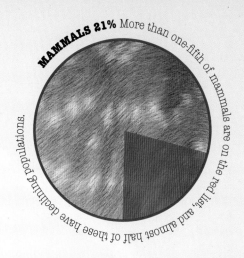

BIRDS 12% The destruction of forests for farmland and timber has reduced bird populations around the world.

REPTILES 5% The low figure for reptiles could be due to the fact that many species have not yet been fully studied.

The red list

Every year the International Union for the Conservation of Nature (IUCN) produces an ever-expanding red list of threatened species. Amphibians and mammals are the classes of life-forms with the highest proportion of endangered species. Insects, however, are faring much better. Although this is the group containing the greatest number of species, only a fraction is considered to be under serious threat. These pie charts identify the proportion of species that are considered to be endangered.

FISH 4% Large-scale commercial fishing has driven many fish species to the brink of extinction.

PLANTS 3% With their amazing biodiversity, the destruction of rain forests has placed plant species under threat.

MOLLUSKS 1% Of all the species to have recently become extinct, 41% were mollusks.

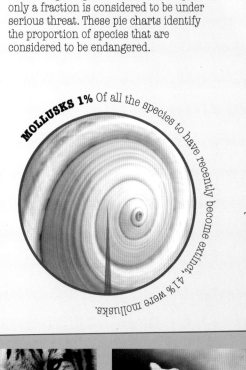

INSECTS 0.06% Of all classes of life, insects have proved to be the most successful, although not all have been assessed.

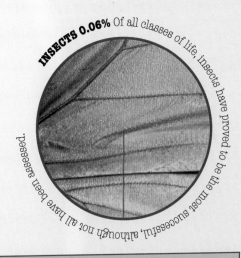

About to go

The major causes for the shrinking numbers of animals include commercial development and clearing land for livestock farming. There are programs being put in place to increase the population of threatened species and, hopefully, to ensure their future survival. However, will it help the animals to the right that are on the brink of dying out?

Siberian tiger
Today, there are just five subspecies of tigers, compared with eight at the start of the 20th century. The rare Siberian tigers live in the forests of eastern Russia, and there may be just 400 of them left in the wild.

Panamanian golden frog
The Panamanian golden frog currently stands on the brink of extinction as a result of a deadly fungus. They have not been seen in the wild since 2007, although some remain in captivity.

Echo parakeet
The destruction of their native Mauritian forests had reduced the echo parakeet population to 12 in 1990. Captive breeding and habitat regeneration have restored the number to about 300 birds today.

Six Degrees of Change

According to the majority of scientists, Earth's average global temperature is steadily rising, due to a buildup of carbon dioxide (CO_2) in the atmosphere. They believe that this is the result of burning fossil fuels, such as coal, gas, and oil. No one is certain exactly what might happen, but the effect of this global warming could be huge, with extreme weather systems leading to flooding and desertification. Many people think individuals and governments need to take action to avert catastrophe.

The greenhouse effect

Earth's atmosphere prevents some of the Sun's heat from escaping back into space, helping warm the planet. However, the more carbon dioxide there is in the atmosphere, the more heat it absorbs and radiates back to Earth, and the hotter the planet gets. This is known as the "greenhouse effect."

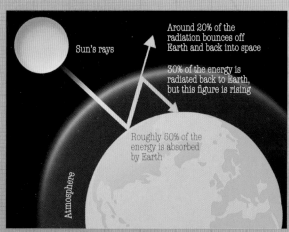

Sun's rays

Around 20% of the radiation bounces off Earth and back into space

30% of the energy is radiated back to Earth, but this figure is rising

Roughly 50% of the energy is absorbed by Earth

Atmosphere

Heating up

Scientists use the Celsius scale to measure temperature. The chart to the right shows the worst case scenarios— both on land and at sea—for every degree Celsius of temperature rise. A 6°C (10.8°F) average rise may not sound like all that much, but scientists believe that it would be enough to unleash a global disaster from which the human race might never recover. It took only a 5°C (9°F) temperature rise to end the last ice age.

6°C (10.8°F)

Methane fireballs
As oceans get warmer they become less able to dissolve oxygen, destroying marine life. Stagnant seas release hydrogen sulfide that poisons the land. If flammable methane rising from the seabed is ignited (by lightning, for example), huge fireballs would sweep across the land, causing further destruction and loss of life.

5°C (9°F)

Migrating people
All rain forests have become deserts and growing crops is now all but impossible in much of the world. Migrant populations spread out across the globe in a desperate hunt for food and safe land. Their hunger leads to increased conflict and indiscriminate hunting, destroying the dwindling food resources.

4°C (7.2°F)

Runaway global warming
Desertification spreads across the globe, causing areas around the Mediterranean to be abandoned. In northern latitudes, the melting permafrost raises sea levels still further. Should temperatures reach this point, some scientists believe that the changes will be irreversible. Earth will face runaway global warming.

3°C (5.4°F)

Lungs of the world collapse
The Amazon rain forest, producer of 10% of the planet's oxygen (and often called "the lungs of the world"), is killed off by a combination of drought and fire. Its demise releases huge amounts of CO_2 into the atmosphere. Elsewhere, billions starve as crop yields dwindle. Swathes of Africa, India, and China are now effectively wastelands.

2°C (3.6°F)

Heat waves across Europe
Glaciers feeding India's rivers melt, causing flooding for a time and then drought as the rivers dry up. Europe suffers heat waves, forest fires, drying riverbeds, and failing crops. Plants are becoming heat-stressed, emitting CO_2 rather than storing it, thereby speeding up the global warming process.

1°C (1.8°F)

Ever-stronger hurricanes
As the sea warms up, hurricanes of the strength of 2005's Hurricane Katrina are more frequent. Fresh water disappears from one third of Earth's surface and is replaced by lifeless deserts. Low-lying areas of coastline are flooded, and many people are affected by heatstroke.

6°C
(10.8°F)

5°C
(9°F)

Maximum sea levels
At this stage, all of Earth's ice will have melted into the oceans, and sea levels will have increased by more than 197 ft (60 m). Across the planet, the sea has taken over large tracts of land. Methane, an even more potent greenhouse gas than carbon dioxide, is released from the seabed, speeding up the greenhouse effect.

4°C
(7.2°F)

Florida covered
Both poles are melting fast, releasing tonnes of stored carbon and raising sea levels by 3 ft (1 m) per year, meaning a state of constant flooding. The U.K. is reduced to an archipelago of small islands, while much of the southeastern United States, including Florida, is now underwater. Supplies of drinkable water are dwindling fast.

3°C
(5.4°F)

Bangladesh under water
Around 80% of the Arctic sea ice has now melted, raising global sea levels by an average of 82 ft (25 m). Vast areas of several low-lying countries, including Bangladesh, Myanmar (Burma), and Thailand are now underwater. Storms get ever fiercer as the seas grow warmer. The U.S. and Australian coasts are battered by superhurricanes.

2°C
(3.6°F)

Shanghai submerged
Melting Arctic glaciers raise sea levels by 20 ft (6 m). Water is encroaching on to the land in more and more areas across the globe. Shanghai, China's largest city, lies submerged, as does much of eastern China, forcing its population inland. One third of all marine species face extinction.

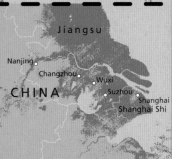

1°C
(1.8°F)

Flooding in northern Europe
The Arctic starts to melt, threatening the survival of the region's wildlife and raising sea levels. Areas of low-lying land around the world, including the Maldives and northern Europe (in blue) are the first to be lost to the rising waves. The Great Barrier Reef, the world's largest coral system, dies.

45

THE World IN ONE Day

EARTH

In the space of just 24 hours, some amazing things are going on in the natural world.

The Sun beams down enough energy to power a **60-watt bulb** for **1.2 million years**

109 tonnes of **cosmic dust** falls to Earth—more than the weight of the **International Space Station**

There are **87 earthquakes,** and around **78** of them happen around the edges of the Pacific Ocean—an area known as the **Pacific Ring of Fire**

Earth travels **1.6 million miles** (2.6 million km) around the Sun

Mosquitos
infect around **684,900** people worldwide with **malaria,** causing roughly **2,740** deaths

The United States suffers around **3 tornadoes**—one happens in **Texas** every 3 days, mostly during the warm summer months

The amount of **forest** land lost is equal to **2,822** soccer fields—most is **lost** due to human activity

Bamboo is the fastest-growing plant, capable of growing **24 in.** (60 cm)

Koala bears sleep for around **21** hours, and eat around **18 oz** (500 g) of eucalyptus leaves in the remaining 3 hours

ZZZZZZ

A single **tree** releases enough **oxygen** to support **two people**

If you were to **stand completely still** at any point on Earth's equator, you would still travel **24,912 miles** (40,080 km) due to **Earth's spin**

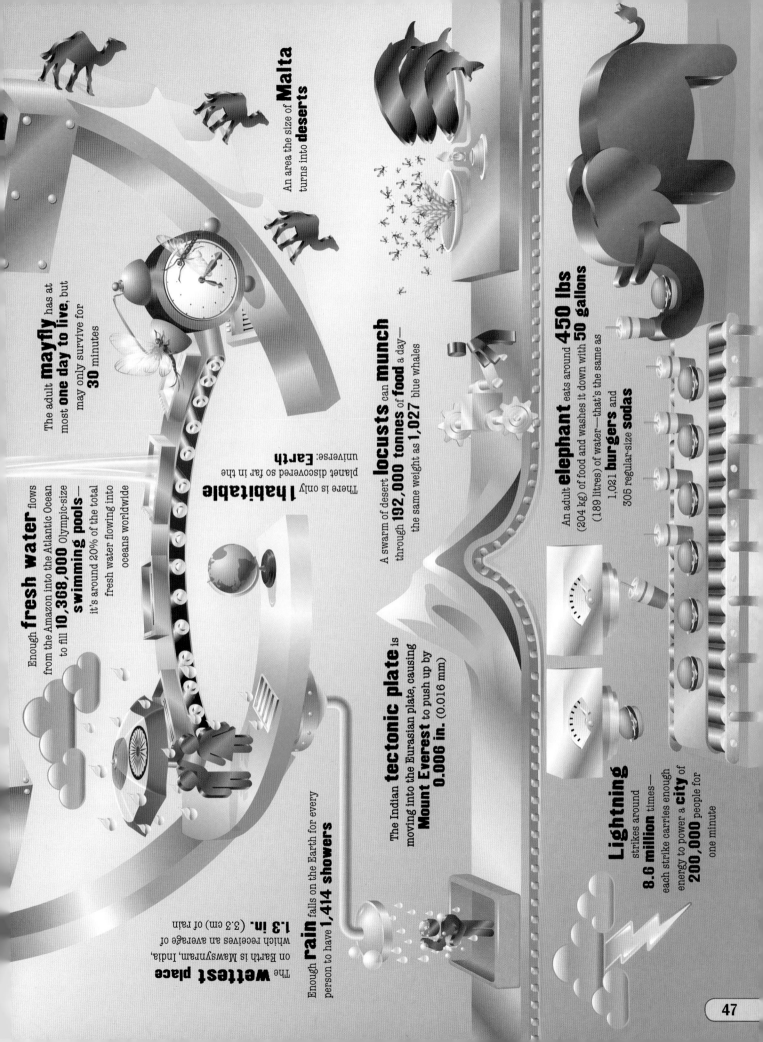

An area the size of **Malta** turns into **deserts**

The adult **mayfly** has at most **one day to live**, but may only survive for **30 minutes**

There is only **1 habitable** planet discovered so far in the universe: **Earth**

Enough **fresh water** flows from the Amazon into the Atlantic Ocean to fill **10,368,000** Olympic-size **swimming pools**— it's around 20% of the total fresh water flowing into oceans worldwide

A swarm of desert **locusts** can **munch** through **192,000 tonnes** of **food** a day— the same weight as **1,027** blue whales

An adult **elephant** eats around **450 lbs** (204 kg) of food and washes it down with **50 gallons** (189 litres) of water—that's the same as **1,021 burgers** and **305** regular-size **sodas**

The Indian **tectonic plate** is moving into the Eurasian plate, causing **Mount Everest** to push up by **0.006 in.** (0.016 mm)

Lightning strikes around **8.6 million** times— each strike carries enough energy to power a **city** of **200,000** people for one minute

The **Wettest place** on Earth is Mawsynram, India, which receives an average of **1.3 in.** (3.3 cm) of rain

Enough **rain** falls on the Earth for every person to have **1,414 showers**

People

As the world's population approaches 7 billion, people are living longer, healthier lives than ever before. But people's life chances are still strongly influenced by where they live. Those living in wealthy Western countries have a massive advantage over those living in poorer countries. This section takes a look at the diversity of the world's people—from the food that we eat and the languages that we speak, to our beliefs and what makes us happy.

Who lives where?

Does this map look strange, or has your brain been bamboozled by all the facts in this book? It's actually a cartogram, showing each country at a size proportional to its population. (To compare with the continents' true sizes, turn to pages 230–231). The cartogram is top-heavy because the northern hemisphere contains around 90% of the world's total population.

Just **11** countries are home to **61%** of the world's population

China

The world's most populous country has a staggering 1.3 billion inhabitants—one-fifth of the people in the world. Thirty years ago, it introduced a policy limiting urban couples to one child each. This is thought to have prevented at least 250 million births.

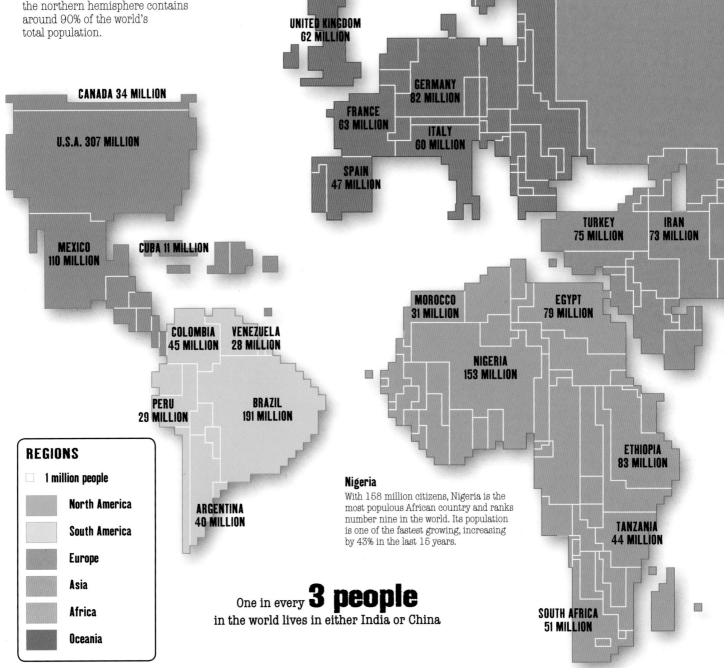

UNITED KINGDOM
62 MILLION

CANADA 34 MILLION

GERMANY
82 MILLION

FRANCE
63 MILLION

ITALY
60 MILLION

U.S.A. 307 MILLION

SPAIN
47 MILLION

TURKEY
75 MILLION

IRAN
73 MILLION

MEXICO
110 MILLION

CUBA 11 MILLION

MOROCCO
31 MILLION

EGYPT
79 MILLION

COLOMBIA
45 MILLION

VENEZUELA
28 MILLION

NIGERIA
153 MILLION

PERU
29 MILLION

BRAZIL
191 MILLION

ETHIOPIA
83 MILLION

ARGENTINA
40 MILLION

TANZANIA
44 MILLION

SOUTH AFRICA
51 MILLION

REGIONS

☐ 1 million people

North America

South America

Europe

Asia

Africa

Oceania

Nigeria

With 158 million citizens, Nigeria is the most populous African country and ranks number nine in the world. Its population is one of the fastest growing, increasing by 43% in the last 15 years.

One in every **3 people** in the world lives in either India or China

How many People on the Planet?

The world's population is a colossal 6.8 billion and counting. The number has quadrupled since 1900. All these people are not spread equally around the world—more than 80% live in the developing regions of Africa, Asia, Latin America, and the Caribbean. Every year our numbers swell by 79 million—a growth rate that is stretching the planet's food and resources.

Japan

Despite having only the 61st-greatest land area, Japan is home to the world's 10th-largest population. Unlike most nations in the top 10, who are struggling with a growing demand for resources, Japan's population is shrinking due to a low birth rate and very little immigration.

**RUSSIAN FEDERATION
142 MILLION**

**CHINA
1.3 BILLION**

**JAPAN
128 MILLION**

**SOUTH KOREA
49 MILLION**

**AKISTAN
MILLION**

**INDIA
1.17 BILLION**

**VIETNAM
87 MILLION**

**THE PHILIPPINES
92 MILLION**

**BANGLADESH
162 MILLION**

INDONESIA 243 MILLION

**AUSTRALIA
22 MILLION**

Population growth

The world's population grew slowly for most of human history. The mid-20th century saw the start of a population "explosion," as death rates fell in developing countries. Growth is now slowing, but population is still increasing by 200,000 people a day. By 2050, it is predicted that the world's population will be almost 9 billion people.

BILLIONS OF PEOPLE

10
9
8
7
6
5
4
3
2
1
0

India

The world's second-most populous country is responsible for a fifth of the world's annual population growth. India's enormous population means that even modest birth rates lead to rapid growth.

Australia

Australia has the world's sixth-largest land area but one of the lowest population densities: just nine people per square mile. Kangaroos outnumber humans three to one!

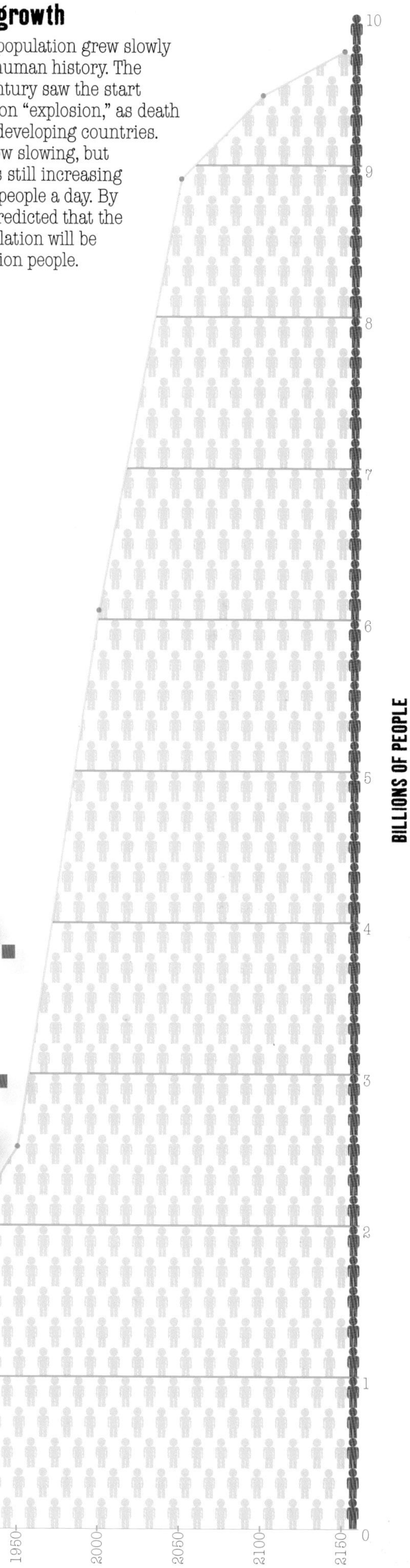

1500 1550 1600 1650 1700 1750 1800 1850 1900 1950 2000 2050 2100 2150

YEAR

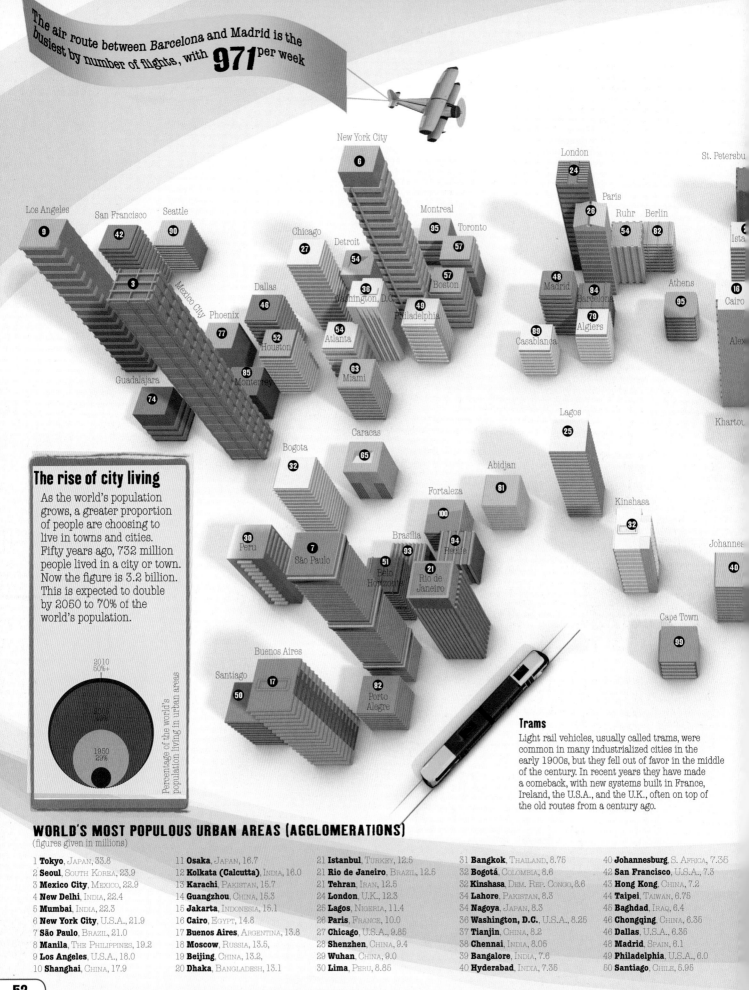

The air route between *Barcelona* and *Madrid* is the busiest by number of flights, with **971** per week

The rise of city living

As the world's population grows, a greater proportion of people are choosing to live in towns and cities. Fifty years ago, 732 million people lived in a city or town. Now the figure is 3.2 billion. This is expected to double by 2050 to 70% of the world's population.

2010 50%+

2005 50%

1950 29%

Percentage of the world's population living in urban areas

Trams

Light rail vehicles, usually called trams, were common in many industrialized cities in the early 1900s, but they fell out of favor in the middle of the century. In recent years they have made a comeback, with new systems built in France, Ireland, the U.S.A., and the U.K., often on top of the old routes from a century ago.

WORLD'S MOST POPULOUS URBAN AREAS (AGGLOMERATIONS)
(figures given in millions)

1 **Tokyo**, Japan, 33.8
2 **Seoul**, South Korea, 23.9
3 **Mexico City**, Mexico, 22.9
4 **New Delhi**, India, 22.4
5 **Mumbai**, India, 22.3
6 **New York City**, U.S.A., 21.9
7 **São Paulo**, Brazil, 21.0
8 **Manila**, The Philippines, 19.2
9 **Los Angeles**, U.S.A., 18.0
10 **Shanghai**, China, 17.9

11 **Osaka**, Japan, 16.7
12 **Kolkata (Calcutta)**, India, 16.0
13 **Karachi**, Pakistan, 15.7
14 **Guangzhou**, China, 15.3
15 **Jakarta**, Indonesia, 15.1
16 **Cairo**, Egypt, 14.8
17 **Buenos Aires**, Argentina, 13.8
18 **Moscow**, Russia, 13.5,
19 **Beijing**, China, 13.2,
20 **Dhaka**, Bangladesh, 13.1

21 **Istanbul**, Turkey, 12.5
21 **Rio de Janeiro**, Brazil, 12.5
21 **Tehran**, Iran, 12.5
24 **London**, U.K., 12.3
25 **Lagos**, Nigeria, 11.4
26 **Paris**, France, 10.0
27 **Chicago**, U.S.A., 9.85
28 **Shenzhen**, China, 9.4
29 **Wuhan**, China, 9.0
30 **Lima**, Peru, 8.85

31 **Bangkok**, Thailand, 8.75
32 **Bogotá**, Colombia, 8.6
32 **Kinshasa**, Dem. Rep. Congo, 8.6
34 **Lahore**, Pakistan, 8.3
34 **Nagoya**, Japan, 8.3
36 **Washington, D.C.**, U.S.A., 8.25
37 **Tianjin**, China, 8.2
38 **Chennai**, India, 8.05
39 **Bangalore**, India, 7.6
40 **Hyderabad**, India, 7.35

40 **Johannesburg**, S. Africa, 7.35
42 **San Francisco**, U.S.A., 7.3
43 **Hong Kong**, China, 7.2
44 **Taipei**, Taiwan, 6.75
45 **Baghdad**, Iraq, 6.4
46 **Chongqing**, China, 6.35
46 **Dallas**, U.S.A., 6.35
48 **Madrid**, Spain, 6.1
49 **Philadelphia**, U.S.A., 6.0
50 **Santiago**, Chile, 5.95

52

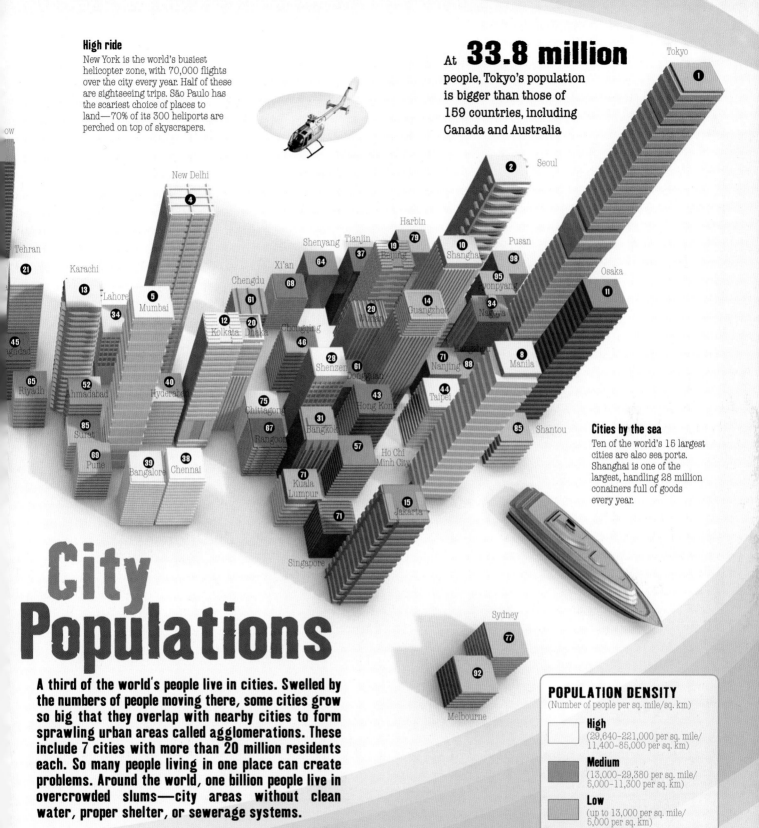

High ride
New York is the world's busiest helicopter zone, with 70,000 flights over the city every year. Half of these are sightseeing trips. São Paulo has the scariest choice of places to land—70% of its 300 heliports are perched on top of skyscrapers.

At **33.8 million** people, Tokyo's population is bigger than those of 159 countries, including Canada and Australia

Cities by the sea
Ten of the world's 15 largest cities are also sea ports. Shanghai is one of the largest, handling 28 million conainers full of goods every year.

City Populations

A third of the world's people live in cities. Swelled by the numbers of people moving there, some cities grow so big that they overlap with nearby cities to form sprawling urban areas called agglomerations. These include 7 cities with more than 20 million residents each. So many people living in one place can create problems. Around the world, one billion people live in overcrowded slums—city areas without clean water, proper shelter, or sewerage systems.

POPULATION DENSITY
(Number of people per sq. mile/sq. km)

High
(29,640–221,000 per sq. mile/ 11,400–85,000 per sq. km)

Medium
(13,000–29,380 per sq. mile/ 5,000–11,300 per sq. km)

Low
(up to 13,000 per sq. mile/ 5,000 per sq. km)

51 **Belo Horizonte**, Brazil, 5.85
52 **Ahmadabad**, India, 5.8
52 **Houston**, U.S.A., 5.8
54 **Atlanta**, U.S.A., 5.7
54 **Detroit**, U.S.A., 5.7
54 **Ruhr**, Germany, 5.7
57 **Khartoum**, Sudan, 5.65
57 **Boston**, U.S.A., 5.65
57 **Ho Chi Mihn City**, Vietnam, 5.65
57 **Toronto**, Canada, 5.65

61 **Chengdu**, China, 5.6
61 **Dongguan**, China, 5.6
63 **Miami**, U.S.A., 5.5
64 **Shenyang**, China, 5.15
65 **Riyadh**, S. Arabia, 4.95
65 **Caracas**, Venezuela, 4.95
67 **Rangoon**, Myanmar, 4.85
68 **Xi'an**, China, 4.825
69 **Pune**, India, 4.75
69 **St. Petersburg**, Russia, 4.75

71 **Kuala Lumpur**, Malaysia, 4.7
71 **Nanjing**, China, 4.7
71 **Singapore**, Singapore, 4.7
74 **Guadalajara**, Mexico, 4.55
75 **Alexandria**, Egypt, 4.5
75 **Chittagong**, Bangladesh, 4.5
77 **Phoenix**, U.S.A., 4.4
77 **Sydney**, Australia, 4.4
79 **Algiers**, Algeria, 4.375
79 **Harbin**, China, 4.375

81 **Abidjan**, Côte d'Ivoire, 4.35
82 **Berlin**, Germany, 4.275
82 **Porto Alegre**, Brazil, 4.275
84 **Barcelona**, Spain, 4.25
85 **Monterrey**, Mexico, 4.075
85 **Shantou**, China, 4.075
85 **Surat**, India, 4.075
88 **Hangzhou**, China, 4.025
89 **Casablanca**, Morocco, 3.975
90 **Seattle**, U.S.A., 3.95

91 **Ankara**, Turkey, 3.925
92 **Melbourne**, Australia, 3.9
93 **Brasília**, Brazil, 3.875
94 **Recife**, Brazil, 3.85
95 **Athens**, Greece, 3.75
95 **Montreal**, Canada, 3.75
95 **Pyongyang**, North Korea, 3.75
98 **Pusan**, South Korea, 3.7
99 **Cape Town**, S. Africa, 3.675
100 **Fortaleza**, Brazil, 3.65

Changing
Populations

Only births and deaths can change our planet's population. The number of babies being born outweighs the number of people dying, so overall, the world's population is growing. But the rate of change is very different from one country to the next. Populations are growing fastest in the developing world. The number of people living in the world's 51 poorest countries will double by 2050. In contrast, the populations of many wealthy countries will shrink as deaths become more common than births.

Fertility rates

Populations are growing fastest where people tend to have large families. Death rates are falling almost everywhere, but fertility (the average number of children per woman) is much higher in some regions than others. Average global fertility is 2.6 children per woman—more than enough to replace both parents when they die.

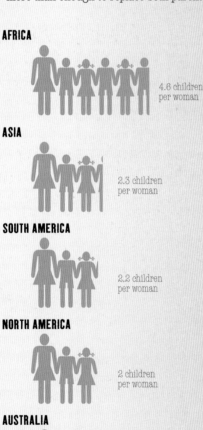

AFRICA

4.6 children per woman

ASIA

2.3 children per woman

SOUTH AMERICA

2.2 children per woman

NORTH AMERICA

2 children per woman

AUSTRALIA

1.8 children per women

EUROPE

1.5 children per woman

Niger

Niger has the world's fastest-growing population and the highest fertility rate. The average woman gives birth to 7.3 children. Each year the number of people increases by nearly 4%.

United States

Natural population growth in the U.S.A. is 0.99% per year. But the number of people is increasing more rapidly than that due to immigration. The rate of immigration is 4.3 migrants to every 1,000 people.

In the balance

Comparing the birth rate and death rate of a country reveals how fast its population is growing. This "natural population growth" does not take into account migration. Most less-developed countries have many more births per year than deaths. In some richer countries, deaths outweigh births—without immigration from poorer countries, their populations would be shrinking rapidly.

India

With more than twice as many births as deaths each year, India's already large population is growing at a rate of 1.3% per year. Some states have reduced population growth by helping women access education, thereby reducing fertility.

Australia

Australia has a similar rate of natural population growth to Brazil, but the effect of its much smaller population is huge. There are just 290,000 births per year in Australia, compared to 2.8 million in Brazil.

Brazil

With 14.2 births per 1,000 people—an average of 2.3 children per woman—natural population growth in Brazil is just 0.75%. But the large existing population means that the population swells by 1.5 million people every year.

Lithuania

Low birth rates mean that many European countries have shrinking populations. With just 10 births per 1,000 people per year, Lithuania has the world's fastest-shrinking population.

Every year **137 million** babies are born and **59 million** people die. The world's population is growing at a rate of **9,100 people** every hour.

BiRTH AND DEATH RATES

 5 deaths per 1,000 people

 5 births per 1,000 people

How Long do you Have?

Life expectancy is rising in most countries, thanks to improved food, hygiene, health care, and education. But life span varies enormously around the world. In wealthy Western Europe, North American, Japan, and Australia, deaths before the age of 60 are unusual. In other parts of the world, people expect to die long before the global average of 69. Many are killed by illnesses that could be treated or prevented if living conditions improved. Look at the lineup below to see how average life spans differ across the world.

Swaziland

In many African countries, life expectancy is falling due to HIV/AIDS. This disease is the world's sixth-biggest killer. In 1990, life expectancy in Swaziland was 60. It is now just 33.

1 2 3 4 5 6 7 8 9 10 11 12   13 14 15   16 17 18 19 20 21   22 23 24 25 26 27 28 29 30 31 32 33 34 35 36 37 38 39 40

Population pyramids

The proportion of people in different age groups within a population can be plotted as a pyramid. The shape reveals whether the population is old or young. The age distribution of a young population produces a pyramid with a wide base and steeply sloping sides. As a population ages, the pyramid gets narrower at the bottom and wider at the top. It starts to look more like a mushroom.

World population

This pyramid shows age distribution for the world as a whole. Although most people in the world are young, rising life expectancy means that elderly people make up a greater proportion of the population than in the past. Currently, almost 8% of the world's population is older than 65. This will rise to 25% by 2050, putting enormous pressure on health and welfare systems.

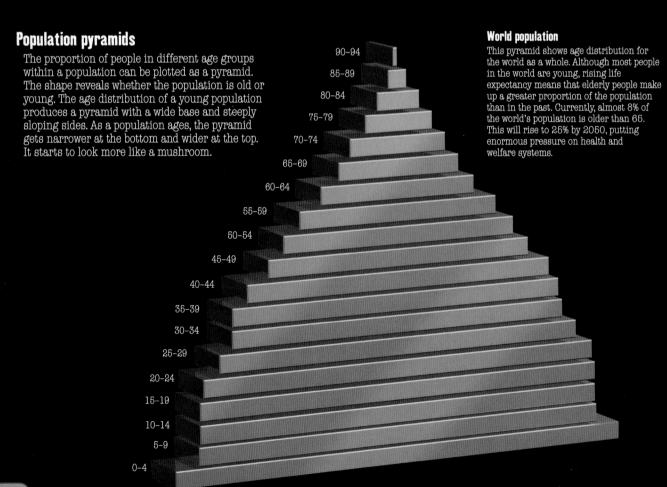

90-94
85-89
80-84
75-79
70-74
65-69
60-64
55-59
50-54
45-49
40-44
35-39
30-34
25-29
20-24
15-19
10-14
5-9
0-4

Living to 100

Celebrating your 100th birthday is a newsworthy event, but if life expectancy trends continue, half of all the babies born in wealthy countries today will live to blow out 100 candles. Jeanne Calment (right) was 122 when she died in 1997, making her the longest-living person ever.

Russia

Cardiovascular disease is the main cause of deaths before the age of 75 in Europe. Death rates are especially high in Russia, where life expectancy has actually fallen since the 1970s due to heart attacks and strokes.

Japan

Japanese women can expect to live longer than anyone in the world—a huge 87 years. Japanese men have a slightly shorter life expectancy, bringing the average down to 82. A 115-year-old Japanese woman is currently the world's oldest living person. In 60 years' time, the average Japanese girl may live to 100.

Afghanistan

Most Afghans have no access to health care or safe drinking water. Just 14% of pregnant women are seen by a health professional—18 mothers die for every 1,000 babies born.

Democratic Republic of the Congo

War in Africa has killed 5.4 million people since 1998. In the Democratic Republic of the Congo, this has wiped 10 years off the average life expectancy. Many people died from preventable diseases that spread during the conflict.

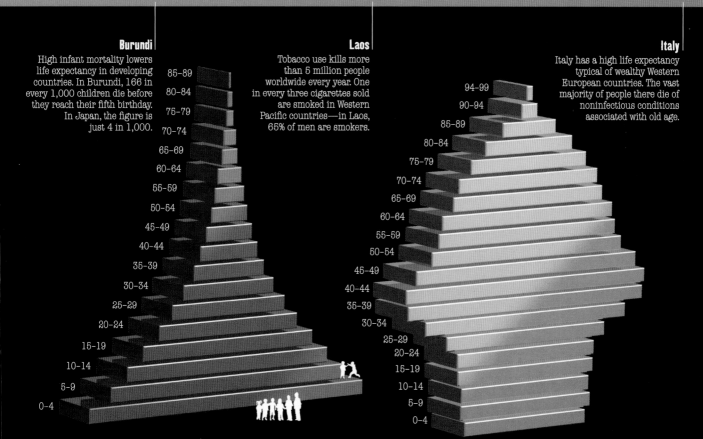

41 42 43 44 45 46 47 48 49 50 51 52 53 54 55 56 57 58 59 60 61 62 63 64 65 66 67 68 69 70 71 72 73 74 75 76 77 78 79 80 81 82

Burundi

High infant mortality lowers life expectancy in developing countries. In Burundi, 166 in every 1,000 children die before they reach their fifth birthday. In Japan, the figure is just 4 in 1,000.

Laos

Tobacco use kills more than 5 million people worldwide every year. One in every three cigarettes sold are smoked in Western Pacific countries—in Laos, 65% of men are smokers.

Italy

Italy has a high life expectancy typical of wealthy Western European countries. The vast majority of people there die of noninfectious conditions associated with old age.

A young population—Burundi

In Burundi, high death rates at all ages means that each age bracket has fewer people than the one below. The narrow tip of the pyramid shows that there are relatively few old people. Less than 3% of people in Burundi live past their 65th birthday.

An aging population—Italy

Populations have aged fastest in developed countries. In Italy, one-fifth of citizens are over 65, and 3.5 million Italians are over the age of 80. By 2050, one-third of Italy's population will be older than 65. This means that for every 100 people of working age, there will be 62 elderly people.

Ways to Go

Of the 55 million deaths each year, certain causes are much more common than others. Risk factors are strongly linked to where you live. In developing regions, disease and malnutrition are deadly, whereas in the wealthiest countries, cancer and cardiovascular disorders are the main causes of death. The spinner shows the overall percentage of deaths due to each cause. The warning signs show a few of the less likely ways to go.

Infectious illnesses
Every year 18 million people die from infectious and parasitic diseases. Pneumonia, diarrhea, and HIV/AIDS claim the most victims, with most of these deaths occurring in developing regions.

Nutritional deficiencies
Malnutrition—not getting the right nutrients—leads to 400,000 deaths annually. A diet lacking enough protein or energy is the biggest killer of children under the age of five, especially in Africa.

Noninfectious illnesses
Noninfectious illnesses are those that cannot be passed on from person to person. Cardiovascular disease (including heart attacks and strokes) is the biggest killer in the world, and cancer accounts for 13% of all deaths.

INFECTIOUS ILLNESSES 25%

NUTRITIONAL DEFICIENCIES 1%

NONINFECTIOUS ILLNESSES 59%

WHAT ARE THE CHANCES?

Snakebite
Worldwide, 450 species of snake are dangerous to humans. Venomous snakebites kill an estimated 125,000 people per year. Of those, 100,000 are in Asia, with 20,000 in India alone.

500,000 : 1

Falling down a manhole
Manholes left open in the road are a real hazard. In 2009, an American teenager had a lucky escape after falling into a manhole while typing a text message. Fortunately, she had a soft landing on the sewage below.

1.5 MILLION : 1

Computer game exhaustion
In South Korea, professional online gamers can earn $100,000 per year. Some take gaming too far—in 2005, a 28-year-old man died of heart failure after playing a game almost nonstop for 50 hours.

5 MILLION : 1

Hippopotamus attack
Although they only eat plants, hippos kill more people in Africa than any other mammal. Weighing as much as three cars, they can outrun a person and will attack to protect their territory.

6 MILLION : 1

In industrialized countries, **one** in **two** people will die of a heart attack or stroke. **70%** of all deaths from car accidents occur in developing countries.

Accidents
Only 6% of deaths are due to accidents, though this adds up to more than 3 million deaths in total. More than a million people die in car accidents alone—two people every minute.

6% ACCIDENTS

War and violence
Men aged between 15 and 60 years have a much higher risk of dying than women of the same age. This is partially due to the greater risk to men of injuries in areas of war and violent conflict.

3% WAR AND VIOLENCE

Birth complications
Every year, 6.3 million babies die shortly before or after being born. Nearly all of these deaths happen in developing countries where good healthcare is unavailable or unaffordable.

6% BIRTH COMPLICATIONS

60% of all deaths are due to infectious diseases.

80% of all deaths from diseases.

In Sub-Saharan Africa, more than

Dirty water is thought to be a factor in

15 BILLION : 1

Laughter
You have more chance of being hit by a meteorite than you have of dying of laughter. But there have been cases of people with weak hearts for whom laughing has been lethal. Laughter increases heart rate and blood pressure, raising the risk of a heart attack.

360 MILLION : 1

Walking into a lamppost
Around 18,000 lamppost-related injuries are reported every year, with some of those affected dying of their injuries.

815 MILLION : 1

Airplane ice
Every year, dozens of people are hit by falling chunks of ice—nowhere near a hailstorm. The ice is likely to form from water leaking from the underside of an aircraft.

256 MILLION : 1

Shark attack
There are around 63 unprovoked shark attacks every year, with more than half taking place in Florida.

250 MILLION : 1

Falling coconuts
It is often claimed that coconut-related deaths are more common than shark attacks. Many tropical resorts warn tourists not to linger under the shady palms, but people who farm the fruit find them harder to avoid.

10 MILLION : 1

Lightning strike
The Democratic Republic of the Congo receives the most lightning, with 395 strikes per square mile each year. In 1998, one bolt of lightning killed all 11 members of a Congolese soccer team.

Diseases and Health Care

Health care has improved so much in the last 30 years that the World Health Organization believes the lives of 6.7 million children have been saved. The world now spends a third more on health than it did just five years ago, and on average people are living longer and healthier lives. But progress is not equal around the world. Poorer countries—and even entire continents—are trailing behind.

Across continents

There is an astonishing difference between the rates of infectious diseases in rich and poor nations. In Europe, only 2.5% of deaths are caused by infectious and parasitic diseases. In the developing countries of Africa, the figure is closer to 50%.

CAUSES OF DEATH

Each circle represents 1% of all deaths

NONINFECTIOUS CONDITIONS

- Cardiovascular diseases
- Cancers
- Digestive diseases
- Respiratory diseases
- Neuropsychiatric disorders
- Diabetes

INFECTIOUS CONDITIONS

- Respiratory infections
- HIV/Aids
- Diarrhea
- Tuberculosis
- Malaria
- Other infectious or parasitic diseases

OTHER

- Accidental injuries
- Intentional injuries
- Birth conditions
- Pregnancy and childbirth
- Other

Europe

Success in preventing and treating infectious diseases means that most illnesses and deaths in Europe are caused by cardiovascular diseases and cancers. These chronic, noninfectious conditions are associated with urbanization, an aging population, and a lifestyle with plenty of food and little exercise. Many of these risk factors could be controlled.

EUROPE

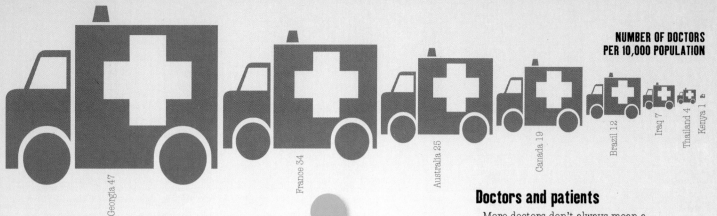

Georgia 47

France 34

Australia 25

Canada 19

Brazil 12

Iraq 7

Thailand 4

Kenya 1

Doctors and patients

More doctors don't always mean a healthier population. In the former Soviet republic of Georgia, most doctors are concentrated in the cities. The poorest people living in rural areas have very little access to health care. Life expectancy is more than 10 years lower than it is in Canada.

More than **16 million** people in sub-Saharan Africa are living with HIV/AIDS

Cost of care

The U.S.A. has one of the world's most expensive health care systems. Around 19% of all government expenditure is on health, and this is more than doubled by private contributions. Pakistan has the smallest health care budget—just 1.3% of government spending.

Africa

In Africa, poor nutrition, unsafe water, and a lack of basic sanitation increase the number of infections and make cases more dangerous than they would be in the developed world. Families often burn wood for cooking and heating, causing a large number of lung infections. Pneumonia is the biggest killer of children.

Pakistan $51

Papua New Guinea $134

Jamaica $240

Namibia $338

Venezuela $396

Jordan $611

Poland $910

Germany $3,328

U.S.A. $6,714

AFRICA

528 pints (250 litres) to produce one ear of corn

Watery Earth

Not all of the water on Earth is suitable for drinking – 97.5% is salty seawater and only 2.5% is drinkable freshwater. Of that 2.5%, the majority is locked up in glaciers, ice caps, and land, leaving just 0.007% in rivers and lakes, readily accessible for us to use.

Water

Water is one of the most important of Earth's resources. Without water to drink, we could not survive for more than a few days. Water is essential for good health, industry, and farming, and we use it to cook with and wash and play in. However, Earth only has a limited amount of this crucial resource, and with the world's population growing, the water is not trickling down to all who need it.

FRESH WATER
2.5%

ACCESSIBLE TO HUMANS
0.007%

SOIL LOCKED
30%

GLACIERS
70%

SALTWATER
97.5%

Global usage

Most of the world's water supply is used for agriculture. The amount that people use in their homes is a mere 8%. However, water usage in different regions varies considerably. In Africa, agriculture consumes 88% of all water withdrawn, while in Europe most water is used in industry.

PERCENTAGE OF GLOBAL WATER SUPPLY USED IN EACH SECTOR

DOMESTIC	INDUSTRY	AGRICULTURE
8%	22%	70%

Domestic usage

A person in the U.S.A. typically uses more water taking a five-minute shower than a person living in a developing country slum uses in an entire day. In developing countries, insufficient infrastructure and sanitation prevents people from accessing the water that they need. This problem plagues 1.6 billion people worldwide, living predominantly in rural communities.

AMOUNT OF WATER USED BY INDIVIDUALS

SUB-SAHARAN AFRICA	EUROPE	NORTH AMERICA AND JAPAN
21–42 pints (10–20 liters)	423 pints (200 liters)	740 pints (350 liters)

Droplet by droplet

Water is used to produce the food that we eat and the products that we use. Even the simplest of things requires large amounts of water. Read around the edge of the page to discover how much water is needed to produce different products.

2,473 pints (1,170 liters) to produce one breast filet of chicken

1,374 pints (650 liters) to produce 500 g (18 oz) of toast

Stressed resources

A country with less than 60,035 ft³ (1,700 m³) of water per capita is said to be experiencing "water stress." One with less than 35,315 ft³ (1,000 m³) is suffering a water crisis. If this drops to below 17,357 ft³ (500 m³), the health of people and economic development in the region is severely compromised.

Greenland

Greenland is covered in glaciers, which hold huge quantities of fresh water. From these, the meltwater provides an immense water supply for very few people—just 55,000 people live in Greenland.

U.S.A.

The U.S. uses a huge amount of water each day, but then it has plenty of freshwater to use; the country is packed with reservoirs, dams, wells, huge water towers, and huge lengths of water pipes.

Kuwait

This desert country has the least amount of fresh water in the world. However, its extreme wealth has enabled it to build desalination plants, to make use of the huge amounts of seawater at its disposal, and to buy in water from Iraq.

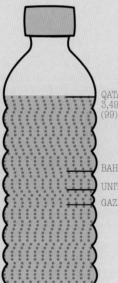

GREENLAND, 380,263,281 (10,767,857)

USA, 55,202,756 (1,563,168)

FRENCH GUIANA, 28,679,782 (812,121)
ICELAND, 21,517,897 (609,319)
GUYANA, 11,183,766 (316,689)

QATAR, 3,496 (99)

BAHAMAS, 2,331 (66)

UNITED ARAB EMIRATES, 2,048 (58)

GAZA STRIP, 1,836 (52)

KUWAIT, 353 (10)

TOP 5 WATER-SECURE COUNTRIES
ft³ (m³) per capita, 2000

TOP 5 WATER-INSECURE COUNTRIES
ft³ (m³) per capita, 2000

Water for the people

Water and populations are unevenly distributed around the globe; arid regions have little fresh water, yet they account for 40% of global land area across the continents. Nearly three billion people—more than 40% of the world's population—live in water-scarce conditions.

34.8%   60.3%

ASIA

5.9%   10.9%

EUROPE

13.3%   7.7%

NORTH AMERICA

10.6%   14.7%

AFRICA

2.9%   0.5%

OCEANIA

32.2%   5.7%

SOUTH AMERICA

WATER SUPPLY

percentage of world's population

percentage of world's water

Water wars

In the past 50 years, there have been 1,831 water-related disputes, 21 of which have resulted in violence. With continued population growth, increased consumption, and anticipated climate change, this is likely to mean more conflicts in the future between nations that share fresh water supplies.

Hunger

We've all felt the unpleasant sensation in our stomach that signals hunger. Around 1.02 billion people battle that feeling every day. It is a huge a barrier to a country's development; hungry people can think of little else beyond their next meal. At the UN Millennium Summit in 2000, world leaders pledged to halve the number of people who suffer from hunger by 2015. They are not on track to do this: while undernourishment fell between 1990 and 2006, it is now rising again.

Africa
With 29% of its population undernourished, sub-Saharan Africa has the highest hunger rate per capita in the world. Millions of Africans rely on food aid, and the global economic crisis saw hunger in the region rise further in 2008.

Arctic circle

NORTH AMERICA

EUROPE

AFRICA

Tropic of Cancer

Where hunger hits the hardest

Although hunger is a global problem, 65% of the world's hungry live in just seven countries—Bangladesh, China, the Congo, Ethiopia, India, Indonesia, and Pakistan. Famine leading to starvation is the most extreme form of hunger, but the long-term effects of a poor diet can be just as serious. Undernourishment describes more than just simple lack of food. One-third of the world's population suffers from chronic malnutrition—a hidden hunger caused by diets that lack the nutrients needed for healthy growth and development. Every day 24,000 people die from hunger-related causes and a large proportion of these are children.

Equator

SOUTH AMERICA

Tropic of Capricorn

EARTH'S AGRICULTURAL POTENTIAL

Utilized

Unutilized

What causes hunger?

It is difficult to understand why so many people go hungry when most people in wealthy countries look forward to long, healthy, food-abundant lives. Less than 60% of our planet's agricultural potential is used to its full capacity, and we already produce enough food each year to feed everyone. But it is not shared out evenly. The main cause of hunger is poverty—a lack of means to buy or grow food. Conflict and natural disasters add to the hunger misery by disrupting food supply and can turn food shortage into a famine.

Brazil
Brazil is the world's fourth-largest agricultural exporter, yet its number of hungry people keeps rising dramatically. Leaders have tackled the problem for the most vulnerable children, though, through a successful school meals program.

More than **80%**
of the world's hungry live in rural communities in developing countries. They often work in food production but are not the end consumers

Asia and the Pacific
Nearly two-thirds of the world's hungry live in this region (which includes India). In southern Asia, 48% of children under the age of five are underweight due to an inadequate diet that stunts growth and development and makes children more susceptible to disease.

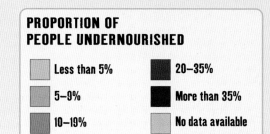

PROPORTION OF PEOPLE UNDERNOURISHED

Less than 5%		20–35%	
5–9%		More than 35%	
10–19%		No data available	

ASIA

Global warming and food production

Crops improve
Climate change threatens to increase extreme weather and drought and to change the seasonal patterns that guide agriculture. While this will devastate the food production of many countries, experts predict that some countries in the mid-latitudes may actually benefit from warmer summers and wetter winters brought about by global warming. In these countries, where fewer people are undernourished in the first place, farms may become more productive.

INCREASE IN CROP YIELDS — THE MID-LATITUDES

The hungrier get hungrier
Countries in this region, already suffering the highest rates of malnutrition, will be the worst hit by global warming. Staple crops such as corn and rice are very sensitive to temperature—a rise of just 1.8°F (1°C) could halve crop production in some areas. Combined with population growth, the consequences of global warming could be devastating.

DECREASE IN CROP YIELDS — THE TROPICS

India
Almost 50% of the world's hungry live in India. Malnutrition begins before birth; nine in 10 of India's pregnant women have an inadequate diet. Those who survive the malnutrition of their youth are likely to become hungry adults.

OCEANIA

Food aid
Wealthy countries produce huge food surpluses, a lot of which is donated to poorer, poverty-stricken countries. But it is not always enough. Year after year developed countries donate billions of dollars to food aid. This goes a long way toward helping many hungry people, but few countries achieve the UN target of donating 0.7% of their national incomes. Food aid is only part of the solution. Providing seeds, tools, and education to help farmers grow their own crops helps build self-sufficiency and reduces the need for food aid.

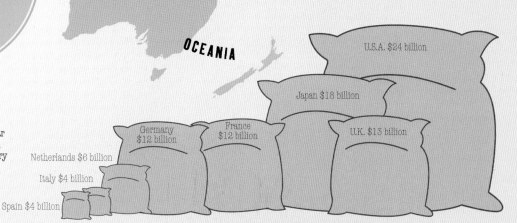

Netherlands $6 billion
Italy $4 billion
Spain $4 billion
Germany $12 billion
France $12 billion
U.K. $13 billion
Japan $18 billion
U.S.A. $24 billion

LARGEST DONORS OF FOOD AID (2006)

Food Waste

Food waste begins on farms, where huge numbers of fruit and vegetables are rejected for being too big, too small, or too ugly. It ends in household garbage cans when we throw away what we can't eat. Wasted food often ends up in landfills, where it generates harmful greenhouse gases. By wasting food, we also waste the energy, water, and other resources that are used to produce, process, and transport it to our tables, further contributing to global warming.

THROWN AWAY

EATEN

Worst offenders

British consumers are among the most wasteful in the world. They spend $19 billion per year buying food that they then throw away. That's about one-third of all the food that they buy and weighs in at a staggering 8.3 million tonnes. Some of this waste is inedible, such as bones or eggshells. But two-thirds—5.3 million tonnes—could be avoided. Eliminating it would enable a cut in carbon dioxide emissions equivalent to taking one-quarter of all the country's cars off the road.

What's in the garbage can?

Almost a quarter of U.K. household food waste by weight is vegetable matter. It is estimated that 45% of lettuce bought in the U.K. is thrown away. Rotting vegetables, fruit, and lettuce are ideal for composting, yet most end up in landfills.

FRESH VEGETABLES AND LETTUCE 23%

DRINKS 16%

FRESH FRUIT 13%

BAKED GOODS 10%

READY-PREPARED MEALS 8%

MEAT AND FISH 7%

DAIRY AND EGGS 7%

ALL OTHER 16%

WASTE IN THE FOOD CHAIN: WHERE WASTE HAPPENS IN THE U.K.

RETAILERS
1.6 million tonnes discarded by stores and restaurants every year

MANUFACTURERS
4–9 million tonnes thrown away every year during the production process

Waste at every stage
Food waste ends in our garbage cans, when we miss an expiry date or cook too much. But your food waste footprint is bigger than you think. Food is lost or thrown away at every stage of the supply chain: during harvesting, processing and distribution, and in the store, where "ugly" fruit and vegetables are left behind on the shelf.

LEFT TO GO BAD
2.9 million tonnes end up in the trash due to not being used in time

SURPLUS TO REQUIREMENTS
2.2 million tonnes are scraped off plates when too much has been prepared. A further 0.2 million tonnes are thrown away in homes for other reasons.

21%
Tipped down drain

Rotten refuse
One-fifth of wasted food is tipped down household drains, flooding sewers with a 1.8-million-tonne river of milk, soda, fruit juice, and eggs. Around 5.8 million tonnes of food are collected by garbage-collection facilities. Some areas have composting schemes, but the majority of places collect food waste with general refuse and send it straight to landfill sites, where it rots and releases methane, a major cause of global warming.

72%
Collected with the trash

8%
Home composting/fed to animals

Food mountain
While 1.02 billion people go hungry every day, rich countries waste enough food to meet the world's food needs several times over. The volume of food wasted in one year in the U.K. alone is more than double the amount that all the countries of the world donated to help relieve hunger for those in desperate situations.

8.3 MILLION TONNES
Amount U.K. consumers throw away each year

4 MILLION TONNES
Amount of emergency food aid donated globally

Eco-friendly options
There are many alternatives to landfills and composting. In some places, these options are being explored, but the number of countries, businesses, and individuals taking advantage of them remains small.

Redistribute to the poor
A growing number of charities rescue spare food from supermarkets and restaurants, distributing it to homeless shelters and other people in need.

Generate energy
Rotting food produces methane, which can be burned to generate electricity. Used cooking oil can be made into biodiesel, a renewable fuel used by buses in many cities.

Feed to the pigs
Japan's food industry recycles more than 70% of its waste into animal feed and fertilizer, increasing the supply to agriculture without growing extra crops.

Become a freegan
Supermarkets often discard edible food because the expiry date has past or the packaging is damaged. Freegans highlight this waste by only eating food they have scavenged.

Globesity

Obesity is a rapidly growing problem around the world. By 2015, 2.3 billion adults will be overweight and 700 million obese. The excess fat stored by their bodies will put them at risk of many serious illnesses. A third of the world's obese people live in the developing world, where health care systems are already struggling. Economic growth, urbanization, and the worldwide availability of cheap, imported, processed food all contribute to this modern epidemic.

Body Mass Index

The Body Mass Index (BMI) is used to spot obesity in adults. This chart can be used to find an adult's BMI – using either metric or imperial measurements, plot where weight and height meet on the grid. Measuring children is more challenging because their age and gender must be taken into account. The World Health Organization (WHO) estimates that there are 22 million obese children worldwide.

HEIGHT IN FEET AND INCHES

Portion sizes

The food portions that we eat in restaurants and buy in supermarkets have expanded massively over the past 50 years. Even the weight of a typical slice of bread has increased. The worst culprits are energy-packed fast foods. In the last few years, three U.S. fast-food chains have introduced sandwiches stuffed with 12 oz (340 g) of beef— the amount of meat an adult should actually eat in two days. Eating more than we need leads to weight gain.

1989

Old portion size—333 calories
Fast-food restaurants in the past offered only one portion size. Now, this portion size is considered "small."

2009

New portion size—590 calories
Meals today are up to twice as big as they were 20 years ago, and five times larger than they were in the 1950s.

The cost of convenience

Obesity rates are at the highest in urban populations. Just 5% of Chinese people are obese, but this rises to 20% in cities, where people exercise less and are more likely to choose processed food. Factory-made foods tend to be high in energy but low in the nutrients needed for health. The drinks shown here contain similar energy levels (measured in calories), but energy is all that the cola provides.

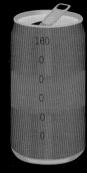

	COLA DRINK	ORANGE JUICE	MILK
CALORIES	160	168	153
VITAMIN A, IU	0	291	750
VITAMIN C, MG	0	146	3
CALCIUM, MG	0	33	450
MAGNESIUM, MG	0	36	51
POTASSIUM, MG	0	711	352

110   120   130   140   150

Weight across the nations

Although being underweight is associated with poverty, many people living in poverty are actually overweight. Obesity is rising fastest in low- and middle-income countries, where poverty is rife, as their populations adopt unhealthy Western habits and eat cheap junk foods, imported from Western countries. The World Health Organization is helping governments tackle the problem by promoting healthy eating in schools.

TOP SIX OBESE COUNTRIES (% OF POPULATION THAT IS OBESE)

NAURU 78.5% TONGA 56% FRENCH POLYNESIA 40.9% SAUDI ARABIA 35.6% UNITED ARAB EMIRATES 33.7% U.S.A. 32.2%

Nauru

The Pacific Islands are home to the world's fattest populations. In the last 50 years, these small countries have been flooded with cheap, fatty, imported foods. In cultures like Nauru's that traditionally celebrate plumpness as a sign of wealth and fertility, obesity has risen dramatically.

Saudi Arabia

In the oil-rich Middle East, wealth and the hot climate encourage a sedentary lifestyle. Religious law makes it particularly difficult for Saudi women to exercise; commercial gyms and sports clubs for women have been banned, and women can only walk in public if accompanied by a male relative.

Health issues

Many serious diseases are more common in overweight and obese people. These include cardiovascular disease, high blood pressure, some cancers, and late-onset diabetes. The first case of diabetes in Nauru was registered in 1925, and the number of sufferers has risen with obesity. Worldwide, there are now 2.6 million patients. Similarly, in the Middle East, a third of all health care costs are linked to obesity.

TOP SIX DIABETIC COUNTRIES (% OF POPULATION THAT IS DIABETIC)

NAURU 30.7% UNITED ARAB EMIRATES 19.5% SAUDI ARABIA 16.7% BAHRAN 15.2% KUWAIT 14.4% OMAN 13.1%

Thrifty gene theory

Some scientists believe that people from Africa, Southeast Asia, and Polynesia are especially likely to become obese when they eat a Western diet. This is due to their genetic make-up; research suggests that people in these nations carry a "thrifty gene" that once helped them store fat easily in case of famine. Even when the food supply is constant, their bodies continue to hold on to as much fat as possible.

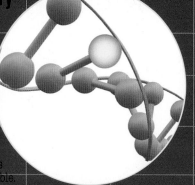

BODY MASS INDEX

Severely underweight	Overweight
Underweight	Obese
Healthy weight	Clinically obese

HEIGHT IN METERS

1.96
1.94
1.92
1.90
1.88
1.86
1.84
1.82
1.80
1.78
1.76
1.74
1.72
1.70
1.68
1.66
1.64
1.62
1.60
1.58
1.56
1.54
1.52

Daily Diets

As more and more people move to towns and cities and living standards improve, global eating habits are changing rapidly. Food is more accessible and diverse than ever before, but for many, fresh fruit, vegetables, and cereals are being replaced by highly processed, energy-dense foods. These foods are full of fat, sugar, and salt. This has led to an increase in diet-related diseases and is a growing problem in developing countries.

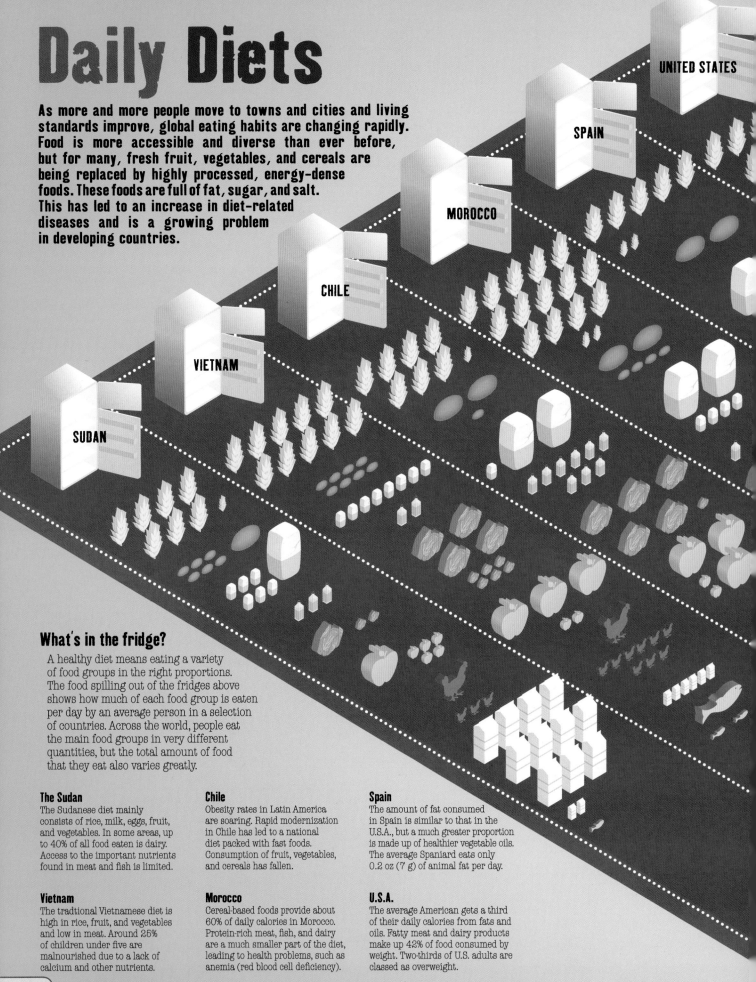

UNITED STATES

SPAIN

MOROCCO

CHILE

VIETNAM

SUDAN

What's in the fridge?

A healthy diet means eating a variety of food groups in the right proportions. The food spilling out of the fridges above shows how much of each food group is eaten per day by an average person in a selection of countries. Across the world, people eat the main food groups in very different quantities, but the total amount of food that they eat also varies greatly.

The Sudan
The Sudanese diet mainly consists of rice, milk, eggs, fruit, and vegetables. In some areas, up to 40% of all food eaten is dairy. Access to the important nutrients found in meat and fish is limited.

Vietnam
The tradtional Vietnamese diet is high in rice, fruit, and vegetables and low in meat. Around 25% of children under five are malnourished due to a lack of calcium and other nutrients.

Chile
Obesity rates in Latin America are soaring. Rapid modernization in Chile has led to a national diet packed with fast foods. Consumption of fruit, vegetables, and cereals has fallen.

Morocco
Cereal-based foods provide about 60% of daily calories in Morocco. Protein-rich meat, fish, and dairy are a much smaller part of the diet, leading to health problems, such as anemia (red blood cell deficiency).

Spain
The amount of fat consumed in Spain is similar to that in the U.S.A., but a much greater proportion is made up of healthier vegetable oils. The average Spaniard eats only 0.2 oz (7 g) of animal fat per day.

U.S.A.
The average American gets a third of their daily calories from fats and oils. Fatty meat and dairy products make up 42% of food consumed by weight. Two-thirds of U.S. adults are classed as overweight.

Cost of consumption

In developed countries, people expect to spend a low proportion of their household budget on food. This puts pressure on food producers in the developing world to sell their crops at low prices, who in turn struggle to feed their own families. In these poorer countries, food is a priority and takes up more of a family's budget.

NIGERIA 73%
ALBANIA 69%
FRANCE 15%
VIETNAM 65%
U.K. 16%
U.S.A. 10%

PROPORTION OF HOUSEHOLD BUDGET SPENT ON FOOD

Counting the calories

The energy in food is often measured in kilocalories (kcal). The average man needs 2,500 kcal to power him through the day; a woman needs 2,000 kcal. In the U.S.A., there are 3,753 kcal available per person per day, whereas in Eritrea, people have access to only 1,519 kcal daily.

Kcal available per person per day

North America	3755.8
Europe	3331.4
Middle East and North Africa	3109.8
South America	2850.9
Asia	2681.8
Sub-Saharan Africa	2262.2

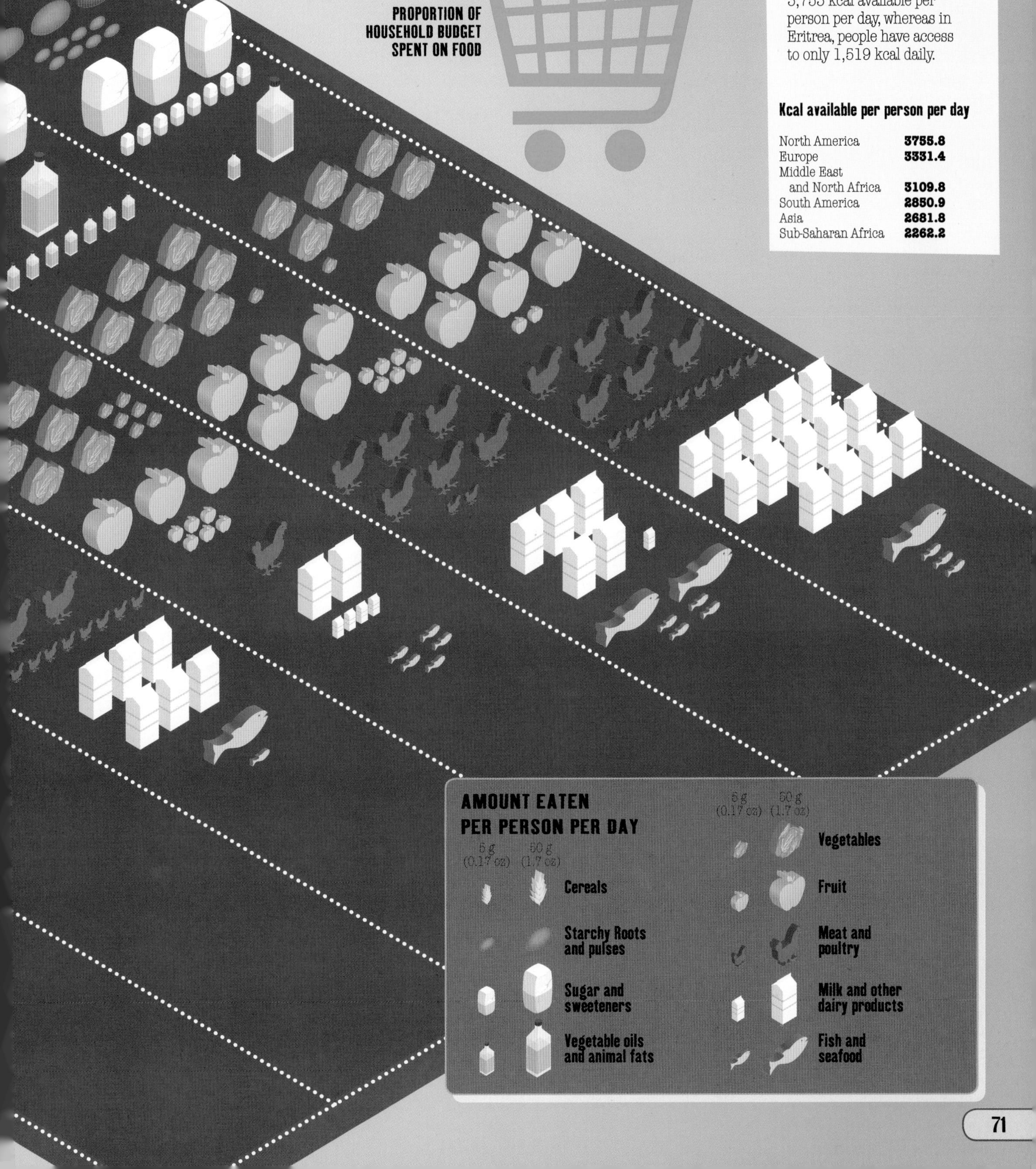

AMOUNT EATEN PER PERSON PER DAY

5 g (0.17 oz)   50 g (1.7 oz)

Cereals

Starchy Roots and pulses

Sugar and sweeteners

Vegetable oils and animal fats

5 g (0.17 oz)   50 g (1.7 oz)

Vegetables

Fruit

Meat and poultry

Milk and other dairy products

Fish and seafood

Look who's Talking

From scary stories to stirring speeches, we use language to express emotions, impart knowledge, and share ideas. The world's 6,900 languages are also a vital part of cultural identity and diversity, yet half of all languages have fewer than 6,000 speakers. Ten disappear every year, and 2,500 are threatened with extinction in the next century. Entire ways of life will fade, as poems, songs, and traditions are lost forever.

Top 25 languages

More than half of the world's population—3.9 billion people—speak one of 25 major languages as their mother tongue. This word cloud shows each language sized proportionally to its number of native speakers. Chinese is by far the biggest, with nearly four times as many speakers as Spanish, the next most common.

TURKISH
RUSSIAN BENGALI
CHII
1.2 BILLION SPEAKERS
GERMAN VIETNAMESE MARATHI
ENGLISH
FRENCH LAHNDA

1. Chinese
With 1.2 billion speakers, Chinese is the world's most spoken language. It is a macrolanguage—one made up of many different regional forms, or dialects. The biggest of these is Mandarin Chinese, with 845 million speakers. Chinese is a tonal language—the meaning of many words changes with their tone or pitch.

3. English
English is spoken as a first language in 112 countries, making it the most widely spread language and the foremost language for international communication. Around 329 million people speak English as their first language, but it is also the most learned foreign language, used by up to 350 million non-native speakers.

IN NUMBERS: HOW THE WORLD'S LANGUAGES COMPARE

Nearly extinct

More than 100 but fewer than 1 million speakers

| 7% | 3% | 87% | 3% |

Fewer than 100 speakers

More than 1 million speakers

Lost your tongue?
Only 300 languages have more than 1 million speakers. The remaining 6,600 are spoken by just 6% of the world's population. Around 470 are classed as nearly extinct, meaning that only a few elderly speakers survive.

2. Spanish

Spanish is the world's second-most spoken language, shared by 329 million people in 44 countries. Although Spanish developed in Europe, there are many more Spanish speakers in Latin America. Differences are minor, so Spanish speakers from any country can understand each other.

4. Arabic

A total of 221 million people in 57 countries across the Middle East and North Africa speak varieties of Arabic. They are often so different that speakers from different countries cannot understand each another. By 2050, Arabic is expected to be one of the top three languages, behind Chinese and Hindi.

SPANISH KOREAN ARABIC MALAY

…ESE

PORTUGUESE JAPANESE GUJARATI BHOJPURI URDU

HINDI TAMIL ITALIAN TELUGU POLISH JAVANESE

5. Hindi

Hindi is the first language of 182 million people and the most spoken of India's 445 living languages. Five other Indian languages make it into the top 25: Telugu, Marathi, Tamil, Gujarati, and Bhojpuri. The Indian movie industry reflects the country's linguistic diversity—just 22% of movies released are in Hindi.

Learning a second language

English, French, and German are the three most-studied foreign languages worldwide. Spanish comes fourth in Europe but tops the chart in the U.S.A. The most multilingual Europeans are the Luxembourgers: 99% speak at least one other language.

Mind your Manners!

Religion, superstition, and centuries of tradition have shaped each country's unique mixture of cultural norms—absorbed as we grow up, but often baffling to those from other cultures. While confused tourists are happy to muddle through, there is a thriving market for etiquette coaches who help businesspeople impress international colleagues and clients with their local know-how.

4 13 14

Numbers

Four is a very unlucky number in China, like the number 13 is in other cultures. Chinese buildings don't have fourth floors. In Japan, the number 14 is avoided because it sounds like the word for death.

Chop-stuck

Eat out in China, Japan, Korea, or Vietnam, and you'll have to master the skill of eating with chopsticks. Not only that, but the etiquette of how to use them differs in each region. Just don't order the soup!

Straight up
Never stand chopsticks upright in a bowl of food. In Asia, this is a reminder of the incense sticks associated with death.

Parallel lines
Finished eating? Be careful to place your chopsticks side by side. Forming a V or X is a bad omen in Japan and Hong Kong.

Skewered
Stabbing food with your chopsticks may make life easier, but it is equivalent to licking food off a knife.

Chopstick shovel
Shoveling dripping food from bowl to mouth is acceptable everywhere except Korea, where fingers are used to eat rice.

Food faux pas

We're often told to clear our plates, but in some countries this would baffle or even insult your host. Make sure that you know where to stuff and where to stop.

Eat it up
Make sure that your eyes aren't bigger than your belly in Greece. Your host would rather remove surplus food than waste it.

Small portions
In Hong Kong, be sure to leave a little on your plate. Finishing everything suggests your host hasn't been generous enough.

Don't take no for an answer
Even a ravenous Chinese person will refuse food at first, for fear of appearing too greedy or eager to eat.

More, please!
Leaving food in Thailand signals that you are full. Force yourself to clear your plate, and the host will bring even more.

Table manners

When it comes to eating, several things considered to be bad manners here are seen as courteous in China. But don't even think about flipping a fish over to eat the other side...

Noisy noodles
Slurping food signals that it is so delicious, you are eating it while it's hot. Slurping noisily cools the food as you go.

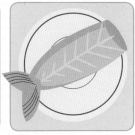

Flipping fish
Flipping a half-eaten fish is said to be bad luck, like turning a fisherman's boat. It's more polite to leave the bottom half.

Burping
Talking with your mouth full and finishing the meal with a loud burp will show how much you've enjoyed it.

Pass me the salt
Chinese hosts reach across the table to serve food. You can reach for the salt—if you stand up first.

Say it with flowers...

...but make sure you know what you're saying. Get the color or number wrong and your beautiful bouquet might be seen as an omen of bad luck or even death to the unlucky recipient.

Marigolds
For Mexicans, marigolds are a symbol of grief and represent the massacre of native Aztecs by the invading Spanish.

Yellow flowers
In Russia, giving a bunch of yellow flowers to a friend is a signal that you want to end the relationship.

Red roses
A dozen red roses are the ultimate romantic gesture in some countries, but a favorite funeral bouquet in Latvia.

White flowers
In many Asian countries, white flowers symbolize tears and death, while an odd number of flowers brings bad luck.

Gifting gaffes

In many cultures, the most innocent-looking objects have hidden meanings. To avoid present-buying problems completely, visit Iceland, where it's considered rude to give your host a gift.

In the doghouse
Cute puppy prints won't go down well in Malaysia and Indonesia, where many people see dogs as unclean.

Umbrella blunder
In China, giving an umbrella means you don't want to see someone again – the word for umbrella sounds like "split up."

Sniffy slipup
In Korea and Mexico, handkerchiefs are symbols of tearful goodbyes and can signal the end of a friendship.

Your time's up
Giving a clock as a gift in China says that you're counting the seconds until the recipient's death.

Silent signals

You're shopping in a foreign country, you don't speak the language, but you've spotted exactly want you want. How are you going to let the shop assistant know without offending them?

Pointing
Pointing with one finger is effective but considered very rude in many countries, as it can indicate anger.

Thumbs up
In Indonesia, the best way to point is with a closed fist held sideways, thumb held toward the object.

Palms up
The Japanese and Chinese point with an open hand, extending all fingers toward the object—ready to receive it.

Pout with lips
Ecuadorians point by puckering or pursing their lips, so don't worry if you see a lot of people pouting.

Don't do it in public!

Do your bad habits include wiping your nose, chewing gum, and...licking stamps? Each of these must be kept behind closed doors in certain countries.

Stick to the right
Bad news for left-handers—touching people, food, and money with the left hand is considered unhygienic in India.

Burst that bubble
Chewing gum is illegal in Singapore. Smuggling it into the country earns you one year in jail and a £10,000 fine.

Royal respect
Thais hold their king in very high regard—even licking the back of a postage stamp is considered disrespectful.

Keep sniffing
Many Japanese think that it's barbaric to blow your nose in public and even worse to keep a used tissue in your pocket.

Tribal Peoples

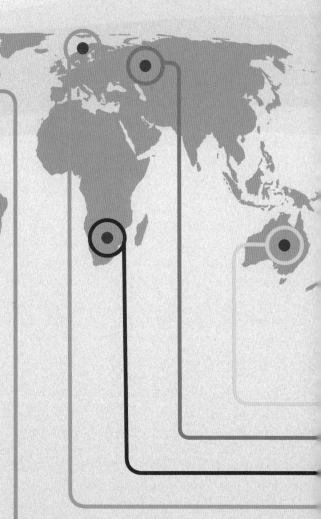

Around 150 million people live in tribal communities that are traditionally self-sufficient, relying on their local land to provide what they need. Their way of life is socially, culturally, and economically different from that of the industrialized world, and they have their own unique values, traditions, and methods of governing themselves. Some tribal peoples have lost their traditional organizations and no longer live off the land but still identify with their culture. The world is beginning to realize how important it is to preserve their diverse knowledge and skills.

Indigenous inhabitants

Many tribal peoples are descended from their country's indigenous (or original) inhabitants. Today, they often live in mountains, forests, and deserts, far from the towns and cities that have been built on their ancestral land. As the world's demand for resources grows, even these remote areas are being invaded. These six tribes live on different continents, but their stories show some of the problems faced by indigenous peoples everywhere.

Tribal peoples make up **2%** of the world's population

Yanomami: Brazil and Venezuela

Since the 1980s, gold miners have invaded the Amazon forest, bringing disease and pollution to tribes such as the Yanomami. They are one of the last tribal peoples to remain on their traditional lands and currently number around 32,000 people. Hunting, gathering, and fishing provide 20% of their food, and the rest is grown in large gardens in forest clearings. In 2004, they formed an organization to establish education and health care and to defend their rights.

Inuit: northern Canada, Alaska, Greenland, and eastern Russia

This is an *inunnguaq*—a distinctive human-shaped stone construction made by the Inuit people as a navigational aid. The Inuit have embraced many aspects of industrial society, but traditional hunting skills are still central to their way of life. Climate change threatens the 160,000 Inuit by disrupting the habitats of the seals, caribou, and other animals that they hunt. Some Inuit are adapting by using their skills to guide tourists eager to go dog sledding or ice fishing.

Aborigines: Australia

Australia's indigenous people once led a nomadic lifestyle, hunting and gathering food. Today's 250,000 Aborigines are the poorest community in Australia, relying on paid labor and state support. Their legitimate claims to land face competition from mining and farming companies. The distinctive styles of Aboriginal artwork—such as this dot painting example—have become an important way for some groups to preserve their identity and unique skills.

Khanty: Siberia

By moving their reindeer herds to find grazing land, Siberia's 22,500 Khanty people survive in an environment too harsh for farming. They waste no part of the reindeer: the Khanty eat reindeer meat, make utensils from their bones, and use the animal's hide to cover their tents (called "chum" tents). Oil drilling, mining, and military bases in these remote areas are destroying the Khanty way of life. Many have been forced off the land and settled in villages.

Saami: Sweden, Norway, and Finland

Northern Europe's 80,000 Saami have a strong political voice compared to other tribal peoples and have protected their traditional way of life as reindeer herders. Now, climate change and modern forestry are threatening the lands that they depend on, destroying the lichens that are the main winter food for their reindeer. The Saami are also concerned about the exploitation of their colorful traditional clothes and culture by the tourist industry.

San: Namibia, South Africa, Botswana, and Angola

Around 87,000 San live in and around southern Africa's Kalahari Desert. Most live in poverty, and few now follow their traditional hunter-gatherer lifestyle—they are often banned from entering the farms and game parks built on former hunting grounds. Some organizations are working to link the San's incredible tracking skills and use of local plants to commercial projects, which may benefit the San and stop their knowledge from dying out.

Beliefs and Believers

Most of the world's people identify with a religion. Their beliefs, customs, or ancestors link them to a particular religious community. Despite high numbers of followers, rates of participation in religious services vary enormously. For many in the Western world, religion is separated from everyday life and practiced at weekends and holidays. In other areas of the world, religious traditions are central to everyday life.

Religions of the world

This diagram shows the number of followers of world religions. Most are single religions, but some are groupings of similar belief systems. Those shown here with symbols are the biggest single religions, and four of these—Hinduism, Christianity, Islam, and Buddhism—account for almost three-quarters of the world's population.

Almost **60 million**
Hindus traveled to Allahabad, India, in 2001 for the 12-day Maha Kumbh Mela festival

394 MILLION

900 MILLION

2.1 BILLION

1.5 BILLION

Chinese traditional religion
This belief system draws heavily on a variety of ancient Chinese mythologies, philosophies, and religious practices. There are hundreds of gods and goddesses and many festivals to worship them.

Hinduism
With the longest history of any living religion, Hinduism is a collection of very diverse traditions and beliefs. Almost 80% of Hindus live in India and Nepal, where the vast population makes it the world's third largest religion.

Christianity
Christianity is the largest religion, followed by almost one-third of the world's population. The Christian cross is one of the most recognized symbols, found everywhere from jewelry to artwork.

Islam
Islam is the second largest religion in the world and thought to be the fastest-growing. The biggest Muslim populations are found in South and Central Asia, North Africa, and Eastern Europe.

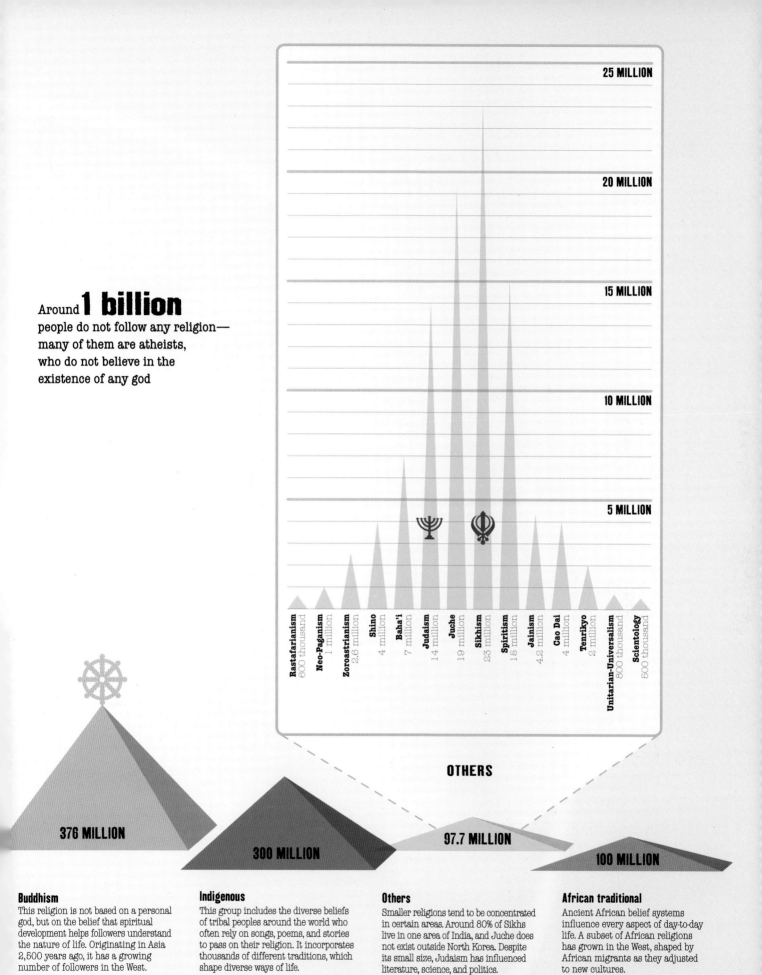

Around **1 billion** people do not follow any religion—many of them are atheists, who do not believe in the existence of any god

25 MILLION

20 MILLION

15 MILLION

10 MILLION

5 MILLION

Rastafarianism 600 thousand
Neo-Paganism 1 million
Zoroastrianism 2.6 million
Shino 4 million
Baha'i 7 million
Judaism 14 million
Juche 19 million
Sikhism 23 million
Spiritism 15 million
Jainism 4.2 million
Cao Dai 4 million
Tenrikyo 2 million
Unitarian-Universalism 800 thousand
Scientology 500 thousand

OTHERS

376 MILLION

300 MILLION

97.7 MILLION

100 MILLION

Buddhism
This religion is not based on a personal god, but on the belief that spiritual development helps followers understand the nature of life. Originating in Asia 2,500 years ago, it has a growing number of followers in the West.

Indigenous
This group includes the diverse beliefs of tribal peoples around the world who often rely on songs, poems, and stories to pass on their religion. It incorporates thousands of different traditions, which shape diverse ways of life.

Others
Smaller religions tend to be concentrated in certain areas. Around 80% of Sikhs live in one area of India, and Juche does not exist outside North Korea. Despite its small size, Judaism has influenced literature, science, and politics.

African traditional
Ancient African belief systems influence every aspect of day-to-day life. A subset of African religions has grown in the West, shaped by African migrants as they adjusted to new cultures.

Hinduism: 900 million believers

The roots of Hinduism go back thousands of years, but despite its long history, the religion has very little formal structure. Different traditions worship different gods and goddesses, such as Shiva and Kali, in a huge variety of ways, with pilgrimages and festivals throughout the year.

Judaism: 14 million believers

Originating during the Bronze Age, Judaism is the oldest of the three Abrahamic faiths. The different branches reflect different interpretations of the rules and duties god set out for Jews more than 3,500 years ago. Orthodox Judaism is more traditional, and Reform Judaism is the most recent.

Buddhism: 376 million believers

Mahayana Buddhism teaches that everyone can attain "enlightenment"—an understanding of the true meaning of life achieved by Gautama Buddha, the religion's founder. Theravada Buddhists believe that discipline is very important, and recommend becoming a monk in order to reach enlightenment.

Christianity: 2.1 billion believers

Since Christianity began with the birth of Jesus Christ, it has divided into many denominations, each with its own beliefs or practices. All Christians share the Bible as a holy text and believe that salvation is offered through the life, teaching, death, and resurrection of Jesus.

The Big Six

The six biggest religions account for around 85% of the world's believers. Christianity, Judaism, and Islam share a common origin and values and believe in just one god. They are often called the Abrahamic faiths, because their holy books feature many of the same stories, places, and people, including Abraham, an important figure in the history of each. Similarly, Hinduism, Buddhism, and Sikhism all began in the same region of the world and are closely related.

Every year, an estimated 300 million people traveling for pilgrimages and other faith-based activities spend

$18 billion

Pilgrimages

Believers travel from all around the world to visit special places and holy sites connected to their religion.

Maha Kumbh Mela

The world's largest gathering takes place every 12 years on the banks of the River Ganges in India. During the festival, up to 60 million Hindu pilgrims bathe where three holy rivers meet.

The Western Wall of the Temple of Jerusalem

Judaism's holiest site, the Western Wall is all that remains of the Temple in Jerusalem, Israel, after it was destroyed in 70 CE. Pilgrims come every year to remember their people's struggles.

Shikoku

Every year, an estimated 100,000 Buddhists travel a 746-mile (1,200-km) circuit around 88 temples on the Japanese island of Shikoku. It takes some pilgrims two months to complete the tour.

ORTHODOX JUDAISM 12 MILLION

REFORM JUDAISM 3.75 MILLION

CONSERVATIVE JUDAISM 4.5 MILLION

MAYAHANA BUDDHISM 185 MILLION

THERAVADA BUDDHISM 124 MILLION

There are more than **33,000** Christian Protestant groups, ranging from a few hundred believers to many millions

PROTESTANTISM 350 MILLION

CATHOLICISM 968 MILLION

EASTERN ORTHODOX 240 MILLION

Islam: 1.5 billion believers

The followers of Islam believe that their religion has always existed but was only revealed to the Prophet Muhammad by Allah (God) 1,400 years ago, near the city of Mecca. The division into Sunni and Shia branches dates right back to the death of Muhammad. Around 80% of Muslims are Sunni.

SUNNI 940 MILLION

SHIA 120 MILLION

Sikhism: 23 million believers

Guru Nanak founded the Sikh religion in the Punjab area of India in the 1400s, when he began teaching a faith that shared some features of Hinduism and Islam but was unique. Different groups follow different rituals and traditions, but there are no formal branches.

Santiago di Compostela

Catholics have traveled long distances to the city of Santiago di Compostela, Spain, since medieval times. The remains of Saint James are thought be buried in the city's cathedral.

Hajj

More than 2 million Muslims from around the world journey to Mecca, Islam's holiest place, to take part in the Hajj pilgrimage every year. Muslims are expected to do this at least once in their life.

Golden Temple

The holiest shrine in Sikhism is the Golden Temple in Punjab, India. It attracts Sikh visitors from all over the world to mark happy occasions such as marriage and the birth of children.

The Gender Gap

When women have equal access to education, health care, employment, and power, societies become richer, healthier, and more peaceful. The world is working toward equal rights, but there is still a long way to go. Of the 72 million children who do not attend elementary school worldwide, 57% are female. Women and girls still make up 70% of the world's poorest people.

Trinidad and Tobago

Many Latin American and Caribbean countries have excellent scores in health and education but lose points because few women join the workforce. Trinidad and Tobago has 60% of women in work and is the region's only country to make it into the top 20.

Iceland

Iceland tops the chart with a score of 0.8276. It has a female prime minister, and women make up one-third of the government. Other Nordic countries also score highly—Finland and Norway come second and third.

Mapping inequality

The Global Gender Gap Index scores countries on equality between men and women. It takes into account whether there are equal opportunities for work, political representation, and access to education and health care. The highest possible score is 1 (where men and women are completely equal) and the lowest is 0.

173

17

GLOBAL GENDER GAP INDEX

- 0.8000 and above
- 0.7000-0.7999
- 0.6500-0.6999
- 0.6000-0.6499
- 0.5000-0.5999
- Below 0.5000
- No data

Heads of state

The number of women in powerful political positions is growing. In 2009, Monaco became the last country to elect its first female member of government. Worldwide, women hold 18% of positions in national parliaments, and there are currently 17 elected female heads of state or government.

Voting rights

In 1883, New Zealand became the first country to allow women to vote in national elections. Some countries have only followed suit very recently.

Date women were allowed the vote:
1979 **Micronesia**
1979 **Marshall Islands**
1980 **Iran**
1984 **Liechtenstein**
1986 **Central African Republic**
1990 **Samoa**
1994 **Kazakhstan**
1994 **South Africa**
2005 **Kuwait**
2010 **United Arab Emirates**

VOTE

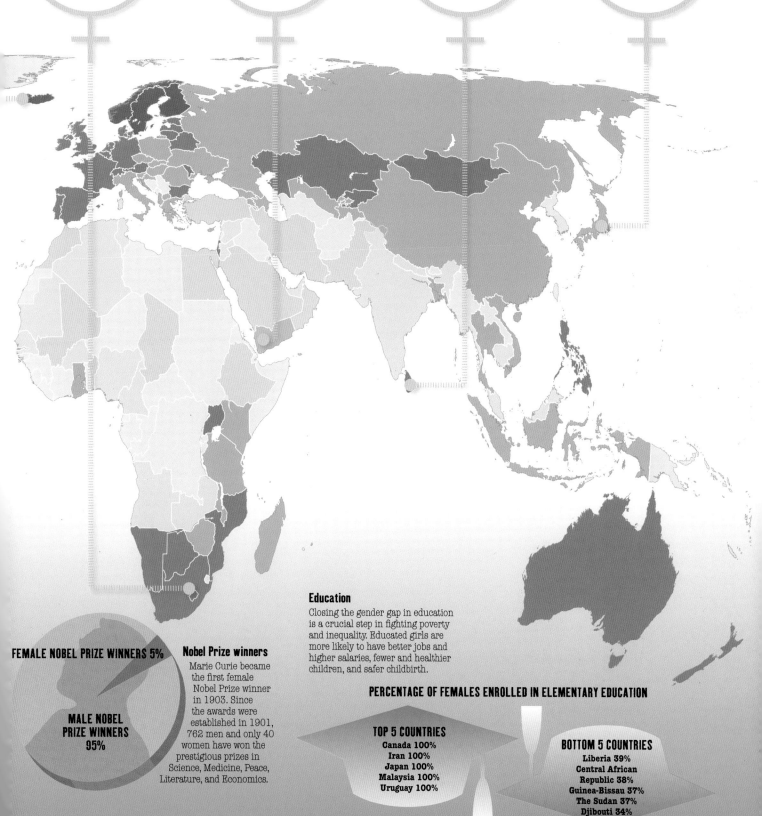

Lesotho
Lesotho and South Africa are the only African countries in the top 20. Lesotho ranks number 10 in the world, boasting no gender gap in education and health. About 69% of women in Lesotho are in paid employment.

Yemen
Middle Eastern and North African countries perform far below the global average. Yemen has the lowest ranking of all 134 countries studied. Just 35% of adult women there can read and write, versus 73% of men.

Sri Lanka
Just two Asian countries— Sri Lanka and the Philippines— make the top 20. Sri Lanka has been led by a female head of state for 21 of the last 50 years, while the Philippines is one of just 12 countries worldwide with no gap in health and education.

Japan
Despite having above average access to health care and education, Japanese women are paid 33% less on average than their male counterparts in the workplace and represent just 9s% of government, putting Japan in 75th position.

FEMALE NOBEL PRIZE WINNERS 5%

MALE NOBEL PRIZE WINNERS 95%

Nobel Prize winners
Marie Curie became the first female Nobel Prize winner in 1903. Since the awards were established in 1901, 762 men and only 40 women have won the prestigious prizes in Science, Medicine, Peace, Literature, and Economics.

Education
Closing the gender gap in education is a crucial step in fighting poverty and inequality. Educated girls are more likely to have better jobs and higher salaries, fewer and healthier children, and safer childbirth.

PERCENTAGE OF FEMALES ENROLLED IN ELEMENTARY EDUCATION

TOP 5 COUNTRIES
Canada 100%
Iran 100%
Japan 100%
Malaysia 100%
Uruguay 100%

BOTTOM 5 COUNTRIES
Liberia 39%
Central African Republic 38%
Guinea-Bissau 37%
The Sudan 37%
Djibouti 34%

Happy Families

The traditional family structure of a married couple and their offspring is what many people think of when they imagine a typical family. But families are becoming more varied. The pace of change is the quickest in Western Europe, where only one-third of households are made up of couples with children—compared to more than half of African and Asian households. In developed countries, people get married later or not at all, while divorce and second marriages are also on the rise. In the developing world, factors including migration for work mean that families are more likely to live separately.

Types of families

Nuclear and extended families are still the most common types worldwide, but soon there may be no typical family. Declining marriage and increasing divorce rates are giving rise to more single-parent families, and "patchwork" families of stepbrothers and stepsisters.

Extended family

Families of three or more generations are still the norm in South Asia, where most young couples start married life with their parents. However, later marriage, migration for work, and demand for more living space mean that families in the developing world are becoming more dispersed every year.

Single-parent family

The number of single-parent families is rising around the world, accounting for 10% or more households in some countries. Around a quarter of children in the U.K. and U.S.A. live with one parent. The U.S.A. has 10.4 million single-mother families and 2.5 million single-father families.

Nuclear family

The nuclear family— two parents and their children—was once the standard model in richer countries. It is becoming less common as parents increasingly live apart, create new families with new partners, or involve other relatives in childcare, as more mothers go to work.

Legally wed

Globally, the most common legal age for marriage is 18—seen as the end of childhood. There are wide differences between and within countries: in Lebanon, nine-year-old girls can get special consent to get married under religious law. Men often have to wait longer than women—Chinese women can marry at 20 as long as their husband-to-be is at least 22.

Average age at first marriage

The typical age at first marriage is rising steadily. Swedish newlyweds are the oldest, at an average of 31.8 years for brides and 34 years for grooms. Western European, North American, and Australian men are likely to marry someone less than two years younger than them, while men in Nigeria, Zambia, Colombia, and Iran prefer women at least four years younger.

In the UK, fathers spend **200%** more time interacting with their children than they did in the 1970s

Marriage rates

Marriage rates are falling across the developed world as people choose to live together for longer before they get married. Mongolians are most likely to get married, with 19 weddings per 1,000 people annually. Colombia has just 1.7 marriages per 1,000 people. One of the most violent countries in the world, its high murder rate means a shortage of available men.

Divorce rates

The tiny Southeast Asian island of Guam has the world's highest divorce rate, with 5.3 divorces per 1,000 people. It is a popular destination for visitors to get a quick divorce, but potential divorcees must visit the island for a week—a divorcemoon? Religion keeps divorce rates low in many Asian countries. Hindus believe that marriage is eternal and people cannot be divorced.

Solitary living

As people get married later and live longer, with women often outliving their spouses, the number of single occupancy households is on the rise. This is driving an increase in residential energy consumption. In Scandinavian countries, the energy consumption of everyone who lives alone could be cut by 60% if they moved to five-person households.

Full house

Most households in Africa and the Middle East (63% of total households), Latin America (53%), and Asia (51%) have five or more inhabitants. The majority are families with many children. Although households are much larger in developing countries, the size of dwellings is smaller: 78% of households in Asia have three rooms or less, with a big impact on living standards.

First-time mother

The age at which a woman starts to have babies affects the total number of children that she might have in her life, so it has a huge impact on the size and future growth of populations. In developed countries, more and more women are waiting until they are financially secure with established careers. The U.K. has the world's oldest first-time moms, with an average age of 30. In most European countries, 20–25% of pregnant women are now over 35. The age is also increasing in developing countries as women's access to education improves.

Childhood

Every child has the right to a safe and healthy childhood. Twenty years ago, world leaders signed the UN Convention on the Rights of the Child, agreeing that all children should be protected, respected, and educated. In countries like the U.S.A. and Japan, most people take these rights for granted. But millions of children in sub-Saharan Africa and South Asia still lack the bare essentials.

CHANCE OF LIVING BELOW THE POVERTY LINE

66%

42%

12.2%   12%   13%

98%   93%   97%

CHANCE OF BEING VACCINATED AGAINST MEASLES

67%

47%

1. Birth
For millions of children in developing countries, childhood begins with a struggle for survival. In Niger, almost 18 in every 100 children die before the age of five. In India, 2 million children a year die before their fifth birthday.

Game of life
Childhood experience is a lottery that depends on where you are born. This board shows the life chances of children in five very different countries by looking at some of life's most basic needs.

6. Poverty
Living below the poverty line means having less than the minimum needed for a decent life. In rich countries, the poverty line is considerably higher than in poor countries, as the ability to afford school field trips and social activities is taken into account.

Around the world, there are

246 million
child laborers,

171 million
of them doing jobs that expose them to dangerous chemicals or machinery

89%

99%

99%

100%

5. Health
One in seven children in the developing world have no access to essential health care, including vaccinations that prevent life-threatening diseases. In the U.S.A., parents can be jailed or fined if they don't get their children vaccinated.

A costly affair
In wealthy countries, parents spend thousands of dollars raising their children. The average amount spent over the course of one child's lifetime in both Japan and the U.S.A. is thought to be roughly $250,000. In the U.S.A., parents spend an average of $286 on toys for each one of their children every year.

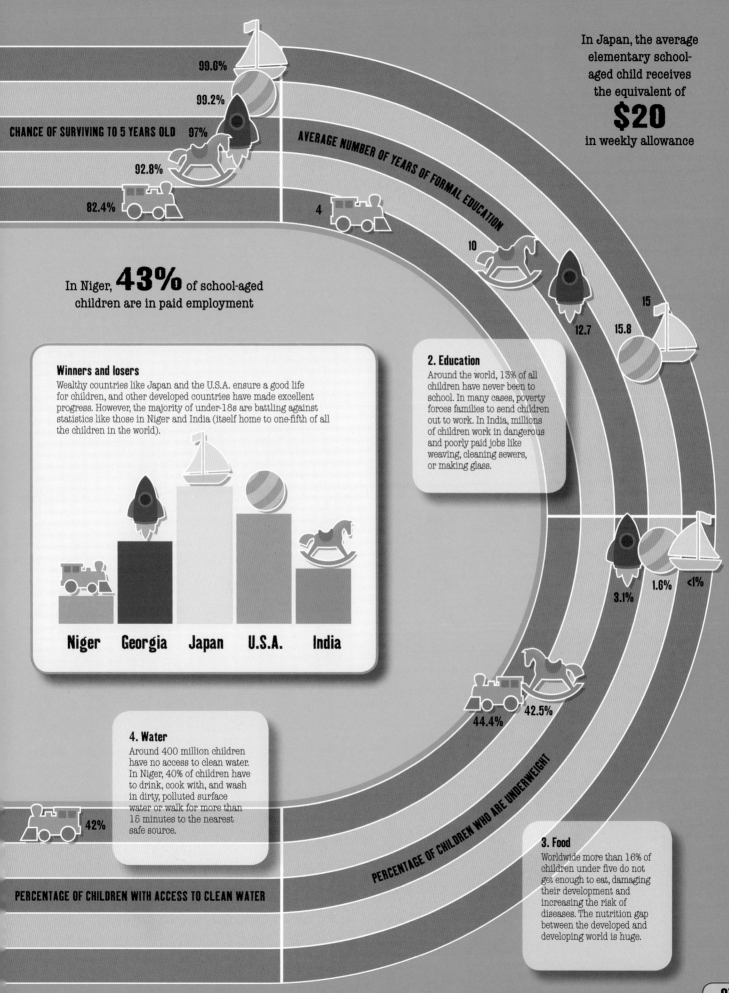

99.6%

99.2%

CHANCE OF SURVIVING TO 5 YEARS OLD   97%

92.8%

82.4%

AVERAGE NUMBER OF YEARS OF FORMAL EDUCATION

4

10

12.7   15.8   15

In Niger, **43%** of school-aged children are in paid employment

Winners and losers
Wealthy countries like Japan and the U.S.A. ensure a good life for children, and other developed countries have made excellent progress. However, the majority of under-18s are battling against statistics like those in Niger and India (itself home to one-fifth of all the children in the world).

Niger   Georgia   Japan   U.S.A.   India

2. Education
Around the world, 13% of all children have never been to school. In many cases, poverty forces families to send children out to work. In India, millions of children work in dangerous and poorly paid jobs like weaving, cleaning sewers, or making glass.

3.1%   1.6%   <1%

44.4%   42.5%

PERCENTAGE OF CHILDREN WHO ARE UNDERWEIGHT

4. Water
Around 400 million children have no access to clean water. In Niger, 40% of children have to drink, cook with, and wash in dirty, polluted surface water or walk for more than 15 minutes to the nearest safe source.

42%

3. Food
Worldwide more than 16% of children under five do not get enough to eat, damaging their development and increasing the risk of diseases. The nutrition gap between the developed and developing world is huge.

PERCENTAGE OF CHILDREN WITH ACCESS TO CLEAN WATER

School Days

Elementary schools and high schools open their doors to one billion children every day. The world agrees that education is central to a child's development, bringing lifelong benefits for individuals, families, and communities. However, at least 72 million children cannot access education, often because their parents are simply too poor to afford it. For those who do get to school, the quality of education depends on where they live. The experience of children in the Netherlands is very different from that in Mali, one of the poorest countries in the world.

THE NETHERLANDS

A developed country in Europe

The Dutch education system prepares students for life in a modern economy, where 80% of the people live in towns and cities and knowledge is more important than manual skills. In international tests, Dutch children score ninth-best in the world and 99% of adults can read and write. Yet, they still face challenges, as 1.5 million Dutch adults cannot read and write well enough to apply for jobs.

Years of compulsory education

In the Netherlands, it is illegal to keep children out of school. All children younger than 18 must stay in education until they have earned a basic qualification.

= 13 years
(ages 5-17)

Average years of schooling

Around 95% of Dutch children move on to high school, and after that 60% move on to college.

= 16.6 years

Education expenditure

The Dutch government spends 11.5% of its total budget on education—5,600 euros ($7,625) for each elementary-age student. They are also one of the leading donors of education aid to poorer countries.

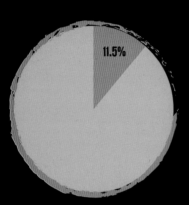

11.5%

PERCENTAGE OF TOTAL BUDGET SPENT ON EDUCATION

Teacher/student ratio

The average class ratio is 1 teacher to 17.2 students—8.5 girls and 8.7 boys. Small classes allow teachers to give students close attention. Dutch elementary-school teachers are trained for four years.

Classroom materials

Dutch schools are well equipped, with an average of one computer per seven children. In Mali, classrooms are very different. Some rural schools only have two seats per three students. Up to 10 students might share one textbook. High-tech teaching materials are virtually nonexistent.

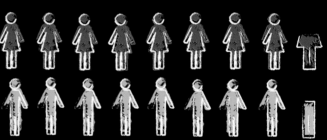

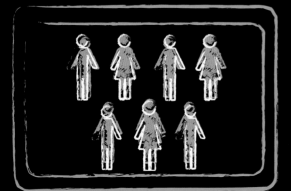

Enrollment ratio for elementary education

98%

99% male　　　　　　　**97% female**

Who is missing out?

In both rich and poor countries, the children who miss out on education are most often those who are already disadvantaged through poverty or social status. In the Netherlands, the children of immigrants achieve less than native children, and the gap is getting bigger.

MALI

A developing country in Western Africa

Around 90% of Mali's population lives on less than the equivalent of $2 per day. For the poorest, education is a low priority compared to the struggle to afford food. Nearly 70% of the population live in rural areas where the nearest school is a 4.1-mile- (6.6-km-) walk away. Mali has the world's lowest literacy rate, with just 26% of adults able to read and write.

Years of compulsory education

Basic elementary education tackle the causes of poverty, as educated adults are more likely to avoid exploitation, eat better diets, and have smaller families.

~~卌~~ |||| = 9 years
(ages 7–15)

Average years of schooling

Many children who start school in Mali do not finish. Poverty forces around half of all Malian children aged 7 to 14 into paid labor.

~~卌~~ || = 7 years

Teacher/student ratio

A shortage of teachers hampers education in Mali, where fewer than half of elementary teachers are trained. The average class ratio is 1 teacher to 54.4 students—23.3 girls and 31.1 boys, on average.

Radio lessons

In many developing countries, radio broadcasts are helping improve education in remote communities. The aid-funded Road to Reading project reaches more than 40,000 classrooms and 500,000 students in Mali.

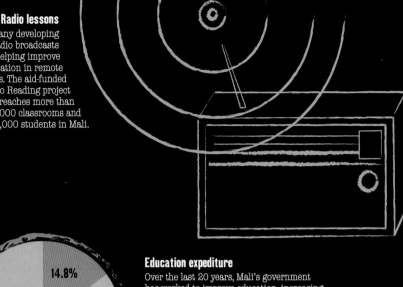

14.8%

PERCENTAGE OF TOTAL BUDGET SPENT ON EDUCATION

Education expediture

Over the last 20 years, Mali's government has worked to improve education, increasing spending to 14.8% of the country's total budget. However, many students in rural areas attend poorly funded community schools, paid for by aid donations, parents, and community schemes.

Laptop initiative

The One Laptop Per Child initiative was set up to provide low-cost laptops to children in developing countries and has been piloted in Mali. Such initiatives give children access to information taken for granted by students in the West.

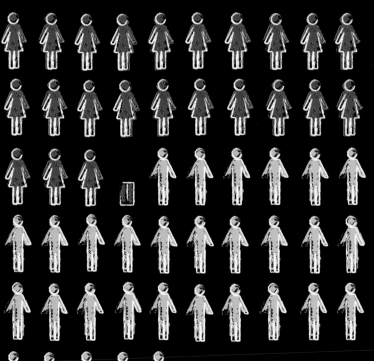

Enrollment ratio for elementary education
63%

67% male   **54% female**

Who is missing out?

Ten years ago, just 43% of Malian children enrolled in primary school. Rates are improving, but more than one-third of children aged 7 to 12 years never go to school. Of these, 60% are girls, who face greater pressure to help with domestic work.

Work

The typical jobs and pay in a country depends on a variety of factors, including education and training of the workforce, as well as the type of economy they live in. In less economically developed countries, up to two-thirds of people do "informal" jobs—small-scale, unofficial ways of making money—that are not regulated in any way or included in official statistics but are hugely important to the economy. Informal sector workers tend to be poorly paid and vulnerable in financial crises.

ANNUAL HOURS AT WORK

- 1 **South Korea** 2,400 hours
- 2 **Australia** 1,850 hours
- 3 **United States** 1,815 hours
- 4 **Switzerland** 1,650 hours
- 5 **Germany** 1,400 hours
- 6 **Norway** 1,340 hours

The above list shows how many hours a person works per year. The average Korean clocks up 20 hours more work than the average Norwegian every week.

Global workforce

The world economy can be divided into three main sectors: agriculture, industry, and services. The number of people working in each sector is changing as the world develops. Higher incomes mean a greater demand for products, education, and health care, and this creates jobs in industry and services.

Agriculture 40.5%

In 28 developing countries, agriculture is still the largest sector of the economy. In eight sub-Saharan countries, at least two-thirds of the workers are employed in farming, forestry, and fishing. The figure is much lower in developed countries, with just 5% of people working in this sector.

Industry 20.5%

Jobs in this sector include construction, processing, and manufacturing, producing everything from cars and chemicals to electricity. Around 45% of China's workforce is employed in this sector.

Services 39%

People working in this sector provide services to the public and to businesses, including transportation, entertainment, restaurants, media, tourism, banking, IT, health care, and law. It also includes academics, government workers, and the arts. More than 80% of the workforce in many developed countries is employed in services.

Size of workforces

Their huge populations give China and India the biggest workforces in the world. An increasing number of Western businesses "outsource" jobs to these countries, where wages are lower. In 2008, Indian workers did $12.2 billion of IT work for overseas companies.

PROPORTION OF PEOPLE WORKING IN EACH AREA

CHINA
807.7 MILLION

INDIA
523.5 MILLION

U.S.A.
155.2 MILLION

INDONESIA
112 MILLION

BRAZIL
100.9 MILLION

RUSSIA
75.7 MILLION

Farmer

The world is producing more crops than ever before, but as countries invest in new technologies, fewer people are needed to farm the land. Twenty-first century farmers need to know as much about business as they do about crops.

What do you want to be?

Media influence means that almost half of British teenagers aspire to be a celebrity above everything else. While a new reality TV star seems to be created every week, the odds of becoming famous are much lower than those of ending up in most other jobs.

Basketball

U.S. citizens have a 1 in 676,635 chance of becoming one of the country's 450 professional—and well-paid—basketball players.

Doctor

Around 10% of U.S. teenagers would like to work in medicine. There are 8.8 million physicians in the world, so 1 in every 770 people is a doctor.

Fisherman or woman

China has 12.2 million fishermen or women, meaning that a Chinese citizen has odds of 1 in 109 of working in fishing.

Astronaut

Don't mind long commutes? You have a 1 in 58.6 million chance of getting a job that's out of this world.

Construction worker

Demand for energy-efficient buildings and sustainable materials has created a "green sector" with new opportunities for those working in industry. The global market for green building materials is expected to reach $600 billion in the next five years.

Teacher

Service-sector jobs like teaching often demand more educated workers than other sectors and are not easily replaced by machines. Even so, the role of teachers is changing as new technologies enter the classroom.

Only around **50–75%** of working-age people in developed countries actually work. The proportion is often higher in poorer countries, as more people have to sell their labor to survive.

180 HOURS
MUMBAI

9 HOURS
NEW YORK CITY

iPod index

The ease of affording popular items can be used to compare wages around the world. Working for nine hours on New York City's average wage would buy you an iPod Nano, but the average earner in Mumbai would need to work 20 nine-hour days to afford the same product.

91

The Teenage Day

The world's 1.2 billion teenagers are trendsetters, influencing their peers, parents, and culture as a whole. The average U.S. high school student spends two-thirds of their time sleeping, at school, or doing homework. The rest of the day is theirs to spend however they want to, and with more than $200 billion in disposable income, the way they spend it influences not only their own lives but also the entire U.S. economy.

8 HRS 6 MINS

Sleep

Teenagers need an average of 9 hrs 15 mins of sleep every night, but the teen's stubborn body clock makes it difficult to fall asleep before 11 p.m. Early school start times mean that they miss out on 1 hr 9 mins of sleep every night, and 15% of U.S. teenagers have fallen asleep at school. To help teens get more time in bed, more than 80 school districts in the U.S. and U.K. have changed school hours.

Education (school, homework)

Teenagers spend the largest chunk of their waking time at school and in education-related activities. It's a good thing, then, that 78% of U.S. students feel a sense of belonging when they're at school. However, 1 in 7 report feeling awkward or out of place there. At home, teenage girls spend 19 minutes longer on homework than boys do, and boys are less likely to do homework at all.

Sport and leisure

Teenage boys devote 1 hr 12 mins more to leisure activities than girls do and are most likely to spend part of this time playing sports. Boys also spend more time watching TV and double the time using computers, but they spend less time shopping than girls. The sexes are equal, though, when it comes to socializing, with an average of 41 minutes per day dedicated to spending time with friends or family.

South Africa: 5 hrs 2 mins
Venezuela: 4 hrs 54 mins
Indonesia: 4 hrs 35 mins
Ireland: 4 hrs 21 mins
Lebanon: 5 hrs 43 mins
Poland: 3 hrs 47 mins
Italy: 3 hrs 34 mins
United States: 5 hrs 30 mins
Australia: 3 hrs 6 mins
Taiwan: 2 hrs 47 mins

Teen TV viewing around the world

The average U.S. teen lives in a home with three TVs and two home-movie players. It's not surprising, then, that American teens watch more TV than ever, but they are far from being the world's biggest couch potatoes; teenagers in South Africa hold that title, spending more than 5 hours in front of the TV screen every day.

72% of teenagers around the world mainly listen to music via an MP3 player or computer; the typical U.S. teen buys just **2** CDs per year

77% of American teenagers have their own cell phone, using it to send or receive an average of **191** calls and **2,899** text messages every month – that's **96** text messages every day

Travel

The average U.S. teenager walks to school in 12 minutes, or spends 29 minutes getting there by car. Most teens do a lot of walking during the day—step by step, boys walk an average of 10,849 steps per day, while girls' rambling rate is 9,662 steps per day.

7 HRS 30 MINS

Other (volunteering, shopping, household activities)

How do teenagers fill the time that's left over? During an average day, 54% of girls do housework for 38 minutes, while boys spend just 25 minutes doing the same. The average boy also spends less time on religious activities (1 minute compared to 4 minutes for girls) and just 10 minutes volunteering, compared to girls' 22 minutes.

4 HOURS

Grooming

The average teenager spends 8 minutes in the shower and 15 minutes sitting on the toilet every day—longer than they spend reading, on the phone, or on religious activities. U.S. teenage girls spend an extra 25 minutes in front of the mirror than boys do every day.

Eating

High-school students spend just 48 minutes a day eating food, and quick, on-the-move snacks are a favored fare—candy, soft drinks, salty snacks, and ice cream are among U.S. teens' top 10 purchases. More than a third of teens eat dinner on their laps in front of the TV but eat alone just 15% of the time. Sleep takes precedence over their first meal of the day, with 20% of teenagers skipping breakfast so that they can spend the time lying in bed.

1 HR 6 MINS

1 HR 12 MINS

Working

Around 15% of U.S. high school students balance school with paid work during the week, and a further 19% are employed at weekends. On average, these teens get 36 minutes less sleep and 42 minutes less leisure time every day than their nonworking peers. Their income, averaging $483 per month, helps them make the most of the leisure time that they do have, though—it is mainly spent on clothes, followed by eating out, cars, movies, and cell phones.

48 MINS

48 MINS

30 MINS

Celebrations

No matter where you are in the world, everyone likes to celebrate. In the past, festivals were connected to the best times for planting and harvesting crops. Many of these ancient events are still marked in weird and wonderful ways around the world and have been joined by a host of newer celebrations. Read on for a selection of celebrations from around the world.

JANUARY

New Year's Day
In cities around the world, huge crowds usher in the new year with fireworks displays. An estimated 45 billion text messages are sent to family and friends. January 1st is a public holiday in most countries.

FEBRUARY

Groundhog Day
Crowds in Punxsutawney, Pennsylvania, gather as the world's most unlikely weather forecaster—a groundhog named Phil—is pulled out of his burrow. If Phil can see his shadow, it means that he predicts there will be six more weeks of winter.

MARCH

Doll Festival
The Japanese festival of Hina Matsuri has been celebrated for centuries. Girls display elaborate doll collections, and parties are held to honor young female family members and pray for their health and prosperity.

APRIL

Songkran
In Thailand, around 40,000 people mark Songkran, the start of the Thai new year. Families clean their houses for good luck and sprinkle water on their elders to show respect.

MAY

International Workers' Day
Many countries celebrate the achievements of ordinary workers on May 1st. Some countries hold parades and other demonstrations of workers' value to society. In the U.S.A., the holiday falls on the first Monday of September.

JUNE

Inti Raymi Day
More than 100,000 people attend the Inti Raymi Festival in Cuzco, Peru. The week-long "Festival of the Sun" survives from Incan times and marks the winter solstice and the beginning of a new year.

Tamil Thai Pongal
The Tamil people in south India and Sri Lanka celebrate the harvest by thanking nature, the Sun, and farm animals for a successful year. A special meal called "Pongal" is eaten, and cattle are decorated with paint and flowers.

Waitangi
New Zealanders mark the founding of their country at the town of Waitangi on February 6th. Around 40,000 people join in games, ceremonies, and music to celebrate an historic agreement between Maori chiefs and British colonists.

Saint Patrick's Day
One of the world's best-known saint's days, Saint Patrick's Day is marked with parades, parties, and celebration of all things Irish. The city of Chicago, Illinois, even dyes its river bright green.

Ram Navami
Across India and Nepal, Hindus celebrate the birthday of Lord Rama, a hero of Hindu mythology. In Nepal, up to 100,000 pilgrims dance through the streets behind decorated elephants.

Cinco de Mayo
In Mexico and some parts of the US, Cinco de Mayo is a celebration of Mexican culture, food, music, and customs. Held on May 5th, it marks the victory of Mexican soldiers over a large French army in 1862.

Wine festival
La Rioja, Spain toasts its favorite drink on June 29th. After a special mass, 10,000 festival-goers spray 13,000 gallons (50,000 litres) of wine at each other from water pistols.

Messy festivals

Many festivals are famous for making a mess. Regardless of if you want to pelt people with oranges, mud, or dirty diapers, there is a festival somewhere for you!

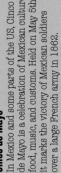

Colorful celebration
The Festival of Colors celebrates the beginning of spring. Hindus smear each other's white clothes with vibrant paints and colored water.

Mud festival
South Korea's Boryeong Mud Festival attracts locals and 80,000 tourists for mud baths, fights, and games on the beach.

Food festival
Around 1,000 people throw food, water, and even dirty diapers at each other during the Wasserschlact festival in Berlin, Germany.

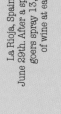

Carnevale d'Ivrea
The people of Ivrea, Italy split into teams before throwing 580,000 lb (265,000 kg) of oranges at each other during the town's carnival.

Movable festivals

Some of the most important religious festivals do not take place on a set date. They are often guided by ancient calendars and based on seasonal changes.

Easter
The life of Jesus Christ is celebrated at Easter, during spring. Today, Christians go to mass and children dye eggs.

Vesak
During the first full Moon in May, the vivid decorations and candle-lit processions of Vesak honor the life of Buddha.

Passover
This feast marks the liberation of the Jews from slavery in Egypt and begins in the middle of the first month of the Hebrew calendar.

Diwali
The "Festival of Lights" is a new year festival in the Hindu calendar, celebrating the victory of good over evil.

Eid-Al-Adha
Muslims celebrate Eid-Al-Adha in the last month of the lunar Islamic calendar, at the end of the annual Hajj pilgrimage.

JULY

Independence Day
Many countries mark the anniversary of the date on which they became independent nations. In the U.S.A., July 4th is celebrated with picnics, parades, concerts, and fireworks, with the American flag flown everywhere.

Bastille Day
All across France, the storming of the Bastille prison on July 14th 1789 — the event that started the French Revolution — is honored with dancing, champagne, fireworks, and fun.

AUGUST

Awa Odori
More than one million tourists descend on the town of Tokushima, Japan, to enjoy costumed performers dancing through the streets. It began more than 400 years ago, when citizens danced in celebration of the town's new castle.

Death of San Martín
The military leader General José de San Martín is a national hero in Argentina, where he defeated royalist forces to liberate the country. The anniversary of his death on August 17th is marked by a national holiday.

SEPTEMBER

French Community Day
On September 27th, Belgium's 3.5 million French-speaking citizens celebrate their culture with folk singing, classical concerts, and exhibitions. They are one of three official groups of Belgian citizens, each with its own government.

Heritage Day
In South Africa, September 24th is a national holiday to celebrate the country's rich cultural heritage. Events are held showcasing the creative arts, dance, languages, and food, as well as the country's landscape.

OCTOBER

International Day of Non-violence
In 2007, the United Nations made Mahatma Gandhi's birthday of October 2nd the "International Day of Non-violence," recognizing his influence on peaceful protest around the world.

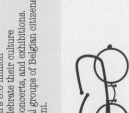

Día de la Raza, or Columbus Day
Across the Americas, the "Day of the Race," or Columbus Day, marks the arrival of Christopher Columbus in the Americas, a significant event in the history of Europe and the civilizations of the American continent.

NOVEMBER

Day of the Dead
Mexico's happy, colorful festival remembers loved ones who have died. Ancient Aztec traditions are mixed with Christian All Saints' Day customs, as families decorate elaborate altars and visit cemeteries to tend their relatives' graves.

Turkey time
Thanksgiving was first celebrated in the U.S.A. to mark the harvest of 1621. These days, families in the U.S.A. come together to eat more than 45 million turkeys to remember the occasion. Thanksgiving is celebrated in Canada in October.

DECEMBER

Christmas Day
Christmas is both a Christian festival marking the birth of Jesus Christ and a secular family celebration. It has many nonreligious traditions, from decorated trees to Santa Claus and presents.

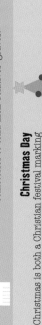

Incwala
Swaziland's king eats pumpkin and other food on the "Festival of the First Fruits." Over three weeks, the nation comes together for dances and other rituals to renew the king's strength and bring blessings for the harvest and the new year.

Chinese festivals

Unlike the Western calendar, the Chinese calendar is based on the phases of the Moon. A year does not have a set number of months, so festivals do not take place on the same date every year.

Moon festival
The Mid-Autumn Festival is celebrated in the eighth month of the Chinese year, falling around September or October in the Western calendar. Traditionally a harvest festival, families gather to watch the bright full Moon and eat round, decorated Moon cakes.

Chinese New Year
The Chinese Spring Festival marks the start of the first month of the Chinese calendar. Red and gold paper decorations are thought to bring happiness, wealth, and long life, and people buy special presents, food, and clothing.

95

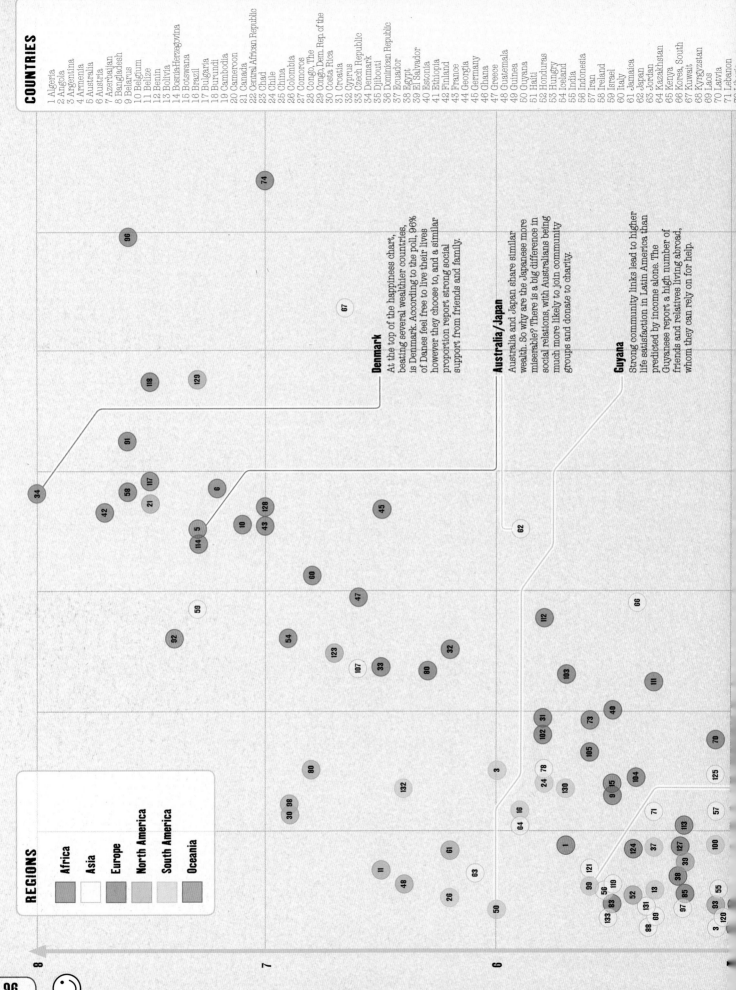

1 Algeria
2 Angola
3 Argentina
4 Armenia
5 Australia
6 Austria
7 Azerbaijan
8 Bangladesh
9 Belarus
10 Belgium
11 Belize
12 Benin
13 Bolivia
14 Bosnia-Herzegovina
15 Botswana
16 Brazil
17 Bulgaria
18 Burundi
19 Cambodia
20 Cameroon
21 Canada
22 Central African Republic
23 Chad
24 Chile
25 China
26 Colombia
27 Comoros
28 Congo, The
29 Congo, Dem. Rep. of the
30 Costa Rica
31 Croatia
32 Cyprus
33 Czech Republic
34 Denmark
35 Djibouti
36 Dominican Republic
37 Ecuador
38 Egypt
39 El Salvador
40 Estonia
41 Ethiopia
42 Finland
43 France
44 Georgia
45 Germany
46 Ghana
47 Greece
48 Guatemala
49 Guinea
50 Guyana
51 Haiti
52 Honduras
53 Hungary
54 Iceland
55 India
56 Indonesia
57 Iran
58 Ireland
59 Israel
60 Italy
61 Jamaica
62 Japan
63 Jordan
64 Kazakhstan
65 Kenya
66 Korea, South
67 Kuwait
68 Kyrgyzstan
69 Laos
70 Latvia
71 Lebanon

Denmark

At the top of the happiness chart, beating several wealthier countries, is Denmark. According to the poll, 96% of Danes feel free to live their lives however they choose to, and a similar proportion report strong social support from friends and family.

Australia/Japan

Australia and Japan share similar wealth. So why are the Japanese more miserable? There is a big difference in social relations, with Australians being much more likely to join community groups and donate to charity.

Guyana

Strong community links lead to higher life satisfaction in Latin America than predicted by income alone. The Guyanese report a high number of friends and relatives living abroad, whom they can rely on for help.

REGIONS

- Africa
- Asia
- Europe
- North America
- South America
- Oceania

8

7

6

Who's Happiest?

Surveying life satisfaction reveals what you might expect: happiness rises with income. People in North America, Western Europe, Japan, Australia, and New Zealand are rich and happy with their lives. Those living in poorer countries are dissatisfied. But money doesn't explain everything. The control that people have over their lives, their trust in government, and the support of friends and family all influence an individual's well-being.

Life satisfaction chart

The polling organization Gallup asked people from 135 countries to score how they felt about their lives, from 0 ("the worst possible life") to 10 ("the best possible life"). No country scored less than 2. Gross national income per capita shows how much money a country makes per person. Plotting a country's life satisfaction score against its per capita income shows that happiness and wealth are linked, but it also throws up some surprising exceptions.

Armenia/Paraguay

Despite similar incomes, people in Paraguay are much happier than those in Eastern European countries. They report greater satisfaction with their health and social life, spending just under 9 hours a day socializing, compared to just 38 minutes in Armenia.

Bulgaria

Bulgarians are significantly less happy than their income might suggest. A lack of confidence in others is to blame—98% of Bulgarians believe that their government is corrupt, and a similar percentage believes local businesses are corrupt.

Togo

Most sub-Saharan African countries appear on the bottom left of the chart. In Togo, approximately 40% of people live on less than $1.25 per day.

Among the poorest countries, small rises in income generally lead to large increases in life satisfaction, as more of life's basic needs can be met.

GROSS NATIONAL INCOME PER CAPITA

$10,000 $20,000 $30,000 $40,000 $50,000 $60,000 $70,000

POOR   RICH

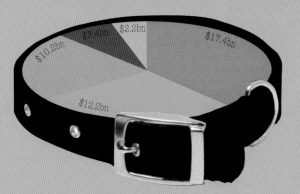

$17.45bn
$2.2bn
$3.4bn
$10.2bn
$12.2bn

Pricey pooches

Every year U.S. pet owners spend a whopping $45 billion on feeding, healing, grooming, and accessorizing their companions. That's double what Americans spend on toys and greater than the GDP of more than half of the world's countries.

Half of U.S. pet owners think of their pets as members of the family

Pets in the U.S.A.

An estimated 63% of U.S. households own at least one pet. The images on the right show the most popular U.S. pets and their population numbers. Keeping fish is a very popular hobby, and fish owners tend to have more than one fish. Although there are fewer dogs in total, two in every five U.S. households own a dog and there are more pet dogs than under-16-year-olds.

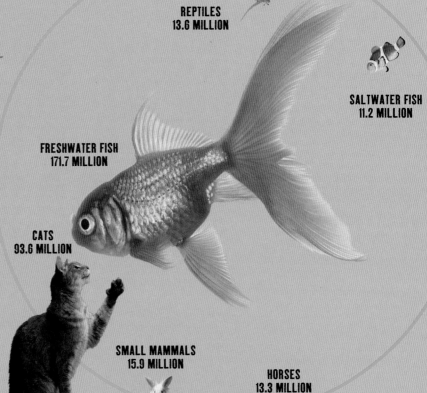

BIRDS
15 MILLION

REPTILES
13.6 MILLION

SALTWATER FISH
11.2 MILLION

FRESHWATER FISH
171.7 MILLION

CATS
93.6 MILLION

DOGS
77.5 million

SMALL MAMMALS
15.9 MILLION

HORSES
13.3 MILLION

Top cat- and dog-owning countries

The U.S.A. is the world's top pet-loving nation, but other countries are nipping at their heels. Almost half of Russian families keep a cat or dog. Pets were once banned in China, but it now boasts a booming market—despite dog featuring on some restaurant menus.

1. U.S.A.	1. U.S.A.
2. BRAZIL	2. CHINA
3. CHINA	3. RUSSIA
4. MEXICO	4. BRAZIL
5. JAPAN	5. JAPAN
6. RUSSIA	6. FRANCE
7. FRANCE	7. U.K.
8. THE PHILIPPINES	8. GERMANY
9. THAILAND	9. THE UKRAINE
10. SOUTH AFRICA	10. ITALY

DOGS

CATS

People
and their Pets

Pets are more popular now than at any time in history. The pet care industry is worth billions, and it's not just the animals that benefit. Scientists have found that owning a pet can reduce stress, lower blood pressure, and cut the risk of a heart attack by nearly a third. But keeping pets comes at a cost. The amount that American pet owners spend on their pets in a year is twice NASA's annual budget.

Dog and cat litters

Cats and dogs breed very quickly, so unneutered stray animals are a huge worldwide problem. Every year up to 7 million former pets end up in U.S. animal shelters, where more than half are put down.

CATS

18 kittens a year, on average

180 kittens in a lifetime

DOGS

12 puppies a year, on average

120 puppies in a lifetime

Pampered pets

What do you buy for the pet that has everything? If your cat can't face another fake mouse and your dog doesn't dig chew toys, look no further than these weird and wonderful pet accessories.

Luxury hotel stay
Pet packages at top hotels include a welcome treat, ice cream, pet massage, and dog-walking services.

Diamond dog collar
The world's most expensive collar features 1,600 diamonds, platinum, white gold, and crocodile leather.

Doggy treadmill
Nearly 40% of dogs in the U.S. are overweight, fattening the market for pet exercise equipment.

Designer clothes
Doggy suit jackets and crystal-studded kimonos hit the catwalk at Pet Fashion Week in New York City.

In 2008, an American dog called Trouble inherited

$12 million

from her billionaire owner

In loving memory

Even the most pampered pet is unlikely to outlive its owner. A typical pet cat lives for 12–18 years, while the average dog will live to age 11. Luckily, the pet care industry has come up with some creative ways to immortalize our furry friends. See below for some of the more inventive options.

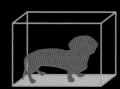

Deep freeze
For $5,600, you can freeze your dead pet in liquid nitrogen, ready to be defrosted when a cure is found. More than 60 U.S. pets are in "cryostasis."

A diamond is forever
Turn man's best friend into a girl's best friend by converting a pet's ashes into a diamond. The process takes six months and costs up to $17,000.

Get stuffed
Some taxidermists will stuff and mount pets in a playful pose, for display in your home. Alternatively, a Nevada business turns pets into cushions for just $80.

Copy cats
The super-rich don't buy memorials to dead pets—they order identical copies. The technology is very new, and the procedure costs up to $700,000.

Mummification
For about $3,800 to $123,000, one American company will mummify your pet and seal it inside a bronze container to keep forever.

In a spin
Pet fur can be spun into yarn for just $10 per 3.5 oz (100 g). Owners can then knit anything from a shaggy-dog sweater to a rabbit-hair handbag.

THE World IN ONE Day

PEOPLE

What's happening to the planet's 6.8 billion inhabitants right now? What a difference a day can make...

380,028 babies are **born**
(that's 264 per minute)

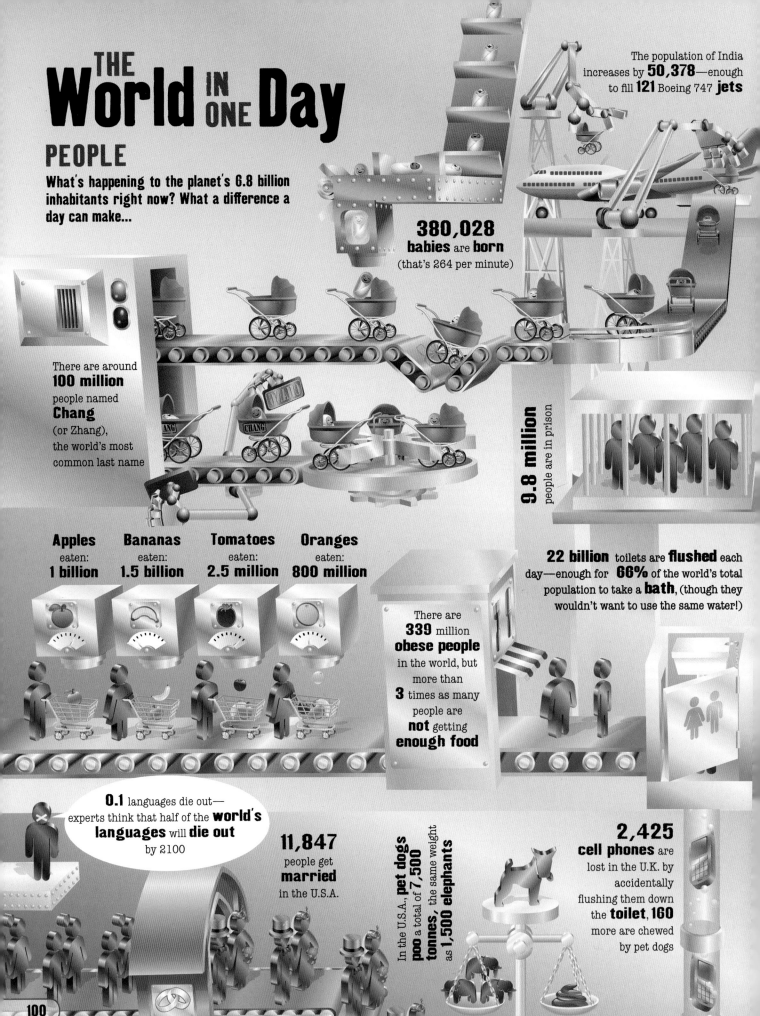

The population of India increases by **50,378**—enough to fill **121** Boeing 747 **jets**

There are around **100 million** people named **Chang** (or Zhang), the world's most common last name

9.8 million people are in prison

Apples	Bananas	Tomatoes	Oranges
eaten:	eaten:	eaten:	eaten:
1 billion	**1.5 billion**	**2.5 million**	**800 million**

22 billion toilets are **flushed** each day—enough for **66%** of the world's total population to take a **bath**, (though they wouldn't want to use the same water!)

There are **339 million obese people** in the world, but more than **3** times as many people are **not** getting **enough food**

0.1 languages die out—experts think that half of the **world's languages** will **die out** by 2100

11,847 people get **married** in the U.S.A.

In the U.S.A., **pet dogs poo** a total of **7,500 tonnes,** the same weight as **1,500 elephants**

2,425 cell phones are lost in the U.K. by accidentally flushing them down the **toilet, 160** more are chewed by pet dogs

30,000 people pelt each other with tomatoes in the world's biggest **food fight** at La Tomatina in **Valencia, Spain**

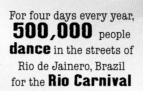

For four days every year, **500,000** people **dance** in the streets of Rio de Jainero, Brazil for the **Rio Carnival**

1 million people go to the world's largest **music festival** at Summerfest in **Milwaukee**

18,368,904 people have a **birthday** (and the average age of the entire world is **28.4** years old)

8,814,000 doctors are at work across the world, which means that there are **771** people for every doctor

110 million people go **bowling**

820,000 golf balls are sold, and **7 million** people enjoy a **game** of golf

1+1=2

77 million elementary-school children **don't** have a place to **go to school**— that's more than the population of Turkey

1,073 people die from **accidental falls**

5,480 people die in **road accidents**

155,539 people **die** in total

411 people die from **global warming**-related issues

Power

The way a country is governed can determine whether its inhabitants are free to live their lives as they choose. International organizations that allow countries to work together can improve conditions and provide opportunities for people. Some rich, powerful countries affect the lives of people all over the world, while multinational companies bring economic stability to their huge global workforces and influence the lives of people all over the world who buy their goods and services.

Countries and Flags

Today, there are more countries in the world than ever before. A country is a place that has its own government, a permanent population, and is widely recognized by other countries. Most governments recognize at least 193 countries—those shown in the main chart. All but one of these, the Vatican City, are members of the United Nations. Each country has its own national flag, used as a symbol of the nation.

REGIONS

- Europe
- Africa
- South America
- North America
- Asia
- Oceania

Country	Capital	Population
ALBANIA 	Tirana	3.19
DENMARK	Copenhagen	5.52
ANDORRA	Andorra la Vella	0.08
ESTONIA	Tallinn	1.34
AUSTRIA 	Vienna	8.37
FINLAND	Helsinki	5.33

Country	Capital	Population
BELARUS	Minsk	9.66
FRANCE 	Paris	62.6
ITALY 	Rome	60.2
MALTA 	Valletta	0.41
POLAND	Warsaw	38.1
SLOVAKIA	Bratislava	5.41
ALGERIA	Algiers	35.3
BURUNDI	Bujumbura	8.30
COMOROS	Moroni	0.67
EQUATORIAL GUINEA	Malabo	0.67
GUINEA	Conakry	10.0
BELGIUM	Brussels	10.7
GERMANY	Berlin	81.9
LATVIA	Riga	2.25
MOLDOVA	Chisinau	4.13
PORTUGAL	Lisbon	10.6
SLOVENIA	Ljubljana	2.04
ANGOLA 	Luanda	17.0
CAMEROON	Yaoundé	18.8
CONGO	Brazzaville	3.68
ERITREA	Asmara	5.07
GUINEA-BISSAU	Bissau	1.61
BOSNIA AND HERZEGOVINA	Sarajevo	3.84
GREECE	Athens	11.2
LIECHTENSTEIN	Vaduz	0.03
MONACO	Monaco	0.03
ROMANIA	Bucharest	21.4
SPAIN	Madrid	46.9
BENIN	Porto-Novo	8.93
CAPE VERDE	Praia	0.50
CÔTE D'IVOIRE 	Yamoussoukro	21.3
ETHIOPIA 	Addis Ababa	82.8
KENYA	Nairobi	39.0
BULGARIA	Sofia	7.59
HUNGARY	Budapest	10.0
LITHUANIA	Vilnius	3.33
MONTENEGRO	Podgorica	0.62
RUSSIA	Moscow	141
SWEDEN	Stockholm	9.28
BOTSWANA	Gaborone	1.99
CENTRAL AFRICAN REP.	Bangui	4.51
DEM. REP. CONGO	Kinshasa	68.6
GABON	Libreville	1.47
LESOTHO	Maseru	2.13
CROATIA	Zagreb	4.43
ICELAND	Reykjavík	0.32
LUXEMBOURG	Luxembourg	0.49
NETHERLANDS	Amsterdam	16.5
SAN MARINO	San Marino	0.03
SWITZERLAND	Berne	7.75
BURKINA FASO	Ouagadougou	15.7
CHAD	N'Djamena	10.3
DJIBOUTI	Djibouti	0.86
GAMBIA	Banjul	1.60
LIBERIA	Monrovia	3.95
CZECH REPUBLIC	Prague	10.5
IRELAND	Dublin	4.52
MACEDONIA	Skopje	2.04
NORWAY	Oslo	4.82
SERBIA	Belgrade	7.32
UKRAINE	Kiev	46.24
UNITED KINGDOM	London	61.8
VATICAN CITY	Vatican City	>0.0001
EGYPT	Cairo	78.6
GHANA	Accra	23.8
LIBYA	Tripoli	6.28

Country	Capital	Population
ARGENTINA	Buenos Aires	40.2
BOLIVIA	La Paz	9.86
CHILE	Santiago	16.9
ECUADOR	Quito	13.6
PARAGUAY	Asunción	6.34
SURINAME	Paramaribo	0.50
ANTIGUA & BARBUDA 	Saint John's	0.08
BAHAMAS	Nassau	0.34
BELIZE	Belmopan	0.32
COSTA RICA	San José	4.50
DOMINICA	Roseau	0.07
BRAZIL	Brasília	191
COLOMBIA	Bogotá	45.0
GUYANA	Georgetown	0.77
PERU	Lima	29.1
URUGUAY	Montevideo	3.36
VENEZUELA	Caracas	28.3
BARBADOS	Bridgetown	0.28
CANADA 	Ottawa	33.7
CUBA	Havana	11.2
DOMINICAN REPUBLIC	Santo Domingo	10.0

East Timor, a former Indonesisan colony that won its independence in 2002, is one of the world's newest countries

MOZAMBIQUE ——— Name

——— National flag

Maputo ——— Capital city

21.9 ——— Country's population in millions

TURKEY
Ankara
74.8

MICRONESIA
Palikir
0.11

BRUNEI
Bandar Seri Begawan 0.38

IRAN
Tehran
73.2

LEBANON
Beirut
3.87

PHILIPPINES
Manila
92.2

TURKMENISTAN
Ashgabat
5.11

NAURU
(no capital)
0.01

CAMBODIA
Phnom Penh
14.8

IRAQ
Baghdad
30.0

MALAYSIA
Kuala Lumpur
28.2

QATAR
Doha
1.40

UNITED ARAB EMIRATES
Abu Dhabi
5.06

NEW ZEALAND
Wellington
4.31

CHINA
Bejing
1,331

ISRAEL
Jerusalem
7.63

MALDIVES
Malé
0.31

SAUDI ARABIA
Riyadh
28.6

UZBEKISTAN
Tashkent
27.6

PALAU
Melekeok
0.02

MADAGASCAR
Antananarivo
19.4

MOZAMBIQUE
Maputo
21.9

AFGHANISTAN
Kabul
28.3

ARMENIA
Yerevan
3.09

BAHRAIN
Manama
1.21

CYPRUS
Nicosia
1.07

JAPAN
Tokyo
127

MONGOLIA
Ulaanbaatar
2.70

SINGAPORE
Singapore
5.11

VIETNAM
Hanoi
87.2

PAPUA NEW GUINEA
Port Moresby
6.61

MALAWI
Lilongwe
14.2

NAMIBIA
Windhoek
2.17

SENEGAL
Dakar
12.5

AZERBAIJAN
Baku
8.78

BANGLADESH
Dhaka
162

EAST TIMOR
Dili
1.08

JORDAN
Amman
5.91

MYANMAR (BURMA)
Naypyidaw
50.0

SOUTH KOREA
Seoul
48.7

YEMEN
Sana'a
22.8

SAMOA
Apia
0.19

MALI
Bamako
12.72

NIGER
Niamey
14.73

SEYCHELLES
Victoria
0.08

SUDAN
Khartoum
39.44

BHUTAN
Thimphu
0.68

GEORGIA
Tbilisi
4.61

KAZAKHSTAN
Astana
15.8

NEPAL
Kathmandu
27.5

SRI LANKA
Colombo
20.5

AUSTRALIA
Canberra
21.8

SOLOMON ISLANDS
Honiara
0.51

MAURITANIA
Nouakchott
3.29

NIGERIA
Abuja
152

SIERRA LEONE
Freetown
5.69

SWAZILAND
Mbabane
1.18

TUNISIA
Tunis
10.4

INDIA
New Delhi
1,171

KUWAIT
Kuwait City
2.98

NORTH KOREA
Pyongyang
22.6

SYRIA
Damascus
21.9

FIJI
Suva
0.84

TONGA
Nuku'alofa
0.10

MAURITIUS
Port Louis
1.27

RWANDA
Kigali
9.87

SOMALIA
Mogadishu
9.13

TANZANIA
Dodoma
43.7

UGANDA
Kampala
30.7

INDONESIA
Jakarta
243

KYRGYZSTAN
Bishkek
6.50

OMAN
Muscat
3.10

TAJIKISTAN
Dushanbe
7.46

KIRIBATI
South Tarawa
0.09

TUVALU
Funafuti
0.001

MOROCCO
Rabat
31.4

SÃO TOMÉ & PRÍNCIPE
São Tomé
0.16

SOUTH AFRICA
Pretoria
50.6

TOGO
Lomé
6.61

ZAMBIA
Lusaka
12.5

ZIMBABWE
Harare
12.5

LAOS
Vientiane
6.32

PAKISTAN
Islamabad
180

THAILAND
Bangkok
67.7

MARSHALL ISLANDS
Majuro
0.05

VANUATU
Port Vila
0.23

EL SALVADOR
San Salvador
7.33

GUATEMALA
Guatemala City
14.0

HONDURAS
Tegucigalpa
7.46

MEXICO
Mexico City
109

PANAMA
Panama City
3.45

SAINT LUCIA
Castries
0.17

TRINIDAD AND TOBAGO
Port of Spain
1.33

GRENADA
Saint George's
0.10

HAITI
Port-au-Prince
9.24

JAMAICA
Kingston
2.70

NICARAGUA
Managua
5.66

SAINT KITTS AND NEVIS
Basseterre
0.05

ST. VINCENT & GRENADINES
Kingstown
0.11

UNITED STATES
Washington, D.C.
306

TAIWAN
Taipei
23.0

KOSOVO
Pristina
2.22

Disputed countries
Sometimes an area may declare independence from an established state but not be universally accepted as a new country. Neither Taiwan, which broke away from China, nor Kosovo, which used to be part of Serbia, are recognized by the UN.

All Change

The number of countries around the world has grown substantially in recent decades. The total has reached about 193, mainly as a result of former colonies seeking independence and the emergence of new territories after war. Each new country requires clearly defined borders, but these are not always permanently set. Politics, conflict, and climate change can alter them, causing some countries to grow larger, others to become smaller, and some to disappear completely.

More than **60 territories** are under the control of another independent country

Breaking up

War and political changes can cause countries to break up. The U.S.S.R. was a superpower that collapsed in 1991, leading 15 new countries, including Russia, the Ukraine, and Belarus, to come into existence. Yugoslavia was a country in Eastern Europe that split into five states after years of ethnic tensions and fighting.

Joining together

When countries become divided after a war, people who once shared the same nationality are separated. In South and North Vietnam, East and West Germany, and North and South Yemen, the borders were rigidly controlled until changes to the political landscape brought them back together again.

YUGOSLAVIA

SLOVENIA

CROATIA

BOSNIA & HERZEGOVINA

SERBIA & MONTENEGRO

MACEDONIA

SERBIA

MONTENEGRO   KOSOVO

Collapse of Yugoslavia

Yugoslavia was once a large country, but in the early 1990s it became the scene of bloody battles and ethnic tensions. It split into five states: Slovenia, Croatia, Bosnia and Herzegovina, Serbia and Montenegro, and Macedonia. Later, Montenegro and the territory of Kosovo split from Serbia, but Kosovo is still seeking international recognition as a sovereign state.

GERMANY

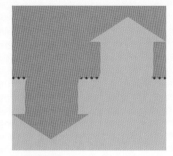

No borders

Within the European Union, 25 countries have signed up to the Schengen Agreement. This has created an area without border checks, so people can pass from one country to another without passports or visas.

Famous borders

China, which shares its land borders with 14 other nations, also boasts the Great Wall of China, a towering wall border that was built in the 5th century. It stretches for 5,500 miles (8,852 km).

Natural change

Global warming has led to changes to country boundaries. It is causing the Alpine glaciers between Switzerland and Italy to melt, so much so that the countries were forced to meet in 2009 to redraw their borders.

Gaining land and disputed territory

There are many places in the world where ownership is not clear. Japan and Russia argue over the Kuril Islands that lie between them, Kashmir is claimed by Pakistan and India, and there are campaigns to free Tibet from Chinese rule. The most hotly disputed land, however, lies in the Middle East.

Israel

In 1948, territory from the Arab country Palestine was given to Israel to form an independent Jewish state. Tensions between Israel and the Arab populations both inside Israel's borders and in neighboring countries have led to its borders being redrawn many times. Control of the West Bank, Gaza Strip, and Golan Heights is still a major issue.

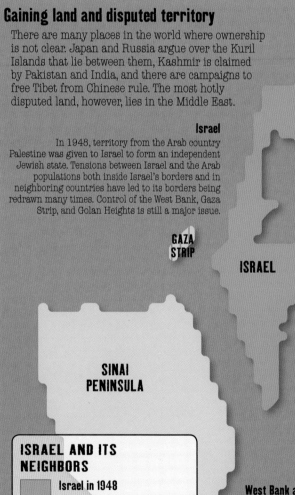

GOLAN HEIGHTS

WEST BANK

GAZA STRIP

ISRAEL

SINAI PENINSULA

ISRAEL AND ITS NEIGHBORS

- Israel in 1948
- Gained in 1967 and returned to Egypt in 1982
- Gained in 1967 and still disputed

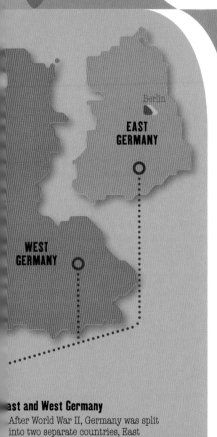

EAST GERMANY

Berlin

WEST GERMANY

East and West Germany

After World War II, Germany was split into two separate countries, East Germany and West Germany. Its old capital city, Berlin, was also divided by a high wall border from 1961. The communist government in East Germany restricted movement between the two countries, and people risked death if they attempted to cross into the West. In 1989, the East German government fell, leading both East and West Germans to pull down the Berlin Wall and reunite Germany.

Golan and Sinai

After the Six-Day War in 1967, Israel made huge territorial gains by capturing the West Bank and the Gaza Strip from Palestine, the Golan Heights from Syria, and the Sinai Peninsula from Egypt. Israel has since given the Sinai Peninsula back to Egypt but has been negotiating with its neighbors over the rest in return for peace and security.

West Bank and Gaza Strip

Israel still holds considerable influence over both the Gaza Strip and the West Bank, though it partially withdrew from the Gaza Strip in 2006. The Palestine Liberation Organization (PLO) and Israel are negotiating a peace deal that may eventually see Israel fully withdraw from both territories.

There were **90** independent countries in **1950**

Biggest and Smallest

Although size isn't everything, Russia is by far the world's largest country by land mass. The Vatican City, a mere speck on the globe by comparison, would fit into it a staggering 38,859,640 times. However, some of the smallest countries have a profile much larger than their tiny stature. Monaco is extremely wealthy, with high living standards and celebrity residents, while the Vatican City is the center of the Catholic Church and attracts thousands of visitors per year.

 Monaco occupies just 2 sq. miles (5 sq. km) of the Cote D'Azur in southern France. A constitutional monarchy, it is a luxury resort and playground for the rich.

 More than 32,000 people enjoy the benefits of life in Monaco. Living standards are high, and unemployment is low.

 Tourism and banking are big businesses. Monaco has many casinos and hosts a Grand Prix.

 The country boasts an underground railroad, helicopter service, bus routes, and two ports.

 A group of nine low-lying islands in the South Pacific, Tuvalu covers 10 sq. miles (26 sq. km). Rising sea levels caused by climate change could see it wiped out.

 The 11,000 islanders live a simple life. Access to drinking water is a big issue as there are no rivers or streams.

 Tuna-fishing licenses, postage stamps, and foreign aid are the main sources of revenue.

 The capital, Funafuti, has an airport, but islanders get around by bicycle and motorcycle.

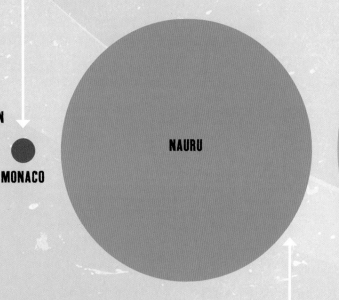

VATICAN CITY

MONACO

NAURU

TUVALU

 Vatican City is the smallest country in the world. It is located within the city of Rome, Italy. At just 0.17 sq. miles (0.44 sq. km) you could walk around its walls in an hour.

 Only 826 people live there, but most do so only temporarily—there are no permanent citizens. Nearly everyone works for the Catholic Church.

 The budget for the Vatican City comes from income donated by Catholics around the world.

 Most people get around on foot. There is a railroad, but no highway or airport.

 The world's smallest island-nation in the South Pacific, Nauru used to be a British colony. It has a total land area of 8 sq. miles (21 sq. km).

 The population of 14,000 live mainly on the coast. They depend on imports, as there is no arable land or fishing industry.

 Mining phosphates—used to produce fertilizer—brought wealth, but supplies are diminishing.

 There are no railroads, but free buses drive on a road 12-miles (19-km) long that circles Nauru.

With only **134 members**, the tiny force of the Swiss Guards protects the Pope and acts as the military of the Vatican

Ever-increasing circles

The green circles are sized in proportion to each country's geographic area. Russia's circle would be much too big to fit on the page. It would be 280,299 times the size of San Marino's circle.

 Almost double the size of the next-largest country, Russia covers one-eighth of Earth's land surface and spans 11 time zones.

 Boasting more than 142 million people, Russia has one of the world's most diverse societies, with 160 ethnic groups living there.

 As of 2009, Russia was the largest exporter of natural gas and the world's largest oil producer.

 With 95,690 miles (154,000 km) of rail, Russians previously preferred trains to cars, though this is slowly changing.

 Completely surrounded by Italy, San Marino is the world's oldest sovereign state. One-tenth the size of New York City, it is only 23 sq. miles (60 sq. km).

 Living standards are high for the 30,324 living there. Inhabitants enjoy close links with Italy and low unemployment.

 Tourism, postage stamps, coins, wine, and ceramics are major sources of income.

 A superhighway runs through San Marino, stretching for 137 miles (220 km).

SAN MARINO

Founded in **301 CE**, San Marino is the world's oldest republic

If Russia's circle was to scale, it would be so big that the actual Vatican City could fit inside it **52.8 times**

RUSSIA

Theocracies

Literally meaning the "rule of God," theocracy is one of the oldest forms of government. In Iran and the Maldives, government officials believe that they are guided by God, and their legal systems are based on Islamic religious law.

Military governments

This type of government is often the result of a military coup, when the armed forces claim power through force and dictate policy. A military government will either rule openly, as in Mauritania and Myanmar (Burma), or through a civilian front.

Communist governments

Only one party—the Communist Party—is allowed to exist under communist rule, and it controls all aspects of life and government. Its core belief is that wealth should be spread equally. The number of communist countries has declined in recent years.

Transitional governments

When a government collapses due to war or the sudden death of a leader, it leaves a vacuum. An emergency government is sometimes put in place to help maintain security and stability when time is needed to set up elections or decide who will rule next.

THEOCRACIES

MILITARY GOVERNMENTS

COMMUNIST GOVERNMENTS

TRANSITIONAL GOVERNMENTS

Myanmar (Burma)

Myanmar is ruled by a military junta who have absolute power; dissenting voices and opposition are suppressed. The National League for Democracy Party won a landslide victory of votes in 1990, but the military will not allow them to govern.

Eritrea

Following independence from Ethiopia in 1993, a provisional government in Eritrea was established, composed entirely of the People's Front for Democracy and Justice. General elections have yet to be held.

Political
Systems

In the modern world there are two main types of political systems: Western-style democracy and single-party rule, which is mostly found in the developing world. In Western-style democracy, great emphasis is placed on individual freedom, and governments are answerable to the people who elect them. Single-party rulers and dictators are all-powerful and strive to preserve their established order. However, this style of government is fragile, and these countries are increasingly veering toward democracy.

Country categorization

Each figure shown here represents a UN-recognized country that adheres to a particular political system. Theocracies are the rarest form of government, while democracy dominates the world's stage. Democracy appears in many forms: established, transitional, and those with constitutional monarchies.

Vatican City

The Vatican City is one of only a few theocracies—the head of the Catholic Church, the Pope, is head of state and holds supreme power. While the Vatican City participates within the UN under the name "Holy See," it is different from other countries as it does not serve its citizens. It is purely an administrative base for the Church, with a population made up of church officials.

Democracy

Established throughout Europe, North America, and Oceania, democracy today is becoming more widely adopted, with 62% of the world's countries now being electoral democracies. Within a democracy, the elected body must represent the views of the majority, and "one person, one vote" is a fundamental principle.

Absolute monarchies

Monarchs who are head of state and government are called absolute monarchs. Usually a king or queen, they often stay in power for decades, until they die or choose to abdicate. Saudi Arabia and Bhutan are well-established absolute monarchies.

One-party republics

Sometimes called a one-party state, these are countries where only one political party is allowed to run and people with opposing views cannot be elected. It is often associated with Communism, but it is also present in former colonies where one party dominated following independence.

Transitional democracies

Countries in Latin America and parts of the developing world, formerly controlled by single parties or military dictatorships, are gradually becoming democracies but are not yet fully established. Well-established democracies, like the U.S.A., generally support a country's transition to democracy.

Established democracies

The majority of countries in the world are democratic, based on the belief that every citizen over a certain age is entitled to vote and participate in politics. Democracy thrives in those countries that willingly permit free speech and dissent, as in most Western countries.

ABSOLUTE MONARCHIES

ONE-PARTY REPUBLICS

TRANSITIONAL DEMOCRACIES

ESTABLISHED DEMOCRACIES

Saudi Arabia

One of the wealthiest nations in the Middle East, Saudi Arabia was named after its ruling Al Saud family, which has been in power since the 18th century. Political parties and opposition to the system are banned.

Belarus

Since 1994, Belarus has been ruled by President Alexander Lukashenko. He suppresses all opposition and is regarded as "Europe's last dictator."

Paraguay

The death of Paraguay's dictator, Alfredo Stroessner, in 2006 was followed by a historic election win for the Patriotic Alliance for Change, led by Fernando Lugo in 2008. The country is only just emerging as a democracy.

Constitutional monarchies within democracies

Many countries that were once ruled by autocratic kings and queens went on to establish democracies. Nations such as Spain and the United Kingdom regard their monarch as a symbolic head, but real power lies in the hands of the people. These countries are shaded purple within the two democracy categories.

United States of America

The U.S.A. is a federal country, which means that political power is shared between the national government, based in Washington, D.C., and the individual governments of each state. The American political system is based on the Constitution, drafted in 1787. The central word cloud, shown here within the outline of a map of the U.S.A., gives the most-occuring and significant words from this key document, describing the fundamental principles of American democracy and governance.

Constitution

The U.S.A. has a written constitution, which is the highest law in the land. The Constitution is a set of rules that state the basic rights and duties of its citizens, and stipulates how the government works, and how the president is elected.

States

The U.S.A. is split into 50 provinces, called states. Each one has a great deal of authority, with its own executive, laws, and courts. The head of the executive is called the Governor. States largely manage their own taxation, criminal justice, education, and health care systems.

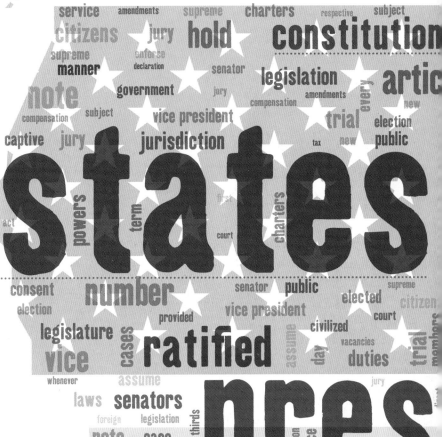

★ ALABAMA	★ MONTANA
★ ALASKA	NEBRASKA
ARIZONA	★ NEVADA
★ ARKANSAS	NEW HAMPSHIRE
CALIFORNIA	★ NEW JERSEY
★ COLORADO	NEW MEXICO
CONNECTICUT	★ NEW YORK
★ DELAWARE	NORTH CAROLINA
FLORIDA	★ NORTH DAKOTA
★ GEORGIA	OHIO
HAWAII	★ OKLAHOMA
★ IDAHO	OREGON
ILLINOIS	★ PENNSYLVANIA
★ INDIANA	RHODE ISLAND
IOWA	★ SOUTH CAROLINA
★ KANSAS	SOUTH DAKOTA
KENTUCKY	★ TENNESSEE
★ LOUISIANA	TEXAS
MAINE	★ UTAH
★ MARYLAND	VERMONT
MASSACHUSETTS	★ VIRGINIA
★ MICHIGAN	WASHINGTON
MINNESOTA	★ WEST VIRGINIA
★ MISSISSIPPI	WISCONSIN
MISSOURI	★ WYOMING

President

The president heads the executive branch and is responsible for running the entire machinery of government. He or she is elected for four years, limited to two terms of office. As military commander-in-chief he or she has considerable power and influence around the world.

Government structure

Power in the U.S.A. is spread over three "branches": the executive (under the president), the legislature (or Congress), and the judiciary (headed by the Supreme Court). This ensures that no single institution has too much power.

Legislative branch
(The Congress is made up of the Senate and House of Representatives)

Executive branch
(The president and vice president are elected for four-year terms)

Judicial branch
(The Supreme Court interprets the Constitution)

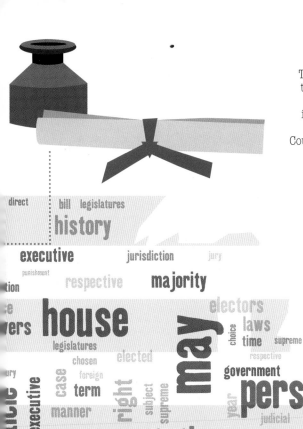

Law

The Supreme Court is the highest court in the United States. Its nine judges, who are appointed by the president, deal with interpreting the Constitution. Below them are several Courts of Appeal and District Courts. Together, these three levels of courts represent the federal judicial system.

Amendment

It is difficult to amend, or change, the Constitution. There have only been 27 amendments in its history. The first 10 changes are called the Bill of Rights; a set of basic rules that protect the liberties of the individual.

1 **Right** of free speech, religion, and press

2 **Right** to keep and bear arms

3 **Conditions** of quarters for soldiers

4 **Search and seizure** to be regulated

5 **Provisions** concerning prosecutions

6 **Right** to a speedy trial and witnesses

7 **Right** to a trial by jury

8 **Protection** from excessive bail, and from cruel punishment

9 **Rule** of construction of the Constitution

10 **Right** of the states under the Constitution

Congress

The lawmaking branch of the U.S. Government is Congress, which is made up of two houses: the House of Representatives, in which each state is represented by a number of electees proportional to its population, and the Senate, which is made up of two senators from each state. Both houses have equal powers and work through committees, which play a major role in steering through bills, which may become laws.

Votes

Every American citizen over the age of 18 has the right to vote. While members of Congress are elected directly by the people, the president is chosen by an Electoral College, as stipulated in the Constitution: voters in each state vote for delegates who, in turn, form an Electoral College. The Electoral College then chooses the president. Most delegates support a candidate from either the Republican Party or the Democratic Party.

China

The People's Republic of China is one of the most powerful countries in the world. China's government is dominated by the Communist Party, which controls all aspects of official activity. In the past, China's economy was run centrally by the government, with most industries government-owned and international trade discouraged. In the last 30 years, however, the economy has become more driven by private ownership, and it is expanding at a rapid rate.

The red flag

For 2,000 years, China was ruled by emperors, but in the 1800s power was lost to Western nations. In 1949, after a long civil war, a communist ruling government was formed. The large yellow star on China's flag represents the Communist Party of China (CPC). The smaller stars are said to represent the unity of the Chinese people, while the color red symbolizes revolution.

How China is governed

The Chinese people vote in direct elections at a local level. Local assemblies then choose delegates for regional and provincial assemblies. The number of candidates who may stand is limited, and only parties approved by the CPC are permitted. The chief assembly is the National People's Congress (NPC), which meets each year in Beijng. The Congress is dominated by CPC members and officials.

Communist Party of China
The CPC has around 74 million members. It does not govern China directly, but it effectively controls government appointments and sets the agenda for the NPC.

Politburo (Political Bureau)
The Politburo is the most important committee of the CPC. It makes important policy decisions, and many of its members also hold posts in the the NPC and the State Council.

Leadership

The Chinese head of state is the president, appointed by the NPC to serve a maximum of two five-year terms. The president nominates a premier to the chair of the State Council, and this must also be approved by the NPC. In practice, the Politburo influences both appointments. The head of the Politburo—called the general secretary—is the country's real leader and will typically take the job of president.

Military affairs commission
This 11-person committee is responsible for China's military policy. Its chairman, elected by the NPC, is commander-in-chief of the armed forces.

National People's Congress
The NPC is the chief body of government in China. It currently has 2,987 members, of whom 888 belong to non-CPC parties. It works closely with the CPC.

State Council
This is the cabinet of the Chinese goverment, with around 50 members. It meets monthly and manages the state budget. Many of its members are also important officials of the CPC.

People's Liberation Army
China has the biggest armed forces in the world. They number around 3 million, including both conscripts and full-time soldiers.

Courts of law
Laws passed by the NPC are implemented by law courts. The highest court is the Supreme People's Court, based in Beijing.

Provinces and cities
The State Council appoints officials to oversee regional and city government. Below them are local-level governments and party organizations.

Media and censorship

China has a huge and rapidly growing press and broadcasting media. Until around 20 years ago, almost all media outlets were state-owned, but independent outlets have since developed. Many news organizations are still censored by the CPC, and access to certain websites is prevented.

Work and wealth

China is developing its industrial power at an astonishing rate. This has created environmental and social problems, as people from rural communities pour into cities to seek work in the factories. There is a growing middle class in the cities, but poverty is still widespread throughout the country.

Around **1 in 5** people in the world live in China—the population in 2009 numbered around **1,338,600,000**

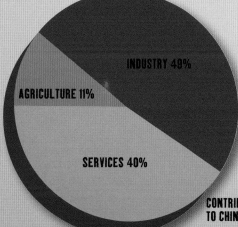

INDUSTRY 49%

AGRICULTURE 11%

SERVICES 40%

CONTRIBUTION OF SECTORS TO CHINA'S GDP

What makes the money?

China has the world's biggest workforce, and 40% of people work on the land. However, it is industry that creates the biggest share of China's wealth. Factories, mines, and mills, using cheap labor, produce coal, iron, steel, concrete, textiles, toys, electronics, and cars. Much of the output is exported, but China is aiming to increase its home market for consumer goods. The growing services sector contributes the next-greatest proportion of China's wealth.

How many children?

With the population exploding in numbers, the government in 1979 decided that each couple should be allowed to bear just one child. The policy was not applied in many rural areas and regions, and today affects around one-third of China's couples nationwide.

The wider world

China invests billions of dollars in foreign countries, especially in Africa and the Middle East, where its interests include energy, oil, gold, nonprecious metals, diamonds, timber, and car production. China is also the largest overseas holder of bonds issued by the U.S. government.

China's minority groups number **114 million** people. Around the world, only 10 independent nations have larger populations.

Many peoples

The government recognizes 56 "nationalities," differentiated by ethnic origin, language, religion, or culture. The Han is by far the largest group. There have been political disputes between the Han government and many of China's minorities, including the Tibetans in the southwest of the country and the Uighurs in the far west.

Han Chinese 91.5%
The Han Chinese is the largest ethnic group in the world and dominates every aspect of life in China. They speak several varieties and dialects of the Chinese language and live in the most densely populated regions of China.

Other nationalities 8.5%
China's 55 other nationalities, which include the Zhuang, Uighurs, Mongolians, Tibetans, Miao, and Dai, make up a small percentage of the population compared to the Han. However, altogether they occupy more than half of China's land area.

North Atlantic Treaty Organization

Set up in 1994, NATO is the world's most powerful regional defense alliance. Member countries from North America and Europe work together to protect each other's safety.

Organization for Economic Cooperation

The OECD's 31 member nations are all developed countries with democratic governments. The alliance, founded in 1961, promotes trade between its members and seeks to improve living standards.

Organization of American States

The main aim of the OAS is to strengthen democracy and development across the Americas. It sends envoys to help negotiate when member states are at war or have a disagreement. Its origins date back to 1890.

International
Alliances

International organizations allow countries that share common interests to come together for their mutual benefit. Some are regional—helping countries in the same part of the world work together for peace and security. Others are made up of countries that have similar trade concerns or cultural links. All aim to improve the lives of people in their member states.

Working together

There are many important international alliances—this diagram shows just a few. The colored boxes indicate which organizations each country belongs to. Some countries are members of many different groups, others only belong to one.

NATO

OECD

OAS

OECD

AUSTRALIA
AUSTRIA
FINLAND
IRELAND
JAPAN
LUXEMBOURG
MEXICO
NEW ZEALAND
SOUTH KOREA
SWEDEN
SWITZERLAND

BELGIUM
CANADA
CZECH REPUBLIC
DENMARK
FRANCE
GERMANY
GREECE
HUNGARY
ICELAND
ITALY
LUXEMBOURG
THE NETHERLANDS
NORWAY
POLAND
PORTUGAL
SLOVAKIA
SPAIN
TURKEY
U.K.

U.S.A.

ARGENTINA
ANTIGUA AND BARBUDA
THE BAHAMAS
BARBADOS
BELIZE
BOLIVIA
BRAZIL
CANADA
CHILE
COLOMBIA
COSTA RICA
CUBA
DOMINICA
DOMINICAN REP.
EL SALVADOR
GRENADA
GUATEMALA
HAITI
HONDURAS
JAMAICA
MEXICO
NICARAGUA
PANAMA
PARAGUAY
PERU
SAINT LUCIA
SAINT KITTS AND NEVIS
SAINT VINCENT AND
THE GRENADINES
TRINIDAD
URUGUAY

OAS

ALBANIA

BULGARIA
CROATIA
ESTONIA
LATVIA
LITHUANIA
ROMANIA
SLOVENIA

NATO

INDONESIA
THE PHILIPPINES
SINGAPORE
THAILAND
CAMBODIA
LAOS
MYANMAR (BURMA)
VIETNAM

ASEAN

GUYANA
SURINAME

ECUADOR
VENEZUELA

NIGERIA
QATAR

OPEC

GCC

ASEAN

Association of Southeast Asian Nations

Established in 1967 and with 10 member countries representing a total population of about 500 million, ASEAN works to increase economic growth and to promote peace, stability, and social progress.

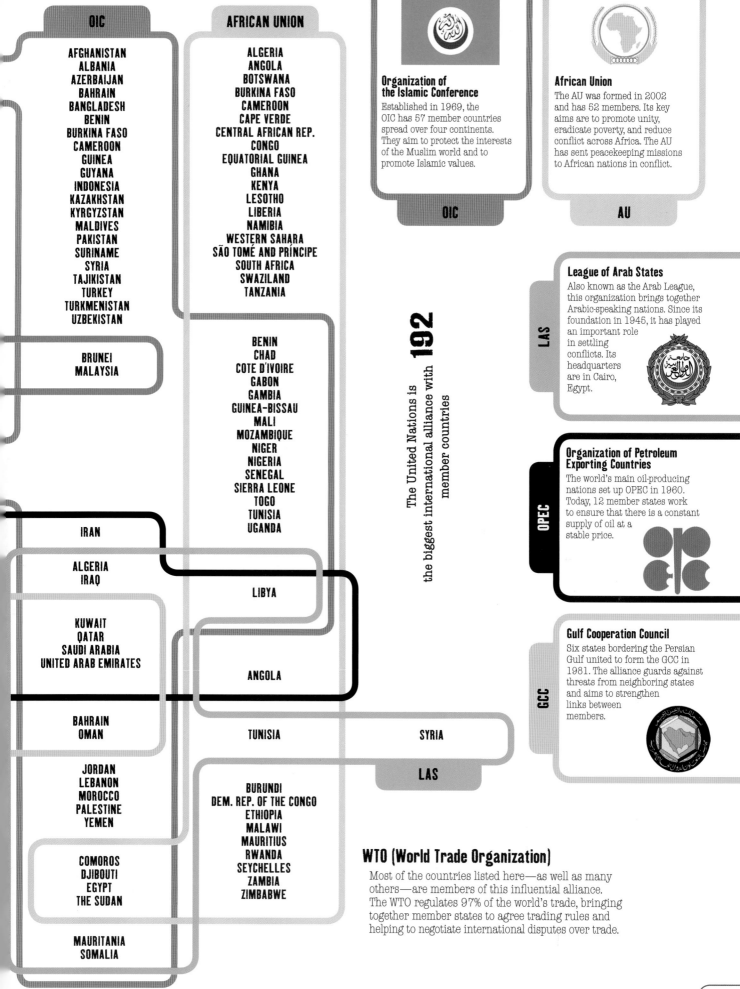

OIC

AFGHANISTAN
ALBANIA
AZERBAIJAN
BAHRAIN
BANGLADESH
BENIN
BURKINA FASO
CAMEROON
GUINEA
GUYANA
INDONESIA
KAZAKHSTAN
KYRGYZSTAN
MALDIVES
PAKISTAN
SURINAME
SYRIA
TAJIKISTAN
TURKEY
TURKMENISTAN
UZBEKISTAN

BRUNEI
MALAYSIA

IRAN

ALGERIA
IRAQ

KUWAIT
QATAR
SAUDI ARABIA
UNITED ARAB EMIRATES

BAHRAIN
OMAN

JORDAN
LEBANON
MOROCCO
PALESTINE
YEMEN

COMOROS
DJIBOUTI
EGYPT
THE SUDAN

MAURITANIA
SOMALIA

AFRICAN UNION

ALGERIA
ANGOLA
BOTSWANA
BURKINA FASO
CAMEROON
CAPE VERDE
CENTRAL AFRICAN REP.
CONGO
EQUATORIAL GUINEA
GHANA
KENYA
LESOTHO
LIBERIA
NAMIBIA
WESTERN SAHARA
SÃO TOMÉ AND PRÍNCIPE
SOUTH AFRICA
SWAZILAND
TANZANIA

BENIN
CHAD
COTE D'IVOIRE
GABON
GAMBIA
GUINEA-BISSAU
MALI
MOZAMBIQUE
NIGER
NIGERIA
SENEGAL
SIERRA LEONE
TOGO
TUNISIA
UGANDA

LIBYA

ANGOLA

TUNISIA

SYRIA

LAS

BURUNDI
DEM. REP. OF THE CONGO
ETHIOPIA
MALAWI
MAURITIUS
RWANDA
SEYCHELLES
ZAMBIA
ZIMBABWE

Organization of the Islamic Conference

Established in 1969, the OIC has 57 member countries spread over four continents. They aim to protect the interests of the Muslim world and to promote Islamic values.

OIC

African Union

The AU was formed in 2002 and has 52 members. Its key aims are to promote unity, eradicate poverty, and reduce conflict across Africa. The AU has sent peacekeeping missions to African nations in conflict.

AU

The United Nations is 192 the biggest international alliance with member countries

League of Arab States

Also known as the Arab League, this organization brings together Arabic-speaking nations. Since its foundation in 1945, it has played an important role in settling conflicts. Its headquarters are in Cairo, Egypt.

LAS

Organization of Petroleum Exporting Countries

The world's main oil-producing nations set up OPEC in 1960. Today, 12 member states work to ensure that there is a constant supply of oil at a stable price.

OPEC

Gulf Cooperation Council

Six states bordering the Persian Gulf united to form the GCC in 1981. The alliance guards against threats from neighboring states and aims to strengthen links between members.

GCC

WTO (World Trade Organization)

Most of the countries listed here—as well as many others—are members of this influential alliance. The WTO regulates 97% of the world's trade, bringing together member states to agree trading rules and helping to negotiate international disputes over trade.

European Union

The European Union (EU) is a political and economic community made up of 27 member states. Set up after World War II by six original states, it aimed to bring peace and raise living standards for its members. Since then, the EU has become a major world power and grown to more than 500 million inhabitants. It operates as a kind of supergovernment, presenting a united front for its member states on matters of concern such as agriculture, trade, and defense.

European Commission
The budget and the day-to-day running of the EU is managed by the Commission. One member is appointed from each state, and they meet regularly to propose new laws to the Council and Parliament. Once these laws are passed, the Commission manages their implementation.

EU Parliament

The EU mainly governs through its Parliament, Commission, and Council. The Parliament votes on how much money the EU should spend, and, with the Council, decides which suggestions from the Commission should be made into new laws. The Parliament's 751 members are elected every five years by EU citizens. The number of seats per state is decided on population size—as the most populous country, Germany has the most seats.

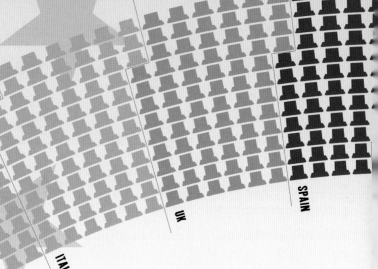

SPAIN

UK

ITALY

FRANCE

GERMANY

EU MEMBERS
This diagram shows how many seats each state has in the Parliament and when they joined the EU.

1 seat	1973	1986	2004
1957	1981	1995	2007

EU POLICIES

Aid donations
Currently the world's biggest aid donor, EU aid to developing countries will reach $7.2 billion by 2012. The EU is aiming to halve extreme poverty, improve education, and halt the spread of AIDS around the world by 2015.

Fisheries
The EU fishing industry is the third-largest in the world and is regulated by the EU fisheries policy. This aims to protect the fish stocks from overfishing but also to ensure a fair standard of living for those working in the fishing industry.

Free movement
Every EU citizen is allowed to live and work in any EU member state. The trade of goods and services also completely free in the EU, a move that has increased trade between member states and helped make it the world's biggest trading group.

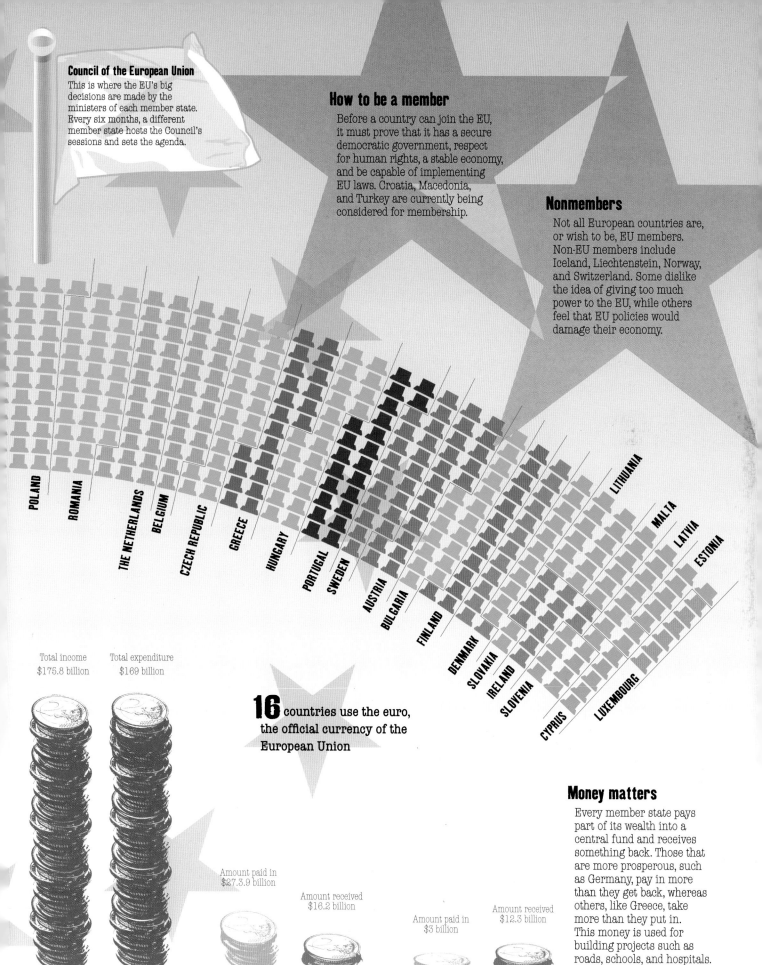

Council of the European Union
This is where the EU's big decisions are made by the ministers of each member state. Every six months, a different member state hosts the Council's sessions and sets the agenda.

How to be a member
Before a country can join the EU, it must prove that it has a secure democratic government, respect for human rights, a stable economy, and be capable of implementing EU laws. Croatia, Macedonia, and Turkey are currently being considered for membership.

Nonmembers
Not all European countries are, or wish to be, EU members. Non-EU members include Iceland, Liechtenstein, Norway, and Switzerland. Some dislike the idea of giving too much power to the EU, while others feel that EU policies would damage their economy.

POLAND
ROMANIA
THE NETHERLANDS
BELGIUM
CZECH REPUBLIC
GREECE
HUNGARY
PORTUGAL
SWEDEN
AUSTRIA
BULGARIA
FINLAND
DENMARK
SLOVAKIA
IRELAND
SLOVENIA
CYPRUS
LUXEMBOURG
LITHUANIA
MALTA
LATVIA
ESTONIA

Total income
$175.8 billion

Total expenditure
$169 billion

16 countries use the euro, the official currency of the European Union

EUROPEAN UNION

Amount paid in
$27.3.9 billion

Amount received
$16.2 billion

GERMANY

Amount paid in
$3 billion

Amount received
$12.3 billion

GREECE

Money matters
Every member state pays part of its wealth into a central fund and receives something back. Those that are more prosperous, such as Germany, pay in more than they get back, whereas others, like Greece, take more than they put in. This money is used for building projects such as roads, schools, and hospitals.

United
Nations

The United Nations (UN) is the world's largest international organization, and nearly every country is a member. The UN and its many agencies work to improve welfare around the world. The organization has two main bodies—the General Assembly and the Security Council. The UN's administrative service, known as the Secretariat, is headed by the Secretary-General, who also speaks as the head of the UN.

General Assembly
The General Assembly is the main governing body of the UN, comprising all 192 Member States. Each state has one vote, regardless of its size. The Assembly's main function is to discuss the world's difficult problems and to make recommendations on them.

International Monetary Fund (IMF)
The IMF offers loans to poorer countries and tries to stabilize the global economy. By working with its members from 186 governments, it aims to promote economic growth, better living standards, international trade, and higher employment.

Specialized agencies
The UN works with many organizations to combat world problems, such as poverty, diseases, and environmental issues. Featured here are 15 of the specialized organizations that are linked to the UN via special agreements.

United Nations Educational, Scientific and Cultural Organization (UNESCO)
UNESCO aims to improve education throughout the world by building schools and training teachers, especially in poorer areas. It promotes international cooperation and stresses mutual respect and shared knowledge.

World Meteorological Organization (WMO)
Everyone can be affected by changes in Earth's atmosphere, weather, climate, oceans, and water resources. The WMO plays a powerful role in helping protect humanity from natural disasters by sharing data, technology, training, and research.

The UN was founded with **51** Member States, and the 192nd Member State was Montenegro, which joined in 2006

International Labor Organization (ILO)
The ILO pushes for better working conditions and equal opportunities and promotes human rights around the world.

Food and Agricultural Organization (FAO)
The FAO was set up to address the problem of hunger around the globe. It advises countries on growing crops, fishing, forestry, modernizing production, and good nutrition.

International Fund for Agriculture Development (IFAD)
Like many UN agencies, IFAD seeks to eliminate poverty in poorer countries. It works not only to improve food production, but it also helps people in rural areas access technology and financial services.

World Intellectual Property Organization (WIPO)
WIPO helps protect work with patents, copyright, and trademarks. It ensures that writers, designers, artists, and inventors benefit from their creative ideas.

The **flags** of all 192 Member States, arranged alphabetically, fly in front of the UN Headquarters in New York City, and the UN European Headquarters in Geneva, Switzerland

International Civil Aviation Organization (ICAO)

Safety in the air has improved as a result of the ICAO's focus on standards for pilots, the condition of planes, and the organized growth of the aviation industry. It is also concerned about the pollution that aircraft can cause to the air.

World Health Organization (WHO)

The WHO aims to improve health in poorer countries. In the 1960s, its actions made the deadly smallpox disease extinct. It is now concerned with the effects of climate change, HIV/AIDS, and malaria.

Around 40,000 people work in the Secretariat.

UN Day is celebrated on October 24th.

Security Council

The Security Council deals with peacekeeping around the world. It aims to settle disputes without force but can send in peacekeeping troops to prevent more violence. The Council has 15 members—10 are elected by the General Assembly and five (France, China, the U.K., the U.S.A., and the Russian Federation) are permanent.

The Blue Helmets

peacekeeping troops are called

International Day of Non-Violence

$1.00

UN

2009

World Bank

This UN agency offers financial assistance and investment to developing countries. Its aim is to eliminate poverty and help countries sustain themselves so that they will be less dependent on foreign aid.

United Nations Industrial Development Organization (UNIDO)

The promotion of industry in underdeveloped countries is handled by UNIDO. It shares knowledge and expertise, provides technical support, and sets up projects to help poorer people earn a living.

The UN has its own post office and postage stamps

The budget for the UN's main operations, paid by Member States, is

$2.5 billion

per year

Universal Postal Union (UPU)

This nonpolitical organization works within the UN to offer advice and develop technical services for postal services worldwide. It works closely with other agencies, such as environment groups, to improve global mail distribution.

There are 17 current peacekeeping missions

International Telecommunication Union (ITU)

The ITU deals with information and technology issues. It tries to coordinate satellite use, build better infrastructure in poorer countries, and improve communications across the globe.

Since 1948, there have been 63 UN peacekeeping missions

International Maritime Organization (IMO)

World experts meet under the IMO to help prevent shipping disasters, improve ship design, and discuss the prevention of pollution by the maritime industry. Its motto is "Safe, Secure, and Efficient Shipping on Clean Oceans."

World Tourism Organization (WTO)

Developing countries are encouraged to improve access for tourists and reap the benefits. The WTO helps minimize the environmental and social impacts with a Code of Ethics for Tourists.

The UN was established in 1945, just after World War II

International Day of Peace

World Peace Day, observed on September 21st, is a global event established by the UN to promote peace around the world.

Tension in Turkey

Turkey is home to the Kurds—a large ethnic group who have no country of their own. Since 1984, the radical Kurdistan Workers' Party (PKK) have launched a violent campaign against the Turkish government for an ethnic homeland in the southeast. Turkey is now seeking a peaceful solution.

2

During World War I, civilians made up fewer than **5%** of all casualties, but they account for **75%** now

1

3

Unrest in the Middle East

The ongoing conflict between Israel and Palestine is one of most complicated in the world. Both sides believe that the other side is occupying land that rightly belongs to them. Palestinian groups have used suicide bombings against Israel, and Israel has responded with rocket attacks and blockades. Many civilians are caught up in the violence.

WARS AND CONFLICTS

Open warfare

These tanks show where battles between two states are happening, with a death toll of at least 1,000 soldiers in a year.

Civil war

Civil wars can last for decades and devastate millions of lives, with civilians suffering the most.

Terrorist attacks

A single violent attack carried out by an individual or group is called a terrorist attack.

Turmoil in the Sudan

The Sudan has been torn apart by decades of civil war, mainly over the control of oil reserves in the south of the country. All of the factions, government or guerrilla, have committed atrocities. The death toll is unknown but is believed to be in the millions, with about 4 million people forced to flee their homes.

Hostilities in the Congo

Fighting over rich mineral resources in the Democratic Republic of the Congo has pitted government forces against rebels. Neighboring countries have taken sides, with Angola, Namibia, and Zimbabwe supporting the government, and Uganda and Rwanda helping the rebels. Despite a peace deal, parts of the country are still volatile.

War and Terrorism

The world is a much safer place today than it was in the 20th century. Open warfare between two or more nations is rare, but war has not gone away completely. Conflicts within countries—known as civil wars—are more common these days, with parts of Africa in particular torn apart by this kind of strife. Border disputes and tension between different ethnic or religious groups cause misery to millions, and terrorist attacks, a new type of warfare, are increasing.

Fighting around the world

This map shows current conflicts and a selection of the most significant civil wars and terrorist attacks. There are many smaller conflicts, particularly in Africa and South America, that are not shown.

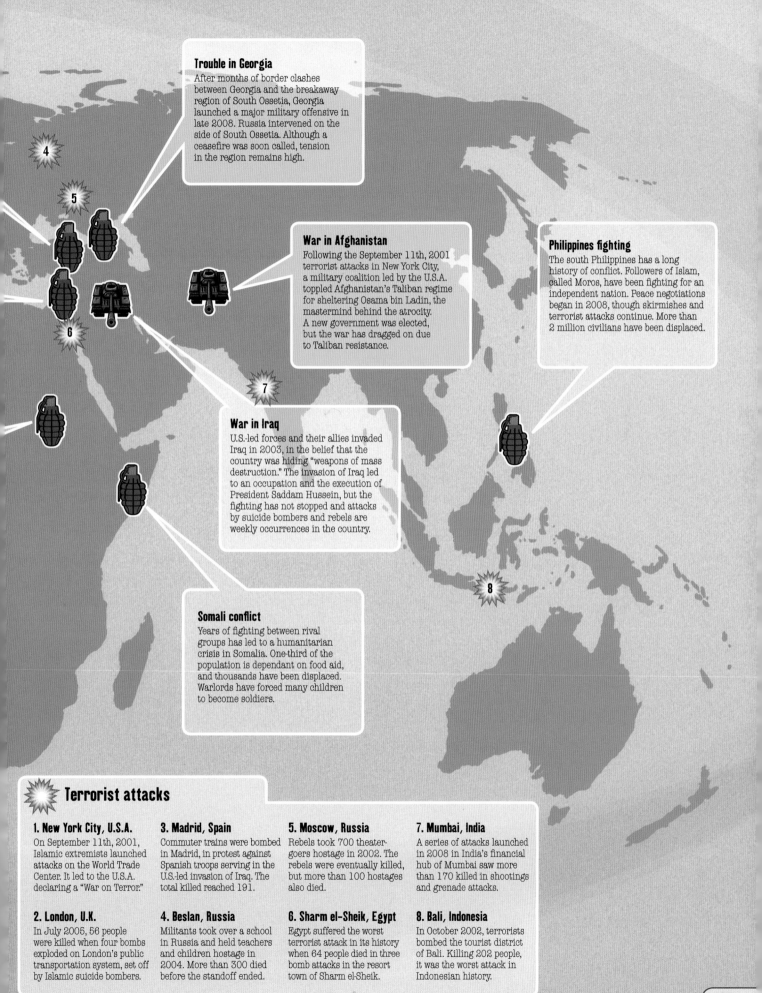

Trouble in Georgia

After months of border clashes between Georgia and the breakaway region of South Ossetia, Georgia launched a major military offensive in late 2008. Russia intervened on the side of South Ossetia. Although a ceasefire was soon called, tension in the region remains high.

War in Afghanistan

Following the September 11th, 2001 terrorist attacks in New York City, a military coalition led by the U.S.A. toppled Afghanistan's Taliban regime for sheltering Osama bin Ladin, the mastermind behind the atrocity. A new government was elected, but the war has dragged on due to Taliban resistance.

Philippines fighting

The south Philippines has a long history of conflict. Followers of Islam, called Moros, have been fighting for an independent nation. Peace negotiations began in 2008, though skirmishes and terrorist attacks continue. More than 2 million civilians have been displaced.

War in Iraq

U.S.-led forces and their allies invaded Iraq in 2003, in the belief that the country was hiding "weapons of mass destruction." The invasion of Iraq led to an occupation and the execution of President Saddam Hussein, but the fighting has not stopped and attacks by suicide bombers and rebels are weekly occurrences in the country.

Somali conflict

Years of fighting between rival groups has led to a humanitarian crisis in Somalia. One-third of the population is dependant on food aid, and thousands have been displaced. Warlords have forced many children to become soldiers.

Terrorist attacks

1. New York City, U.S.A.
On September 11th, 2001, Islamic extremists launched attacks on the World Trade Center. It led to the U.S.A. declaring a "War on Terror."

2. London, U.K.
In July 2005, 56 people were killed when four bombs exploded on London's public transportation system, set off by Islamic suicide bombers.

3. Madrid, Spain
Commuter trains were bombed in Madrid, in protest against Spanish troops serving in the U.S.-led invasion of Iraq. The total killed reached 191.

4. Beslan, Russia
Militants took over a school in Russia and held teachers and children hostage in 2004. More than 300 died before the standoff ended.

5. Moscow, Russia
Rebels took 700 theater-goers hostage in 2002. The rebels were eventually killed, but more than 100 hostages also died.

6. Sharm el-Sheik, Egypt
Egypt suffered the worst terrorist attack in its history when 64 people died in three bomb attacks in the resort town of Sharm el-Sheik.

7. Mumbai, India
A series of attacks launched in 2008 in India's financial hub of Mumbai saw more than 170 killed in shootings and grenade attacks.

8. Bali, Indonesia
In October 2002, terrorists bombed the tourist district of Bali. Killing 202 people, it was the worst attack in Indonesian history.

Lockheed Martin

This aerospace manufacturer, based in the U.S.A., is the world's largest defense contractor. It supplies a whole index of countries with spy planes and fighter jets, including the F-16 Falcon.

THE U.S.A. HAS 732 F-16 FALCONS IN ACTIVE DUTY

F-16 FALCON

PRICE TAG: $18.8 MILLION EACH

Explosive Budgets

War, unfortunately, plays a major part in our world history, both past and in the making. The increase in threat from terrorism following the attack on the World Trade Center and the war in Iraq and Afghanistan, has seen military spending soar, particularly in the United States. They invest more on defense than the next 45 highest spending countries combined, while strong economic growth in nations such as China and India has enabled those countries to dramatically increase the size of their military. The total amount spent on defense for each person in the world is today estimated to be $217 per year.

Spending per person

Countries in the Middle East, such as Oman and Kuwait, have increased their wealth due to oil. With this, their military spending has also grown. But topping the charts of spending on defense per person in the world is Israel.

| FRANCE $1,050 | U.K. $1,075 | GREECE $1,125 | NORWAY $1,250 | SAUDI ARABIA $1,500 | KUWAIT $1,600 | SINGAPORE $1,625 | OMAN $1,650 | U.S.A. $1,950 | ISRAEL $2,300 |

In 2008, the total world spending on defense reached **$1.46 trillion**

Total spending

The biggest spender by far in this well-funded moneypot is the United States. With a budget of $607 billion, it accounts for almost 50% of world military spending.

U.S.A. $607 billion

SOUTH KOREA $24.2 BILLION

INDIA $30 BILLION

SAUDI ARABIA $38.2 BILLION

ITALY $40.6 BILLION

JAPAN $46.3 BILLION

GERMANY $46.8 BILLION

RUSSIA $58.6 BILLION

U.K. $65.3 BILLION

FRANCE $65.7 BILLION

CHINA $84.9 BILLION

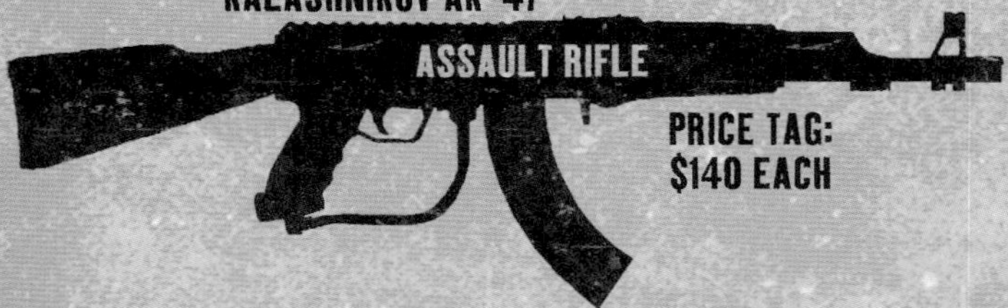

GLOCK-19 PISTOL — $400 EACH

ARSENAL-SHIPKA SUBMACHINE GUN — PRICE TAG: $300 EACH

Handheld guns

It is estimated that there are more than 650 million guns circulating the globe, claiming a devastating 1,000 lives per day.

Aircraft carriers

The average cost of an aircraft carrier is an impressive $4 billion. More than 20 of these warships roam the oceans, from 10 different countries.

AIRCRAFT CARRIER — PRICE TAG: $4 BILLION EACH

U.S. aircraft carriers are named after presidents

STEYER AUG-A1 ASSAULT RIFLE — PRICE TAG: $2,245 EACH

JAVELIN ANTI-TANK MISSILE — PRICE TAG: $125,000 EACH

NORTH KOREA 2
PAKISTAN 60
INDIA 65
ISRAEL 80
U.K. 160
CHINA 186
FRANCE 300

106,000
Worldwide, there are approximately 106,000 tanks in existence

TANK — PRICE TAG: UP TO $4 MILLION EACH

KALASHNIKOV AK-47 ASSAULT RIFLE — PRICE TAG: $140 EACH

Ammunition

Many countries have a domestic arms industry to make cartridges, land mines, and grenades for their army. However, illegal trade in small arms is a widespread problem.

The nuclear family

The number of countries with nuclear warheads is slowly growing. The number that each country is thought to have is shown here, with an estimated 20,392 nuclear warheads worldwide.

U.S.A. — AN ESTIMATED 2,702 NUCLEAR WARHEADS

RUSSIA — AN ESTIMATED 4,834 NUCLEAR WARHEADS

A 1-MEGATON BOMB LEVELS EVERYTHING WITHIN A 2 MILE (3.2 KM) RADIUS

HAND GRENADE — PRICE TAG: UP TO $25 EACH

Refugees

Those forced to leave their country of origin due to war, violence, or persecution are known as refugees. They are different from migrants, who leave their homes in search of a better life. Most refugees flee to neighboring countries, though some seek sanctuary farther afield.

9,146,000

Where do they come from?

In 2008, more than one-third of the world's 15.2 million refugees came from just five countries: Afghanistan, Iraq, Colombia, the Sudan, and Somalia. These countries have seen intense conflict in recent years. In countries divided by war, people may get caught up in the fighting or persecuted due to their race or religion.

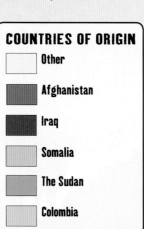

COUNTRIES OF ORIGIN
- Other
- Afghanistan
- Iraq
- Somalia
- The Sudan
- Colombia

2,800,000

REST OF WORLD
465,200

32,700   43,900

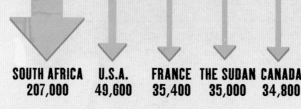

Asylum seekers

When a person seeks refuge in a foreign country, they must prove that their life was at risk before they are recognized as a refugee and allowed to stay. While the host country decides, the person is known as an asylum seeker. Asylum seekers have limited rights and are often held in specially built detention centers.

SOUTH AFRICA	U.S.A.	FRANCE	THE SUDAN	CANADA
207,000	49,600	35,400	35,000	34,800

Host countries

Sometimes it can be difficult to tell whether a person is genuinely in danger or has come to a new country to find work. It can take host countries months to decide whether or not someone will be allowed to stay. Asylum seekers whose claims are rejected are usually deported (sent home).

Far from Home

Every year armed conflict, natural disasters, and the threat of persecution force millions of people to leave their homes and seek protection elsewhere. Some are homeless within their own countries, while others seek refuge abroad. Most countries take in refugees, but the process of being recognized as a refugee can be strict and not everyone is allowed to stay. Those whose cases have not been decided yet are called asylum seekers.

Causes

In 2008, the number of people around the world who were uprooted from their homes stood at 42 million. There are many reasons why people flee their homes, but most do so because they no longer feel safe.

 In some parts of the world, people who speak out against their government are threatened with violence.

 Some people's homes are destroyed by natural disasters such as earthquakes or hurricanes.

 War is one of the main reasons why people flee their homes.

 Communities may be uprooted when the effects of climate change make their land uninhabitable.

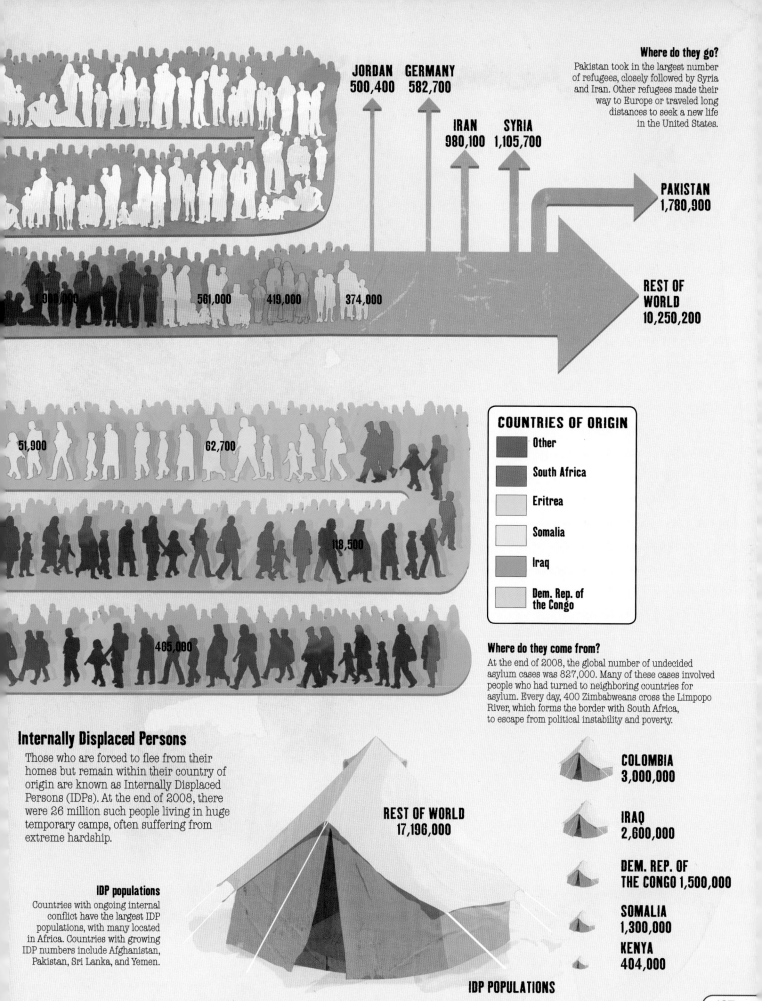

Where do they go?
Pakistan took in the largest number of refugees, closely followed by Syria and Iran. Other refugees made their way to Europe or traveled long distances to seek a new life in the United States.

JORDAN
500,400

GERMANY
582,700

IRAN
980,100

SYRIA
1,105,700

PAKISTAN
1,780,900

REST OF WORLD
10,250,200

1,900,000   561,000   419,000   374,000

51,900   62,700

118,500

465,000

COUNTRIES OF ORIGIN
- Other
- South Africa
- Eritrea
- Somalia
- Iraq
- Dem. Rep. of the Congo

Where do they come from?
At the end of 2008, the global number of undecided asylum cases was 827,000. Many of these cases involved people who had turned to neighboring countries for asylum. Every day, 400 Zimbabweans cross the Limpopo River, which forms the border with South Africa, to escape from political instability and poverty.

Internally Displaced Persons

Those who are forced to flee from their homes but remain within their country of origin are known as Internally Displaced Persons (IDPs). At the end of 2008, there were 26 million such people living in huge temporary camps, often suffering from extreme hardship.

IDP populations
Countries with ongoing internal conflict have the largest IDP populations, with many located in Africa. Countries with growing IDP numbers include Afghanistan, Pakistan, Sri Lanka, and Yemen.

REST OF WORLD
17,196,000

COLOMBIA
3,000,000

IRAQ
2,600,000

DEM. REP. OF THE CONGO 1,500,000

SOMALIA
1,300,000

KENYA
404,000

IDP POPULATIONS

127

Human Rights

The Universal Declaration of Human Rights was adopted by the United Nations in 1948. It set out the rights and freedoms that every human being is entitled to, such as a right to education, free speech, and self-expression. Despite international support of the declaration, abuses of the rights that it contains still take place around the world. There are agencies that try to monitor human rights violations, but many abuses take place in secret, sometimes with powerful governments behind them.

Massacre of journalists

On November 23rd, 2009, a convoy carrying candidates for a mayoral election in the Philippine province of Maguindanao was brutally massacred. Of the 57 people killed, 34 were journalists—the worst single attack on journalists ever recorded. The Philippines is one of the most dangerous countries for journalists, second only to Iraq.

Discrimination in education

Romany people in Europe have often faced discrimination at work and school. Discrimination in education is unlawful, but Romany children receive inferior schooling in the Czech Republic. Almost one-third of Romany children are placed in schools designed for children with mild mental disabilities or in segregated schools that provide second-rate education.

Extraordinary rendition

The alleged practice of extraordinary rendition involves the abduction and transportation of suspected terrorists to places such as Jordan, Egypt, and Guantánamo in Cuba, where they are interrogated and imprisoned on behalf of the U.K. and U.S. governments. Around 3,000 people are alleged to have been treated in this way.

Silenced in Myanmar (Burma)

Since the military seized power in Myanmar in 1988, the pro-democracy campaigner Aung San Suu Kyi has criticized its grip on the country. She was elected Prime Minister in 1990, but instead the military placed her under house arrest, where she has been for 14 of the last 20 years, often in solitary confinement. There are currently 2,000 political prisoners in the country.

Girls in Equatorial Guinea

In Equatorial Guinea, thousands of girls as young as eight are forced to work up to 18 hours a day as domestic workers. The majority are not paid and are frequently beaten by their employers, refused education, and receive no help when they are sick.

Religious expression in France

France has traditionally kept religion and everyday life separate. In 2004, the wearing of religious symbols in schools was banned. This has led to tensions over the right of the individual to express themselves and observe the traditions of a religious faith. The issue is especially heated around the question of whether Muslim schoolgirls should wear a hijab (headscarf).

Press freedom

The freedom of the press to express ideas and report truthfully plays a key role in society. It contributes to greater accountability and good governance, yet press freedom is in decline in almost every part of the world. Only 17% of the world's citizens currently enjoy a totally free press.

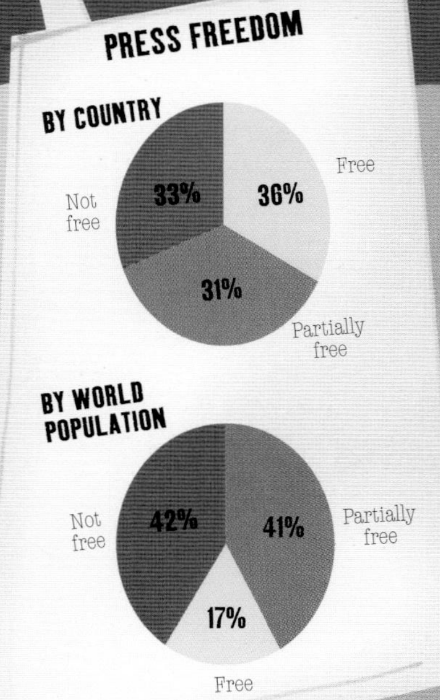

PRESS FREEDOM

BY COUNTRY

- Free 36%
- Partially free 31%
- Not free 33%

BY WORLD POPULATION

- Free 17%
- Partially free 41%
- Not free 42%

CHILD LABOUR
(percentage of children aged 5–14 engaged in work)

- No data
- Less than 10%
- 10–29%
- 30% or more

Child labor

There are an estimated 158 million children aged between five and 14 working worldwide. This map shows that many exploited children live in developing countries, such as the 75 million children working in India. Child labor accounts for 22% of the workforce in Asia and 32% in Africa.

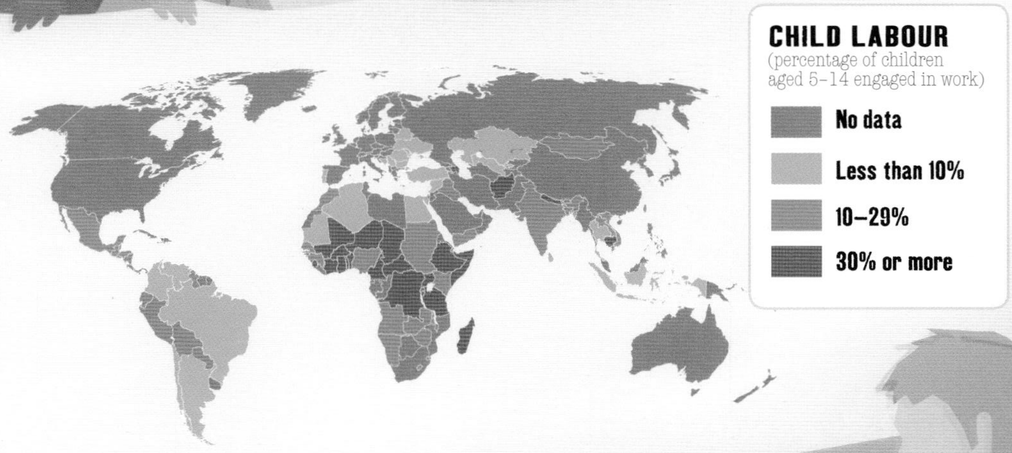

Freedom of religion

Though it has decreased in recent decades, religious prejudice remains a serious problem around the world. Some countries discriminate against any religion that does not correspond to their official faith. Around 70% of the global population live in countries that experience high levels of religious intolerance.

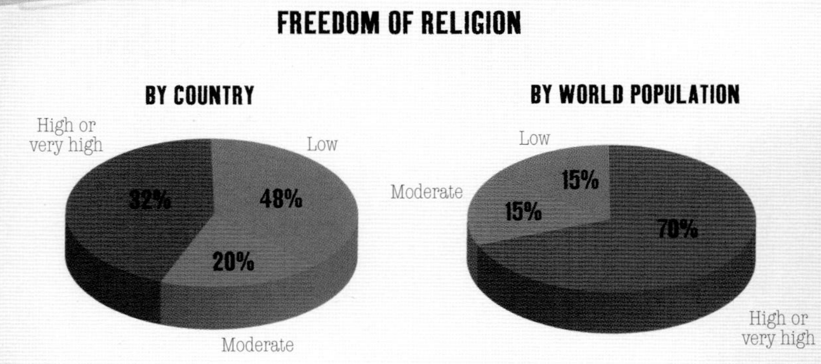

FREEDOM OF RELIGION

BY COUNTRY

- High or very high 32%
- Low 48%
- Moderate 20%

BY WORLD POPULATION

- Moderate 15%
- Low 15%
- High or very high 70%

Crime

Large urban populations and abundant consumer goods are all linked with high crime rates—if there are more things to steal, more things will be stolen. These are common features of life in Europe, where robbery, violent crime, and drug trafficking have increased by around 4% in the last decade. The willingness of victims to report crimes also influences statistics: it is estimated that 30–60% of crimes in European countries are never recorded.

Reporting crimes

The figures shown on this map reflect the number of crimes that were reported to the police, rather than the number of crimes that were actually committed. Across Europe, 28% of robberies are not reported to the police because victims feel the police can't or won't do anything.

Crime hot spots

The most common crimes vary widely between countries. U.K. households are the most burgled in Europe, and the U.K. also has the highest number of assaults. Lithuania is the murder capital of Europe, with one homicide per 12,500 people. You are most likely to get robbed in Spain but to have your car stolen in Switzerland, where there is one car theft per 130 people every year.

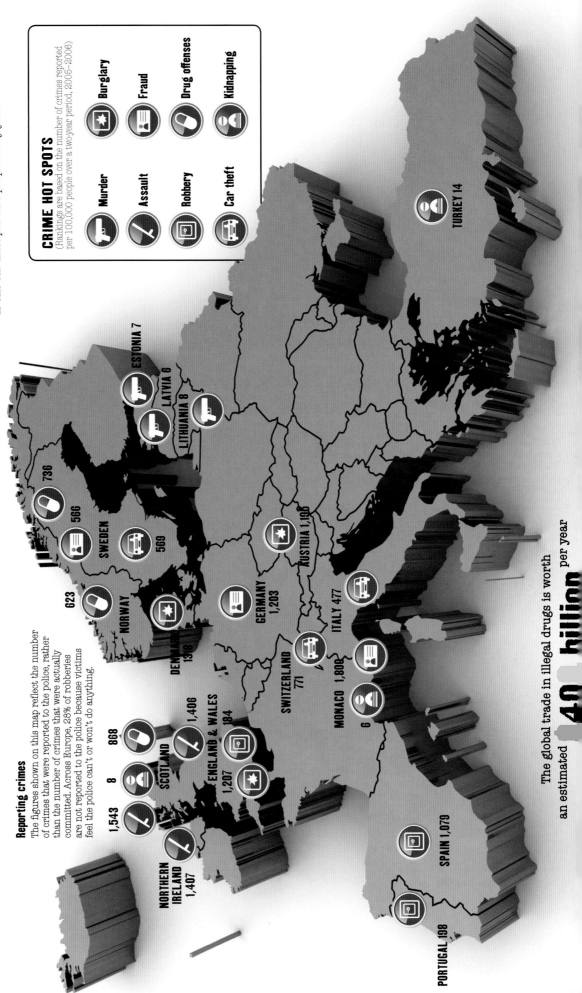

CRIME HOT SPOTS
(Rankings are based on the number of crimes reported per 100,000 people over a two-year period, 2005–2006)

- Murder
- Assault
- Robbery
- Car theft
- Burglary
- Fraud
- Drug offenses
- Kidnapping

TURKEY 14

ESTONIA 7

LATVIA 6

LITHUANIA 8

736

566

SWEDEN

569

623

NORWAY

DENMARK 198

GERMANY 1,203

AUSTRIA 1,196

ITALY 477

SWITZERLAND 771

MONACO 1,808

9

NORTHERN IRELAND 1,407

SCOTLAND

1,543   8   868

ENGLAND & WALES
1,207   184   1,406

SPAIN 1,079

PORTUGAL 198

The global trade in illegal drugs is worth an estimated **400 billion** per year

Crime rate in Europe

More Swedish victims report crimes to the police than in any other European country. A huge proportion of these are property crimes, such as burglary, robbery, and car theft. Interestingly, fear of crime in Europe does not reflect actual crime rates. The populations of Poland and Greece feel least safe on the streets after dark, while Finns, facing Europe's third-highest crime rates, are the least fearful.

TOTAL RECORDED NUMBER OF CRIMES PER 100,000 PEOPLE
Top ten European countries

80% of crime victims surveyed in
Finland, Denmark, and Austria were pleased with the response of their police force

SCOTLAND
8,200

FINLAND
9,825

SWEDEN
13,493

AUSTRIA
7,079

GERMANY
7,628

THE NETHERLANDS
7,439

NORTHERN IRELAND 7,144

ENGLAND & WALES 10,399

Organized crime
Criminal gangs make a business operation out of their illegal activity, organizing themselves centrally to make even bigger profits from activities like drug trafficking and fraud. Easier travel between countries in the European Union means that this "organized crime" is thriving in Europe.

Police personnel
Police officers are the frontline in protecting the public against crime. More than 1% of Kuwait's population works for the police and crime rates are low. But more police doesn't always mean less crime. Despite its large police force, Mexico has some of the world's highest murder and kidnapping rates.

NUMBER OF POLICE OFFICERS PER 100,000 PEOPLE

KUWAIT 1,116

CYPRUS 618

ITALY 558

MEXICO 491

U.S.A. 326

AUSTRALIA 304

U.K. 257

S. AFRICA 224

JAPAN 182

MOROCCO 141

Punishment

When someone commits a crime, most countries have strict laws outlining how they should be punished. Justice differs around the world—some countries focus on rehabilitating offenders, while others have zero-tolerance policies for even the slightest of crimes. In some countries, criminals pay with their lives for their misdemeanors.

Under lock and key

Imprisonment is one of the most common forms of punishment for serious crimes. The number of people in prison around the world—either serving their sentence or awaiting trial—currently stands at 9.8 million. Just three countries account for nearly half of all the world's prisoners—the U.S.A. has 2.29 million prisoners, China has 1.57 million, and Russia has 890,000.

U.S.A. 23%

RUSSIA 9%

CHINA 16%

REST OF THE WORLD 52%

For every 100,000 people in the world, **145** are serving time in prison

Laying down the law

Punishments are determined by the laws of the land. In some countries, an elected parliament makes the laws. In others, the law is dictated by the ruling group. Some countries also observe religious law, which uses a code of ethics that followers believe has been laid down by god.

In China, there are

850,000

people in "administrative detention" (held without trial for security reasons). Including them would bring the world prisoner number to 10.6 million.

Prisoners in the U.S.A.

The U.S. has the world's highest prison population. The cost of holding their 2.29 million inmates clocks in at around $68 billion per year. More than 70% of inmates in U.S. prisons are nonwhite, compared to only 20% in the population at large.

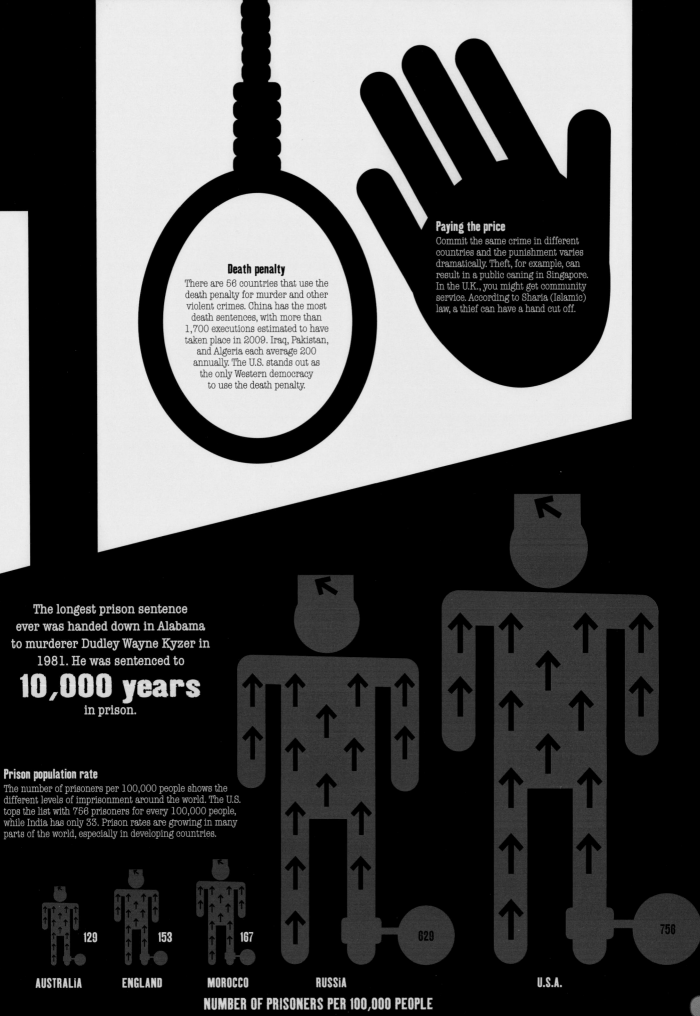

Death penalty

There are 56 countries that use the death penalty for murder and other violent crimes. China has the most death sentences, with more than 1,700 executions estimated to have taken place in 2009. Iraq, Pakistan, and Algeria each average 200 annually. The U.S. stands out as the only Western democracy to use the death penalty.

Paying the price

Commit the same crime in different countries and the punishment varies dramatically. Theft, for example, can result in a public caning in Singapore. In the U.K., you might get community service. According to Sharia (Islamic) law, a thief can have a hand cut off.

The longest prison sentence ever was handed down in Alabama to murderer Dudley Wayne Kyzer in 1981. He was sentenced to

10,000 years

in prison.

Prison population rate

The number of prisoners per 100,000 people shows the different levels of imprisonment around the world. The U.S. tops the list with 756 prisoners for every 100,000 people, while India has only 33. Prison rates are growing in many parts of the world, especially in developing countries.

129   153   167   629   756

AUSTRALIA   ENGLAND   MOROCCO   RUSSIA   U.S.A.

NUMBER OF PRISONERS PER 100,000 PEOPLE

Surveillance

Once the domain of secret agents, surveillance—the monitoring of people's activities—now affects nearly everyone. Our use of the internet, cell phones, and smart cards has increased dramatically in recent years. Along with the increasing number of CCTV cameras, almost every move that we make is monitored. Officials say that surveillance is a crucial tool in combating terrorism and controlling crime, but there are growing concerns about invasions of privacy and restrictions on personal freedom.

Google-eyed

Google's recent "Earth" and "Street View" projects have caused some controversy. These ambitious undertakings have mapped countries from the air, and photographed towns and cities at street level, with the information then freely available to view online. Some people have complained about having images of their private property posted online without their permission.

Tangled in the net

Every time you use the Internet, it is possible for your browsing to be seen by a third party. Emails can be intercepted on any of the servers they are stored on before they reach their final destination. Photographs posted online can be seen by anyone online unless you are extremely careful. Social networking sites and search engines gather data about their users' interests and sell it on to companies, who use it to target their advertising.

Camera action

Closed Circuit Television (CCTV) cameras are put in many public places primarily to record criminal activity, but in doing this they essentially monitor all of us. It is estimated that the U.K. has nearly 5 million cameras, making it the most watched society in the world. The U.K. spent 78% of its crime prevention budget in the 1990s on CCTV cameras, but studies have shown that only one crime is solved for every 1,000 cameras.

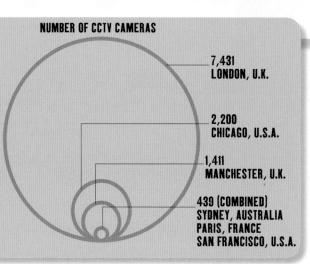

NUMBER OF CCTV CAMERAS

7,431
LONDON, U.K.

2,200
CHICAGO, U.S.A.

1,411
MANCHESTER, U.K.

439 (COMBINED)
SYDNEY, AUSTRALIA
PARIS, FRANCE
SAN FRANCISCO, U.S.A.

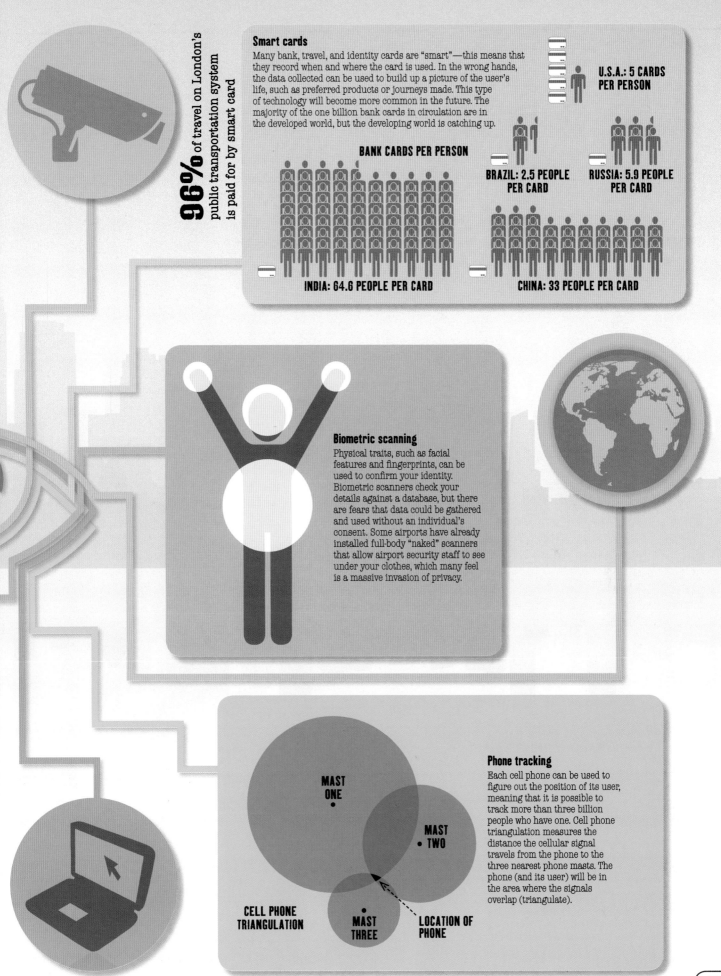

96% of travel on London's public transportation system is paid for by smart card

Smart cards

Many bank, travel, and identity cards are "smart"—this means that they record when and where the card is used. In the wrong hands, the data collected can be used to build up a picture of the user's life, such as preferred products or journeys made. This type of technology will become more common in the future. The majority of the one billion bank cards in circulation are in the developed world, but the developing world is catching up.

U.S.A.: 5 CARDS PER PERSON

BANK CARDS PER PERSON

BRAZIL: 2.5 PEOPLE PER CARD

RUSSIA: 5.9 PEOPLE PER CARD

INDIA: 64.6 PEOPLE PER CARD

CHINA: 33 PEOPLE PER CARD

Biometric scanning

Physical traits, such as facial features and fingerprints, can be used to confirm your identity. Biometric scanners check your details against a database, but there are fears that data could be gathered and used without an individual's consent. Some airports have already installed full-body "naked" scanners that allow airport security staff to see under your clothes, which many feel is a massive invasion of privacy.

Phone tracking

Each cell phone can be used to figure out the position of its user, meaning that it is possible to track more than three billion people who have one. Cell phone triangulation measures the distance the cellular signal travels from the phone to the three nearest phone masts. The phone (and its user) will be in the area where the signals overlap (triangulate).

MAST ONE

MAST TWO

CELL PHONE TRIANGULATION

MAST THREE

LOCATION OF PHONE

Big Business

Multinational companies have operations in multiple countries; they tend to have a strong presence in their home nation but have expanded across the globe, often to take advantage of cheaper labor. Investment from multinationals leads to jobs and training for people in the host country, but the power and influence multinationals have over foreign governments, as well as the low wages they sometimes pay, make them the target of intense criticism.

Powerhouses

The number of multinational companies in the world exceeds 60,000. With their subsidiaries spread across the globe, the top 500 account for almost one quarter of world trade and earn huge profits, rivaling the GDPs of entire countries. The top 10 companies by revenue are shown here. The most successful company, U.S. retail giant Wal-Mart, earned a whopping $401 billion in 2008—more than the GDP of Sweden.

Biggest employers

Multinationals employ more than 200 million people worldwide. Wal-Mart, whose huge empire comprises a chain of retail stores, is the largest employer, with 2.1 million people on its books. Four of the top 10 employers are businesses run by the Chinese state.

Biggest employers
(with country of origin)

1. **Wal-mart (U.S.A.)** 2,055,000
2. **State Grid (China)** 1,486,000
3. **China National Petroleum** 1,117,345
4. **U.S. Postal Service** 785,929
5. **Sinopec (China)** 834,011
6. **Hon Hai Precision Industries (Taiwan)** 550,000
7. **Carrefour (France)** 490,042
8. **Deutsche Poste** 475,100
9. **Agricultural Bank of China** 447,519
10. **Gazprom (Russia)** 436,098

1. WAL
2. EXXON
3. ROYAL DU
4. BRITISH P
5. TOYOTA MOTORS
7. iNG GROUP
9. GENERAL MOTORS

1 in 8
Americans have worked in a McDonalds restaurant at some point in their lives

Global reach of select multinationals

Some multinationals have expanded their businesses to foreign countries more than others. The transnationality index helps us measure this by looking at the number of assets, employment figures, and sales for each company outside its home country. Wal-Mart may be at the top of the list of multinationals for revenue, but its transnationality percentage is just 41%. By comparison, Vodafone has a global reach of 85%.

WAL-MART (U.S.A.) 41%

EXXON MOBIL (U.S.A.) 68%

ROYAL DUTCH SHELL (U.K. AND NETHERLANDS) 70%

BRITISH PETROLEUM (U.K.) 80%

The most profitable sectors

Certain industries perform consistently better than others when it comes to profitability. Oil and gas, which provide energy for transportation, heating, and industrial production, generate huge revenues for companies such as Royal Dutch Shell and British Petroleum. Other essential services, such as medicine, hospitality, and information technology (IT), are also high earners.

MINING AND CRUDE OIL PRODUCTION 19.8%

PHARMACEUTICALS 17.7%

BEVERAGES 11.9%

HOUSEHOLD AND PERSONAL PRODUCTS 11.8%

COMMUNICATION EQUIPMENT 11.6%

MOST PROFITABLE INDUSTRIES BY REVENUE

MART
MOBIL
CH SHELL
TROLEUM
6. CHEVRON
8. TOTAL
10. CONOCOPHILLIPS

If all the sandwiches Subway make in a year were placed end to end, they would wrap around Earth **6 times**

Developing countries

(amount invested, 2008, figures given in millions)

1 **Hong Kong** $1,184
2 **Brazil** $328.4
3 **China** $327
4 **Russia** $324
5 **Mexico** $265.7
6 **Singapore** $249.7
7 **Turkey** $146.5
8 **South Korea** $119.6
9 **Chile** $105.6
10 **South Africa** $93.5

Foreign investment

Multinational businesses take advantage of new technology to relocate to developing countries where costs are lower. The 10 countries listed here receive 70% of the foreign investment that is made by multinationals in developing countries.

Multibranding

The name of a successful company in one country does not necessarily translate well in another. Wal-Mart's discount department stores are emblazoned with more than 60 different names around the world.

Hello, my name is

WAL-MART, also known as:
ASDA, BEST PRICE,
BOMPREÇO, SEIYU,
TODO DIA, WALMEX,
WOOLCO...

TOYOTA (JAPAN) 45%	COCA-COLA (U.S.A.) 78%	NESTLÉ (SWITZERLAND) 83%	VODAFONE (U.K.) 85%	SONY (JAPAN) 59%	TOTAL (FRANCE) 74%

Making Money

Money enables us to pay for goods and services. When something is sold at a higher price than it cost to buy or make, the difference between the two is profit. Businesses try to make a profit to pay their workers and meet their costs. Money deposited in bank accounts is used by banks to provide credit (loans). The banks make a profit by charging fees for their services and interest on money borrowed from them.

All the money in the world

Cash is just one part of all the money in the world. There is also money held in bank accounts and money tied up in assets (property) and investments (things bought in the hope that they will become more valuable).

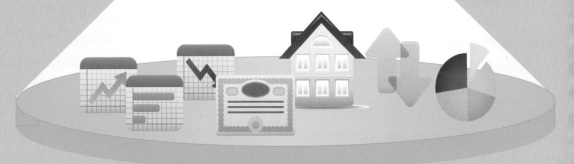

Cash in circulation
The total value of all the banknotes and coins in circulation around the world is a hefty $4 trillion.

Bank accounts
The money held in bank accounts worldwide amounts to $45 trillion—11 times more than all the cash in circulation.

Assets
All the land, buildings, company shares, and other assets comes have an estimated value of an astonishing $290 trillion.

Global currencies

Nearly three quarters of all the cash in circulation belongs to just four currencies. These are the European euro, U.S. dollar, Japanese yen, and Chinese yuan—the currencies of the world's biggest economies. The U.S. dollar is one of the longest-running currencies, dating from 1792. Only the British pound sterling is older, dating back to 1694.

Every year the United States Mint makes around

14—20 billion
new coins

Pie chart values: 27.5%, 11%, 18.5%, 20%, 23%

CURRENCIES
- Euro
- U.S. dollar
- Japanese yen
- Chinese yuan
- Other

How banking works

When people deposit money in banks, the banks use it to make more money by loaning most of it to other people and to businesses and charging interest (a regular fee).

CUSTOMER MAKES A DEPOSIT

BANK 1

BANK 1 KEEPS 10% AND LOANS THE REST TO BANK 2

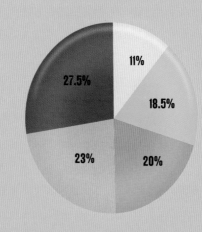

BANK 2

BANK 2 KEEPS 10% AND LOANS THE REST TO BANK 3

BANK 2 PAYS BANK 1 INTEREST ON THE LOAN

BANK 3 PAYS BANK 2 INTEREST ON THE LOAN

Life expectancies of dollar bills

Banknotes and coins wear out and have to be replaced. Notes, or bills, with smaller values are used more often than larger ones and so have to be replaced more frequently. Banknotes wear out faster than coins. A dollar bill lasts about 22 months, compared to a dollar coin's life expectancy of at least 30 years.

Safe money

Security features, including watermarks and metal thread, make banknotes more difficult to forge. Some countries have even introduced banknotes made of plastic instead of paper.

1.8 YEARS — $1

2 YEARS — $20

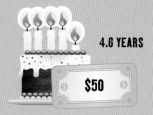

4.6 YEARS — $50

HOW LONG A U.S. BANKNOTE REMAINS IN CIRCULATION

JAPAN 765.2
SWITZERLAND 1,040.1
CHINA 1,054
FRANCE 2,435.4
ITALY 2,451.8
IMF 3,005.3
GERMANY 3,407.6
UNITED STATES 8,133.5

THE BIGGEST GOLD RESERVES (TONNES)

Who has the gold?

Governments and central (national) banks keep gold as part of a nation's wealth. Some large international financial organizations, such as the International Monetary Fund (IMF), have gold reserves, too. Approximately 28,000 tonnes—around 19% of all the gold that has ever been mined—is held in this way. The U.S.A.'s gold reserve is the biggest of any country.

All the gold

If all 120,000–140,000 tonnes of gold ever mined was melted down, it would fill fewer than three Olympic-size swimming pools. Together, it would be worth around $1.8 trillion.

One tonne of gold is worth around
$35 million

BANK 3

BANK 3 KEEPS 10% AND LOANS THE REST TO OTHER BANKS

BANK 3 PAYS BANK 2 INTEREST ON THE LOAN

Hyperinflation

Inflation is the increase in the cost of goods and services in a country from year to year. It is a normal part of a country's economy. However, if prices rise too quickly, a unit of currency is able to buy fewer and fewer things and the value of the currency goes down. This is called hyperinflation. Throughout the 2000s Zimbabwe suffered from record hyperinflation. At its peak, prices were doubling every 24 hours and the Zimbabwean dollar became worthless.

Wealth of Nations

The wealth of a nation can be measured in several ways. The most common is to calculate the total value of all the goods and services that a country produces in a year. This is called the Gross Domestic Product (GDP) and is usually measured using the world's most common currency—the U.S. dollar.

U.S.A.: $14.4 trillion
Topping the world rankings is the U.S.A. Much of its wealth—around 68%—is generated by services such as banking, though the U.S.A. is also the world's biggest manufacturer and has plenty of natural resources.

Japan: $4.9 trillion
Japan may be a tiny country with few natural resources, but it makes second place due to its advanced manufacturing sector and successful policies on industry in the wake of World War II.

China: $4.3 trillion
China is the world's fastest growing economy. By 2030, it is expected to exceed Japan and the U.S.A. to become the world's largest. It has booming manufacturing businesses and is the largest exporter of goods.

Germany: $3.7 trillion.
Once called the "sick man of Europe," Germany now has Europe's biggest economy and is the world's second-largest exporter. Employment rates are steady, and manufacturing and engineering are strong.

The EU has a total GDP of
$18.4 trillion

NORWAY
$94,387
LUXEMBOURG
$113,044

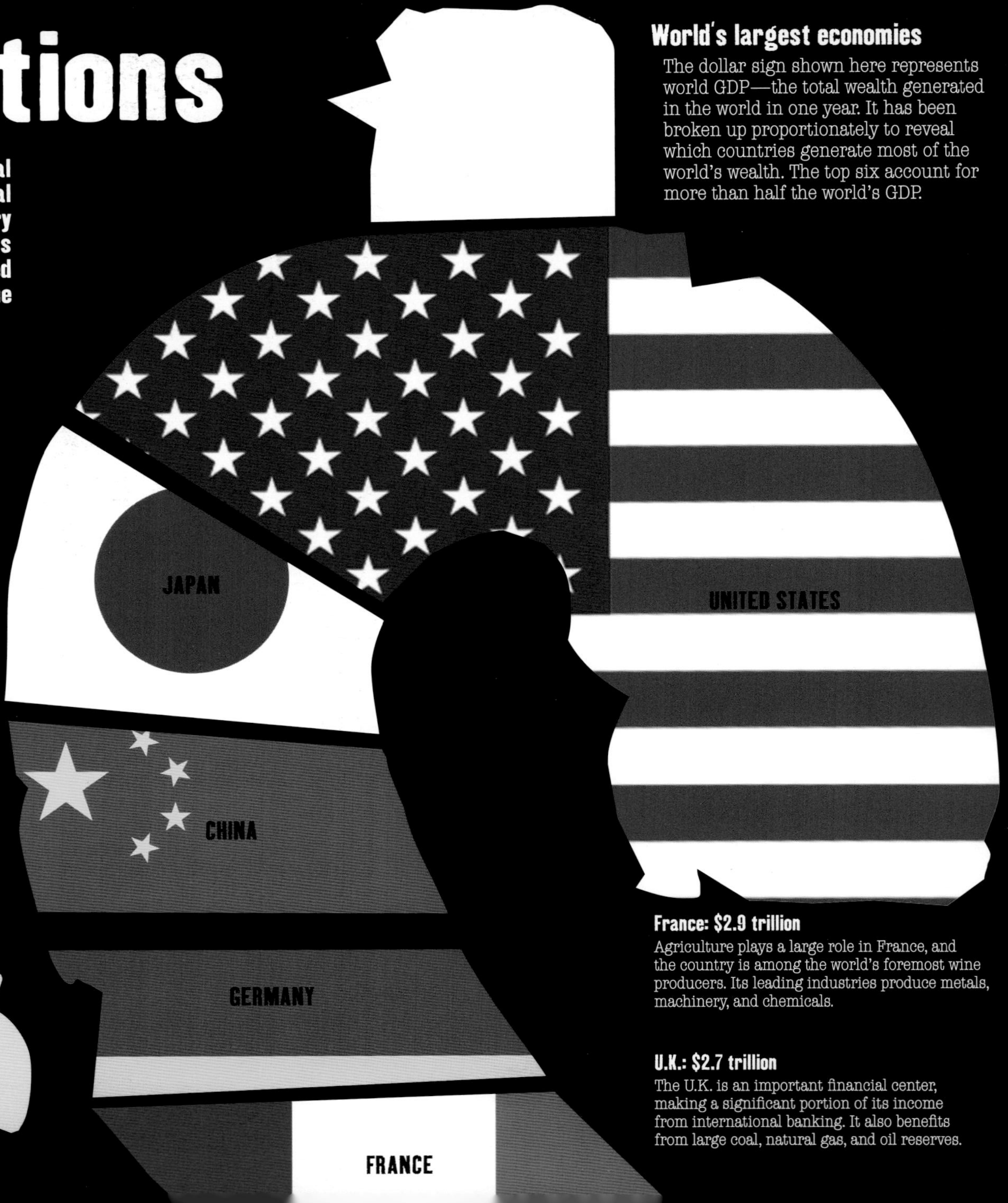
UNITED STATES
JAPAN
CHINA
GERMANY
FRANCE

World's largest economies

The dollar sign shown here represents world GDP—the total wealth generated in the world in one year. It has been broken up proportionately to reveal which countries generate most of the world's wealth. The top six account for more than half the world's GDP.

France: $2.9 trillion
Agriculture plays a large role in France, and the country is among the world's foremost wine producers. Its leading industries produce metals, machinery, and chemicals.

U.K.: $2.7 trillion
The U.K. is an important financial center, making a significant portion of its income from international banking. It also benefits from large coal, natural gas, and oil reserves.

THE REST OF THE WORLD

Total world GDP is about
$60 trillion

Rest of the world: $27 trillion

All the other countries in the world account for the remaining 46% of world GDP. In many developing countries, GDP stays flat from year to year. But in some countries, the picture is changing. Brazil, India, and Mexico have all seen their economies boom in recent years.

GDP per capita

When the size of a country's population is considered, a new picture of wealth emerges. Dividing GDP by the number of people in a country shows how much wealth is being generated per person and produces a very different list of top countries. GDP per capita doesn't represent how much the average person earns, but it can be used to compare rough standards of living.

Income groups

The World Bank groups countries into income brackets according to their GDP per capita. High-income countries are sometimes referred to as developed nations, and those in the other three bands as developing nations. This map shows how countries in the same bracket tend to be grouped together geographically, with many high-income countries in the Northern Hemisphere, and the world's poorest located in sub-Saharan Africa.

INCOME KEY

High income	$11,906 or more
Middle income	$3,856–11,905
Low income	$976–3,855
Very low income	$975 or less

QATAR
$93,204

SWITZERLAND
$68,433

DENMARK
$62,097

Haves and have-nots

The world's riches are shared out very unequally. Of all the household wealth—the money and assets owned by individuals—a massive 40% is owned by just 1% of the world's people. At the other end of the scale, half the world's population share just 1% of household wealth between them. The wealthy few live mostly in the industrialized nations of Europe, North America, and Asia.

WEALTH DISTRIBUTION
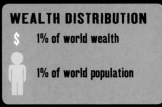
$ 1% of world wealth
👤 1% of world population

The average American has **$144,000** per person in assets, whereas in India the average is just **$1,100**

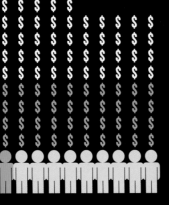

10% OF THE WORLD'S PEOPLE OWN 85% OF THE WORLD'S WEALTH. THE TOP 1% OF PEOPLE OWN 40%.

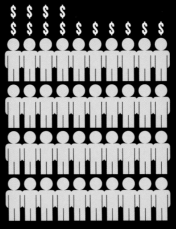

40% OF THE WORLD'S PEOPLE OWN 14% OF THE WORLD'S WEALTH.

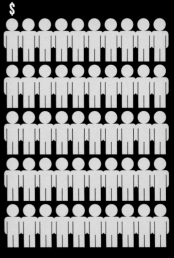

50% OF THE WORLD'S PEOPLE OWN 1% OF THE WORLD'S WEALTH.

Inequality

The world's people are sharply divided into rich and poor, and the two sides of the divide are grossly imbalanced. The rich few own most of the world's wealth, while the majority of people share the remainder. Many people are so poor that they are unable to meet life's basic needs—food, shelter, clean water, adequate health care. Most of the world's rich are concentrated in the wealthiest countries, but there are impoverished people everywhere. In Russia, 16% of the population live in poverty, while the country's wealthy elite includes 32 billionaires.

In 2005, roughly **1.4 billion** people—one-fifth of the world's population—were living in extreme poverty

Less than $1.25 a day

The World Bank defines extreme poverty as having less than $1.25 a day to live on. Most of the countries with a large proportion of people living in extreme poverty are in sub-Saharan Africa.

Proportion of people living on less than $1.25 a day:

1. **Tanzania** 88%
2. **Liberia** 84%
3. **Burundi** 81%
4. **Rwanda** 77%
5. **Mozambique** 75%
6. **Malawi** 74%
7. **Guinea** 70%
8. **Madagascar** 68%
9. **Niger** 66%
10. **Nigeria** 64%

Who wants to be a billionaire?

Forget being a millionaire – today's wealthiest people are measured by their billions. There are currently an estimated 793 dollar billionaires in the world. Nearly half of them come from the U.S.A.. Together, the fortunes of the world's billionaires amounts to around $2.4 trillion.

World's richest people

Some individuals are so rich that their personal fortunes rival the wealth of entire nations. Bill Gates—the world's richest man for 14 of the last 15 years—made his billions founding the computer giant Microsoft. His wealth is greater than the GDP of roughly half of the world's countries.

COUNTRY

- U.S.A.
- Other countries
- Germany
- China and Hong Kong
- Russia
- U.K.
- India
- Japan
- Canada

1 Carlos Slim Helú, Mexico: $53.5 billion
This telecommunications tycoon controls 90% of Mexico's landlines. Beat Gates to the top spot in 2010.

2 Bill Gates, U.S.A.: $53 billion
Founded Microsoft in 1975. Like many of the world's richest people, he now dedicates himself to charity work.

3 Warren Buffett, U.S.A.: $47 billion
Made his fortune investing in companies. Known as the "sage of Omaha" for his successful track record.

4 Mukesh Ambani, India: $29 billion
Owns a 48% stake in Reliance Industries, a multibillion-dollar oil company founded by his father in 1966.

5 Lakshmi Mittal, U.K.: $28.7 billion
Indian-born, U.K.-based steel magnate who built his business up from scratch, buying steel plants all over the world.

Wealth within countries

How rich or poor a country is as a whole is not the end of the story. Within countries, wealth is often spread out unequally. In the poorest countries, wealth tends to be concentrated in the hands of the few, though many richer countries also have a wide wealth gap. These diagrams show how a country's income is spread out.

POPULATION BANDS

POOREST 20%	SECOND 20%	THIRD 20%	FOURTH 20%	RICHEST 20%

% OF INCOME

1.4 3.0 5.4 11.5%   78.7%

Namibia
Namibia has one of the most uneven distributions of wealth in the world. The richest 20% of the population enjoy a high standard of living, with access to more than 70% of the country's assets. The remaining 80% of people share just 30% of the wealth. Nearly one-third of Namibia's 1.8 million people live on $1 a day or less.

POPULATION BANDS

POOREST 20%	SECOND 20%	THIRD 20%	FOURTH 20%	RICHEST 20%

% OF INCOME

10.6% 14.2% 17.6% 22%   35.7%

Japan
In Japan, there is a narrower gap between the rich and the poor. The country has one of the world's most even distributions of wealth, but even so the richest 20% of people there still possess more than a third of the country's wealth, leaving the poorest with just under 11%.

Balancing the Books

Two big issues seriously affect a country's chance of beating poverty. One is the amount of aid they get, the other is the amount of debt they owe. International aid helps developing countries build up their economies so they will prosper independently in the future. However, many countries receiving aid have to pay huge amounts of interest to rich nations on money that they have borrowed, which can outweigh the amount of aid received. Some people have called for the debts of the poorest nations to be canceled.

A helping hand
Many rich countries give financial help to the world's poorer nations. Aid is given freely and does not have to be paid back. Humanitarian aid is used to respond to emergencies, such as natural disasters, whereas development aid is money intended to help countries out of poverty in the long term. More than 90% of development aid comes from the 22 members of OECD (Organization for Economic Cooperation and Development). The countries that give the most in relation to their population size are all European.

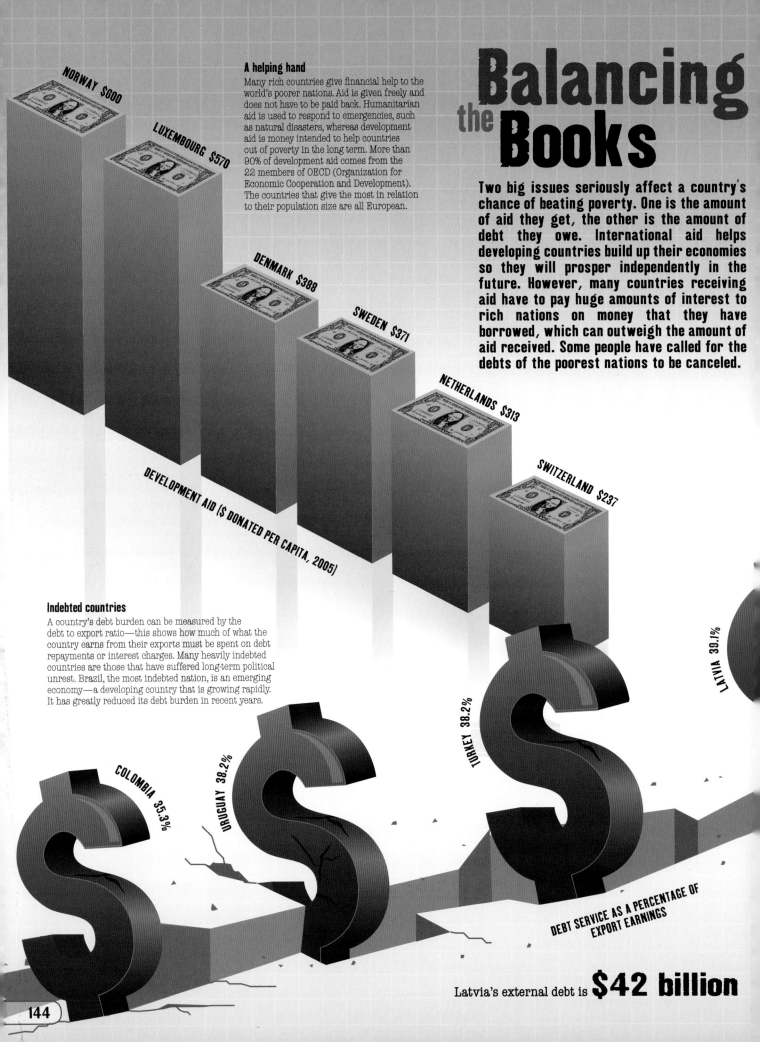

NORWAY $600

LUXEMBOURG $570

DENMARK $388

SWEDEN $371

NETHERLANDS $313

SWITZERLAND $237

DEVELOPMENT AID ($ DONATED PER CAPITA, 2005)

Indebted countries
A country's debt burden can be measured by the debt to export ratio—this shows how much of what the country earns from their exports must be spent on debt repayments or interest charges. Many heavily indebted countries are those that have suffered long-term political unrest. Brazil, the most indebted nation, is an emerging economy—a developing country that is growing rapidly. It has greatly reduced its debt burden in recent years.

COLOMBIA 35.3%

URUGUAY 38.2%

TURKEY 38.2%

LATVIA 39.1%

DEBT SERVICE AS A PERCENTAGE OF EXPORT EARNINGS

Latvia's external debt is **$42 billion**

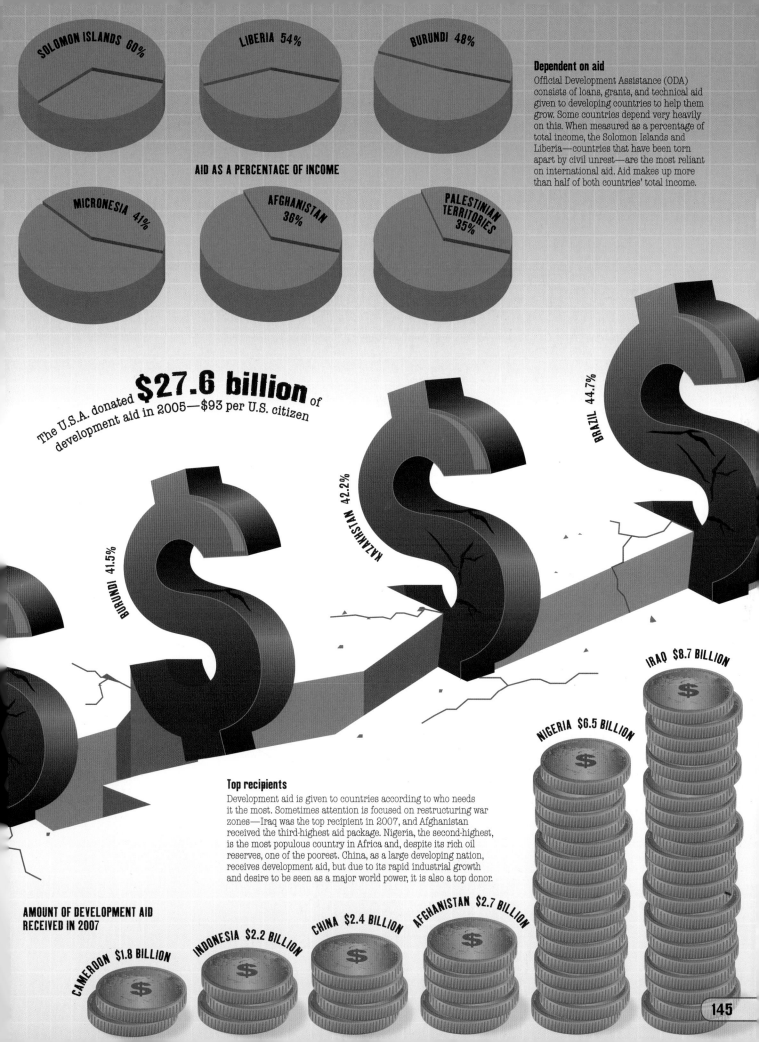

SOLOMON ISLANDS 60%

LIBERIA 54%

BURUNDI 48%

AID AS A PERCENTAGE OF INCOME

MICRONESIA 41%

AFGHANISTAN 36%

PALESTINIAN TERRITORIES 35%

Dependent on aid

Official Development Assistance (ODA) consists of loans, grants, and technical aid given to developing countries to help them grow. Some countries depend very heavily on this. When measured as a percentage of total income, the Solomon Islands and Liberia—countries that have been torn apart by civil unrest—are the most reliant on international aid. Aid makes up more than half of both countries' total income.

The U.S.A. donated **$27.6 billion** of development aid in 2005—$93 per U.S. citizen

BURUNDI 41.5%

KAZAKHSTAN 42.2%

BRAZIL 44.7%

IRAQ $8.7 BILLION

NIGERIA $6.5 BILLION

Top recipients

Development aid is given to countries according to who needs it the most. Sometimes attention is focused on restructuring war zones—Iraq was the top recipient in 2007, and Afghanistan received the third-highest aid package. Nigeria, the second-highest, is the most populous country in Africa and, despite its rich oil reserves, one of the poorest. China, as a large developing nation, receives development aid, but due to its rapid industrial growth and desire to be seen as a major world power, it is also a top donor.

AMOUNT OF DEVELOPMENT AID RECEIVED IN 2007

CAMEROON $1.8 BILLION

INDONESIA $2.2 BILLION

CHINA $2.4 BILLION

AFGHANISTAN $2.7 BILLION

145

THE World IN ONE Day

POWER

Governments, money, big business, international affairs—these are the things that make the world go around.

The **United Nations** (UN) is currently involved in **17 peacekeeping** operations around the world, involving **121,169** UN representatives

In 2008, **7** people were **executed** and **24** sentenced to **death** per day around the world

2,880 **court cases** are filed in the U.S.A. every day

There are around **11.9 million illegal** immigrants in the U.S.A.

The Federal Reserve Bank in New York transfers **$1.8 trillion** between itself and other **banks** around the world

There are **6,500** people employed by the United States' **Secret Service**

Giant **stone disks** are still recognized as legal currency in **Yap**, Micronesia

There are **182** **official currencies** in circulation

23,000 people work in **The Pentagon**, the headquarters of the U.S. Department of Defense—they make **200,000** telephone calls and receive around **40,000** pieces of mail

Iraq receives **$23.5 million** in **development aid**

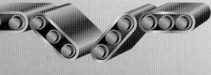
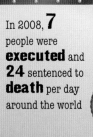

75,750 ambulances could be bought with the **$8.7 billion** spent by governments on **health care** worldwide

There are **75 million military troops** ready for action worldwide

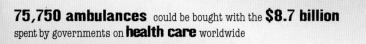

$3.8 billion is spent on the world's **militaries**

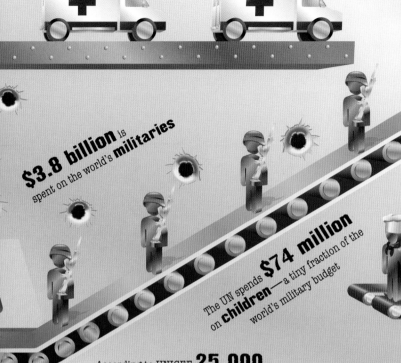

The UN spends **$74 million** on **children**—a tiny fraction of the world's military budget

There are **31,000 McDonald's** restaurants, employing **1.5 million** people, a population that's bigger than **51 countries** of the world

Chefs in the **White House** are able to serve **140** guests in one sitting

According to UNICEF, **25,000 children** die each day due to **poverty**

The average **Londoner** is caught on CCTV cameras **300 times**—the city has around **7,500 cameras**

Governments spend about **$6.8 billion** on **education**

There are **5 communist states** in the world—**China, Cuba, Laos, Vietnam, and North Korea**

Only **2 flags** show **guns**: Guatemala's flag shows rifles, but Mozambique's flag is the only one to show a modern weapon—an **AK–47**

There is only **1** nonrectangular **flag** in the world—**Nepal's** consists of two triangles

Industry

The products of industry are all around us—from the goods that we buy to the services we rely on. Taking Earth's resources and turning them into manufactured products allows countries to make money. But the way in which we're using Earth's resources is having an effect on the planet's health. Our consumer society uses a huge amount of energy, and with fossil fuels running out in the near future, we'll need to turn to different energy sources to power our way of life.

World Market

The buying and selling of products and services between countries is called international trade. Things bought from other countries are called imports, and those sold are called exports. Trading between countries enables them to sell what they produce and buy the things that they need but cannot make themselves.

Top imports

Below are the top 10 imports in 2008. Industrial produce makes up the majority of the list, with coal and oil at the top, but farm produce also features prominently. The prices for these rise and fall according to supply and demand: prices rise when demand rises or when supply falls.

COAL:
3.1 BILLION
TONNES

CRUDE OIL:
2.2 BILLION
TONNES

SALT:
163 MILLION
TONNES

ELECTRICAL ENERGY:
482 MILLION
MEGAWATT HOURS

WHEAT:
157 MILLION
TONNES

IRON ORES:
814 MILLION
TONNES

CEMENT:
264 MILLION
TONNES

CORN:
243 MILLION
TONNES

IRON PRODUCTS:
153 MILLION
TONNES

SOYBEANS:
72 MILLION
TONNES

Balancing the scales

One of the most important figures in a country's finances is its balance of trade, which is the difference between the value of its exports and the cost of its imports. The U.S.A. has a trade deficit as it pays more for imports than it earns from exports. Ideally, a country will aim to have a trade surplus like China, which sells more than it buys, meaning that the country is not overly dependent on its trading partners.

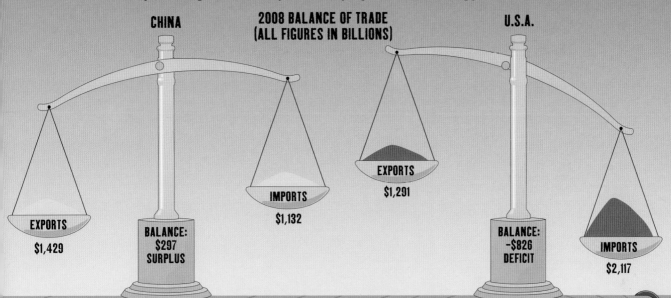

CHINA

2008 BALANCE OF TRADE (ALL FIGURES IN BILLIONS)

U.S.A.

EXPORTS $1,429

IMPORTS $1,132

BALANCE: $297 SURPLUS

EXPORTS $1,291

BALANCE: −$826 DEFICIT

IMPORTS $2,117

Raw materials and finished goods

NIGERIA EXPORTS 30 BILLION GALLONS (115 BILLION LITERS) OF CRUDE OIL PER YEAR

Many countries in the developing world do not have the facilities to turn their raw materials into finished goods. Nigeria produces a large amount of oil, but cannot turn it into the gasoline that it needs. Its total gasoline imports are made using 5.8 billion gallons (22 billion liters) of oil—almost a fifth of what it exports.

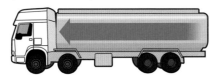

NIGERIA IMPORTS 2.9 BILLION GALLONS (11 BILLION LITERS) OF GASOLINE PER YEAR

Trading fair

Fair Trade is a global movement with the aim of ensuring higher payments for food producers in developing nations, by ensuring that they get a decent minimum price for their produce, as well as money to invest in improving their communities. Bananas, coffee, and cocoa are all popular Fair Trade products.

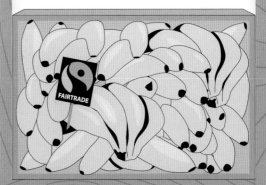

FAIRTRADE

Tariffs

Customers like to pay as little as possible, but cheap imported goods can stifle home businesses. In some cases, special taxes called tariffs are placed on foreign products. In the example here, despite starting off cheaper, the 50% tariff makes the foreign shoes more expensive. This raises money for the government but also protects the country's own industry. On the downside, it gives the consumer less choice.

HOME SHOES: BASE PRICE $31	NO TARIFF ADDED	FINAL PRICE: $31
FOREIGN SHOES: BASE PRICE $28	50% TARIFF ADDED +$14	FINAL PRICE: $42

Japanomics

Japan is one of the world's leading economies, with a high standard of living and high life expectancy for its people. The word "economy" refers to a country's wealth and resources and all the goods and services that it produces and consumes. Japan has few natural resources, so it relies on exports to pay for the raw materials, food, and fuel that it must import.

Using land

Japan is a chain of hundreds of mountainous volcanic islands. About 68% of its rugged landscape is blanketed with forests. Cities are located on the earthquake-prone coastal plains.

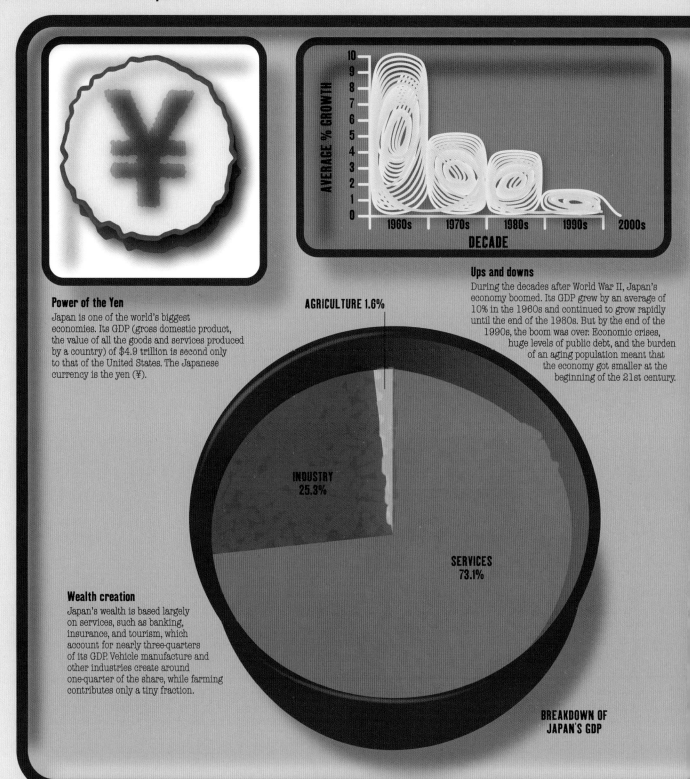

AVERAGE % GROWTH

10
9
8
7
6
5
4
3
2
1
0

1960s   1970s   1980s   1990s   2000s

DECADE

Power of the Yen

Japan is one of the world's biggest economies. Its GDP (gross domestic product, the value of all the goods and services produced by a country) of $4.9 trillion is second only to that of the United States. The Japanese currency is the yen (¥).

Ups and downs

During the decades after World War II, Japan's economy boomed. Its GDP grew by an average of 10% in the 1960s and continued to grow rapidly until the end of the 1980s. But by the end of the 1990s, the boom was over. Economic crises, huge levels of public debt, and the burden of an aging population meant that the economy got smaller at the beginning of the 21st century.

AGRICULTURE 1.6%

INDUSTRY
25.3%

SERVICES
73.1%

Wealth creation

Japan's wealth is based largely on services, such as banking, insurance, and tourism, which account for nearly three-quarters of its GDP. Vehicle manufacture and other industries create around one-quarter of the share, while farming contributes only a tiny fraction.

BREAKDOWN OF
JAPAN'S GDP

Filling the rice bowl

Only 12% of Japan's land is suitable for growing crops. Rice is the chief food crop, but wheat, corn, sugar beet, and tea are also grown. Very large amounts of food need to be imported in order to meet the country's needs.

11,563,629

cars were manufactured in Japan in 2008

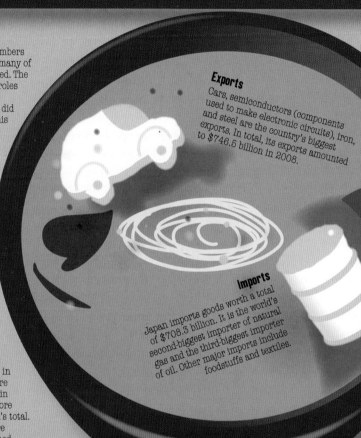

People at work

Japan's workforce numbers around 66.5 million, many of whom are highly skilled. The country's set gender roles have meant that until recently most women did not go out to work. This is now changing— 40% of workers are female—but the number of women in senior positions remains low.

Exports

Cars, semiconductors (components used to make electronic circuits), iron, and steel are the country's biggest exports. In total, its exports amounted to $746.5 billion in 2008.

Imports

Japan imports goods worth a total of $708.3 billion. It is the world's second-biggest importer of natural gas and the third-biggest importer of oil. Other major imports include foodstuffs and textiles.

Ro-bot-ics!

Japan leads the world in robotics. In 2005, there were 370,000 robots in Japan's factories—more than 40% of the world's total. That means there were roughly 30 programmed automatic helpers for every 1,000 Japanese human factory workers.

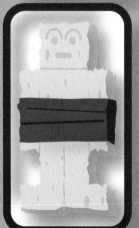

Cost of consumption

Like other developed nations, Japan has a heavy ecological footprint. The amount of carbon dioxide emitted per person in 2007 was 9.7 tonnes, placing Japan 35th in the world. But the country is one of the largest consumers of fish and tropical timber. Its economic activity leads to the depletion of these resources in other parts of the world.

Fishing fleets

The Japanese eat more fish than any other nation. They are the biggest importers of fish, and their own fleet takes almost 15% of the global catch. However, the size of their catch has fallen in recent years, due to restrictions brought in to prevent overfishing.

Oil

Without oil, much of the world's transportation would come to a standstill. North America has a huge number of vehicles and used eight times the amount of oil that Africa used in 2008.

Coal

The most common use for coal is to generate electricity—as much as 93% of the U.S.A.'s coal is used in this way. Burning coal is one of the most polluting ways to generate electricity.

Gas

Many homes need gas for cooking and heating, and it is also used widely to power industry. The Middle East has the largest gas reserves but uses less than one-third of what Europe uses.

Renewables

Renewable energy sources still represent only a small fraction of the world's total energy production. Denmark is leading the way, with wind power generating 20% of its electricity.

Nuclear

Nuclear power plants use uranium to generate electricity. Nuclear power is cleaner than fossil fuels, but concerns over dealing with radioactive waste have led to a reduction in nuclear power.

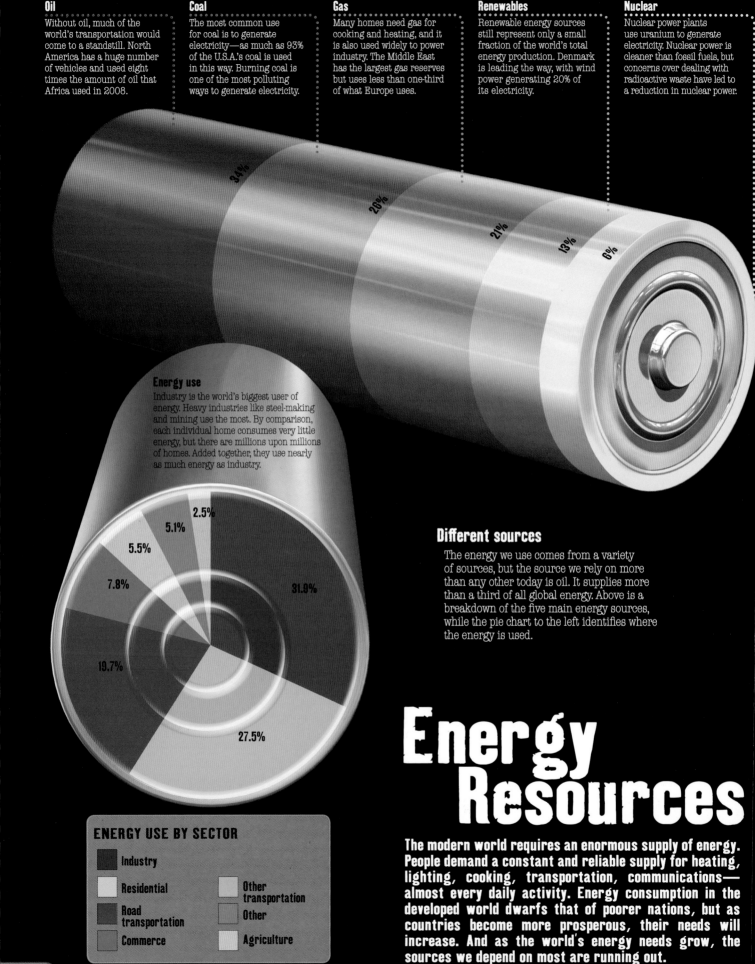

34%
26%
21%
13%
6%

Energy use

Industry is the world's biggest user of energy. Heavy industries like steel-making and mining use the most. By comparison, each individual home consumes very little energy, but there are millions upon millions of homes. Added together, they use nearly as much energy as industry.

2.5%
5.1%
5.5%
7.8%
31.9%
19.7%
27.5%

Different sources

The energy we use comes from a variety of sources, but the source we rely on more than any other today is oil. It supplies more than a third of all global energy. Above is a breakdown of the five main energy sources, while the pie chart to the left identifies where the energy is used.

Energy Resources

The modern world requires an enormous supply of energy. People demand a constant and reliable supply for heating, lighting, cooking, transportation, communications— almost every daily activity. Energy consumption in the developed world dwarfs that of poorer nations, but as countries become more prosperous, their needs will increase. And as the world's energy needs grow, the sources we depend on most are running out.

ENERGY USE BY SECTOR

- Industry
- Residential
- Road transportation
- Commerce
- Other transportation
- Other
- Agriculture

AFRICA 0.77

WORLD AVERAGE 1.82

GERMANY 4.03

U.S.A. 7.75

PER CAPITA ENERGY CONSUMPTION
(tonnes oil equivalent)

UNITED ARAB EMIRATES 11.83

World energy usage

If all the energy used in the world was divided up between everyone equally, each person would use as much energy in a year as there is in 1.8 tonnes of oil. However, consumption is very uneven around the world. People in developed countries use a lot more than this.

Increase in energy consumption

As economies grow and people become wealthier, more cars and electrical equipment are bought. Manufacturing expands to meet the rising demand, and, as a result, energy consumption increases. In 2010, the world consumed 508 quadrillion BTU (British thermal units) of energy. By 2030, this is set to increase by around a third.

2010

(QUADRILLION BTU)

2030

(QUADRILLION BTU)

How long will supplies last?

Most of the energy sources we depend on now will run out one day. Oil is expected to be the first to go, probably in around 40 years. Renewable energy, such as solar and wind energy, is the only source that will not run out.

COAL 120 YEARS

URANIUM 80 YEARS

NATURAL GAS 60 YEARS

OIL 40 YEARS

Fuel wood

Around 2.4 billion people—just over one-third of the world's population—depend on wood for heating and cooking. In most of the world, the use of fuelwood is in decline, but it is increasingly used in Africa.

The world's nuclear power plants use **65,000 tonnes** of uranium every year.

Fossil Fuels

Fossil fuels are substances that formed from dead plants or animals as a result of natural processes. Coal, oil, and natural gas are fossil fuels and are burned to release energy. This energy—in the form of heat—is used for warmth, light, powering machines, and making electricity. When fossil fuels burn, they emit gases that contribute to global warming.

In one year, a coal-fired power plant supplying

140,000 homes
with electricity burns

1.5 million tonnes of coal

How gas and oil are formed

Most of the oil and gas that we use today formed from trillions of microscopic plants and animals. These tiny organisms lived in the sea hundreds of millions of years ago, before the age of the dinosaurs.

1. Buried remains
When the tiny organisms died, their bodies sank to the seabed. Their remains were then covered by sand and fine silt. Over millions of years, they were buried deeper and deeper below the seabed as more sand and silt piled up above them.

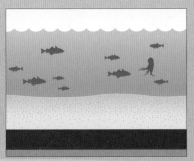

2. Heat and pressure
The deep layers of sediments that built up on the seabed slowly changed to rock. Below them, heat and pressure changed the organic remains into oil and gas. If the oil and gas could not escape through the rock above them, they became trapped.

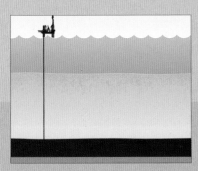

3. Fields of fuel
The oil and gas are still trapped underground today, forming the oilfields and gasfields that fuel our energy-hungry way of life. These valuable fuels are reached by drilling down through the rock until the oil and gas rush up through the hollow drill pipe.

Oil reserves
The amount of oil still under the ground is estimated to be 1,342.2 billion barrels (213 trillion liters). A barrel of oil contains 42 gallons (159 liters). Saudi Arabia has the biggest share.

Gas reserves
Gas reserves amount to 6,254 trillion ft³ (177 trillion m³). Nearly half of this is located in the Middle East and more than one quarter is beneath Russia's territory.

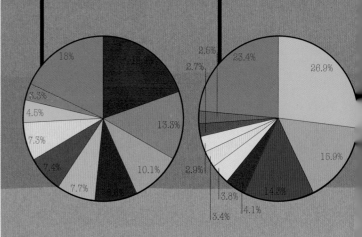

COUNTRIES

Africa	Canada	India
Algeria	China	Iran
Australia and New Zealand	Other Europe and Eurasia	Iraq

156

Coal consumption

The Asia Pacific region, and China in particular, is by far the world's biggest coal user. China burns more than twice as much coal as the U.S.A. and more than four times as much as all 27 countries of the European Union combined.

61.5%	18.4%	15.8%	3.3%	0.7%	0.3%
Asia Pacific	North America	Europe	Africa	Central and South America	Middle East

PROPORTION OF WORLD COAL CONSUMPTION

Coal reserves

The worldwide coal reserves amount to 843 billion tonnes. The U.S.A. holds the largest share, at just over one quarter. The types and quality of the coal vary from place to place.

4.1%
5.9%
6.7%
9.2%
13.7%
13.6%
18.6%
28.3%

Kuwait

Libya

Nigeria

Qatar

Russia

Saudi Arabia

United Arab Emirates

U.S.A.

Venezuela

Rest of the world

How coal is formed

Coal was created in a similar way to gas and oil, forming on land from plants and trees that lived hundreds of millions of years ago in huge, swampy forests.

1. Decaying plants

Giant ferns, primitive trees, mosses, and many other strange plants covered most of the land with a thick green carpet. When these plants died, they fell to the forest floor and formed layers of decaying vegetation that were soon covered with soil.

2. Squash and squeeze

The heavy soil on top of the plants squashed them, squeezing out the moisture and slowly changing them into coal. As the levels of land and sea changed over millions of years, some of the land with coal forming beneath it disappeared underwater.

3. Harder and blacker

A soft brown coal called lignite is formed first. After more time, the coal becomes harder and blacker, finally forming coal called anthracite. To reach the coal today, the land lying above it is stripped away, or shafts are dug down to mine it.

Renewable Energy

Renewable energy is produced from natural sources that will never run out. These sources include the Sun, wind, water, plants, animal waste, and the heat found below the Earth's surface. Renewable sources currently generate 13% of energy used globally, for heating, electricity, and powering industry. With fossil fuels running out, renewable power will be even more important in the future.

Power for the people

Much of the energy generated by renewables is used to produce electricity. Today, renewables contribute 18% to the amount of electricity produced worldwide. This chart shows how much of the total electricity from renewables is contributed by each source and how much each is projected to contribute by the year 2030.

Biomass

Anything derived from recently living plants and animals and used as a fuel is known as biomass. Wood, plants, and chicken manure are used in developing countries to fuel cooking and heating in the home, while some crops, such as sugarcane, are fermented to make ethanol, a type of alcohol that can be used as a fuel.

FUELS MADE FROM BIOMASS ARE CALLED BIOFUELS

ONE WIND TURBINE CAN PRODUCE ENOUGH ELECTRICITY TO POWER UP TO 300 HOMES

CALIFORNIA HAS 34 GEOTHERMAL POWER PLANTS

Covering **4%** of deserts with solar panels would meet all the world's electricity needs

Wind power

Windmills have been used as a source of energy since ancient times. Modern wind turbines use the wind's power to generate electricity. The movement of the blades drives a generator on top of the tower. More than 70 countries use wind power, and it is the fastest-growing renewable energy source.

Geothermal energy

Earth's natural store of heat, which radiates upward from its core, can be harnessed to produce electricity. Water is piped from a geothermal energy plant to deep underground, where it heats up. The water then becomes steam that rises up a pipe to turn a generator, which converts the movement into electricity.

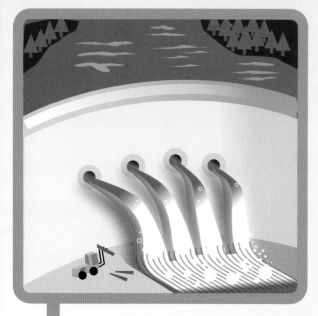

Hydroelectric power

Hydroelectric power uses the power of water that flows downhill to turn an electricity generator. It supplies around 15% of the world's electricity needs. The top five producers of hydropower are China, Canada, Brazil, the U.S.A., and Russia.

WATER PROVIDES ELECTRIC POWER FOR 28.3 MILLION PEOPLE

BIOFUELS PROVIDE AROUND 4% OF THE ENERGY USED IN THE U.S.A.

A WIND TURBINE CAN WORK WITH AN AVERAGE WIND SPEED OF JUST 13.7 MPH (22 KM/H)

THE ANCIENT ROMANS WERE THE FIRST PEOPLE TO HEAT HOUSES WITH GEOTHERMAL ENERGY

ENOUGH SUNLIGHT FALLS ON EARTH IN ONE HOUR TO SUPPLY THE WORLD WITH ENERGY FOR ONE YEAR

% CONTRIBUTION TO TOTAL ELECTRICITY FROM RENEWABLES

2002 2030 2002 2030 2002 2030 2002 2030 2002 2030 2002 2030

Electric future

By far the biggest contributor to renewably-sourced electricity is hydroelectricity. Solar and tidal power each contribute less than 1%. By 2030, improved technologies, such as solar panels and wind turbines, should allow solar and wind power to increase their share. This is reflected in the graph by the drop in hydroelectricity's share, as the other renewable energies grow in use.

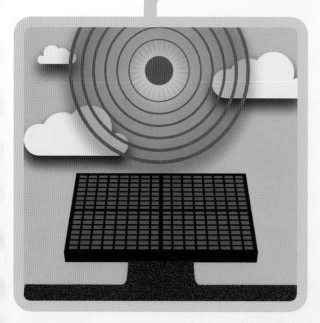

Solar radiation

Solar energy is captured in two main ways. Photovoltaic cells (solar panels) convert sunlight directly into electricity, while solar collectors use solar energy to heat air or water, which can then be transferred to where the heat is needed. Solar water heaters are used by around 50 million people worldwide, most of them in China.

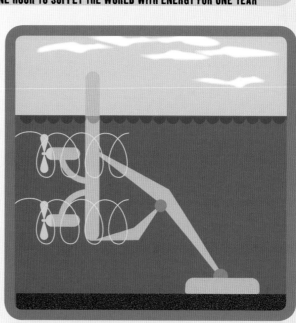

Tidal and wave power

The energy in tides and waves can both be converted into electricity, but currently this is the least developed form of renewable energy. Several large, commercial tidal power plants are being developed, but only two are in operation – one in France and the other in Canada. The world's first wave power plant opened in Portugal in 2008.

Nuclear Energy

Nuclear energy is the energy that is stored inside the nucleus (central part) of an atom. Nuclear power plants release this energy by a process called nuclear fission and use it to make electricity. Nuclear power is a cleaner way of generating electricity than burning fossil fuels, but it produces radioactive waste that remains hazardous for many years and cannot be allowed to escape into the environment.

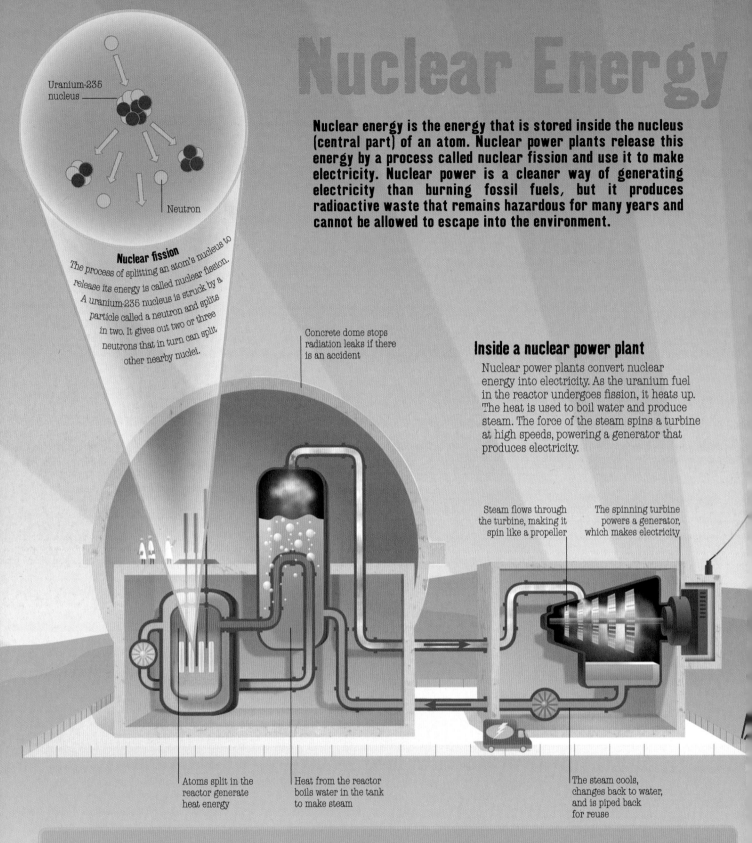

Uranium-235 nucleus

Neutron

Nuclear fission

The process of splitting an atom's nucleus to release its energy is called nuclear fission. A uranium-235 nucleus is struck by a particle called a neutron and splits in two. It gives out two or three neutrons that in turn can split other nearby nuclei.

Concrete dome stops radiation leaks if there is an accident

Inside a nuclear power plant

Nuclear power plants convert nuclear energy into electricity. As the uranium fuel in the reactor undergoes fission, it heats up. The heat is used to boil water and produce steam. The force of the steam spins a turbine at high speeds, powering a generator that produces electricity.

Steam flows through the turbine, making it spin like a propeller

The spinning turbine powers a generator, which makes electricity

Atoms split in the reactor generate heat energy

Heat from the reactor boils water in the tank to make steam

The steam cools, changes back to water, and is piped back for reuse

Energy equivalents

A pellet of uranium is the size of your fingertip and weighs only 0.2 oz (7 g). But it can generate the same amount of energy as much larger quantities of fossil fuels.

1 URANIUM PELLET (shown actual size) = **3.5 BARRELS OF OIL** (147 gallons/ 556 liters) = **1,780 LBS COAL** (807 kg) = **17,000 FT³ NATURAL GAS** (481 m³)

350,000 ft³ (10,000 m³) 7.4 million ft³ (210,000 m³)

Hazardous waste

The world's nuclear power facilities produce 7.4 million ft³ (210,000 m³) of radioactive waste every year. Most of the waste is intermediate or low-level – only slightly radioactive. Less than 5% is classified as high-level waste. It must be carefully processed so as not to cause harm to people or the environment.

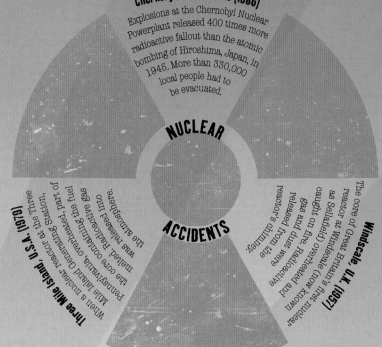

NUCLEAR ACCIDENTS

Chernobyl, the Ukraine (1986)
Explosions at the Chernobyl Nuclear Powerplant released 400 times more radioactive fallout than the atomic bombing of Hiroshima, Japan, in 1945. More than 330,000 local people had to be evacuated.

Three Mile Island, U.S.A. (1979)
When a nuclear reactor at the Three Mile Island Generating Station, in Pennsylvania, overheated, part of the core containing the fuel melted. Radioactive gas was released into the atmosphere.

Windscale, U.K. (1957)
The core of Great Britain's first nuclear reactor at Windscale (now known as Sellafield) overheated and caught on fire. Radioactive gas and dust were released from the reactor's chimney.

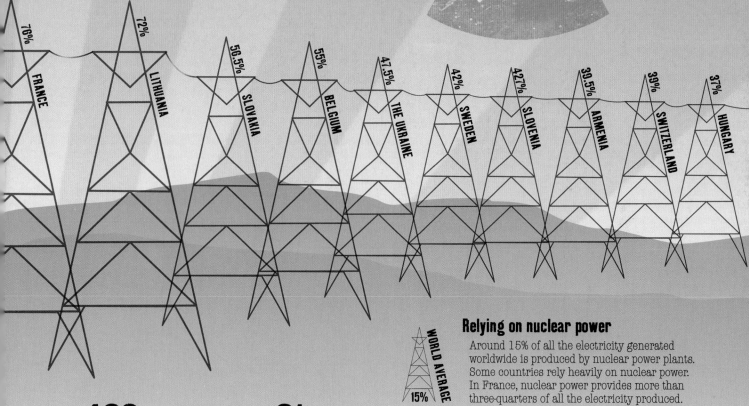

76% FRANCE
72% LITHUANIA
56.5% SLOVAKIA
55% BELGIUM
47.5% THE UKRAINE
42% SWEDEN
42% SLOVENIA
39.5% ARMENIA
39% SWITZERLAND
37% HUNGARY

WORLD AVERAGE 15%

Relying on nuclear power

Around 15% of all the electricity generated worldwide is produced by nuclear power plants. Some countries rely heavily on nuclear power. In France, nuclear power provides more than three-quarters of all the electricity produced.

There are **439** nuclear power plants in **31** countries

Clean and green

Nuclear power plants emit almost no greenhouse gases, though they do generate some preparing and transporting fuel. Their main environmental impact is the hazardous waste they produce.

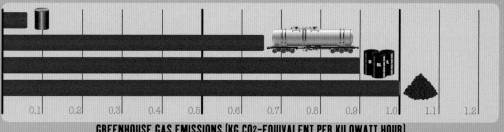

0.1 0.2 0.3 0.4 0.5 0.6 0.7 0.8 0.9 1.0 1.1 1.2

GREENHOUSE GAS EMISSIONS (KG CO²-EQUIVALENT PER KILOWATT HOUR)

START

ENERGY

industry is the name for any business activity that processes raw materials, manufactures products, or provides a service. All the businesses dealing with the same type of raw material or product belong to the same industry. industries are interlinked. They supply products and services to each other, as well as to the public.

Industry

Steel and oil

In order for drivers to fill up their tanks at a gas station, a whole range of industries have played their part—from the ships that carried the crude oil across the world, to the mines where the raw materials to build the ships were extracted.

Iron ore mine

Iron ore is iron-rich rock found in Earth's crust. Like most industries, the mining business that extracts it from the ground requires large amounts of energy.

Making steel

Iron is used to make steel, a very strong, hard alloy (substance made by mixing a metal with another metal or nonmetal).

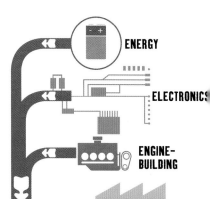

ENERGY

ELECTRONICS

ENGINE-BUILDING

Steel supply

Many different industries use steel, including car manufacturing, construction, and shipbuilding industries.

CAR MANUFACTURING

CONSTRUCTION

Shipbuilding

Shipbuilders use thousands of tonnes of steel, as well as products from the electronics, plastics, and marine engineering industries to make ships.

Oil refineries produce **2 pints** (1 liter) of gasoline from **4 pints** (2 liters) of crude oil

Shipping oil

An oil tanker made by the shipbuilding industry transports oil from the country where it is extracted to a refinery in another part of the world.

PORT

Refining oil

At the refinery, the oil is processed to make a variety of chemicals and fuel, including gasoline.

REFINERY

Satellite

Oil tankers and other ships are guided across the oceans by products of the space and electronics industries— navigation satellites.

SATELLITE

TRUCK-BUILDING INDUSTRY

GASOLINE DEPOT

Gas station

Drivers visit gas stations and pay to fill up their cars with fuel.

Gasoline supply

Gasoline is trucked from the oil refinery to a depot, where tanker trucks fill up and haul it by road to gas stations.

GAS STATION

START

ENERGY WATER CHEMICALS MACHINERY

The meat business
The food that we buy starts off on farms, but many other industries contribute to getting it into the stores. Some of the food that we buy comes from nearby farms, but much of it may have traveled long distances from other countries, using energy, materials and other inputs from many industries.

Growing grain
Wheat is grown by farmers. Most is used to make bread, but some is processed into animal feed.

Farming inputs
Farming uses large amounts of energy and water. Many farmers use chemical sprays to protect crops from pests and diseases.

Cattle food
On another farm, cattle are reared. The cows mainly eat grass, but their diet is supplemented by wheat-based feed.

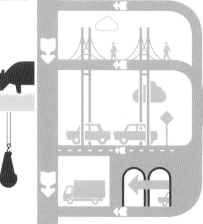

ROAD, BRIDGE, TUNNEL CONSTRUCTION

On the road
The construction industries that build and maintain the transportation infrastructure allow goods from all industries to be transported by road from one place to another.

Cattle slaughtered
At 1–2 years old, the cattle are taken to a nearby slaughterhouse, usually by road.

Chilled to **−13°F** (-25°C), refrigerated shipping containers can keep meat frozen solid

Road transportation
The meat is transported from the slaughterhouse to a port by refrigerated truck.

Shipping meat
The meat can be transported across the world and arrive fresh, thanks to refrigerated containers. Like oil tankers, containerships are guided by satellite.

At the wholesaler
A wholesaler is a business that buys large quantities of meat and sells it on in smaller quantities to stores and food processors.

PORT

SATELLITE

Store
Shoppers can buy the meat of their choice in their local supermarket.

SUPERMARKET

Food processors
Some of the meat goes to factories to be turned into processed food, such as burgers and sausages. The rest goes directly to the retailer as cuts of meat.

Land Use

Land covers 57.5 million sq. miles (149 million sq. km) of Earth. This may sound like a lot, but in reality it is less than one-third of the world's surface area, and it must support the housing, commercial, industrial, transportation, farming, and other needs of 6.8 billion people. As the human population is growing, the need for land is increasing. By 2050, there will be 9 billion people on Earth. As there is no more land, it will be increasingly important to make the best use of the resources that we have through careful planning.

Agriculture

The area of agricultural land is nearly 60 times bigger than the area used by cities and suburbs. However, the expansion of towns and industry in growing economies such as Brazil and India is often at the expense of agricultural croplands.

Residential

Places where many people live are called residential areas. More than 50% of the world's population are now tightly packed into apartments and houses in towns and cities, which sprawl out across more and more land. Many countries now have laws to protect the countryside from being built on.

More than **35%** of the world's ice-free land area has been cleared or converted for agriculture

Industry

Even in highly industrialized countries, things like factories and power plants take up very little land. In Japan, for example, one of the world's biggest manufacturers and exporters, only 0.4% of the land area is used by industry.

There are **392** cars per mile (245 cars per km) on Hong Kong's crowded road network

Infrastructure
The network of roads, bridges, railroad lines, communication, electric power, and other services are collectively called infrastructure. They make life easier on a day-to-day basis.

The U.S.A. has paved more than
61,000 sq. miles
(160,000 sq. km) of land for roads and parking lots

Unused land
Wilderness describes places that are mainly unchanged by human activities. Surprisingly, despite the billions of people on Earth and their cities, roads, and farms, nearly 50% of the world's land area is still wild.

Institutions
As well as housing, roads, stores, and businesses, communities need public buildings such as libraries and sports facilities. Hospitals and schools are also extremely important. Town planners must include these public buildings and institutions in plans for new communities.

95% of the people on Earth are concentrated on just **10%** of the land

55% of Bangladesh's land is suitable for growing crops, more than anywhere else on Earth

Reaching for the Sky

For most of the 20th century, the world's tallest buildings were American. Since 1998, the height charts have been topped by buildings in Malaysia, Taiwan, and, most recently, Dubai. As engineers defy the vertical challenge again and again with new and more innovative ways to build higher and higher, there seems to be no limit to a building's height.

Highest tower

The CN Tower in Toronto, Canada, stands 1,815 ft (553.3 m) tall. It was built as a communications tower with public areas, including a restaurant and observation gallery, near the top. It would be the world's second-tallest building but because it does not have floors all the way up from the ground it is categorized as a tower, not a building.

East versus west

At 1,713 ft (522 m) high, the East Tower to the already standing West Tower is due to dwarf its neighbor after completion in 2015.

Empire State Building

Constructed in 1931 and rising 1,250 ft (381 m) tall, the Empire State Building in New York City was the world's tallest building for more than 40 years. Today, it is the 13th-tallest building in the world.

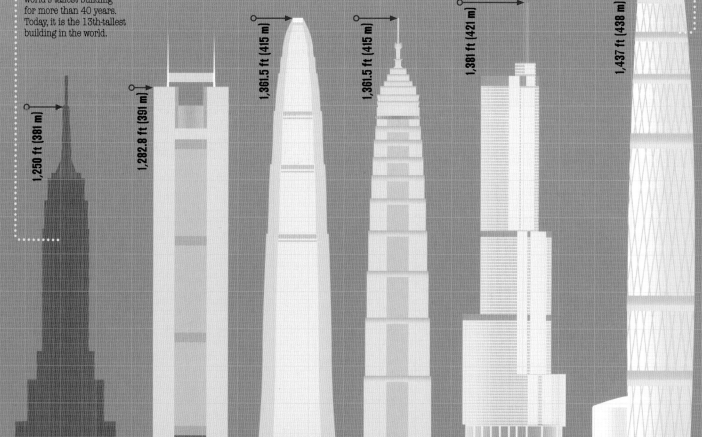

1,250 ft (381 m)

1,282.8 ft (391 m)

1,361.5 ft (415 m)

1,361.5 ft (415 m)

1,381 ft (421 m)

1,437 ft (438 m)

EMPIRE STATE BUILDING
New York City, U.S.A.
Completed: 1931

CITIC PLAZA
Guangzhou, China
Completed: 1997

TRUMP INTERNATIONAL HOTEL AND TOWER
Chicago, U.S.A.
Completed: 2009

TWO INTERNATIONAL FINANCE CENTER
Hong Kong, China
Completed: 2003

JIN MAO TOWER
Shanghai, China
Completed: 1999

GUANGZHOU WEST TOWER
Guangzhou, China
Completed: 2010

MEASURING HEIGHT

Each building's height is measured from the sidewalk level of the building's main entrance to its structural top. This includes spires on top of the building, but it does not include antennae or flagpoles.

Green skyscrapers

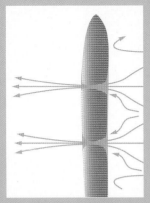

The 1,017-ft- (310-m-) high Pearl River Tower in Guangzhou, China, is the world's most environmentally friendly skyscraper. Wind turbines and solar panels built into its structure generate more than enough electricity to cover the entire building's energy needs.

Reaching new heights

A new building proposed for construction in Dubai, the Nakheel Tower could be the first skyscraper to be more than 0.62 miles (1 km) high. As the design has evolved, the height it could reach is estimated to be around 4,593 ft (1,400 m) – almost double that of the current record holder, Burj Khalifa.

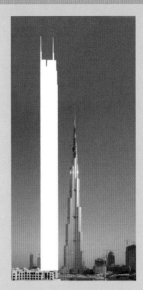

Petronas Towers

The Petronas Towers were the world's tallest buildings between 1998 and 2004. The two towers are linked 558 ft (170 m) above the ground by the world's highest two-story "skybridge."

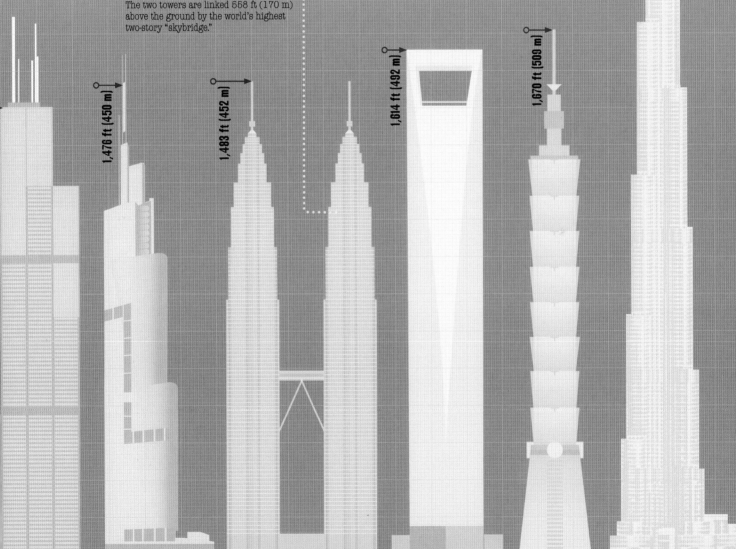

1,476 ft (450 m)

1,483 ft (452 m)

1,614 ft (492 m)

1,670 ft (509 m)

2,716.5 ft (828 m)

WILLIS TOWER
Chicago, U.S.A.
Completed: 1974

NANJING GREENLAND FINANCIAL CENTER
Nanjing, China
Completed: 2010

PETRONAS TOWERS
Kuala Lumpur, Malaysia
Completed: 1998

SHANGHAI WORLD FINANCIAL CENTER
Shanghai, China
Completed: 2008

TAIPEI 101
Taipei, Taiwan
Completed: 2004

BURJ KHALIFA
Dubai, United Arab Emirates
Completed: 2010

The **first skyscraper** was the 10-story Home Insurance Building, built in Chicago in 1885

forests

The world's forests are a precious resource that have evolved over millions of years, and we rely on trees for many things. They protect wildlife, land, and water. They bear many fruit, providing us with food, and their wood is used to build houses, as well as for the paper that this book is printed on. But forests are easily damaged: a wooded area the size of New Zealand is lost to fire each year, and human activity has led to many forests being damaged beyond repair.

Forest cover

The world's forests blanket 15.4 million sq. miles (40 million sq km) of Earth, which is almost a third of its total land area. Two-thirds of Earth's forests are located in just 10 countries, and 45 countries have more than 50% of their land area covered by these wooded environments.

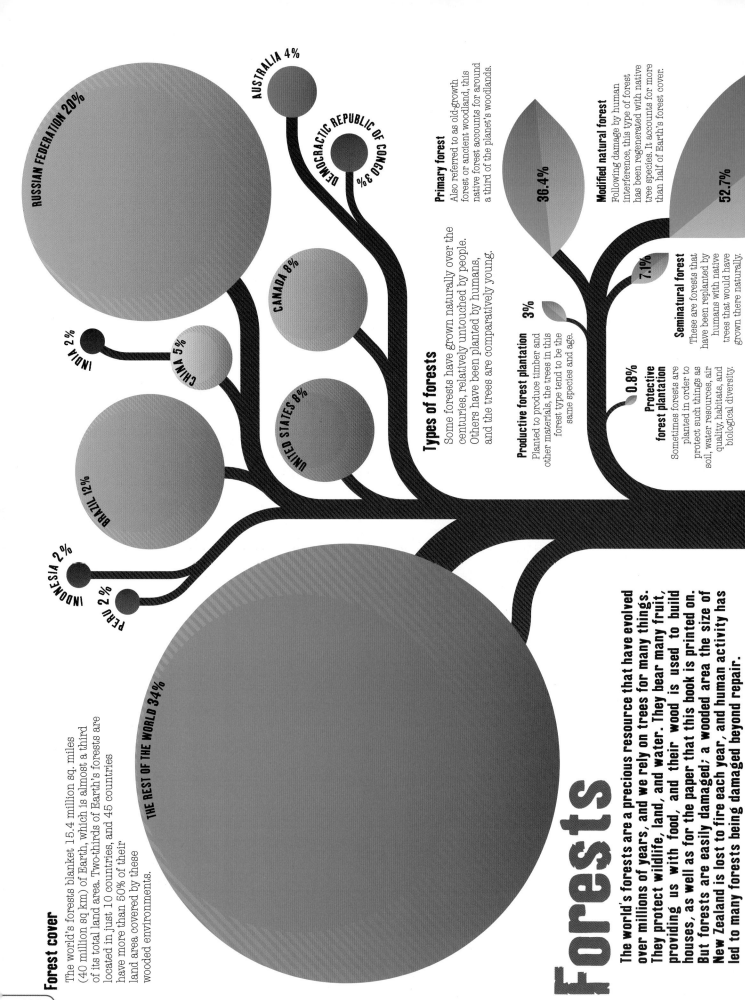

RUSSIAN FEDERATION 20%

AUSTRALIA 4%

DEMOCRACTIC REPUBLIC OF CONGO 3%

CANADA 8%

INDIA 2%

CHINA 5%

UNITED STATES 8%

BRAZIL 12%

INDONESIA 2%

PERU 2%

THE REST OF THE WORLD 34%

Types of forests

Some forests have grown naturally over the centuries, relatively untouched by people. Others have been planted by humans, and the trees are comparatively young.

Primary forest

Also referred to as old-growth forest or ancient woodland, this native forest accounts for around a third of the planet's woodlands.

36.4%

Modified natural forest

Following damage by human interference, this type of forest has been regenerated with native tree species. It accounts for more than half of Earth's forest cover.

52.7%

Productive forest plantation

Planted to produce timber and other materials, the trees in this forest type tend to be the same species and age.

3%

Protective forest plantation

Sometimes forests are planted in order to protect such things as soil, water resources, air quality, habitats, and biological diversity.

0.8%

7.1%

Seminatural forest

These are forests that have been replanted by humans with native trees that would have grown there naturally.

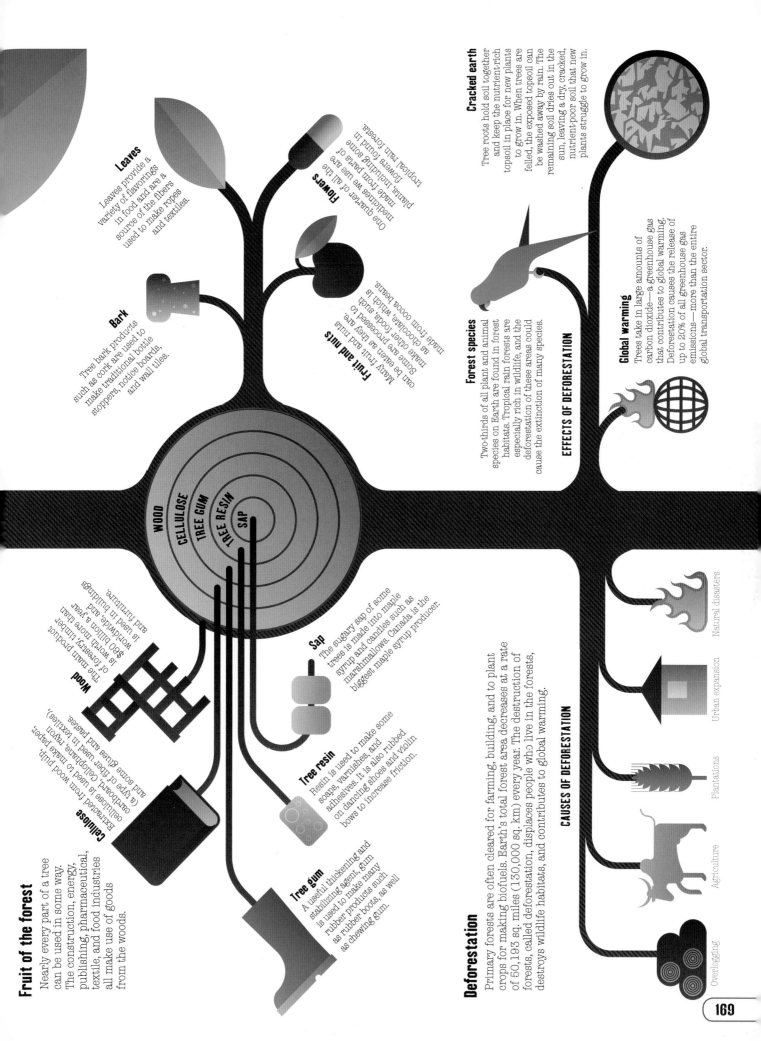

Fruit of the forest

Nearly every part of a tree can be used in some way. The construction, energy, publishing, pharmaceutical, textile, and food industries all make use of goods from the woods.

Leaves

Leaves provide a variety of flavorings in food and are a source of the fibers used to make ropes and textiles.

Flowers

One quarter of all the medicines we use are made from parts of plants, including some flowers found in tropical rain forests.

Bark

Tree bark products such as cork are used to make traditional bottle stoppers, notice boards, and wall tiles.

Fruit and nuts

Many fruit and nuts can be eaten as they are. Some are processed to make other foods, such as chocolate, which is made from cocoa beans.

WOOD
CELLULOSE
TREE GUM
TREE RESIN
SAP

Wood

The main product of forestry, timber is worth more than $60 billion a year worldwide, and is used in buildings and furniture.

Cellulose

Extracted from wood pulp, cellulose is used to make paper, cardboard, cellophane, rayon (a type of fiber used in textiles), and some glues and pastes.

Sap

The sugary sap of some trees is made into maple syrup and candies such as marshmallows. Canada is the biggest maple syrup producer.

Tree resin

Resin is used to make some soaps, varnishes, and adhesives. It is also rubbed on dancing shoes and violin bows to increase friction.

Tree gum

A useful thickening and stabilizing agent, gum is used to make many rubber products such as rubber boots, as well as chewing gum.

Deforestation

Primary forests are often cleared for farming, building, and to plant crops for making biofuels. Earth's total forest area decreases at a rate of 50,193 sq. miles (130,000 sq. km) every year. The destruction of forests, called deforestation, displaces people who live in the forests, destroys wildlife habitats, and contributes to global warming.

CAUSES OF DEFORESTATION

Overlogging

Agriculture

Plantations

Urban expansion

Natural disasters

Cracked earth

Tree roots hold soil together and keep the nutrient-rich topsoil in place for new plants to grow in. When trees are felled, the exposed topsoil can be washed away by rain. The remaining soil dries out in the sun, leaving a dry, cracked, nutrient-poor soil that new plants struggle to grow in.

EFFECTS OF DEFORESTATION

Forest species

Two-thirds of all plant and animal species on Earth are found in forest habitats. Tropical rain forests are especially rich in wildlife, and the deforestation of these areas could cause the extinction of many species.

Global warming

Trees take in large amounts of carbon dioxide—a greenhouse gas that contributes to global warming. Deforestation causes the release of up to 20% of all greenhouse gas emissions—more than the entire global transportation sector.

Farming

The world's farms have to produce enough food to sustain the global population of 6.8 billion people. Just three crops (wheat, rice, and corn) provide nearly two-thirds of human food. With the population rising, farming will have to produce even more in the future to feed everybody. However, global warming may make it even more difficult to increase farm production.

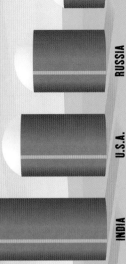

Top wheat producers

Wheat is an important food crop that is cultivated all over the world. It can be ground up into flour and used to make all types of foodstuffs, including bread and pasta. China is the world's leading wheat producer, producing more than the U.S.A. and Russia combined.

WHEAT PRODUCED PER YEAR (MILLIONS OF TONNES)

CHINA 109.3

INDIA 75.8

U.S.A. 55.8

RUSSIA 49.4

FRANCE 32.8

Key crops

The most important food crops are wheat, rice, and coarse grains such as barley, oats, and corn. Oilseed crops include palm, soybean, and sunflower and are grown to provide oils for cooking, industry, and making fuel, while cotton is grown to make into textiles.

COTTON 120.5

OILSEEDS 391.6

MILLED RICE 435.4

WHEAT 610.7

COARSE GRAINS 1,076.6

AMOUNT PRODUCED PER YEAR (MILLIONS OF TONNES)

More than **1.3 billion** people work in farming worldwide

Farmland

Only 11% of Earth's land is suitable for growing crops. Even the areas that can be farmed are not equally productive. Farmers in the developing world may not have access to technology or techniques that would allow them to get the higher yields out of the land.

CHEMICAL PROBLEMS 23%

CLIMATE TOO WET 10%

PERMAFROST 6%

SUITABLE FOR AGRICULTURE 11%

CLIMATE TOO DRY 28%

SOIL TOO SHALLOW 22%

Top rice producers

Rice is the staple food for roughly half of the world's population. Milled (white) rice is the most common form eaten by people. China and India provide more than three-quarters of all the rice grown in the world.

RICE PRODUCED PER YEAR (MILLIONS OF TONNES)

CHINA — 187.4
INDIA — 144.6
INDONESIA — 57.1
BANGLADESH — 43
VIETNAM — 35.9

Organic farming

More than 115,830 sq. miles (300,000 sq. km) of land worldwide is managed organically. This is an area of land similar in size to the state of New Mexico. Organic farmers use natural methods and materials to grow crops and raise livestock.

AFRICA — 3,475 sq. miles (9,000 sq. km)
ASIA — 11,197 sq. miles (29,000 sq. km)
EUROPE — 50,116 sq. miles (78,000 sq. km)
LATIN AMERICA — 24,711 sq. miles (64,000 sq. km)
NORTH AMERICA — 8,494 sq. miles (22,000 sq. km)
OCEANIA — 46,718 sq. miles (121,000 sq. km)

AREA USED FOR ORGANIC FARMING

Livestock accounts for **18%** of all greenhouse gas emissions— more than all types of transportation combined

Poultry populations

The global poultry population numbers in the billions. The majority of birds are farmed using "intensive" methods, in which they are reared to be slaughtered as soon as possible.

DUCKS: 1 BILLION

CHICKENS: 15.8 BILLION

Poultry icons sized proportionally

Livestock populations

Hundreds of millions of animals are farmed for meat. Cows are the most numerous. Cattle ranching is the main cause of deforestation in the Amazon rain forest. The forest is cleared to make way for pasture to feed cattle. Around 75% of Brazil's greenhouse gas emissions are due to deforestation.

1.34 BILLION

1.03 BILLION

743 MILLION

941 MILLION

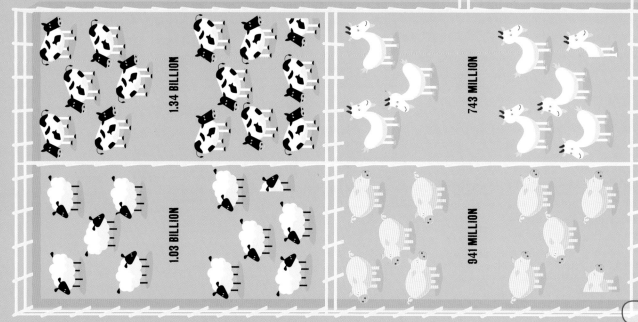

LIVESTOCK NUMBERS

= 100 million cows

= 100 million goats

= 100 million sheep

= 100 million pigs

Cocoa and Chocolate

Chocolate is the world's favorite treat—more than 7 million tonnes of it is consumed worldwide annually and global sales are worth more than $100 billion per year. Chocolate is made from cacao beans, which come from the cacao tree, an evergreen plant found only near the equator. The beans have a strong, bitter taste and must be fermented and roasted to bring out the chocolate flavor.

Cocoa crop

Cocoa is grown in more than 35 countries in a narrow belt around the equator. Nearly three-quarters of all cocoa is grown in Africa, most of it in West Africa, but only 10% of the beans go on to be processed there. Most are shipped to processors in Europe, Asia, and the Americas. The world's biggest cocoa handling port is Amsterdam in the Netherlands.

A cacao tree produces about **30** pods a year, and each pod holds up to **50** seeds

GROWING COCOA

THE AMERICAS 11%
ASIA 19%
AFRICA 70%

PROCESSING COCOA

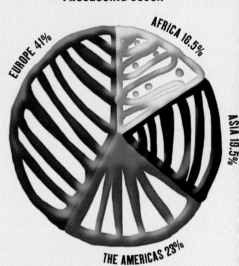

EUROPE 41%
AFRICA 16.5%
ASIA 19.5%
THE AMERICAS 23%

Cocoa consumption

The U.S.A. consumes more cocoa in total than any other country. However, at 11 lbs (5 kg) per head, their per capita consumption is only about half that of the Swiss, who eat a massive 22 lbs (10 kg) a year each. This is not just because the Swiss have a sweet tooth: Swiss chocolate tends to contain much more cocoa than American chocolate, about 60% cocoa solids compared to as little as 10% in the U.S.A.

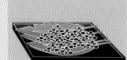

U.S.A. 634,000
The Netherlands 500,000
Germany 236,000
France 234,000
Brazil 212,000
U.K. 134,000
Italy 72,000
Spain 70,000
Canada 69,000
Belgium 68,000

THE WORLD'S TOP COCOA CONSUMERS
(total consumed in tonnes)

Chocolate quality

Cocoa powder is used in different amounts to make different grades of chocolate. Sweet milk chocolate contains about 20% cocoa solids (cocoa powder), while dark chocolate contains at least 60% cocoa solids. White chocolate is made from cocoa butter and contains no cocoa powder.

FROM CACAO BEAN TO CANDY BAR

1. Harvesting
Cocoa pods are harvested by hand. Workers cut the pods off using machetes or knives on long poles.

2. Deshelling
The cocoa pods are split open, and the beans are scooped out. The pod shells are thrown away.

3. Fermenting
For 2–8 days, the beans are left in wooden boxes to ferment, as the sugars in the pulp turn to acids.

4. Drying
The fermented beans are left to dry in the sun. In bad weather, hot-air blowers are used instead.

5. Shipping
When the beans are ready, they are shipped to a manufacturer to be made into chocolate.

6. Roasting
The beans are roasted to bring out the distinctive flavor and aroma of chocolate.

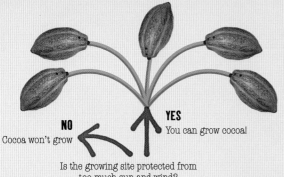

NO
Cocoa won't grow

YES
You can grow cocoa!

Is the growing site protected from too much sun and wind?

NO
Cocoa won't grow

YES

...but less than 10 ft (3 m) of rainfall each year?

NO
Cocoa won't grow

YES

Is there more than 3 ft (1 m) of rainfall a year...?

NO
Cocoa won't grow

YES

Is the climate humid?

NO
Cocoa won't grow

YES

Is the average annual temperature between 64°F–68°F ?

NO
Cocoa won't grow

YES

Is the soil loose?

NO
Cocoa won't grow

YES

Are you less than 1,300 ft (400 m) above sea level?

NO
Cocoa won't grow

YES

Are you between 20° north and 20° south of the equator?

An estimated **3 million tonnes** of cocoa is produced every year

Who profits?

For every $1 you spend on chocolate, the farmer who produces the cocoa beans earns just 8¢. The chocolate manufacturer and the shop that sells the chocolate each receive more than a quarter of the total price of the bar.

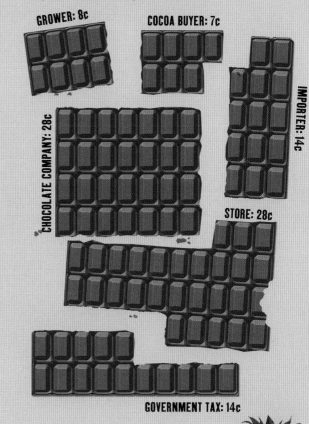

GROWER: 8c

COCOA BUYER: 7c

IMPORTER: 14c

CHOCOLATE COMPANY: 28c

STORE: 28c

GOVERNMENT TAX: 14c

Can you grow cocoa?

The cacao trees that produce cacao beans for chocolate only grow in certain very specific conditions. If the soil type, average temperature, humidity level, and amount of sunlight and rainfall are not all exactly right, the trees will not thrive.

A ripe cocoa pod is **6–12 in** (15–30 cm) long— around the same size as a pineapple

---

7. Husks removed
The outer husks are removed and then the roasted beans are ground into a liquid.

8. Fat extracted
The liquid is pressed to remove the fat (cocoa butter), some of which is used to make cosmetics.

9. Mixing
The remaining powder is mixed with sugar, cocoa butter, vanilla, and, for milk chocolate, milk.

10. Rolling
This mixture is squeezed through a series of heavy rollers, changing it into a dry flaky solid.

11. Stirring
Ingredients are added that help bind the mixture and then it is stirred into a smooth paste.

12. Tempering
The chocolate is tempered (repeatedly heated and cooled) for a glossy finish, then left to set in a mould.

Fishy Business

Fish is an important part of the diet in many countries. More than one billion people rely on fish and other seafood as their main source of animal protein. The world's commercial fishing fleet has always met the growing demand for fish, but there are clear signs that too many fish are being taken from the wild, threatening the survival of many species. Farmed fish are having to make up more and more of global production.

13 million
people worldwide work in the fishing industry

One of the world's
biggest trawl nets could encircle more than a dozen Boeing **747s**

Rich waters
The Pacific Ocean is the world's biggest ocean as well as the most productive. In 2007, Pacific fish and shellfish production amounted to 64.5 million tonnes—almost twice as much as the catches of all the other oceans and seas added together.

- Pacific
- Atlantic
- Indian
- Mediterranean and black sea

Fish production
In 2007, the total world catch of fish and shellfish amounted to 90 million tonnes, while another 50 million tonnes were farmed. More than half of the world's total production is caught and farmed by just five nations (see below).

10 times
In every catch of prawns, up to 10 times their weight in other species is also caught in the net and then discarded, often already dead

Biggest fishers
China is the world's biggest fishing nation by a long way, catching more than three times as much as, and farming almost nine times more than, the next biggest fishing nation, India. Even though 75% of China's fish is consumed by its domestic market, it is the largest exporter of fish in the world.

- Fish farmed
- Fish captured

CHINA 14,659,036 tonnes / 31,420,275 tonnes
INDIA 3,953,476 tonnes / 3,354,764 tonnes
PERU 7,210,544 tonnes / 59,651 tonnes
INDONESIA 4,936,699 tonnes / 1,392,904 tonnes
U.S.A. 4,767,596 tonnes / 528,261 tonnes

Deadly cuisine
Despite the fact that its liver and intestines contain a deadly poison, the spiny puffer fish is a great delicacy in Japan, where it is called fugu. Only specially trained "fugu-certified" chefs are allowed to prepare this potentially fatal fish dish.

174

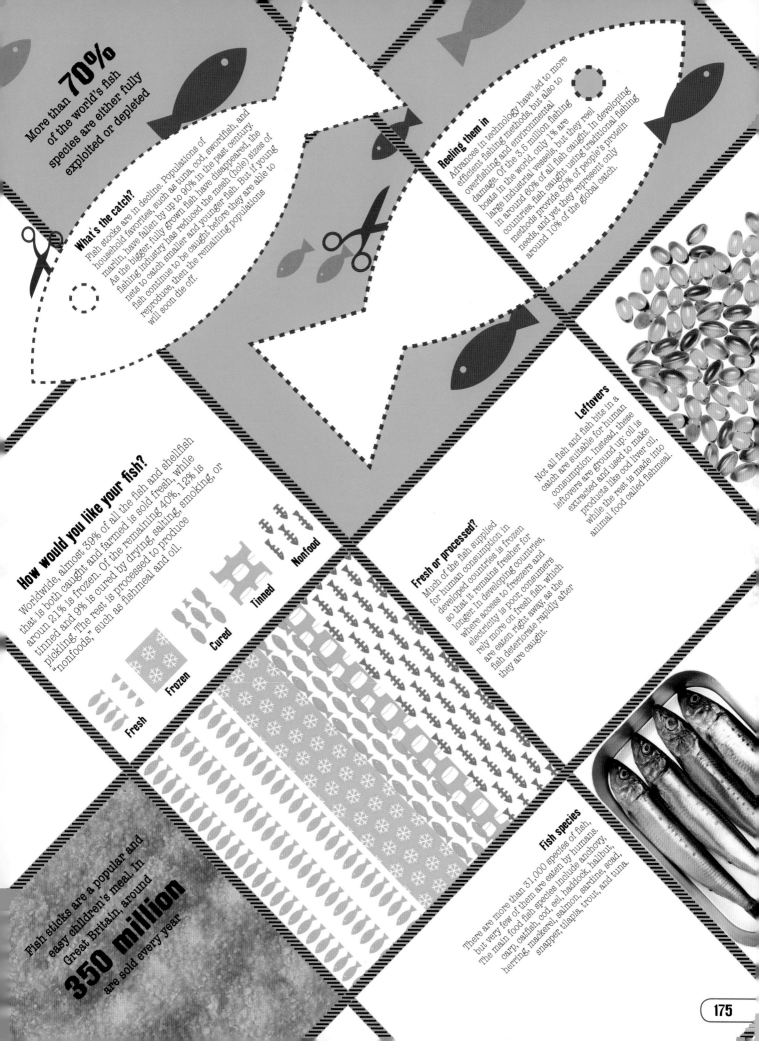

More than 70%
of the world's fish species are either fully exploited or depleted

What's the catch?
Fish stocks are in decline. Populations of household favorites, such as tuna, cod, swordfish, and marlin, have fallen by up to 90% in the past century. As the bigger, fully grown fish have disappeared, the fishing industry has reduced the mesh (hole) sizes of nets to catch smaller and younger fish. But if young fish continue to be caught before they are able to reproduce, then the remaining populations will soon die off.

Reeling them in
Advances in technology have led to more efficient fishing methods, but also to overfishing and environmental damage. Of the 3.5 million fishing boats in the world, only 1% are large industrial vessels, but they real in around 60% of all fish caught. In developing countries, fish caught using traditional fishing methods provide 80% of people's protein needs, and yet, they represent only around 10% of the global catch.

Leftovers
Not all fish and fish bits in a catch are suitable for human consumption. Instead, these leftovers are ground up, oil is extracted and used to make products like cod liver oil, while the rest is made into animal food called fishmeal.

How would you like your fish?
Worldwide, almost 39% of all the fish and shellfish that is both caught and farmed is sold fresh, while around 21% is frozen. Of the remaining 40%, 12% is tinned and 9% is cured by drying, salting, smoking, or pickling. The rest is processed to produce "nonfoods," such as fishmeal and oil.

Fresh

Frozen

Cured

Tinned

Nonfood

Fresh or processed?
Much of the fish supplied for human consumption in developed countries is frozen so that it remains fresher for longer. In developing countries, where access to freezers and electricity is poor, consumers rely more on fresh fish, which are eaten right away as the fish deteriorate rapidly after they are caught.

Fish species
There are more than 31,000 species of fish, but very few of them are eaten by humans. The main food fish species include anchovy, carp, catfish, cod, eel, haddock, halibut, herring, mackerel, salmon, sardine, scad, snapper, tilapia, trout, and tuna.

Fish sticks are a popular and easy children's meal. In Great Britain, around
350 million
are sold every year

Mining

From precious gemstones to the metal that makes a jumbo jet, the results of mining are all around us. Mining is the process of digging rock out of the ground. Rock is made of a mixture of substances called minerals, each of which has a particular chemical make-up and structure. Miners search for minerals called ores, which contain valuable elements. The ores are processed to extract the elements. Coal is mined too, although it is not a mineral but a type of rock formed from dead plants.

Coal

Coal is an important fuel that is mined in great quantities. However, it will not last forever. Peak coal—when the most coal is produced—may be reached by 2025, after which production will fall as resources become depleted.

Mining methods

Most minerals, including 98% of metal ores, are produced by surface mining. Surface mines are dug by stripping away the ground above the minerals. Deeper minerals are mined by digging tunnels and sinking shafts down to them.

Metal ores

Iron ore is mined in much greater quantities that any other metallic ore. Most iron ore is used to create steel, which is needed for a number of objects, from kitchen appliances to bridges. To a much lesser extent, iron is also an ingredient in medicine, paint, and fertilizer.

Metal mining consumes up to **10%** of global energy

At least **40** different minerals are needed to make a telephone

IRON ORE
2,000 million tonnes

ALUMINIUM ORE (BAUXITE)
212 million tonnes

MANGANESE ORE
38.8 million tonnes

CHROMIUM ORE
23 million tonnes

MAGNESIUM ORE
5.3 million tonnes

TOP 5 METAL ORES MINED IN 2007

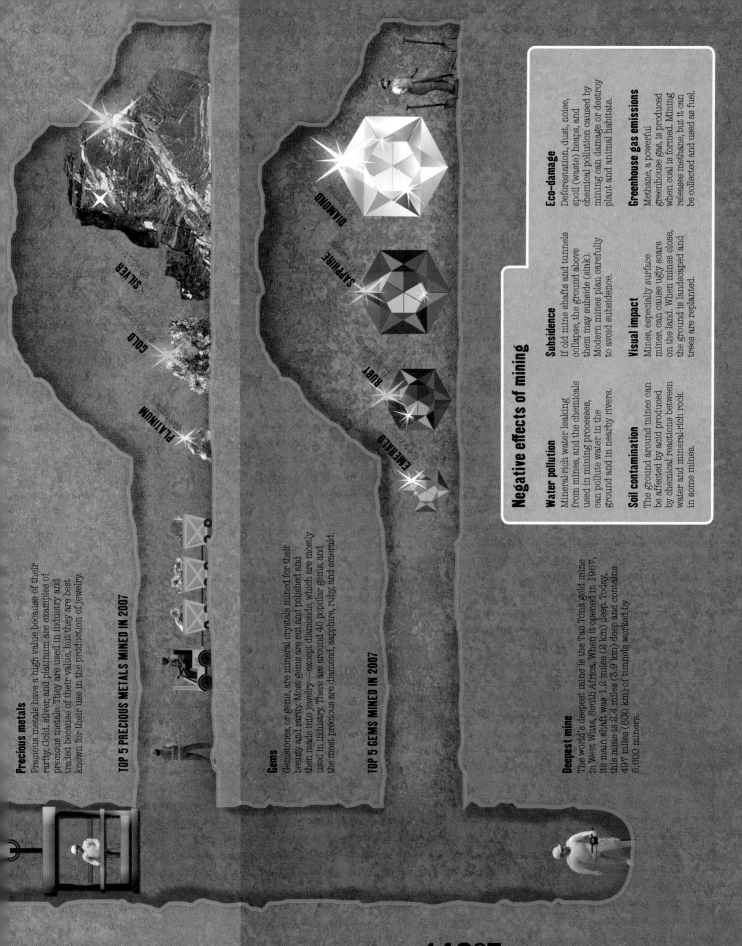

Precious metals

Precious metals have a high value because of their rarity. Gold, silver, and platinum are examples of precious metals. They are used in industry and traded because of their value, but they are best known for their use in the production of jewelry.

TOP 5 PRECIOUS METALS MINED IN 2007

SILVER
20,488 tonnes

GOLD
2,340 tonnes

PLATINUM
200 tonnes

Gems

Gemstones, or gems, are mineral crystals mined for their beauty and rarity. Most gems are cut and polished and then made into jewelry — except diamonds, which are mostly used in industry. There are around 40 popular gems, and the most precious are diamond, sapphire, ruby, and emerald.

TOP 5 GEMS MINED IN 2007

DIAMOND
177 tonnes

SAPPHIRE
800 tonnes

RUBY
1 tonnes

EMERALD
557 tonnes

Deepest mine

The world's deepest mine is the Taut Tona gold mine in West Wits, South Africa. When it opened in 1957, its main shaft was 1.2 miles (2 km) deep. Today, this mine is 2.4 miles (3.9 km) deep and contains 497 miles (800 km) of tunnels worked by 5,600 miners.

Negative effects of mining

Water pollution

Mineral-rich water leaking from mines, and the chemicals used in mining processes, can pollute water in the ground and in nearby rivers.

Soil contamination

The ground around mines can be affected by acid produced by chemical reactions between water and mineral-rich rock in some mines.

Subsidence

If old mine shafts and tunnels collapse, the ground above them may subside (sink). Modern mines plan carefully to avoid subsidence.

Visual impact

Mines, especially surface mines, can cause ugly scars on the land. When mines close, the ground is landscaped and trees are replanted.

Eco-damage

Deforestation, dust, noise, spoil (waste) heaps, and chemical pollution caused by mining can damage or destroy plant and animal habitats.

Greenhouse gas emissions

Methane, a powerful greenhouse gas, is produced when coal is formed. Mining releases methane, but it can be collected and used as fuel.

The temperature at the bottom of the world's deepest mine is **140°F** (60°C)

Diamonds

Diamond is the hardest material found in nature. It is made of carbon, the same substance that forms graphite (the lead in a pencil)—one of the world's softest materials. The difference between them is the way in which the carbon atoms are linked together. The rarity of large, gem-quality diamonds and their sparkling appearance increases their value. Around $13 billion of diamonds are produced each year, and the diamond industry employs around 10 million people.

Mining from the land

Diamonds form deep underground at high temperatures and great pressure. Most are more than one billion years old. Ancient volcanoes brought them to the surface in pipelike rock structures, from which they are mined today.

Sifting from rivers

When water erodes diamond-bearing rock, the diamonds may be washed out into a river. These diamonds are called alluvial diamonds, because they are found by sifting the alluvium, the silt and sediment deposited by a river.

Sieving from the sea

Alluvial diamonds are sometimes carried all the way down rivers and into the sea. They are mined by boats that suck up the seabed sediments, which are then sieved to obtain the diamonds.

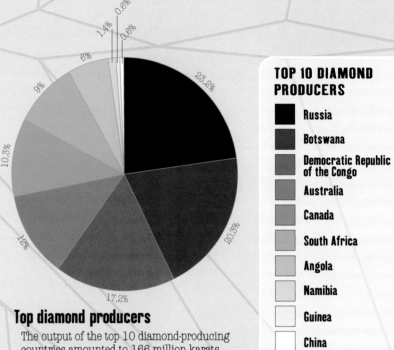

Pie chart values: 23.2%, 20.3%, 17.2%, 12%, 10.3%, 9%, 6%, 1.4%, 0.6%, 0.6%

TOP 10 DIAMOND PRODUCERS

- Russia
- Botswana
- Democratic Republic of the Congo
- Australia
- Canada
- South Africa
- Angola
- Namibia
- Guinea
- China

Top diamond producers

The output of the top 10 diamond-producing countries amounted to 166 million karats, or just over 33 tonnes, in 2007. Russia was the top producer, with an output of more than 38 million karats, or around 7.6 tonnes. One karat is equal to 0.0004 lbs (0.2 g). Diamonds with larger karats are more expensive than lower karat diamonds.

From the rough

Diamonds that are mined from the ground are rough and dull, so they have to be cut and polished to transform them into sparkling gemstones. A diamond is cut to give it a new shape (shown here in blue) and to get rid of faults called inclusions (shown here in red). It is then polished and set in a ring, necklace, or other piece of jewelry.

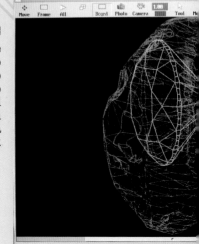

The biggest diamond ever found in the universe is the heart of an old star named BPM 37093—the 10 billion trillion trillion karat diamond star has a diameter of **2,485 miles** (4,000 km)

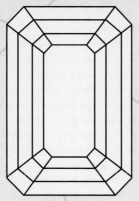

THE NINE LARGEST CULLINAN DIAMONDS
(shown actual size)

Jewels in the crown

The largest rough diamond ever found is the Cullinan. It was discovered in South Africa in 1905, weighing 3,106 karats, or 1.4 lbs (621 g). It was cut into nine large gemstones and 96 smaller stones. The nine largest stones of the Cullinan are in the British Crown Jewels and other jewelry worn by the British royal family.

CULLINAN I
(also called the star of Africa)
530.3 karats
(Royal scepter)

CULLINAN II
317.4 karats
(Imperial State Crown
of Great Britain)

CULLINAN III
94.4 karats
(finial of Queen Mary's Crown)

CULLINAN IV
63.5 karats
(band of Queen Mary's Crown)

CULLINAN V
18.50 karats
(center of brooch)

CULLINAN VI
11.5 karats
(diamond and
emerald necklace)

CULLINAN VII
8.8 karats
(pendant drop
on brooch)

CULLINAN VIII
6.8 karats
(mounted as center diamond on
same brooch as Cullinan VII)

CULLINAN IX
4.39 karats
(set in ring)

In 2008, the 35.6-karat Wittelsbach diamond became the world's most expensive diamond when it was sold at an auction for

$24.3 million

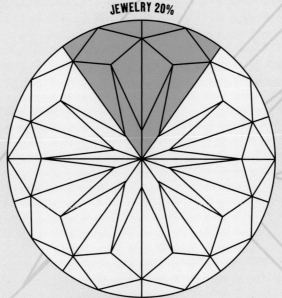

JEWELRY 20%

INDUSTRY 80%

What are diamonds used for?

Around 135 million karats, which represent 80% of global diamond production, are used by industry. Industrial diamonds are used to make cutting, drilling, grinding, and sanding products because the material is so hard. Only 20% of mined diamonds are made into gemstones.

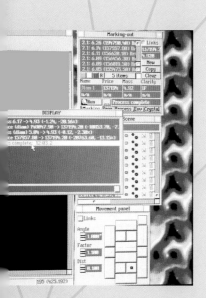

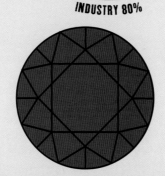

Conflict diamonds

Conflict diamonds come from war zones and are sold to buy weapons. In the 1990s, 4% of the world's diamonds were conflict diamonds. By tracking new diamonds from the mine to the buyer, this has now been cut to a fraction of a percent.

179

Making the Modern World

A global effort

We use manufactured products in every aspect of our lives. They range from machine parts, engines, toys, and cars to electronic components, cell phones, TVs, and computers. Follow the assembly line to see how the entire world is involved in creating, selling, and buying manufactured goods.

Manufactured goods are all around us, from the clothes that we wear to the chairs that we sit on. Most items are made in a handful of countries, but the parts that they contain will often have been manufactured separately all over the world. The global market for manufactured products was worth more than $11 trillion in 2009, with developing countries such as China increasing their share every year.

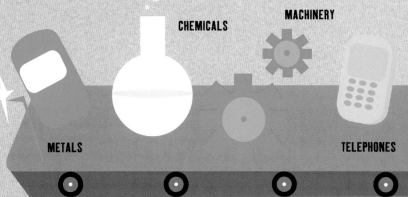

CHEMICALS

MACHINERY

METALS

TELEPHONES

Auto increase

Car production is one of the biggest manufacturing industries. More than 600 million cars are in use today, and another 50 million were manufactured in 2008. Japan alone produced nearly 10 million cars.

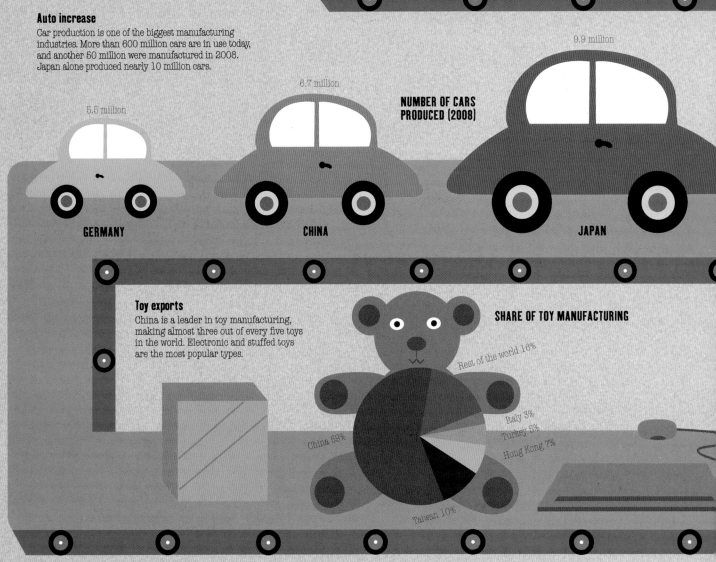

NUMBER OF CARS PRODUCED (2008)

5.5 million — GERMANY

6.7 million — CHINA

9.9 million — JAPAN

Toy exports

China is a leader in toy manufacturing, making almost three out of every five toys in the world. Electronic and stuffed toys are the most popular types.

SHARE OF TOY MANUFACTURING

- China 59%
- Taiwan 10%
- Hong Kong 7%
- Turkey 5%
- Italy 3%
- Rest of the world 16%

The biggest U.S. manufacturing sector is **chemical** products, worth **$249 billion** in 2007

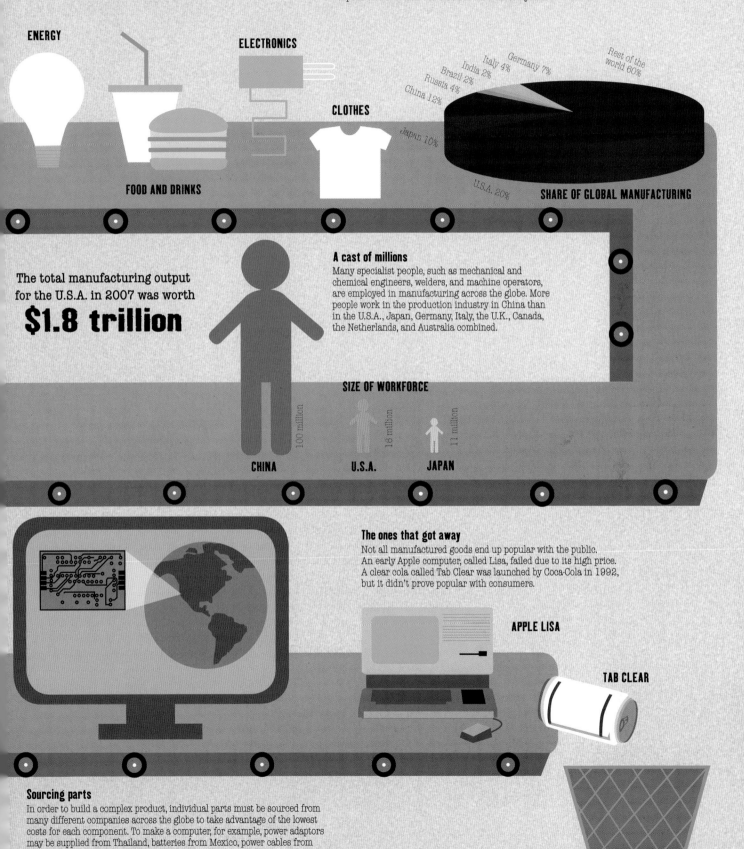

China has the fastest-growing manufacturing industry, increasing by **27%** in 2007

The leaders of tomorrow

Today, the top five manufacturing countries—U.S.A., China, Japan, Germany, and Italy—account for more than half of all global manufacturing output. The world's leading emerging economies are known as BRIC (Brazil, Russia, India, and China). BRIC's total manufacturing output combined is equal to the world's largest manufacturing country, the U.S.A. China alone is expected to overtake the U.S.A. in the next few years.

ENERGY

ELECTRONICS

CLOTHES

FOOD AND DRINKS

Italy 4% Germany 7% Rest of the world 60%
India 2%
Brazil 2%
Russia 4%
China 12%
Japan 10%
U.S.A. 20%

SHARE OF GLOBAL MANUFACTURING

The total manufacturing output for the U.S.A. in 2007 was worth **$1.8 trillion**

A cast of millions

Many specialist people, such as mechanical and chemical engineers, welders, and machine operators, are employed in manufacturing across the globe. More people work in the production industry in China than in the U.S.A., Japan, Germany, Italy, the U.K., Canada, the Netherlands, and Australia combined.

SIZE OF WORKFORCE

100 million — **CHINA**

16 million — **U.S.A.**

11 million — **JAPAN**

The ones that got away

Not all manufactured goods end up popular with the public. An early Apple computer, called Lisa, failed due to its high price. A clear cola called Tab Clear was launched by Coca-Cola in 1992, but it didn't prove popular with consumers.

APPLE LISA

TAB CLEAR

Sourcing parts

In order to build a complex product, individual parts must be sourced from many different companies across the globe to take advantage of the lowest costs for each component. To make a computer, for example, power adaptors may be supplied from Thailand, batteries from Mexico, power cables from India, and microprocessors from California.

Robots

A robot is a machine that can be programmed to carry out tasks for humans. There are around 6.5 million of them in operation around the world today. Some robots are remotely controlled by a person, while others are programmed to carry out tasks automatically. Robots are commonly used for tasks that are either too dangerous, dirty, or dull for humans to do. Some robots are strong enough to move cars, while others have a touch delicate enough to perform surgeries.

Japan expects to have
1 million
robots by 2025

Robot density

The number of industrial robots in relation to workers in a country is called the robot density. Japan has the world's highest robot density, with almost 300 industrial robots for every 10,000 manufacturing workers.

Japan

Singapore

South Korea

Germany
163

Sweden
126

Italy
124

Finland
98

Belgium
89

U.S.A.

Spain
84

NUMBER OF ROBOTS PER 10,000 WORKERS

Service robots

Instead of making products, service robots help humans. Domestic service robots, like the Roomba vacuum cleaner, help out around the home. Professional service robots work in hospitals, offices, farms, transportation, military forces, and space exploration.

Roomba

The Roomba is a robot vacuum cleaner that can steer itself around a room automatically, turning to avoid obstacles and walls. It even returns to its charging station to recharge its battery when it is finished.

Asimo

One of the world's most advanced robots, Asimo looks like a 4-ft- (1.3-m-) tall astronaut wearing a backpack. Its joints are moved by 34 electric motors. Asimo can walk, talk, understand spoken commands, and even dance.

Industrial robots

As the cost of using machines has fallen and the cost of employing people has risen, industrial robots have replaced workers in many factories. There are around one million of them in operation around the world. They can drill, cut, and weld parts, paint products, and move items from place to place.

On average, one industrial robot can do the work of
10 people

Robots by industry

This table shows which industries bought the most robots in 2008. Around 40,500 robots were bought by vehicle and vehicle parts manufacturers. The food industry bought 3,000 robots, mainly for stacking and packing products.

INDUSTRIAL ROBOT SALES 2008

Motor vehicle: 20,500
Motor vehicle parts: 20,000
Electrical machinery: 14,000
Chemical, rubber, and plastics: 12,500
Metal products: 10,500
Machinery: 5,000
Food: 3,000   Communications: 1,000
Nonmetallic products: 750
Medical, precision, and optical instruments: 750
Other vehicles: 500

Motor vehicles

Car-building robots assemble a car's body panels and weld them together. Painting robots, eight to a car, can paint 50 cars an hour. Each car can be a different color, if required, and the robots can keep going 24 hours a day.

Food

Robots are just starting to be used in the food-processing industry. They can load and unload workers. The latest robots have smooth, easy-to-clean bodies that meet the industry's strict hygiene standards for handling food.

Robots by service

There are 6.5 million service robots at work around the world, worth a combined $11.2 billion. Around 30% of the service robots sold in 2008 were for defense, rescue, and security—doing dangerous jobs such as bomb disposal.

SERVICE ROBOT SALES 2008

Defense, rescue, security: 20,000
Farming: 14,950
Logistic: 2,500
Medical: 5,050
Mobile robot platforms: 4,000
Cleaning: 6,000
Building and demolition: 4,950
Underwater: 5,000
Household robots: 4,200
Entertainment and leisure: 2,950

Medical robots

In some hospitals, robots deliver packages such as patients' records. Other robots visit patients and let a doctor elsewhere see them and talk to them. The most advanced hospital robots are surgical robots, remotely controlled by surgeons to carry out operations.

Robot soccer

Designers are trying to build a team of robots good enough to play against a team of human soccer players. Until then, the robots play against each other at the Robot Soccer World Cup. In 2008, 373 teams of robots were entered.

At your Service!

Whether you need to buy a box of chocolates or book a flight, you will need the help of service industries. People who work in this sector do not produce any manufactured goods but exist to serve the public. Around 39% of the global workforce are employed in service industries, in a wide range of jobs, from retail sales to tourism.

Hotel check-in

The hotel industry encompasses a wide variety of services. From the moment you arrive and are greeted by reception, to eating a meal prepared by the hotel chef, the aim of most hotels is to provide a high level of service and comfort. But be careful how much you pay—a night in the best suite at the Atlantis Hotel in the Bahamas will cost you $25,000!

BANK

Money, money, money!

The banking industry deals with money, from setting up a personal savings account to more complex financial planning for businesses and governments. The types of jobs vary enormously, including administration, accounting, and computer programming, to name just three. By 2008, this industry employed 1.8 million people in the U.S.A.

Get up and go!

All over the world, transportation is a major service industry, and we would not get very far without it—literally! In India, the railroads alone carry more than 6 billion passengers every year and employ more than 1.4 million people.

Retail detail

Retailing is the selling of goods directly to the customer. In developed countries, retail has moved away from traditional downtown stores to out-of-town supermarkets. By 2005, supermarkets accounted for 73% of all grocery sales in the U.K.

Changing times

As they develop, economies tend to move from agriculture toward manufacturing. As they become more prosperous, salaries rise and manufacturers move elsewhere to find cheaper sources of labor. Most developed countries have economies dominated by the service industries. However, with a globalized economy and modern communication, service industries may be located anywhere. Many telephone call centers have now been moved from Europe to India, where salaries are lower.

In Cuba, there is
1 doctor
for every
170 patients

Read all about it!
The communication and media industries include newspapers, magazines, books, radio, TV, and web sites. The rise of electronic media is challenging traditional printed media—there are already 1.7 billion Internet users worldwide.

Take a vacation
Are you planning a vacation any time soon? If so, you can book your ticket at a travel agent—in person, on the phone, or online. The Internet is quickly becoming the most popular way to research and book vacations. In 2007, 55% of Internet users booked a vacation online in the U.K.

Care for your health
The level of health care depends on the experience and quality of the staff—from medical to administrative—and the condition of hospitals and equipment. The U.K.'s National Health Service is the world's biggest health care employer, with a labor force of around 1.3 million.

School time
Education is a crucial public service because teachers help shape the minds of future generations. The ability to read and write is one of the most vital skills taught in school. Literacy rates vary widely, from 99.8% in Cuba to under 24% in Burkina Faso.

Shop 'til you Drop!

The sale of goods directly to the public is known as retail. Retail is big business, and it is getting bigger, but it is also changing. Today, an increasing number of small independent or family-run stores are losing out to chain stores and large supermarkets. The way that people shop has also changed, with many consumers using the Internet to buy goods online.

Big spenders

The shopping bags identify the highest spending countries in the world. Between them, they account for around two-thirds of the world's retail sales. In 2008, the biggest spender of all, the U.S.A., accounted for around one-quarter of these sales.

FRANCE $2.4 billion
RUSSIA $2.9 billion
ITALY $3.4 billion
U.K. $3.6 billion
MEXICO $4.4 billion
KOREA $7 billion
GERMANY $8.9 billion
BRAZIL $10.1 billion
JAPAN $22.8 billion
U.S.A. $29.6 billion

The world's biggest shopping malls

A shopping mall is like a town in itself. The top five largest malls in the world, listed below, bring together all types of different stores under a single roof, with covered walkways, escalators, dining areas, and even ice rinks, casinos, and swimming pools. The great shopping mall boom of the 1990s and 2000s created giants; however, economic recession has forced many malls around the world to downsize or rethink their future.

More than **40 million** people went to the Mall of America in Bloomington, Minnesota in 2006, making it the world's most-visited shopping mall

Mall food

What is the secret to a successful shopping mall? Food, of course. The main activity in a mall is not actually shopping, but eating.

1) New South China Mall
Dongguan, China
7.1 million sq. ft
(2.2 million sq. m)
Special features: a theme park,
but this has not been taking
shoppers away from the stores

2) Golden Resources Mall
Beijing, China
6 million sq. ft
(557,400 sq. m).
Special features:
more than 1,000 stores
over five stories

3) SM Mall of Asia
Pasay City, The Philippines
4.2 million sq. ft
(390,200 sq. m)
Special features: swimming
pool and movie theater and
its very own tram system

4) Dubai Mall
Dubai, United Arab Emirates
3.8 million sq. ft
(353,000 sq. m)
Special features: ice rink,
aquarium, and top
fashion outlets

5) Cevahir Istanbul,
Istanbul, Turkey
3.8 million sq. ft
(353,000 sq. m)
Special features: Europe's
largest mall, with
wavepool and
roller coaster

Market day

Many outdoor or covered markets date back to ancient times and are often at the heart of community life. Chatuchak Weekend Market in Bangkok, Thailand, covers a huge 1,176,119 sq. ft (109,265 sq. m), with around 15,000 stalls and 200,000 visitors daily. Market vendors are generally small independent traders who are prepared to haggle over the price of goods.

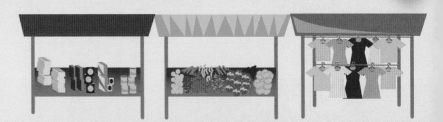

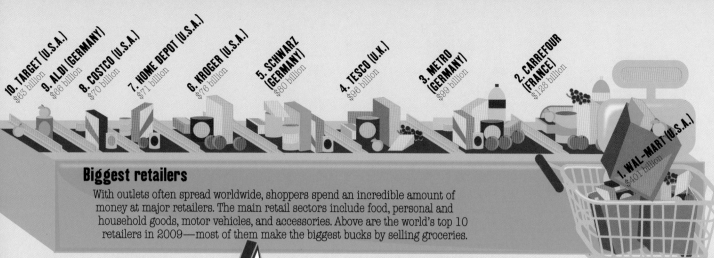

10. TARGET (U.S.A.)
$63 billion

9. ALDI (GERMANY)
$86 billion

8. COSTCO (U.S.A.)
$70 billion

7. HOME DEPOT (U.S.A.)
$71 billion

6. KROGER (U.S.A.)
$76 billion

5. SCHWARZ (GERMANY)
$80 billion

4. TESCO (U.K.)
$96 billion

3. METRO (GERMANY)
$99 billion

2. CARREFOUR (FRANCE)
$128 billion

1. WAL-MART (U.S.A.)
$401 billion

Biggest retailers

With outlets often spread worldwide, shoppers spend an incredible amount of money at major retailers. The main retail sectors include food, personal and household goods, motor vehicles, and accessories. Above are the world's top 10 retailers in 2009—most of them make the biggest bucks by selling groceries.

The future of shopping?

The ultimate in-store electronic technology is being tried out at a Metro group store in northern Germany. The Future Store has scales that recognize products visually, electronic price labeling, computer handsets to guide shoppers around the store, as well as electronic product information.

Shopping online

In 2007, online shopping accounted for under 7% of retail sales, but it is growing at a phenomenal rate. Today, 40% of the world's population have bought items on the Internet. In 2008, books were purchased by the most people online, with clothing and shoes just behind.

Top online purchases
(proportion bought online)
1 **Books** 41%
2 **Clothing and shoes** 36%
3 **Videos, DVDS, and games** 24%
3 **Airline tickets** 24%
4 **Electronic goods and gadgets** 23%
5 **Music** 19%
5 **Cosmetics and nutrition** 19%
6 **Computer hardware** 11%
7 **Hotel and tour reservations** 16%
8 **Tickets and events** 15%

Around **10,000** payment card transactions are made around the world every second

Plastic fantastic

When you pay for goods with a bank card, the money is immediately transferred out of your bank account. When you pay with a credit card, you borrow the money from the bank and pay it back later with interest. The first credit cards were introduced by Diners Club in 1950. They are convenient, quick, and easy to use—but they can lead users into serious debt.

Advertising

Scaling the side of buildings, splashed across webpages, and coming through your mailbox, advertising has increasingly become a feature of the modern world. Manufacturers and retailers spent a combined $487 billion in 2008 to persuade the public to buy their products or services. Advertising has always existed, but since the 1950s, advertisers have made use of a growing understanding of human psychology in order to achieve success.

Getting the message across

Though the ways in which we see and hear advertising are constantly changing, they can be roughly divided into a few key areas: print, outdoor, Internet, and TV, movie, and radio. The pie chart segments show how much of the worldwide advertising budget for 2008 was spent on each area. The best form of advertising is generally considered to be the one that money can't buy – word of mouth.

Logging on

The Internet has only existed since 1990, yet it has completely changed advertising. Internet promotion includes banner displays, spam messages, and virals, which rely on people to pass on the ad.

11%

Great outdoors

Whenever you step outside, you can rarely avoid seeing advertising and promotions. They appear on traditional billboards, but may also be moving, on screens, or on the side of trucks or buses.

7%

The printed word

Newspapers have been around for about 400 years, but the rise of the Internet has hit newspaper sales and their advertising income. Newspapers now have to seek a new readership and advertising revenue online.

36%

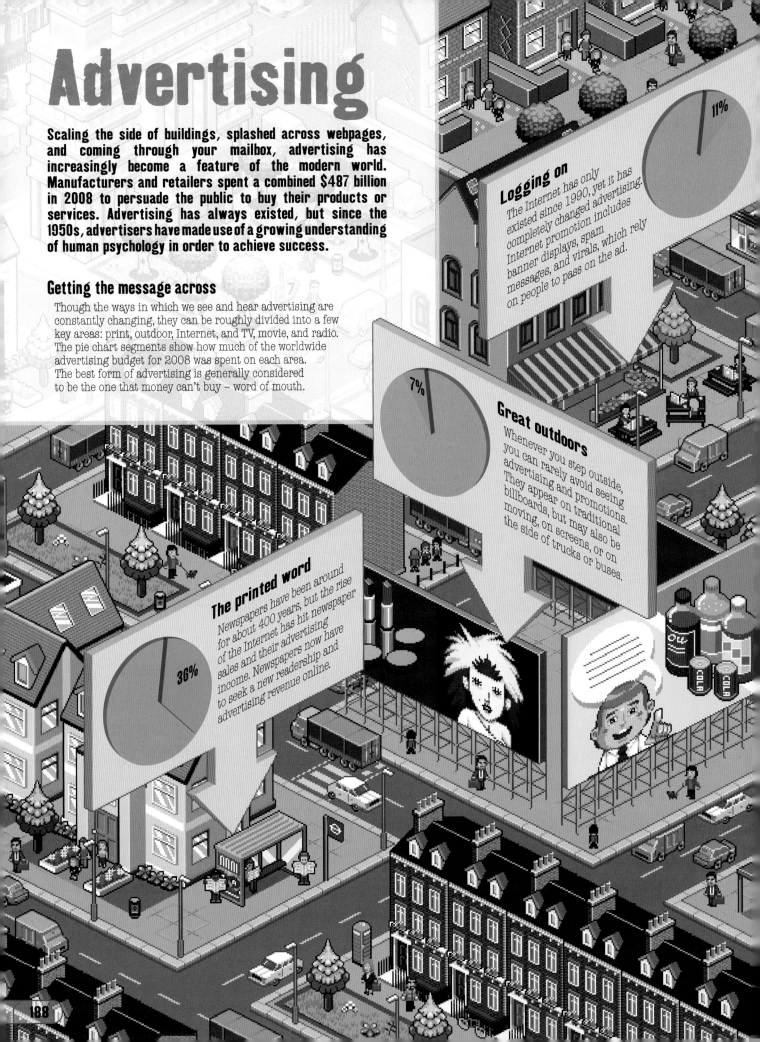

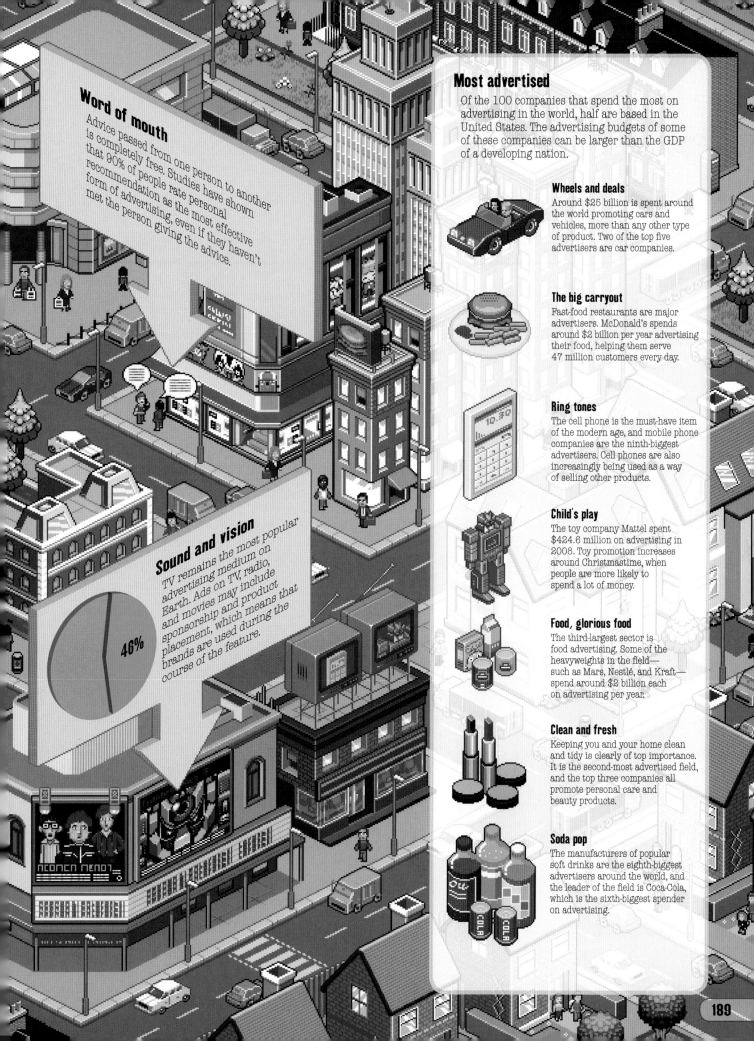

Word of mouth

Advice passed from one person to another is completely free. Studies have shown that 90% of people rate personal recommendation as the most effective form of advertising, even if they haven't met the person giving the advice.

Sound and vision

TV remains the most popular advertising medium on Earth. Ads on TV, radio, and movies may include sponsorship and product placement, which means that brands are used during the course of the feature.

46%

Most advertised

Of the 100 companies that spend the most on advertising in the world, half are based in the United States. The advertising budgets of some of these companies can be larger than the GDP of a developing nation.

Wheels and deals

Around $25 billion is spent around the world promoting cars and vehicles, more than any other type of product. Two of the top five advertisers are car companies.

The big carryout

Fast-food restaurants are major advertisers. McDonald's spends around $2 billion per year advertising their food, helping them serve 47 million customers every day.

Ring tones

The cell phone is the must-have item of the modern age, and mobile phone companies are the ninth-biggest advertisers. Cell phones are also increasingly being used as a way of selling other products.

Child's play

The toy company Mattel spent $424.6 million on advertising in 2008. Toy promotion increases around Christmastime, when people are more likely to spend a lot of money.

Food, glorious food

The third-largest sector is food advertising. Some of the heavyweights in the field—such as Mars, Nestlé, and Kraft—spend around $2 billion each on advertising per year.

Clean and fresh

Keeping you and your home clean and tidy is clearly of top importance. It is the second-most advertised field, and the top three companies all promote personal care and beauty products.

Soda pop

The manufacturers of popular soft drinks are the eighth-biggest advertisers around the world, and the leader of the field is Coca-Cola, which is the sixth-biggest spender on advertising.

Human Impact

Nearly everything that we do creates some type of waste. Land, water, and even the atmosphere have become our dumping grounds. The planet is running out of room. With one U.S. garbage dump already visible from space, the world's most wasteful nation may have just 18 years of landfill capacity left. We need to reuse and recycle more and, most importantly, reduce the amount that we consume. When millions of people take small steps, the effects can be huge.

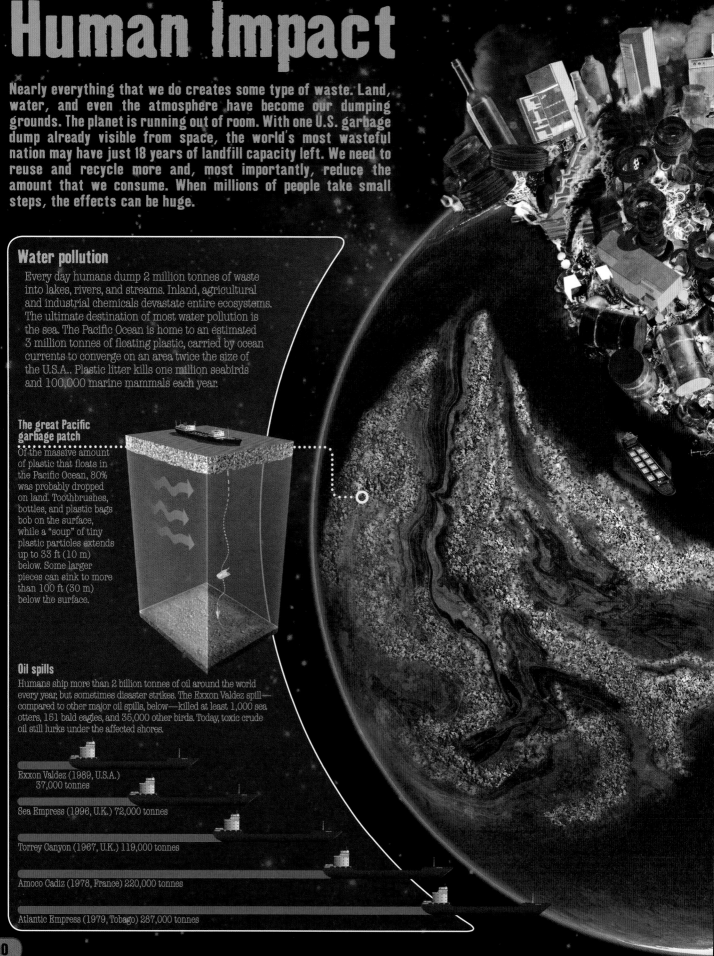

Water pollution

Every day humans dump 2 million tonnes of waste into lakes, rivers, and streams. Inland, agricultural and industrial chemicals devastate entire ecosystems. The ultimate destination of most water pollution is the sea. The Pacific Ocean is home to an estimated 3 million tonnes of floating plastic, carried by ocean currents to converge on an area twice the size of the U.S.A.. Plastic litter kills one million seabirds and 100,000 marine mammals each year.

The great Pacific garbage patch

Of the massive amount of plastic that floats in the Pacific Ocean, 80% was probably dropped on land. Toothbrushes, bottles, and plastic bags bob on the surface, while a "soup" of tiny plastic particles extends up to 33 ft (10 m) below. Some larger pieces can sink to more than 100 ft (30 m) below the surface.

Oil spills

Humans ship more than 2 billion tonnes of oil around the world every year, but sometimes disaster strikes. The Exxon Valdez spill—compared to other major oil spills, below—killed at least 1,000 sea otters, 151 bald eagles, and 35,000 other birds. Today, toxic crude oil still lurks under the affected shores.

Exxon Valdez (1989, U.S.A.) 37,000 tonnes

Sea Empress (1996, U.K.) 72,000 tonnes

Torrey Canyon (1967, U.K.) 119,000 tonnes

Amoco Cadiz (1978, France) 220,000 tonnes

Atlantic Empress (1979, Tobago) 287,000 tonnes

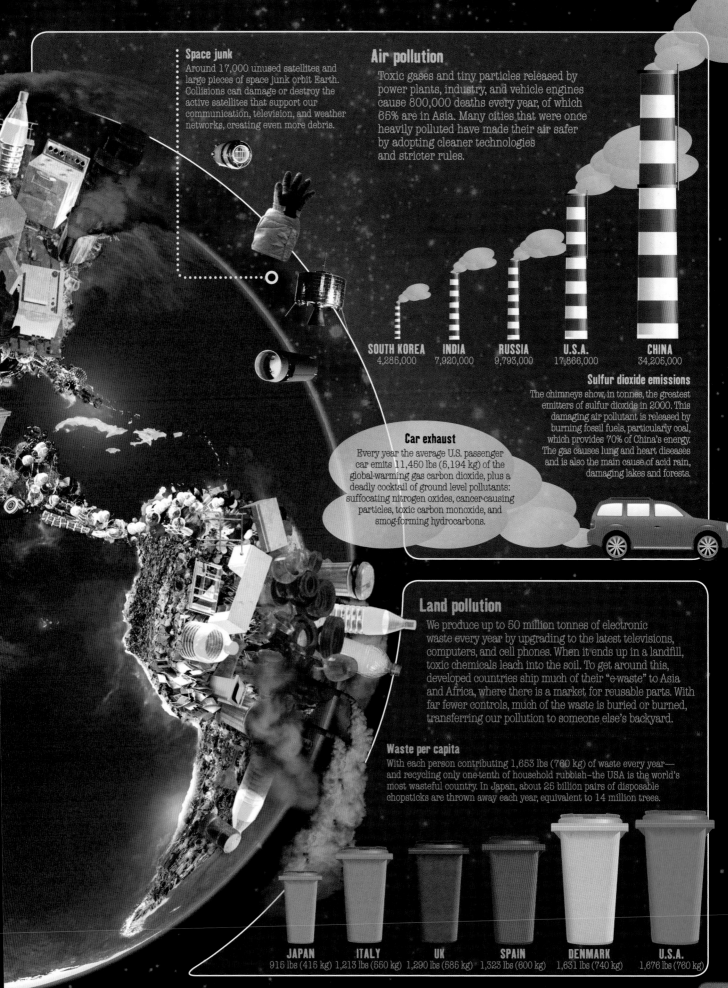

Space junk

Around 17,000 unused satellites and large pieces of space junk orbit Earth. Collisions can damage or destroy the active satellites that support our communication, television, and weather networks, creating even more debris.

Air pollution

Toxic gases and tiny particles released by power plants, industry, and vehicle engines cause 800,000 deaths every year, of which 65% are in Asia. Many cities that were once heavily polluted have made their air safer by adopting cleaner technologies and stricter rules.

SOUTH KOREA	INDIA	RUSSIA	U.S.A.	CHINA
4,286,000	7,920,000	9,793,000	17,866,000	34,205,000

Sulfur dioxide emissions

The chimneys show, in tonnes, the greatest emitters of sulfur dioxide in 2000. This damaging air pollutant is released by burning fossil fuels, particularly coal, which provides 70% of China's energy. The gas causes lung and heart diseases and is also the main cause of acid rain, damaging lakes and forests.

Car exhaust

Every year the average U.S. passenger car emits 11,450 lbs (5,194 kg) of the global-warming gas carbon dioxide, plus a deadly cocktail of ground level pollutants: suffocating nitrogen oxides, cancer-causing particles, toxic carbon monoxide, and smog-forming hydrocarbons.

Land pollution

We produce up to 50 million tonnes of electronic waste every year by upgrading to the latest televisions, computers, and cell phones. When it ends up in a landfill, toxic chemicals leach into the soil. To get around this, developed countries ship much of their "e-waste" to Asia and Africa, where there is a market for reusable parts. With far fewer controls, much of the waste is buried or burned, transferring our pollution to someone else's backyard.

Waste per capita

With each person contributing 1,653 lbs (760 kg) of waste every year—and recycling only one-tenth of household rubbish–the USA is the world's most wasteful country. In Japan, about 25 billion pairs of disposable chopsticks are thrown away each year, equivalent to 14 million trees.

JAPAN	ITALY	UK	SPAIN	DENMARK	U.S.A.
915 lbs (415 kg)	1,213 lbs (550 kg)	1,290 lbs (585 kg)	1,323 lbs (600 kg)	1,631 lbs (740 kg)	1,676 lbs (760 kg)

THE World IN ONE Day

INDUSTRY

Most people have to work to earn a living, and all jobs produce something. What's on the planet's production line today?

Hens lay **189 million eggs**, the combined weight is heavier than **110** passenger airplanes

550,000 robots work on **car assembly** worldwide

If all **142,387 cars** made were in one long **traffic jam**, they would stretch the length of the United Kingdom

483 robots are sold around the world – **310** of them will work in **industry**, and **173** of them are **service** robots

270 million cotton **shirts** could be made with the **61,370 tonnes** of **cotton** picked

513,500 tonnes of **rice** are produced in **China**, the same weight as five cruise ships

6.4 tonnes of **gold** is mined, enough to make **853,300** gold **rings**

288,800 tonnes of **fish** is turned into **food**, the same weight as **18,750** articulated trucks

Enough **oil** is pumped to fill **5,343** Olympic-size swimming pools

450,000 karats of diamonds are mined

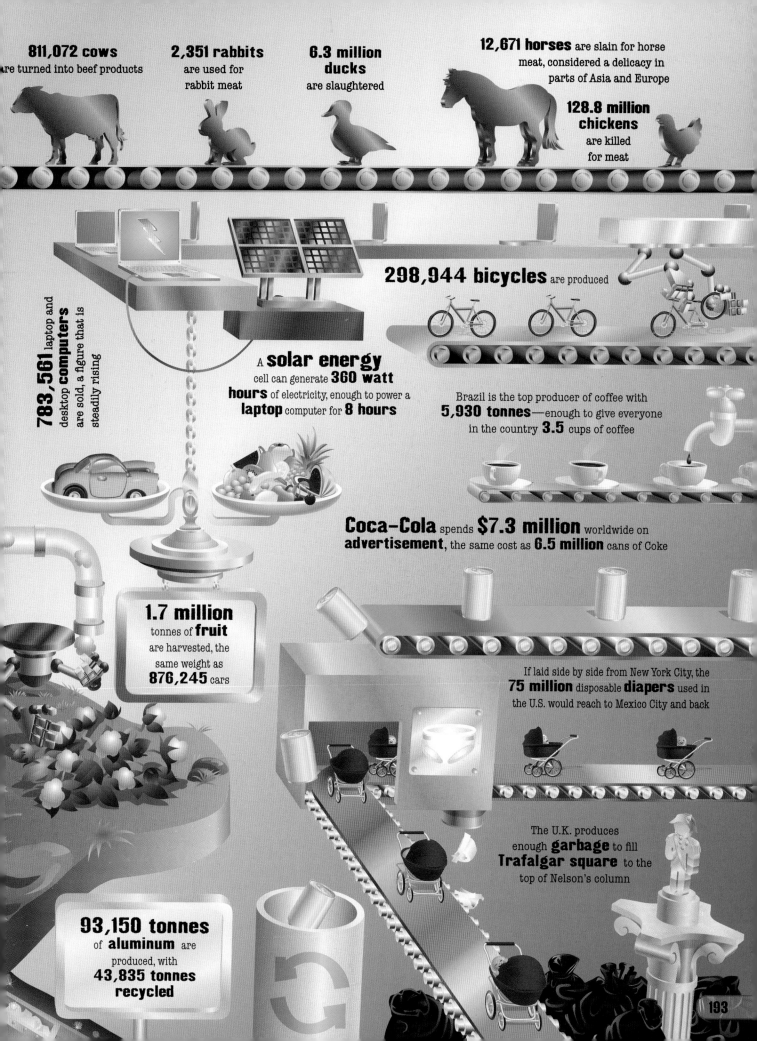

811,072 cows are turned into beef products

2,351 rabbits are used for rabbit meat

6.3 million ducks are slaughtered

12,671 horses are slain for horse meat, considered a delicacy in parts of Asia and Europe

128.8 million chickens are killed for meat

783,561 laptop and desktop **computers** are sold, a figure that is steadily rising

298,944 bicycles are produced

A **solar energy** cell can generate **360 watt hours** of electricity, enough to power a **laptop** computer for **8 hours**

Brazil is the top producer of coffee with **5,930 tonnes**—enough to give everyone in the country **3.5** cups of coffee

Coca-Cola spends **$7.3 million** worldwide on **advertisement**, the same cost as **6.5 million** cans of Coke

1.7 million tonnes of **fruit** are harvested, the same weight as **876,245** cars

If laid side by side from New York City, the **75 million** disposable **diapers** used in the U.S. would reach to Mexico City and back

The U.K. produces enough **garbage** to fill **Trafalgar square** to the top of Nelson's column

93,150 tonnes of **aluminum** are produced, with **43,835 tonnes recycled**

193

Connections

The world is shrinking. Transportation is getting quicker and more people are traveling, but those who stay at home are more connected, too. Modern telecommunications means that data can travel around the world much quicker than humans ever could—we can watch events unfolding, even if they are happening on the other side of the world. Our interests connect us, too, as sports events and movies attract an ever-increasing global audience.

Taking flight

Every day, tens of thousands of aircraft take off for destinations all over the world. They range from the smallest business jets to the biggest airliners. In 2007, the world's 240 airlines scheduled 25 million flights. U.S. aircraft traveled the farthest, clocking up a staggering 6.9 billion miles (11 billion km) in 2009.

AIR 1.6%

TRANSPORTATION 13%

ROAD 10%

In the driving seat

There are more than 600 million cars on Earth—one car for every 10 people. Roughly 250 million of the world's cars are in the U.S.A. Another 50 million new cars are added to the world total every year.

Stretching a total of
4,017,661 miles
(6,465,799 km), the U.S.A.'s road network is the longest in the world

Car ownership

Luxembourg leads the world with 647 cars for every 1,000 people. In China, however, there are only 18 cars per 1,000 people, though car use there is increasing rapidly.

LUXEMBOURG 647

CHINA 18

On the road

Up to 40% of a country's road traffic is carried on high-speed routes called motorways or expressways. The maximum speeds allowed on these long, wide, and, where possible, straight routes are much higher than on other roads.

On the Move

A huge network of transportation routes extends across the world, keeping people and cargo moving along roads, railroads, air routes, and sea lanes. Transportation of all types is getting faster and more frequent, but concerns about global warming are leading to a change to less polluting engines and fuels. No cars at all will be allowed in a new city called Masdar being built in Abu Dhabi. Instead, citizens will rely on the world's most advanced public transportation network.

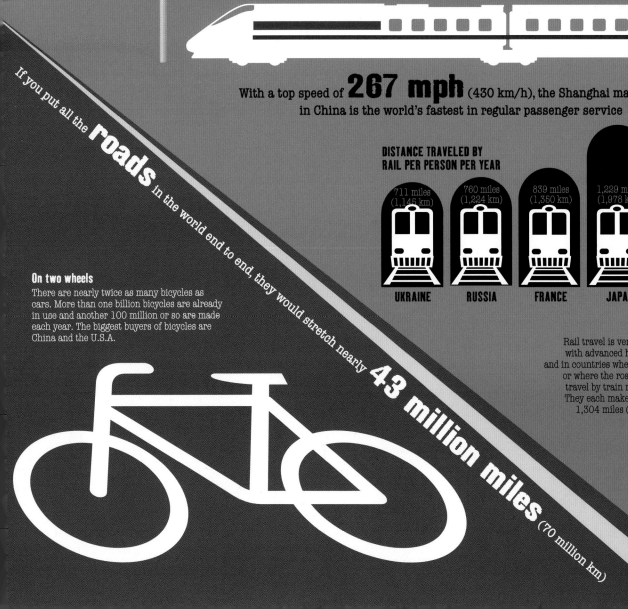

OTHER 1.4%

Emissions from transportation
When fuel is burned in the engines of cars, planes, and other vehicles, greenhouse gases are produced. Around 13% of all human-made greenhouse gases come from transportation, with road vehicles contributing most of the emissions.

In Venice, Italy, **400** licensed gondolas transport people and goods on the city's **170** canals

Global fleet
The worldwide passenger and cargo fleet numbers 53,000 ships. This includes 17,100 general cargo ships and 14,100 tankers. There are 6,800 passenger ships, 7,800 bulk carriers, 4,700 containerships and 2,500 other types of ship.

With a top speed of **267 mph** (430 km/h), the Shanghai maglev train in China is the world's fastest in regular passenger service

If you put all the **roads** in the world end to end, they would stretch nearly **43 million miles** (70 million km)

DISTANCE TRAVELED BY RAIL PER PERSON PER YEAR

711 miles (1,145 km)	760 miles (1,224 km)	839 miles (1,350 km)	1,229 miles (1,978 km)	1,307 miles (2,103 km)
UKRAINE	RUSSIA	FRANCE	JAPAN	SWITZERLAND

On two wheels
There are nearly twice as many bicycles as cars. More than one billion bicycles are already in use and another 100 million or so are made each year. The biggest buyers of bicycles are China and the U.S.A.

Travel by train
Rail travel is very popular in countries with advanced high-speed rail services and in countries where few people own cars or where the roads are poor. The Swiss travel by train more than anyone else. They each make rail journeys totalling 1,304 miles (2,103 km) every year.

Up and Away!

Air travel is big business. Almost 2.3 billion people—a third of all the people in the world—traveled by airplane in 2007. Around 40% of all goods by value are also transported by air. Aviation produces 2% of global carbon emissions, one of the causes of global warming. This figure has not changed much in 20 years, even though air traffic is increasing, because today's aircraft engines are more efficient and burn less fuel.

Longest passenger flight

The world's longest scheduled nonstop passenger flight is the Singapore Airlines service from Newark, New Jersey, to Singapore. The flight covers a distance of 9,535 miles (15,345 km) and takes around 19 hours.

Largest planes

The largest airliner in service today is the Airbus A380. This giant double-decked airliner can carry up to 840 passengers. Fully loaded, it can weigh up to 560 tonnes.

The world's busiest airline, Southwest Airlines, carried

101.9 million

passengers in 2008

Sick bags

There are air sickness bags in the seat-back pockets of every airliner, in case of emergencies. The bags are made in huge numbers. One company, Jinan Horizon International in China, can supply up to 300,000 per day.

1: AIRBUS A380
Wingspan 261 ft. 8 in.
(79.8 m)

2: BOEING 747-400
Wingspan 211 ft. 5 in.
(64.4 m)

3: AIRBUS A340-600
Wingspan 208 ft. 2 in.
(63.4 m)

4: BOEING 777-300
Wingspan 199 ft. 11 in.
(60.9 m)

Strange cargo

Airlines have very strict rules about what items can be taken on board an airplane. But that hasn't stopped people from trying to smuggle on some very strange items. All the things in the list on the right have been seized by airport security.

1 Baby alligator
2 Suitcase full of cockroaches
3 Two live pigeons
4 Dead cat
5 Full set of tires
6 Frozen monkey's head

CONCORDE
Mach 2.04
1,350 mph (2,172 km/h)

LARGE JET AIRLINER
Mach 0.85
567 mph (913 km/h)

SMALL REGIONAL AIRLINER
Mach 0.43
285 mph (460 km/h)

Cruising speeds
Sound travels at 768 mph (1,236 km/h), known as Mach 1. Small regional airliners cruise at around half the speed of sound. Concorde, a supersonic jet that retired in 2003, flew at twice the speed of sound.

Busiest airport on each continent

HARTSFIELD–JACKSON
90,039,280
(Atlanta, Georgia, U.S.A.)

HEATHROW
67,056,379
(London, U.K.)

TOKYO INTERNATIONAL
66,754,829
(Tokyo, Japan)

KINGFORD SMITH
32,900,000
(Sydney, Australia)

SÃO PAULO/GARULHOS
20,400,304
(São Paulo, Brazil)

TAMBO AIRPORT
18,400,000
(Jo'burg, S. Africa)

Busiest routes by passenger numbers
Some air routes are more popular with passengers than others. The Hong Kong–Taipei route is the busiest of all, with more than 2 million passengers every year.

5. MILAN–ROME: 1,518,767 PASSENGERS

4. MELBOURNE–SYDNEY: 1,563,106 PASSENGERS

3. LONDON–NEW YORK: 1,609,337 PASSENGERS

2. LOS ANGELES–NEW YORK: 1,697,593 PASSENGERS

1. HONG KONG–TAPEI: 2,138,484 PASSENGERS

AIRBUS A380
$300 million+

BOEING 747-8
$293–308 million

BOEING 767
$127.5–175 million

BOEING BUSINESS JET 3
$74.5–84.5 million

Priciest planes
Large passenger jets cost hundreds of millions of dollars to buy. The Airbus A380 and Boeing 747-8 are the most expensive, each costing around $300 million, twice as much as the next most expensive, the Boeing 767.

Busiest airport by passenger numbers
The world's busiest airport is Hartsfield-Jackson in Atlanta, U.S.A. More than 90 million passengers passed through it in 2008. In contrast, the busiest airport in Africa, Johannesburg's Tambo Airport, saw only around 18 million passengers.

DAY 1: ROTTERDAM, THE NETHERLANDS

The ship carries tulip bulbs, machinery parts, and furniture as it makes its way to New York.

DAY 7: NEW YORK, U.S.A.

A week later, the Rotterdam cargo is unloaded in New York and is replaced with aircraft parts, cars, and computers.

DAY 18: SANTOS, BRAZIL

In Santos, footwear, coffee, and timber are loaded on to the ship after the New York load is delivered.

Trip around the world

Above is a typical journey around the world for an average containership. They can cruise at 29 mph (46 km/h)—fast enough to cross an ocean in less than two weeks—and can carry 2,500 containers.

Shipping and Ports

Around 80% of goods by weight are transported by sea. At the end of 2009, the world's shipping fleet had a carrying capacity of almost 2 billion tonnes. The fleet includes more than 4,700 containerships, carrying 13 million standard shipping containers. People travel by sea, too. Around 12 million people go on a cruise each year, and millions more travel short distances by ferry.

Global seaborne trade in 2008 was around

8 billion tonnes

New York, U.S.A.

Los Angeles, U.S.A.
New Orleans, U.S.A.

Cartagena, Colombia

PACIFIC OCEAN

Santos, Brazil

ATLANTIC OCEAN

Busiest ports

Singapore is the world's busiest container port. It handled nearly 30 million standard shipping containers in 2008. The port of Shanghai was just behind with 28 million containers handled.

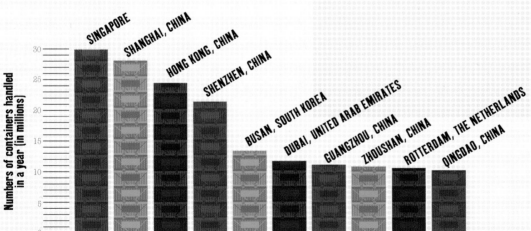

Numbers of containers handled in a year (in millions)

SINGAPORE • SHANGHAI, CHINA • HONG KONG, CHINA • SHENZHEN, CHINA • BUSAN, SOUTH KOREA • DUBAI, UNITED ARAB EMIRATES • GUANGZHOU, CHINA • ZHOUSHAN, CHINA • ROTTERDAM, THE NETHERLANDS • QINGDAO, CHINA

Types of ships

Cargo ships include containerships, which carry cargo in shipping containers, and bulk carriers, which carry unpackaged cargo such as coal. Passenger ships include cruise ships and ferries.

Knock Nevis

The biggest oil tanker ever built is the Knock Nevis. It is 1,503 ft (458 m) long, and can carry more than 564,000 tonnes of oil. It is now coming to the end of its working life and will be scrapped.

MSC Danit

At 1,200 ft. (365 m) long and 167 ft (51 m) wide, the MSC Danit is the world's biggest container ship. It can carry 14,000 shipping containers, weighing up to 165,000 tonnes.

DAY 38:
SHANGHAI, CHINA

It takes almost three weeks to reach China, where the Santos cargo is replaced with toys, clothes, and optical equipment.

DAY 42:
YOKOHAMA, JAPAN

The Shanghai cargo is delivered in Yokohama, where games consoles, cars, and office machinery are loaded.

DAY 57: LOS ANGELES, U.S.A.

The Japanese goods are delivered to Los Angeles, where paper, animal food, and scrap metal are loaded, as the ship continues its journey back to Rotterdam.

Containerships usually have a crew of around
30 people

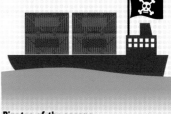

Pirates of the oceans

Piracy is a growing problem, particularly in the waters around Somalia in Africa. In 2008, 49 ships—including a supertanker—were hijacked, and 889 crew members were taken hostage by pirates worldwide.

Lost containers

Around 10,000 shipping containers fall off ships every year. When nearly 29,000 floating toys spilled out of a container in the Pacific Ocean in 1992, their movements helped scientists study ocean currents.

PACIFIC OCEAN

INDIAN OCEAN

SHIPPING FROM MAJOR PORTS
(Traffic in millions of tonnes)

400+	20–100
300–400	10–20
200–300	5–10
100–200	

World shipping routes

The busiest shipping routes in the world carry goods and materials between Europe, the Middle East, the Far East, and North America. The busiest routes of all carry more than 400 million tonnes of cargo per year.

Alternative container uses

The average life of a shipping container is around 10–15 years. Containers taken out of circulation have been converted into offices, homes, storage units, hotels, and museums. One was even used as a traveling home for an elephant!

MS Berge Stahl
The largest bulk carrier ship in the world is the MS Berge Stahl. It carries iron ore between Brazil and Rotterdam. A full load weighs around 364,000 tonnes.

Oasis of the Seas
The 100,000-tonne Oasis of the Seas is the biggest cruise ship. It carries up to 5,400 passengers, who are looked after by a crew of 2,165.

MV Ulysses
The world's largest car ferry is the MV Ulysses. It can carry 1,342 cars and 1,875 passengers.

Tourism and Travel

Tourism on a mass international scale began in the 1950s, and people have been traveling in ever greater numbers ever since. Today, most tourists travel between countries within their own region of the world. Only around one in five tourists choose to venture any farther and visit another continent. The most adventurous tourists are always looking for new places to go. A handful of wealthy travelers became the first space tourists in the early 2000s.

1.6 BILLION ···· 2020

1.05 BILLION ···· 2010

On the rise

The number of international tourists traveling every year has more than doubled since 1990. The number is predicted to continue growing at more than 4% per year, reaching 1.6 billion by 2020.

Top destinations

More tourists visit European countries than visit Asia, the Pacific, the Americas, Africa, and the Middle East combined. France is the world's favorite vacation destination, with nearly 82 million tourists in 2007.

FRANCE 81.9 MILLION

USA 56 MILLION

GERMANY 24.4 MILLION

MEXICO 21.4 MILLION

SPAIN 59.2 MILLION

CHINA 54.7 MILLION

UNITED KINGDOM 30.7 MILLION

ITALY 43.7 MILLION

UKRAINE 23.1 MILLION

TURKEY 22.2 MILLION

NUMBER OF VISITORS PER YEAR

Every year, a massive **16.64 million** people visit
Disney World, Florida—the most popular amusement park in the world

POLAND
40.8 MILLION

RUSSIA
28.4 MILLION

FRANCE
22.3 MILLION

UNITED STATES OF AMERICA
63.5 MILLION

MALAYSIA
30 MILLION

ITALY
23.3 MILLION

UNITED KINGDOM
66.5 MILLION

CHINA
31 MILLION

CZECH REPUBLIC
36.7 MILLION

GERMANY
77.4 MILLION

MOST FREQUENT TRAVELERS IN 2005

Travel bug

More than half of the world's tourists are Europeans. Germans top the list, followed by the British and the Americans. The numbers of tourists from growing economies are rising fast. Chinese tourists, who numbered only 720,000 in 1993, grew to 31 million by 2005.

The biggest earners

International tourism generated a global revenue of $944 million in 2008. It is the main source of income for some developing countries and island nations. The biggest earner is the U.S.A., even though it is not the most popular destination.

MONEY EARNED FROM TOURISM IN 2008
(in millions)

U.S.A.	SPAIN	FRANCE	ITALY	CHINA	U.K.	GERMANY	AUSTRALIA	AUSTRIA	TURKEY
$96.7	$57.8	$54.2	$42.7	$41.9	$37.6	$36	$22.2	$18.9	$18.5

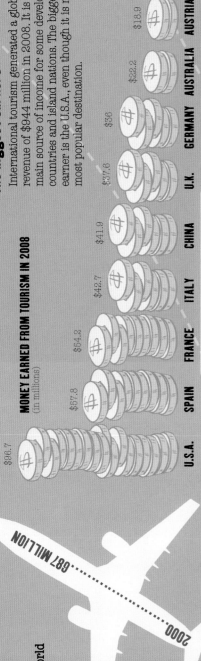

With **35.2 million**

visitors each year, Times Square is the most popular attraction in the world

687 MILLION
2000

435.5 MILLION
1990

278.1 MILLION
1980

105.8 MILLION
1970

63.3 MILLION
1960

25.3 MILLION
1950

Space cadet

Dennis Tito became the first space tourist in 2001, when he paid £13 million ($20 million) to visit the International Space Station.

In the Mail

Millions of people take letters to post offices or drop them into mail boxes every day. The mail is handled by more than 5.5 million mail workers worldwide, processing a staggering 445 billion individual pieces of mail every year. The mail is delivered using all types of vehicles, from bicycles and trucks to aircraft. There were even unsuccessful attempts in the 1930s to see if mail could be carried long distances by rocket.

Letters: 66%

Just under 300 billion letters are mailed worldwide every year. Most are mailed to addresses within the same country, but almost 5.5 billion are international mail, going from one country to another. Four billion of these are transported by aircraft (and are called airmail).

Advertising mail: 32%

You may have noticed the volume of advertising mail in your letterbox. More than 143 billion pieces of mail, selling everything from pizza to phones, are sent every year. In most cases, this type of mail is not requested by the receiver and is often called junk mail.

Packages: 2%

Usually taking longer to deliver than the other types of mail, packages make up more than 6.5 billion of the total worldwide mail. They take longer to process due to their different shapes, sizes, and weights.

Mail maths
These three boxes are sized to show the division of the three types of mail items. The majority of the mail is letters and postcards, just under a third are advertising items, and only 2% are packages.

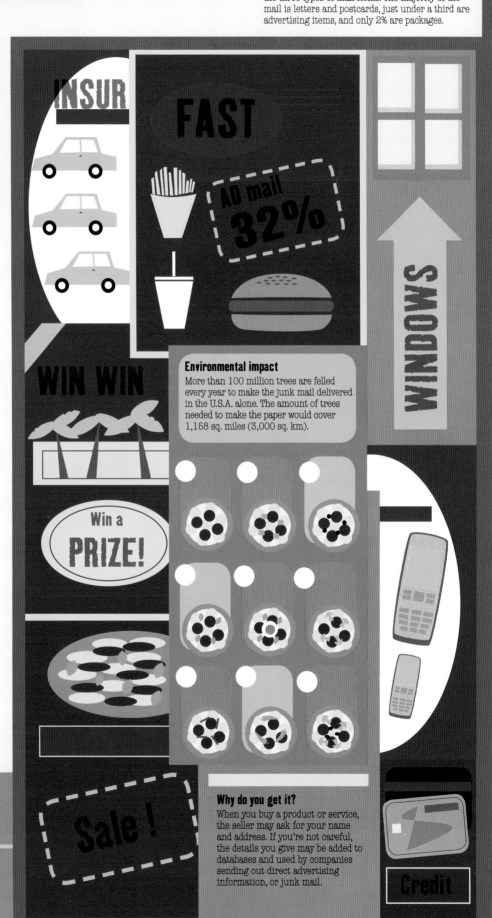

AD mail **32%**

Environmental impact
More than 100 million trees are felled every year to make the junk mail delivered in the U.S.A. alone. The amount of trees needed to make the paper would cover 1,158 sq. miles (3,000 sq. km).

Why do you get it?
When you buy a product or service, the seller may ask for your name and address. If you're not careful, the details you give may be added to databases and used by companies sending out direct advertising information, or junk mail.

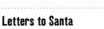

Letters to God

More than 1,000 letters arrive every year in Jerusalem, Israel, addressed to God. They are blessed before being stuffed into the cracks of the Western Wall of the Temple of Jerusalem. They are sent by people of all faiths from all over the world.

Letters to Santa

Children have been writing messages to Santa Claus for 800 years. Children mail 6 million Christmas letters every year. These special letters are collected and answered by Santa's mail elves in the North Pole.

Machine help

So many letters are sent every day that it is impossible to sort them all by hand. Machines sort mail wherever possible, using scanners and bar codes. The fastest machines can sort 50,000 letters per hour.

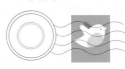

Letters
66%

A letter sent from Queensland, Australia, in 1889 to Aberdeen, Scotland, took a record **112 years** to arrive

Lost letters

Thousands of letters are delivered to the wrong addresses every day. Sometimes, the addressee is known to the receiver, who then delivers the letter, and there is no record of the error. However, some letters never reach the correct address and are lost forever.

12.4 million
letters are lost in the U.K. every year

Dead letters

Mail that cannot be delivered or returned to their senders are called dead letters. They are taken to mail recovery centers (often called "dead letter offices"), where staff open them and try to find a sender or addressee. If none can be found, the paper is destroyed to protect privacy and any valuable items are sold at a special postal auction.

The United States Postal Service handles **46%** of the world's total letter mail

Internet

Although the Internet is only 20 years old, for its 1.7 billion users it has become indispensable for communication, shopping, work, and entertainment. By linking computer networks across the globe into one huge global network, it gives easy access to information and allows nearly any type of data to be exchanged in an instant.

Online access

The number of people using the Internet varies enormously around the world. Each of these pie charts shows the percentage of people who have access to the Internet in a given region. In North America, more than 70% of the population is online, whereas in Africa the figure is just 7%. However, the number of Internet users in Africa is growing faster than anywhere else, except the Middle East.

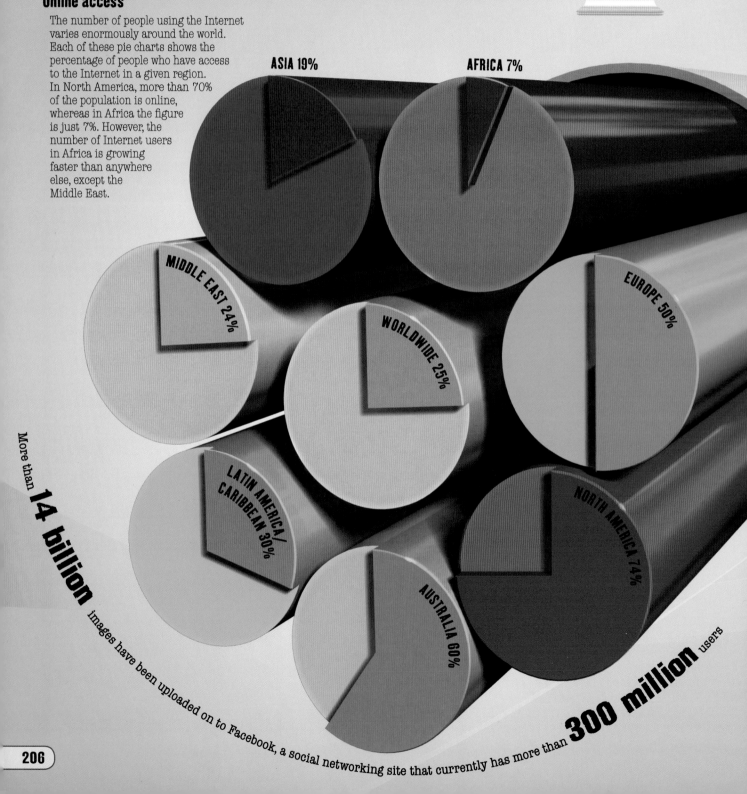

ASIA 19%

AFRICA 7%

MIDDLE EAST 24%

WORLDWIDE 25%

EUROPE 50%

LATIN AMERICA/ CARIBBEAN 30%

AUSTRALIA 60%

NORTH AMERICA 74%

More than **14 billion** images have been uploaded on to Facebook, a social networking site that currently has more than **300 million** users

28% of all webpages are written in English...

...**22%** are in Chinese

There are currently
150
webpages to every
person in the world

The average American spends **68 hours** a month online

Internet speed

At first, Internet users connected their computers to the Internet via an ordinary telephone line and a device called a modem. A modem changes data into sounds that can be sent along a telephone line. At most, dial-up access transfers 57,344 bits of data per second. Broadband Internet connections provided by digital telephone lines, satellites, or fiber-optic cables are much faster. They carry digital data without having to change it into sounds. Japanese Internet users enjoy the world's fastest broadband service, with an average download speed of 64 million bits per second.

GREECE 1.0

NEW ZEALAND 2.5

U.K. 2.6

U.S.A. 4.9

GERMANY 6.0

CANADA 7.6

FRANCE 17.6

FINLAND 21.7

SOUTH KOREA 49.5

JAPAN 63.6

AVERAGE BROADBAND SPEEDS
(million bits per second)

File sharing

One of the most popular online activities is file sharing—uploading music, images, and video files on to web sites for other people to download and enjoy. The most popular video sharing site, YouTube, exceeded 10 billion views in a single month for the first time in August 2009.

Piracy

The music industry loses billions of dollars per year because of Internet piracy—downloading music without paying for it. Up to 95% of all the music available online is downloaded from an illegal source, often websites set up to allow people to upload files for other people to download for free. A survey of 16 countries found that around 40 billion music files were shared illegally in 2008. It's not just music—movies and software are also commonly shared illegally. Since 2003, there have been an estimated 30,000 lawsuits filed against pirates, often resulting in heavy fines.

Confidence tricks

Fraud is a crime that involves deceiving people, usually to steal money. One-third of all online fraud involves persuading people to pay for goods that are never delivered. A further quarter sees fraudsters sell goods at auctions that don't live up to their description. But there is a whole range of more elaborate scams. Identity theft involves stealing someone else's personal details. Confidence fraud means conning someone into giving you money by pretending to be someone that you're not. Advance-fee fraudsters send e-mails that offer huge amounts of money in return for use of the recipient's bank details. Phishing scams try to con Internet users into giving out their bank details by posing as a financial institution.

- 33% Nondelivery of goods
- 25.5% Misrepresenting goods at auctions
- 9% Fraudulent use of a bank card/credit card
- 8% Confidence fraud
- 6% Altering data without permission, e.g., on a social networking profile
- 5% Buying goods with a check that is rejected by the seller's bank
- 3% Advance-fee fraud
- 2.5% Identity theft
- 2% Phishing
- 2% Conning users into installing malicious software
- 4% Other

Online fraud: the culprits

More than half of all online fraudsters operate from the U.S.A. More than 90% of the people who report online crimes are in the U.S.A., too, mainly in California, Texas, and Florida. But online crime is truly international, so cooperation between countries is essential to deal with it. Police forces in many countries now have dedicated cyber crime units.

- 66% United States
- 11% United Kingdom
- 7.5% Nigeria
- 3% Canada
- 3% China
- <1% South Africa
- <1% Ghana
- <1% Spain
- <1% Italy
- <1% Romania
- 8% Other

Viruses and malware

In 2008, one Internet security company claimed to have discovered 1,656,227 online threats—viruses and other harmful software. This was more than double the number discovered in 2007.

Malware is the name for all malicious computer codes that damage unprotected machines. Viruses are a specific type of malware that infect computers and then create new versions of themselves to infect even more computers. Unlike real viruses, which occur naturally, Internet viruses are created by people and released deliberately on to the Internet.

COUNTRIES OF ORIGIN

- United States
- Brazil
- Turkey
- India
- Poland
- South Korea
- Russia
- Romania
- Spain
- Czech Republic
- Rest of the world

Chart axis values: 35%, 7%, 7%, 2.5%, 2.5%, 4.5%, 5%, 5.5%, 6%, 10%, 25%

Who sends the spam?

Roughly 65% of spam e-mails originate from just 10 countries. The U.S.A. tops the list of spam-producing countries, accounting for 25% of the nuisance e-mails sent at the beginning of 2009. The U.S.A. is having some success in reducing the numbers of spam e-mails originating from within its borders, but the numbers coming from some other countries are increasing. Spammers often hijack unprotected home computers, using them to send out millions of e-mails without their owners suspecting that anything is wrong. Just one response per 10 million e-mails is enough to make the venture profitable.

The **electricity** used to send all the spam e-mails sent worldwide in one year is equivalent to the yearly output of **four** large power plants

Online Crime

Online crime, also called cyber crime, is one of the fastest-growing types of criminal activity. It costs businesses an estimated $1 trillion per year. Cyber criminals steal money and valuable information, such as bank and credit card details, spread damaging software, or send nuisance e-mails without even having to leave home.

Spam

Spam is electronic junk mail—unwanted e-mails sent out in large numbers to advertise products or dupe people into falling for money-making scams. Spammers send millions of e-mails at a time to computers all over the world. In a bad month, up to 97% of all e-mails sent worldwide are spam. Over the course of 2008, an incredible 62 trillion spam e-mails were sent.

Sports Watch

Sports have always been entertaining, and watching the strongest, fastest, most skilful athletes on the planet compete can be exhilarating. Although nothing compares with watching sports live among the cheering fans, TV allows audiences of millions to watch their favorite teams play around the world. Sports are also big business in the 21st century, and global brands clamor to sponsor the best players.

Most watched sports on TV

Football and Formula One events always attract a global audience. However, an enormous home audience and a tense game propeled one of China's most popular sports—volleyball—to the top of the 2008 chart with 184 million viewers. Meanwhile, the 2008 Super Bowl was the most watched sporting event ever in the U.S.A.

SPORTING EVENTS WITH THE BIGGEST TV AUDIENCES, 2008

Volleyball
Summer Olympics game between China and Cuba (184 million viewers)

Track and field
Men's 100 m final at the Summer Olympics (178 million viewers)

Soccer
European Championship final between Germany and Spain (166 million viewers)

1972: VALERI BORZOV

1984: CARL LEWIS

1992: LINFORD CHRISTIE

95 m   96 m   97 m

$110 million

AMOUNT EARNED IN 2009

$45 million

$45 million

$45 million

$42 million

TIGER WOODS   **KOBE BRYANT**   **MICHAEL JORDAN**   **KIMI RAIKKONEN**   **DAVID BECKHAM**

Show me the money!

Modern sport stars earn megabucks, but not all of the money is from their regular jobs alone. The huge amounts shown to the left combine salaries, endorsements, prize money, bonuses, and licensing income in just one year. Tiger Woods has earned almost $900 million during his 13-year golf career. Branding helps Michael Jordan earn $85 per minute, seven years after his last professional basketball game.

Football
Super Bowl; New England Patriots vs. New York Giants (104 million viewers)

Soccer
Champions League final between Manchester United and Chelsea (98 million viewers)

Formula One
World Championships; Brazillian Grand Prix (80 million viewers)

Tennis
Wimbledon men's finals between Roger Federer and Rafael Nadal (23 million viewers)

Ice hockey
World Championship final between Canada and Russia (23 million viewers)

Basketball
NBA finals between Boston Celtics and Los Angeles Lakers (20 million viewers)

Motorcycling
MotoGP World Championship in Catalunya, Spain (19 million viewers)

Golf
U.S. Masters final day in Augusta, Georgia (19 million viewers)

NASCAR
Daytona 500 car race, located in Daytona Beach, Florida (18 million viewers)

Baseball
Final between Philadephia Phillies and Tampa Bay Rays (17 million viewers)

Cycling
Stage 9 of the grueling Tour de France (14 million viewers)

Cricket
Indian Premier League final between Rajasthan and Chennai (12 million viewers)

= 1 million viewers

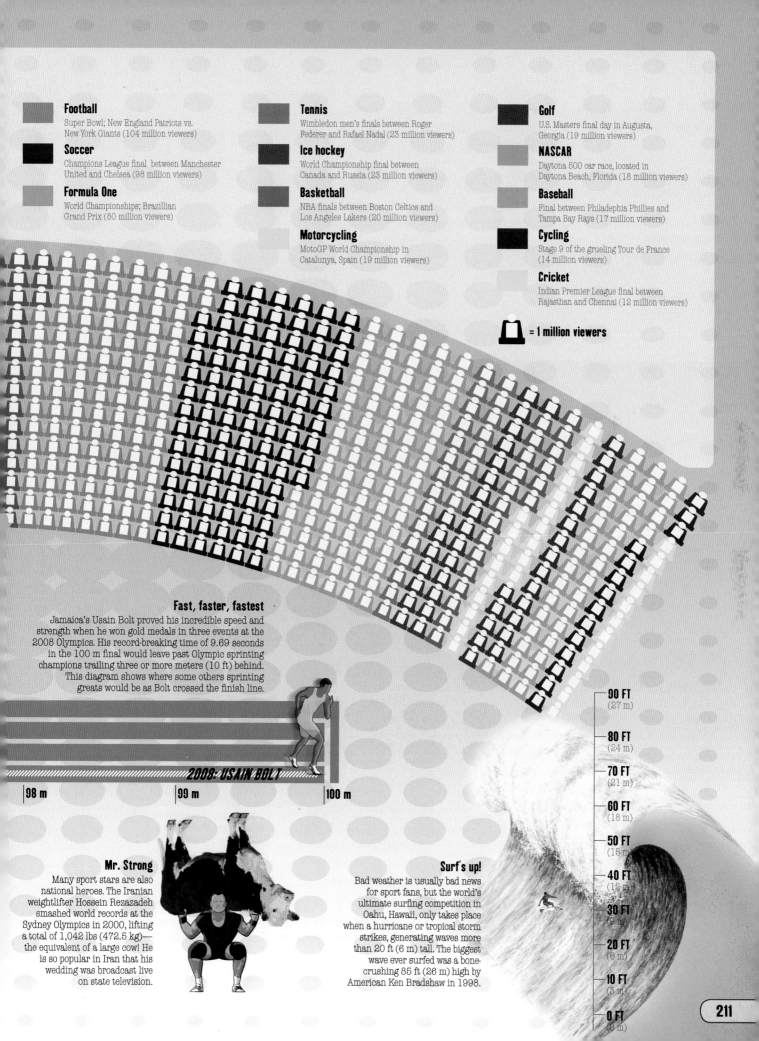

Fast, faster, fastest
Jamaica's Usain Bolt proved his incredible speed and strength when he won gold medals in three events at the 2008 Olympics. His record-breaking time of 9.69 seconds in the 100 m final would leave past Olympic sprinting champions trailing three or more meters (10 ft) behind. This diagram shows where some others sprinting greats would be as Bolt crossed the finish line.

2008: USAIN BOLT

| 98 m | 99 m | 100 m |

Mr. Strong
Many sport stars are also national heroes. The Iranian weightlifter Hossein Rezazadeh smashed world records at the Sydney Olympics in 2000, lifting a total of 1,042 lbs (472.5 kg)—the equivalent of a large cow! He is so popular in Iran that his wedding was broadcast live on state television.

Surf's up!
Bad weather is usually bad news for sport fans, but the world's ultimate surfing competition in Oahu, Hawaii, only takes place when a hurricane or tropical storm strikes, generating waves more than 20 ft (6 m) tall. The biggest wave ever surfed was a bone-crushing 85 ft (26 m) high by American Ken Bradshaw in 1998.

90 FT (27 m)
80 FT (24 m)
70 FT (21 m)
60 FT (18 m)
50 FT (15 m)
40 FT (12 m)
30 FT (9 m)
20 FT (6 m)
10 FT (3 m)
0 FT (0 m)

211

Movie Magic

The global movie industry is dominated by the movie studios in Hollywood, California, and Bollywood. Big-budget Hollywood movies top the box-office charts around the world and generate billions of dollars in total revenue. Bollywood produces the most movies and has an enormous home audience. The world's largest potential audience lies in China where moviegoing is becoming more popular and the movie industry is thriving.

Avatar, the highest-grossing movie of all time, made **$2.2 billion** in its opening eight weeks

Production costs per movie

Hollywood has the highest average production costs, but the salaries of actors and technical staff can make up as much as 75% of a Bollywood movie's production budget. In China, filmmakers typically receive about 7% of a movie's budget from the Chinese government, but they sometimes struggle to secure the rest to make big-budget movies.

HOLLYWOOD $13.6 MILLION

CHINA $7 MILLION

BOLLYWOOD $1.3 MILLION

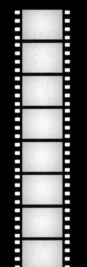

The big three

HOLLYWOOD, U.S.A.

The U.S. movie industry has been based in Hollywood, California, since the very first silent movies of the 1910s and 1920s and made the world's first "talkie" (talking movie) in 1927. It still leads the world in developing new filmmaking techniques and has produced some of the most expensive movies in history.

BOLLYWOOD, INDIA

The most famous part of the Indian movie industry based its name on its American equivalent, changing the "H" for a "B" after Bombay (Mumbai), the industry's home city. As in Hollywood, the first Indian movies were silent, but today's Bollywood movies are famous for their singing, dancing, colors, and costume changes.

CHINA

The first Chinese movie, called *The Difficult Couple*, was filmed in 1913. During the 1920s, U.S. filmmakers trained Chinese filmmakers in Shanghai, and the industry grew slowly for most of the 20th century. More recently, government control over the industry has relaxed, making it easier to make movies.

Nollywood

Nigeria's booming movie industry—known as "Nollywood"—produces more than 17 movies every week. Although the country has just four theaters, a huge DVD and home video market in Nigeria and neighboring countries generates around $250 million in revenue every year.

Top moviegoing nations

Around one-quarter of New Zealand's population goes to the movies once a month or more, and the average person visits the movie theater almost nine times a year. Contrast this with China, where the average person goes to the movies only once every six years. The U.S.A. boasts 39,476 screens (one for every 7,700 people), which is more than the whole of the European Union put together.

MOVIE THEATER TRIPS PER PERSON PER YEAR

- **NEW ZEALAND: 8.9 TRIPS**
- **AUSTRALIA: 7 TRIPS**
- **ICELAND: 4.6 TRIPS**
- **CANADA/IRELAND: 4.2 TRIPS (each)**

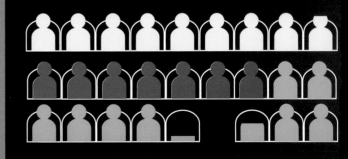

Marketing costs per movie

Hollywood movie studios often spend enormous amounts to attract audiences, usually around half the cost of making the movie. Television, print, poster, radio, and online advertising usually take 75% of the marketing budget.

CHINA
$2.3 MILLION

BOLLYWOOD, INDIA
$500,000

HOLLYWOOD, U.S.A.
$32.7 MILLION

Revenues

Beyond the box office, movies make money through home viewing, licensing, and merchandising. Although DVD sales are falling, online DVD rental and movie downloads are growing. These revenue sources are threatened by piracy, particularly in China and India, where pirate DVDs are much cheaper than movie tickets. Piracy is thought to cost the Indian movie industry $1 billion every year.

Tickets sold

The world spends almost $30 billion on movie tickets every year. China leads the way with 1,497 million tickets, but the U.S.A. (1,446 million) and India (1,341 million) are not far behind. The growing number of 3-D movies is expected to keep sales rising by about 5% annually, as more people pay higher ticket prices for an experience that they can't have at home.

Movies produced

Movies are made so fast in Bollywood that actors may shoot as many as four different movies at a time using the same sets. The Chinese movie industry is growing rapidly and now makes double the amount of movies that it did in 2004.

CHINA
456 MOVIES PER YEAR

HOLLYWOOD
485 MOVIES PER YEAR

BOLLYWOOD
1,091 MOVIES PER YEAR

And the winner is...

No movie industry would be complete without its own awards show—and the global audiences of millions watching them. The winners may be chosen by past victors, expert panels, or the fans themselves.

The Oscars

The Academy Awards, popularly called "the Oscars," began in 1929. Since then, more than 2,700 awards have been handed out. The gold-plated Oscar trophy— a knight holding a sword, standing on a reel of film— weighs as much as a newborn baby. The movies *Ben Hur*, *Titanic*, and *Lord of the Rings: the Return of the King* share the record of 11 Oscars each.

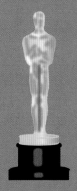

IIFA trophy

The International Indian Film Awards (IIFA) take place in a different country every year. Despite being held for the first time in 2000, the IIFA already attracts a total global audience of 350 million. The fans decide who get the trophies, which display a Sun-influenced design. The 2003 movie *Kal No Naaa Ho* (*Tomorrow May Not Come*) broke records with 14 IFAA awards.

Golden Horse

The Taiwanese Golden Horse Awards are the most prestigious of the Chinese-language movie industry. The horse-shaped statuettes are awarded to movies from Taiwan, Malaysia, Singapore, Hong Kong, and China. The record haul goes to *Gun Gun Hong Chen* (*Red Dust*), with eight wins at the 1990 awards show.

El Mariachi, made in 1992 in Mexico, is the most profitable movie ever—it only cost $7,000 to make, but took more than

$2 million

in sales worldwide

Media

In the past, it could take hours or days for news to travel, but now we can read about events right away or even watch them happening. The various means of mass communication are referred to collectively as the media, and include TV, radio, newspapers, and the Internet. The media is dominated by a small number of massive international companies, who each own a variety of publishers, broadcasting companies, and news websites.

$59.1 billion
1. Walt Disney
The world's biggest media and entertainment organization, the Walt Disney Company was founded in 1923 by brothers Roy and Walt Disney. The company's wide-ranging activities include movies, TV, publishing, and the world-famous Disney theme parks.

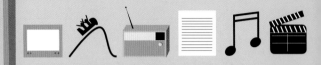

$50.1 billion
4. Time Warner
The Time Warner media group was formed in the 1990s when the magazine publisher Time, Inc. merged with the movie studio and music producer Warner Communications. The AOL Internet service provider was also part of the organization until it was sold in 2009.

Newspapers
The best-selling newspapers sell millions of copies every day. The world's most avid newspaper readers are the Japanese. Three times more newspapers are delivered to the average Japanese home than in the U.S.A., and nearly 10 times more than in France.

Top 10 newspapers by circulation (in millions):
1 **Yomiuri Shimbun** (Japan) 14.1
2 **The Asahi Shimbun** (Japan) 12.1
3 **Mainichi Shimbun** (Japan) 5.6
4 **Nihon Keizai Shimbun** (Japan) 4.6
5 **Chunichi Shimbun** (Japan) 4.5
6 **Das Bild** (Germany) 3.5
7 **Reference News** (China) 3.2
8 **The Times of India** (India) 3.1
9 **The Sun** (U.K.) 3.0
10 **The People's Daily** (China) 2.8

TOP FIVE MEDIA COMPANIES' INTERESTS
- Theme parks
- TV
- Radio
- Movies
- Telecoms
- Sports
- Magazines
- Music
- Online
- Print media

Magazines
A more glossy type of print media, magazines are usually published weekly or monthly. News magazines concentrate on issues in the news, often dealing with them in greater depth than a newspaper can. Special interest magazines deal with one particular subject, such as sports, entertainment, or fashion.

Top 10 magazines by circulation (in millions):
1 **National Geographic** (U.S.A.) 6.7
2 **Time** (U.S.A.) 3.3
3 **Newsweek** (U.S.A./U.K.) 2.7
4 **US News & World Report** (U.S.A.) 1.7
5 **The Economist** (U.K.) 1.4
6 **India Today** (India) 1.1
7 **Veja** (Brazil) 1.08
8 **The New Yorker** (U.S.A.) 1.05
9 **Der Spiegel** (Germany) 1.03

Media through time
The first news sheets were published in China in the 8th century. They were handwritten on silk. Over time, the world gradually developed into the multimedia society that we live in today.

Radio
Radio was the first of the broadcast media. Today, it is the most popular news medium in developing countries. Radio is going digital, with the introduction of Digital Audio Broadcasting (DAB), which is growing in popularity, especially in Europe.

c. 3100 BCE	c. 50 BCE	c. 748	1455	1839	1920s

Writing	**Paper**	**Newspapers**	**Gutenburg press**	**Photography**	**Public radio broadcasting**
Invented more than 5,000 years ago in Mesopotamia.	Invented in China, at first as wrapping paper and then to write on.	First printed in China on silk sheets, giving government news.	Invented by Johannes Gutenberg and revolutionized printing.	Invented by Frenchman Louis Daguerre and Englisman William Fox Talbot.	Began in the U.S.A. and Europe, with music and news.

2. News Corp

$58.9 billion

This massive global corporation owns lots of TV channels, book publishers, newspapers, magazines, sports organizations, movie studios, record labels, and digital media. It was created in 1980 by Australian business tycoon Rupert Murdoch.

3. Comcast

$57.7 billion

The Comcast name amalgamates "communication" and "broadcast"—its main activities—into one word. Comcast began in cable television in the U.S.A. in the 1960s, before branching out to supply telephone and broadband Internet services to its U.S. subscribers.

5. Vivendi

$45.7 billion

This French media group operates worldwide in TV, movies, telecommunications, music publishing, and video games. It was formed in 1998 from a company with interests in water, energy, transportation, and construction, which then moved into media activities.

Television

Many TV news channels reach huge audiences. The most popular is BBC World News—a 24-hour news and information channel that broadcasts to 292 million households in more than 200 countries. In second place, U.S. channel CNN reaches 200 million households, while Qatar-based Al Jazeera broadcasts to 150 million.

Online

The Web is an increasingly popular and convenient source of news. One measure of the success of news websites is the number of people who look at a site for the first time each month. These numbers are called monthly uniques.

Top 10 news sites by monthly uniques:
1 **Yahoo News** 42 million
2 **CNN Digital** 38 million
3 **MSNBC Digital** 36 million
4 **AOL News** 25 million
5 **NYTimes** 21 million
6 **Fox News Digital** 17 million
7 **Tribune** 16 million
8 **ABCNews Digital** 14 million
9 **Google news** 14 million
10 **Gannett News** 12 million

Cell phones

enable users to access up-to-the-minute news coverage and to submit news and photographs taken with, and sent via, their phones

---

1936

TV broadcasting
Began with shows broadcast by the BBC in London, England.

1962

Telstar
Launched into Earth's orbit as the first communication satellite.

1977

Personal computers
Invented with the introduction of the Commodore PET.

1979

Cellular phones
Developed in the 1980s, allowing people to make phone calls on the move.

1990

World Wide Web
Invented by Tim Berners-Lee and made available to the public.

1991

Cells go digital
Second-generation cellular phones introduced.

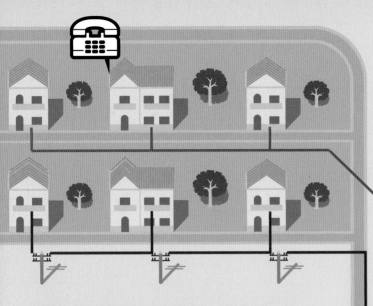

Calling from a home phone

The telephone network can connect any telephone line to any other. There are so many phones over such a wide area that calls must travel through a series of exchanges—hubs that electronically connect one telephone line to another.

Local telephone exchange
The call first goes to a local telephone exchange. It is carried there as an electronic signal along copper wires underground or strung between telephone poles overhead or as pulses of light along underground fiber-optic cables.

Telephone Networks

When you make an international telephone call, whether from a home phone or a cell phone, the signal travels through a huge network of cables, radio links, and satellites to reach its destination. It may travel thousands of miles, but it gets there—and is relayed back—in the blink of an eye. Here are the main stages of that journey.

Main exchange
Calls are relayed from the local exchange to a main exchange located in a nearby town or city. If the call is destined for a nearby city, it is forwarded from one main exchange to another.

System of cells
Each cell has a radio antenna, called a base station, that picks up signals from nearby cell phones and sends them to the cellular switching center.

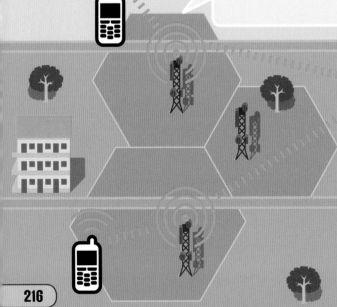

Cellular switching center
The cellular switching center is a type of exchange. If the call is for a nearby cell phone, it will be directed back to the relevant base station. If the call needs to go farther afield or to a home phone, it goes to the main exchange.

Calling from a mobile phone

A mobile phone call uses the same main exchange as a landline, but to get there it is routed through the mobile network. The mobile network divides the land into areas called cells. The size of each cell depends on the type of terrain and the number of people it contains.

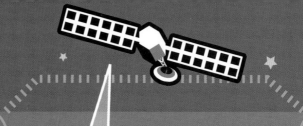

Communications satellite

Orbiting 22,370 miles (36,000 km) above the equator, a satellite receives the radio signal and transmits it to a different location. Communication satellites follow a geostationary orbit, meaning that they always stay over the same location on the ground. This is so that dishes on Earth can be fixed in one position.

Satellite earth station

A telephone call going a very long distance, especially over land, may be sent to a satellite earth station. From here, the signal is sent via a satellite dish to a communication satellite orbiting Earth.

Satellite earth station

In the destination country, a satellite earth station receives the radio signal. It is changed back into an electronic signal and sent along wires or into pulses of light and sent down optical fibers.

Telecommunication tower

International calls are sent from the main exchange to a dish antenna at the top of a tall telecommunication tower. The antenna sends a microwave radio signal to a satellite earth station or an exchange near the coast.

Satellite or submarine signal?

Telephone calls for overseas are most often connected by submarine cable because it is cheaper and more reliable than using a satellite. A call from the U.S.A. to Europe, for example, might travel 3,700 miles (6,000 km) end to end if linked by submarine cable. The same call connected by satellite has to travel 12 times farther—22,370 miles (36,000 km) up and then the same distance back down.

CONNECTIONS

— Overhead cable

— Underground optical fiber

⋯ Microwaves

— Submarine cable

Coastal exchange

A coastal exchange on the other side of the sea receives the call from the submarine cable and sends it on through a chain of telephone exchanges, as before.

Coastal exchange

A telephone call going overseas may be sent by submarine (underwater) cable—a fiber-optic cable laid on the seabed. A telephone exchange located near the coast sends the signal on its way.

By the end of 2009, **4.6 billion** cell phones were in use worldwide.

Satellites

Anything that orbits a planet is known as a satellite. The Moon is a natural satellite of Earth. Thousands of artifical satellites also circle Earth, doing all types of jobs. Some photograph clouds and storms to help with weather forecasting, others relay telephone calls, Internet traffic, and television shows from place to place. The U.S. space agency NASA uses a fleet of satellites to keep in touch with its spacecraft, while orbiting telescopes such as Hubble use the clear view above Earth's atmosphere to study distant galaxies.

Rocket power

Satellites are launched on rockets. When a satellite reaches orbit, it is traveling at the speed its rocket boosted it to. In space, there is nothing to stop it, so it just keeps going. Gravity pulls the satellite toward Earth, but the satellite is moving forward, so its falling path matches the curve of Earth's surface. The satellite stays in orbit because its forward speed balances the pull of Earth's gravity.

3. Old satellites

Satellites in low orbits are gradually slowed down by the faint wisps of atmosphere that they fly through. As they slow down, they orbit lower and lower and eventually spiral into the atmosphere and burn up. Satellites at higher altitudes may remain in orbit, but most only function for around 15 years.

With a fleet of around **1,400**, Russia owns nearly half of all the satellites in orbit

2. Into orbit

A satellite takes around 8 minutes to go from the launchpad into orbit. To get a satellite into space, a large amount of fuel is needed—the weight of a rocket on launch is mostly made up of the fuel that it will burn on its journey.

4% satellite
6% rocket structure

90% fuel

PROPORTIONAL WEIGHT OF THE ROCKET

1. Ready for liftoff

Putting a satellite into orbit is an expensive task. Tens of millions of dollars are spent on the launch and on insuring the mission against the risk of accidents. These costs are dwarfed by that of the satellite itself, which may run into hundreds of millions of dollars.

LAUNCH COSTS

- **Insurance** $80 million
- **Launch** $80 million
- **Satellite itself** $250 million

A satellite in low Earth orbit moves through space at **17,400 mph** (28,000 km/h)

Geostationary orbit

A satellite 22,370 miles (36,000 km) above the equator goes as fast as Earth turns. This means that it stays above the same spot on the ground all the time, but because it is far away, its signal can reach a wide area. Communication satellites often use this orbit.

Highly elliptical orbit

Countries near the poles use this orbit for communication satellites. While a satellite in this orbit is far from Earth, it travels slowly over the polar regions. Then it swoops around Earth fast and starts the long, slow part of its next orbit.

Medium Earth orbit

Medium Earth orbit extends from a height of around 620 to 12,430 miles (1,000 to 20,000 km). Medium Earth orbits are mainly used by navigation satellites, such as GPS (see below).

Polar orbit

Some satellites orbit from pole to pole. Polar orbits are used by satellites observing Earth, including some weather satellites, because this orbit takes satellites over Earth's entire surface.

Low Earth orbit

Satellites in low Earth orbit are between 186 and 620 miles (300 and 1,000 km) above the ground. The International Space Station and the Hubble Space Telescope both use this orbit.

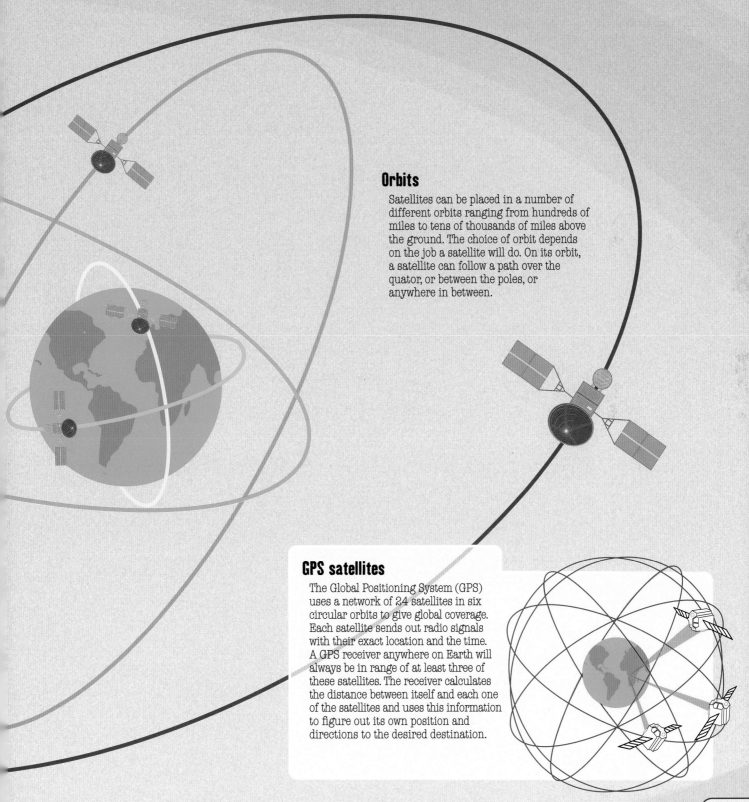

Orbits

Satellites can be placed in a number of different orbits ranging from hundreds of miles to tens of thousands of miles above the ground. The choice of orbit depends on the job a satellite will do. On its orbit, a satellite can follow a path over the quator, or between the poles, or anywhere in between.

GPS satellites

The Global Positioning System (GPS) uses a network of 24 satellites in six circular orbits to give global coverage. Each satellite sends out radio signals with their exact location and the time. A GPS receiver anywhere on Earth will always be in range of at least three of these satellites. The receiver calculates the distance between itself and each one of the satellites and uses this information to figure out its own position and directions to the desired destination.

International Space Station

The International Space Station (ISS) is the largest structure ever built in space. Orbiting Earth at an altitude of around 211 miles (340 km), it is the ongoing work of 16 countries, all working together to complete this ambitious project. Construction began in 1998 and is expected to be completed by 2011. It is assembled from dozens of parts that are launched separately and then linked together by astronauts.

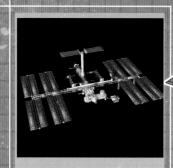

Completion

After more than 80 flights of U.S. Space Shuttles and Russian rockets, the International Space Station will be completed in 2011. It will measure 243 ft (74 m) by 356 ft (108.5 m), with as much space inside as a Boeing 747 passenger cabin.

ISS structure

When the International Space Station is complete, it will consist of around a dozen cylindrical modules, where the crew live and work, connected to a main beam called the truss structure. Solar panels and radiators, which keep the space station cool, are attached to the ends of the same beam.

Zarya

The Zarya (Sunrise) Module, also known as the Functional Cargo Block, was built by Russia and was the first piece of this massive feat to be launched into space, in November 1998.

Truss structure

Truss structure

Quest airlock

Astronauts will have made 1,705 hours of spacewalks from the Space Shuttle and airlocks like Quest to complete the station.

Solar panels

Electrical power is provided by solar panels. They contain an impressive 262,400 individual solar cells and cover a total area of around 2,500 sq. m (26,910 sq. ft). Together, they generate more than 100 kilowatts from sunlight.

Radiator

Node 3

Tranquillity, or Node 3, is attached to Node 1 and houses a seven-window dome called a cupola. From here, the robotic arm Canadarm 2 will be operated.

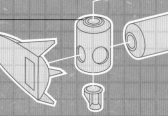

A total of **52 computers** control all the systems on board the International Space Station

Docking at the ISS

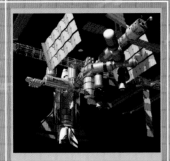

Docking ports allow spacecraft such as the Space Shuttle and European ATV supply craft to link up with the space station. A Russian Soyuz spacecraft is always docked with the station to serve as a lifeboat in an emergency.

Life on board

The crew's daily activities at the ISS are planned in detail before they leave Earth. Life on board is split between scientific experiments, maintenance work, and exercise—essential to stop muscles from wasting away in the weightlessness of space.

Space clothing

Everyday wear in the space station consists of T-shirt and shorts or pants. To make spacewalks, astronauts don a 280-lb (127-kg) spacesuit that feels as light as a feather in microgravity, and comes with its own special underwear.

Space food

The crew on board the ISS eat three meals a day. Today's astronauts can pick and choose what they eat, from cereal and fresh fruits to meat and vegetables. Some food is fresh, some packaged in foil or cans, and some is dehydrated and needs to be mixed with water.

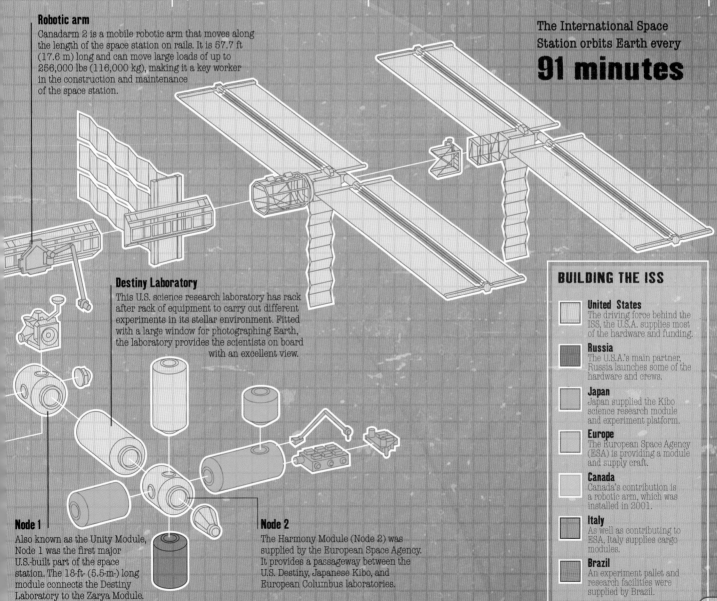

Robotic arm
Canadarm 2 is a mobile robotic arm that moves along the length of the space station on rails. It is 57.7 ft (17.6 m) long and can move large loads of up to 256,000 lbs (116,000 kg), making it a key worker in the construction and maintenance of the space station.

The International Space Station orbits Earth every

91 minutes

Destiny Laboratory
This U.S. science research laboratory has rack after rack of equipment to carry out different experiments in its stellar environment. Fitted with a large window for photographing Earth, the laboratory provides the scientists on board with an excellent view.

Node 1
Also known as the Unity Module, Node 1 was the first major U.S.-built part of the space station. The 18-ft- (5.5-m-) long module connects the Destiny Laboratory to the Zarya Module.

Node 2
The Harmony Module (Node 2) was supplied by the European Space Agency. It provides a passageway between the U.S. Destiny, Japanese Kibo, and European Columbus laboratories.

BUILDING THE ISS

United States
The driving force behind the ISS, the U.S.A. supplies most of the hardware and funding.

Russia
The U.S.A.'s main partner, Russia launches some of the hardware and crews.

Japan
Japan supplied the Kibo science research module and experiment platform.

Europe
The European Space Agency (ESA) is providing a module and supply craft.

Canada
Canada's contribution is a robotic arm, which was installed in 2001.

Italy
As well as contributing to ESA, Italy supplies cargo modules.

Brazil
An experiment pallet and research facilities were supplied by Brazil.

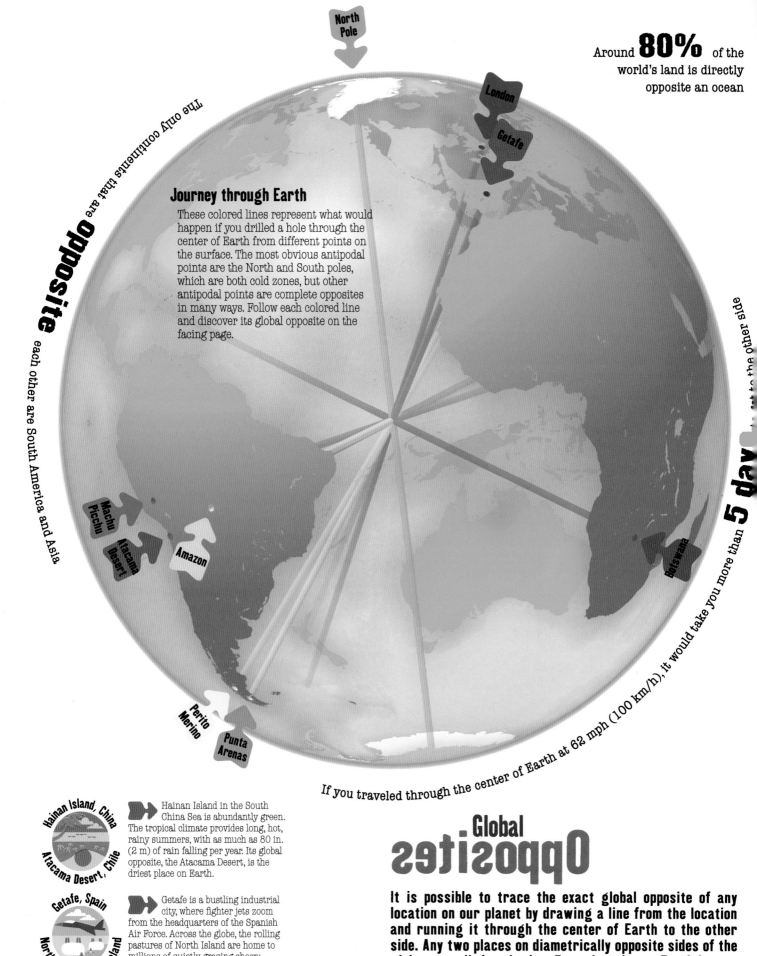

North Pole

Around **80%** of the world's land is directly opposite an ocean

The only continents that are **opposite** each other are South America and Asia

London

Getafe

Journey through Earth

These colored lines represent what would happen if you drilled a hole through the center of Earth from different points on the surface. The most obvious antipodal points are the North and South poles, which are both cold zones, but other antipodal points are complete opposites in many ways. Follow each colored line and discover its global opposite on the facing page.

Machu Picchu

Atacama Desert

Amazon

Botswana

Perito Merino

Punta Arenas

If you traveled through the center of Earth at 62 mph (100 km/h), it would take you more than **5 days** to get to the other side

Hainan Island, China
Atacama Desert, Chile

Hainan Island in the South China Sea is abundantly green. The tropical climate provides long, hot, rainy summers, with as much as 80 in. (2 m) of rain falling per year. Its global opposite, the Atacama Desert, is the driest place on Earth.

Getafe, Spain
North Island, New Zealand

Getafe is a bustling industrial city, where fighter jets zoom from the headquarters of the Spanish Air Force. Across the globe, the rolling pastures of North Island are home to millions of quietly grazing sheep; exporting sheep meat is one of New Zealand's largest industries.

Global Opposites

It is possible to trace the exact global opposite of any location on our planet by drawing a line from the location and running it through the center of Earth to the other side. Any two places on diametrically opposite sides of the globe are called antipodes. Every location on Earth has an antipodal point.

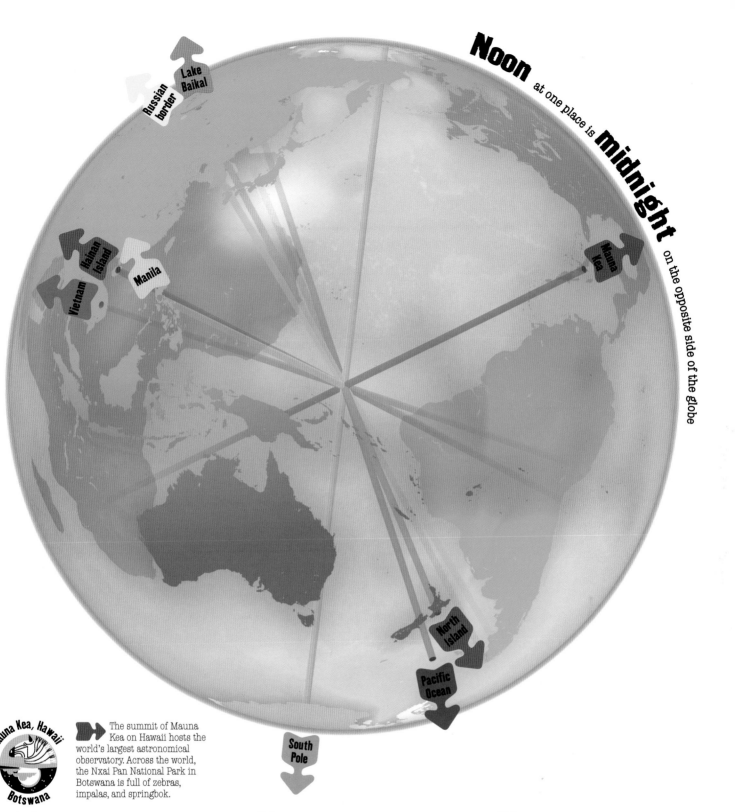

Lake Baikal

Russian border

Vietnam

Hainan Island

Manila

Mauna Kea

North Island

Pacific Ocean

South Pole

Mauna Kea, Hawaii / Botswana — The summit of Mauna Kea on Hawaii hosts the world's largest astronomical observatory. Across the world, the Nxai Pan National Park in Botswana is full of zebras, impalas, and springbok.

Russian border / Perito Merino, Argentina — The Yenisey river basin in Russia is a green and fertile land where many animals live. By contrast, the icy and vast Perito Merino Glacier is located among rugged mountains and glacial lakes.

Dak Lak, Vietnam / Machu Picchu, Peru — The coffee-growing regions of Vietnam are thriving, producing up to one million tonnes a year. The ancient ruins of Machu Picchu lie atop a steep Andean mountain, 8,000 ft (2,430 m) high.

Lake Baikal, Russia / Punta Arenas, Chile — Mini submarines explore the world's deepest freshwater lake. Across the globe—near the very tip of South America—Punta Arenas is a starting point for explorers to Antarctica.

North Pole / South Pole — Though they share a cold climate, the poles have their differences. The North Pole is home to polar bears, while penguins live in the South Pole. The South Pole is much colder than the North because it sits on land.

Manila, Philippines / Amazon, Brazil — Manila in the Philippines is one of the most densely populated cities in the world. Shoot across the globe and you are in the Amazon rain forest, where you will find lush green trees and a huge diversity of animal life.

London, U.K. / Pacific Ocean — London's busy streets are packed with commuters and tourists, miles from the sea. Its global opposite is the immense Pacific Ocean—a habitat for humpback whales and giant tube worms.

THE World IN ONE Day

CONNECTIONS

Whether you're a globe-trotter or sofa-surfer, technology has made the planet a smaller place, and information travels fast.

30 new **extrasolar planets** were announced in one day on October 2009—the most ever

There are **5 people** in **space,** all on the International Space Station

Actor Harrison Ford earned **$550,847** a day on the fourth *Indiana Jones* movie

Around **10.7 million** people go to the **movies** in India, more people than live in **Paris, France**

4 official international **soccer games** are contested somewhere around the world

63,000 sea travelers journey to and from British **ports**

545,780,360 newspapers are circulated

Popstar **Madonna** earned **$301,370** per day in 2009

81,096 passenger **flights** are made very day, with around **200 million** airline **meals** served

9,589 people spend **30 minutes** each on the **London Eye** in London, England— it can carry **800** people at a time

76,712 people go to **Niagra Falls** to see the most powerful waterfall in North America

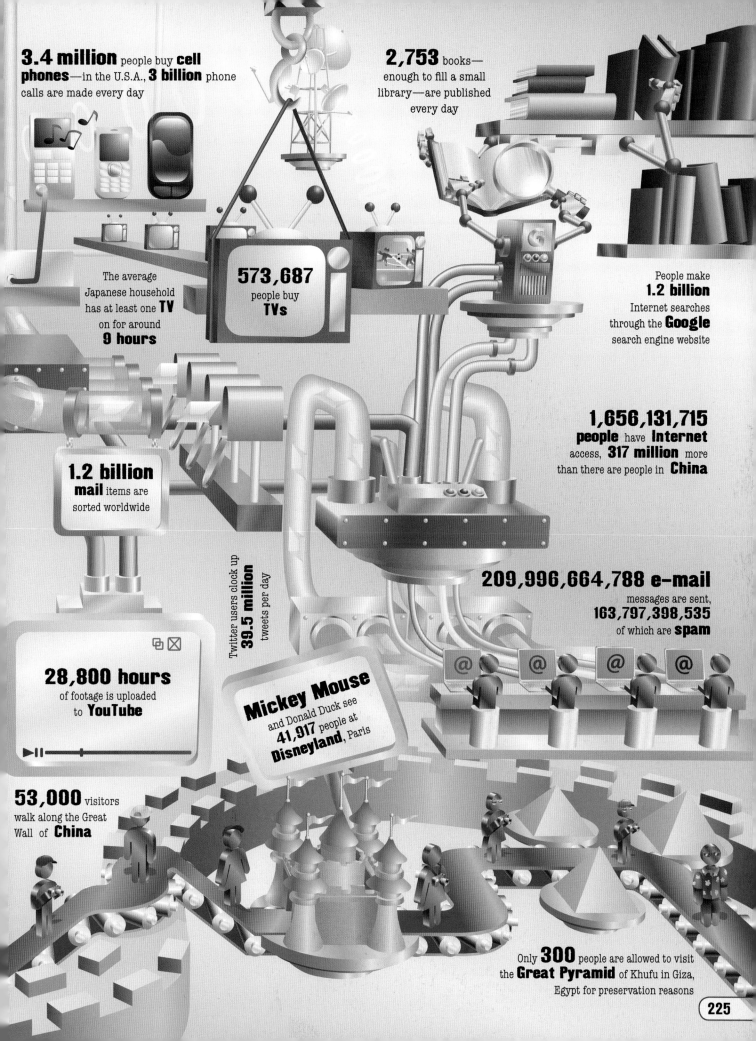

3.4 million people buy **cell phones**—in the U.S.A., **3 billion** phone calls are made every day

2,753 books—enough to fill a small library—are published every day

The average Japanese household has at least one **TV** on for around **9 hours**

573,687 people buy **TVs**

People make **1.2 billion** Internet searches through the **Google** search engine website

1,656,131,715 people have **Internet** access, **317 million** more than there are people in **China**

1.2 billion mail items are sorted worldwide

Twitter users clock up **39.5 million** tweets per day

209,996,664,788 e-mail messages are sent, **163,797,398,535** of which are **spam**

28,800 hours of footage is uploaded to **YouTube**

Mickey Mouse and Donald Duck see **41,917** people at **Disneyland**, Paris

53,000 visitors walk along the Great Wall of **China**

Only **300** people are allowed to visit the **Great Pyramid** of Khufu in Giza, Egypt for preservation reasons

Our World in the Future

it's 2050, and people are, on average, bigger, older, and fatter than they are now. Computers are smaller, faster, and virtually everywhere—from your clothes to the cells in your body. They think for themselves and are connected to each other in countless ways, acting and reacting to help you through life. No classrooms, no washing, and no nasty surprises from overhead birds. . .This is a snapshot of what the future may bring.

Medicine
The human genome is mapped—leading the way to cures for diseases such as cancer and AIDS. In 2050, patients are diagnosed and treated according to their unique genetic profile, with doctors able to see exactly where diseases and infections lie, making it possible to live even longer. Research into special cells called "stem cells" offer new ways to treat common ailments.

Economics
China overtook the U.S.A. to become the world's largest economy in 2030. India is now catching up, at 90% the size of the U.S. economy. However, the populations of India and China are so big that their per capita incomes are still 40% lower than that of the U.S.A.

LARGEST ECONOMIES iN 2050

China   US   India   Japan   Brazil

SPRAY'N'GO STORE

Future clothing
Washing and ironing is dead: spray-on fibers create disposable fashion with a perfect fit. Nanotechnology fabrics have brains as well as beauty, alerting you to changes in your body and even using the energy from your movements to power gadgets.

Hydrogen fuel
Around 1.5 billion vehicles are zipping around in 2050, but there are diminishing fossil fuels left to power them. Hydrogen fuel is the clean, green, and renewable source of power that is used. It can be generated on huge solar farms and used to top up fuel cells in electrical devices of all sizes, from cars to computers.

School classroom
Classrooms are a thing of the past, along with textbooks, pens, and paper. Students interact with teachers online, while avatars—the students' identities in cyberspace—manage their personal learning plans. Despite your school being virtual, your homework is still a reality.

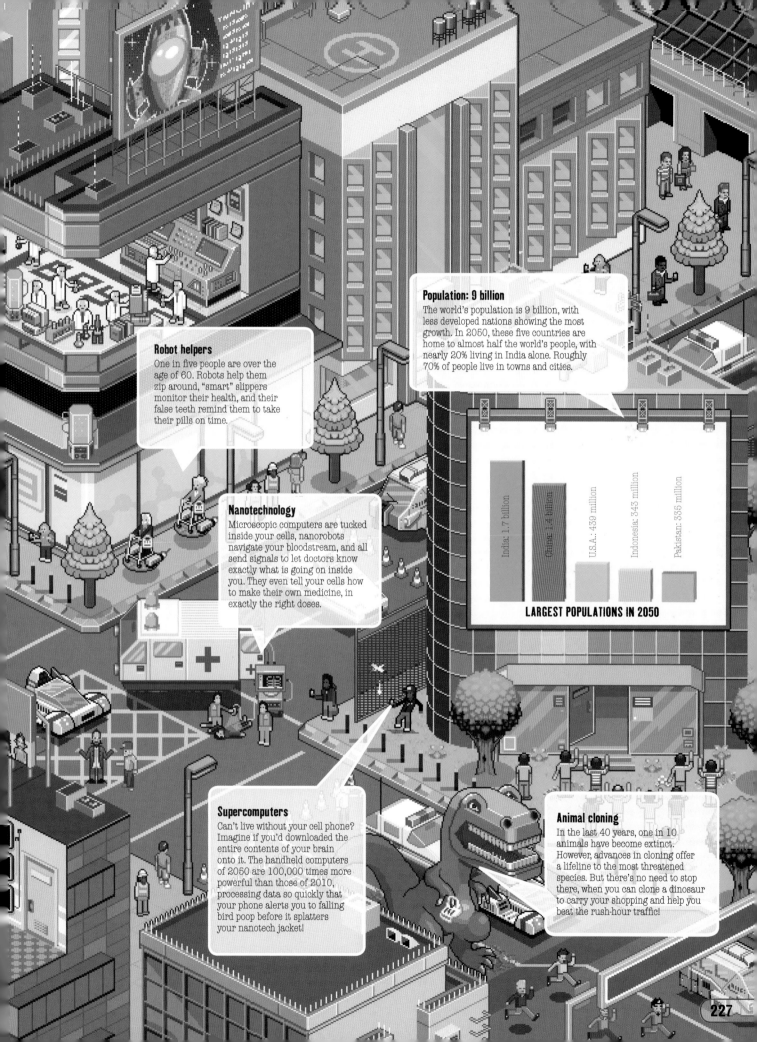

Robot helpers
One in five people are over the age of 60. Robots help them zip around, "smart" slippers monitor their health, and their false teeth remind them to take their pills on time.

Nanotechnology
Microscopic computers are tucked inside your cells, nanorobots navigate your bloodstream, and all send signals to let doctors know exactly what is going on inside you. They even tell your cells how to make their own medicine, in exactly the right doses.

Population: 9 billion
The world's population is 9 billion, with less developed nations showing the most growth. In 2050, these five countries are home to almost half the world's people, with nearly 20% living in India alone. Roughly 70% of people live in towns and cities.

India: 1.7 billion
China: 1.4 billion
U.S.A.: 439 million
Indonesia: 343 million
Pakistan: 335 million

LARGEST POPULATIONS IN 2050

Supercomputers
Can't live without your cell phone? Imagine if you'd downloaded the entire contents of your brain onto it. The handheld computers of 2050 are 100,000 times more powerful than those of 2010, processing data so quickly that your phone alerts you to falling bird poop before it splatters your nanotech jacket!

Animal cloning
In the last 40 years, one in 10 animals have become extinct. However, advances in cloning offer a lifeline to the most threatened species. But there's no need to stop there, when you can clone a dinosaur to carry your shopping and help you beat the rush-hour traffic!

Reference

This section contains a handy reference guide to the world's countries. Use the world map to locate them geographically and look up key statistics in the alphabetical chart. The sources pages list the agencies, reports, and websites that are the original sources for the data in this book.

World Map

The seven continents that make up the world's landmasses are, from largest to smallest, Asia, Africa, North America, South America, Antarctica, Europe, and Australia. Oceania is not a continent but a name for the region that includes Australia, New Zealand, and the Pacific islands.

Political map

This map is called a political map, because it shows country borders rather than physical features. Like many of the maps in this book, it uses an Eckert IV Projection.

MAP KEY

—————	Full international border
∙∙∙∙∙∙∙∙	Disputed border
---------	Maritime border
FRANCE	Independent state
Gibraltar (to UK)	Self-governing dependent territory
Johnston Atoll (to US)	Non self-governing dependent territory

Map labels

ARCTIC OCEAN
Arctic Circle
Great Bear Lake
Great Slave Lake
Baffin Bay
Alaska (to US)
Hudson Bay
60°N
Aleutian Islands (to US)
CANADA
NORTH AMERICA
Lake Winnipeg
Great Lakes
St Pierre & Miquelon (to France)

PACIFIC OCEAN

UNITED STATES OF AMERICA
ATLANTIC OCEAN

30°N
Midway Islands (to US)
Guadalupe (to Mexico)
Tropic of Cancer
Gulf of Mexico
Bermuda (to UK)
BAHAMAS
Turks & Caicos Islands (to UK)
British Virgin Islands (to UK)
Virgin Islands (to US)
Anguilla (to UK)
ST KITTS & NEVIS
ANTIGUA & BARBUDA
Montserrat (to UK)
Guadeloupe (to France)
DOMINICA
Martinique (to France)
ST LUCIA
ST VINCENT & THE G
BARBADOS
GRENADA
TRINIDAD & TOBAGO

Hawaii (to US)
MEXICO
Cayman Islands (to UK)
CUBA
DOMINICAN REPUBLIC
JAMAICA
HAITI
Puerto Rico (to US)
Revillagigedo Islands (to Mexico)
BELIZE
Caribbean Sea
GUATEMALA
HONDURAS
Aruba (to Neth.)
Neth. Ant. (to Neth.)
EL SALVADOR
NICARAGUA
COSTA RICA
Clipperton Island (to France)
VENEZUELA
GUYANA
French Guiana (to France)
PANAMA
COLOMBIA
SURINAM

Johnston Atoll (to US)

Kingman Reef (to US)
Palmyra Atoll (to US)
Baker & Howland Islands (to US)
Jarvis Island (to US)
Equator
Galapagos Islands (to Ecuador)
ECUADOR
KIRIBATI

Tokelau (to NZ)
Cook Islands (to NZ)
PACIFIC OCEAN
BRAZIL
SOUTH AMERICA
PERU
Wallis & Futuna (to France)
SAMOA
American Samoa (to US)
BOLIVIA
TONGA
Niue (to NZ)
French Polynesia (to France)
Tropic of Capricorn
PARAGUAY

Pitcairn Islands (to UK)
Sala y Gomez (to Chile)
San Felix Island (to Chile)
Easter Island (to Chile)
San Ambrosio Island (to Chile)
CHILE
ARGENTINA
30°S
Kermadec Islands (to NZ)
Juan Fernandez Islands (to Chile)
URUGUAY

Chatham Islands (to NZ)
Falkland Islands (to UK)

60°S
South Shetland Islands (to UK)
Antarctic Circle

150°W 120°W 90°W

Squaring a circle

The only really accurate way to show the world is by using a globe. Flat maps always involve distortions. The choice of how to portray the curve of Earth on a flat surface is called a projection. Different projections distort different things depending on their purpose—some show area correctly, while others show compass direction correctly.

Eckert IV

The projection used for the maps in this book is called the Eckert IV Projection. It distorts area and direction as little as possible. This strikes a balance between the Peters' and the Mercator projections.

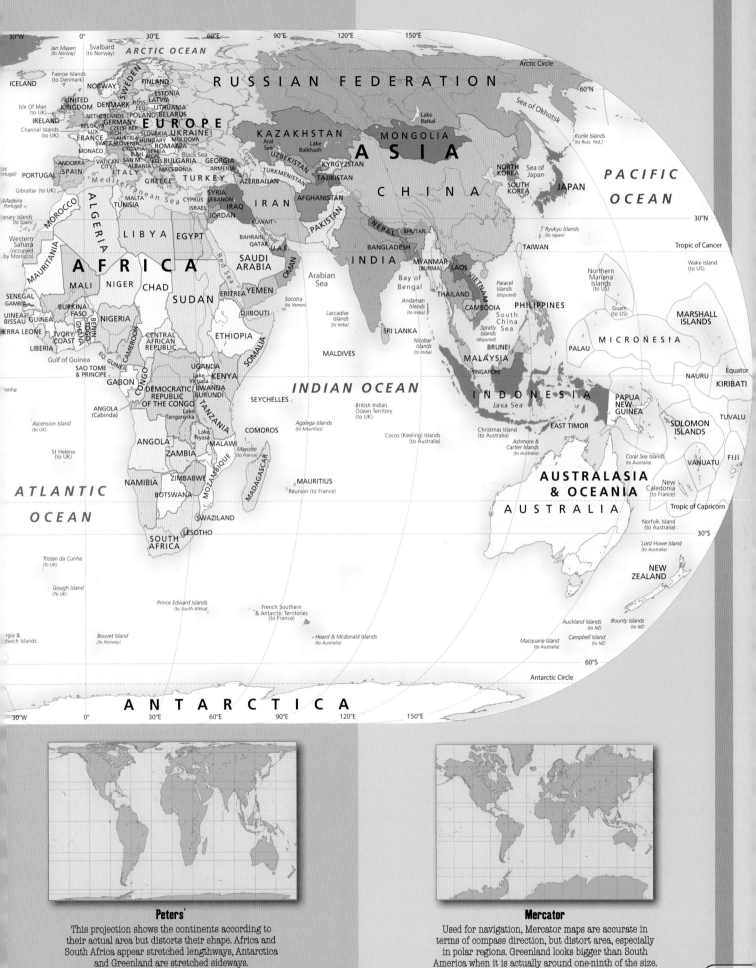

Peters'
This projection shows the continents according to their actual area but distorts their shape. Africa and South Africa appear stretched lengthways, Antarctica and Greenland are stretched sideways.

Mercator
Used for navigation, Mercator maps are accurate in terms of compass direction, but distort area, especially in polar regions. Greenland looks bigger than South America when it is actually around one-ninth of the size.

Reference

COUNTRY	CAPITAL CITY	CURRENCY	GDP	GDP PER CAPITA
Afghanistan	Kabul	Afghani	$12,061,000,000	$416
Albania	Tirane	Lek	$12,964,000,000	$4,090
Algeria	Algiers	Algerian dinar	$159,669,000,000	$4,588
Andorra	Andorra la Vella	Euro	–	–
Angola	Luanda	Kwanza	$83,384,000,000	$5,054
Antigua and Barbuda	Saint John's	East Caribbean dollar	$1,256,000,000	$14,556
Argentina	Buenos Aires	Argentine peso	$324,767,000,000	$8,171
Armenia	Yerevan	Dram	$11,928,000,000	$3,685
Australia	Canberra	Australian dollar	$1,013,461,000,000	$46,824
Austria	Vienna	Euro	$414,828,000,000	$50,039
Azerbaijan	Baku	Azerbaijani manat	$46,378,000,000	$5,349
Bahamas	Nassau	Bahamian dollar	$7,463,000,000	$22,359
Bahrain	Manama	Bahraini dinar	$21,236,000,000	$27,248
Bangladesh	Dhaka	Taka	$81,938,000,000	$521
Barbados	Bridgetown	Barbadian dollar	$3,682,000,000	$13,314
Belarus	Minsk	Belarussian rouble	$60,288,000,000	$6,235
Belgium	Brussels	Euro	$506,183,000,000	$47,289
Belize	Belmopan	Belize dollar	$1,381,000,000	$4,241
Benin	Porto-Novo	CFA franc	$6,940,000,000	$828
Bhutan	Thimphu	Ngultrum	$1,368,000,000	$2,114
Bolivia	La Paz	Boliviano; Bolivian peso	$17,413,000,000	$1,656
Bosnia and Herzegovina	Sarajevo	Convertible mark	$18,469,000,000	$4,625
Botswana	Gaborone	Pula	$13,461,000,000	$7,554
Brazil	Brasilia	Real	$1,572,839,000,000	$8,295
Brunei	Bandar Seri Begawan	Brunei dollar	$14,553,000,000	$37,053

LAND AREA	POPULATION	LIFE EXPECTANCY	LITERACY RATE
251,827 sq. miles (652,230 sq. km)	28,396,000	43	28.0%
11,099 sq. miles (28,748 sq. km)	3,196,000	75	99.0%
919,595 sq. miles (2,381,741 sq. km)	35,370,000	72	69.9%
180 sq. miles (468 sq. km)	86,000	–	–
481,353 sq. miles (1,246,700 sq. km)	17,074,000	43	67.4%
171 sq. miles (443 sq. km)	88,000	73	99.0%
1,073,518 sq. miles (2,780,400 sq. km)	40,276,000	75	97.6%
11,483 sq. miles (29,743 sq. km)	3,097,000	71	99.5%
2,988,901 sq. miles (7,741,220 sq. km)	21,852,000	81	99.0%
32,382 sq. miles (83,871 sq. km)	8,374,000	80	99.0%
33,436 sq. miles (86,600 sq. km)	8,781,000	72	99.5%
5,359 sq. miles (13,880 sq. km)	341,000	72	95.8%
286 sq. miles (741 sq. km)	1,217,000	75	88.8%
55,597 sq. miles (143,998 sq. km)	162,221,000	63	47.5%
166 sq. miles (430 sq. km)	281,000	76	99.7%
80,154 sq. miles (207,600 sq. km)	9,662,000	70	99.7%
11,786 sq. miles (30,528 sq. km)	10,792,000	80	99.0%
8,867 sq. miles (22,966 sq. km)	329,000	73	75.1%
43,483 sq. miles (112,622 sq. km)	8,935,000	56	34.7%
14,824 sq. miles (38,394 sq. km)	683,000	66	47.0%
424,164 sq. miles (1,098,581 sq. km)	9,863,000	65	90.7%
19,767 sq. miles (51,197 sq. km)	3,843,000	74	96.7%
224,607 sq. miles (581,730 sq. km)	1,991,000	49	81.2%
3,287,612 sq. miles (8,514,877 sq. km)	191,481,000	72	90.0%
2,225 sq. miles (5,765 sq. km)	383,000	75	94.9%

COUNTRY	CAPITAL CITY	CURRENCY	GDP	GDP PER CAPITA
Bulgaria	Sofia	Lev	$51,989,000,000	$6,561
Burkina Faso	Ouagadougou	CFA franc	$8,103,000,000	$578
Burundi	Bujumbura	Burundi franc	$1,097,000,000	$138
Cambodia	Phnom Penh	Riel	$11,182,000,000	$823
Cameroon	Yaounde	CFA franc	$23,243,000,000	$1,224
Canada	Ottawa	Canadian dollar	$1,499,551,000,000	$45,085
Cape Verde	Praia	Escudo caboverdiano	$1,723,000,000	$3,464
Central African Republic	Bangui	CFA franc	$1,997,000,000	$459
Chad	N'Djamena	CFA franc	$8,390,000,000	$863
Chile	Santiago	Chilean peso	$169,458,000,000	$10,117
China	Beijing	Chinese yuan	$4,327,448,000,000	$3,259
Colombia	Bogota	Colombian peso	$240,832,000,000	$4,989
Comoros	Moroni	Comorian franc	$532,000,000	$816
Congo	Brazzaville	CFA franc	$10,774,000,000	$2,952
Cote d'Ivoire	Yamoussoukro	CFA franc	$23,508,000,000	$1,132
Dem. Rep. of the Congo	Kinshasa	Congolese franc	$11,589,000,000	$185
Costa Rica	San Jose	Costa Rican colón	$29,828,000,000	$6,544
Croatia	Zagreb	Croatian kuna	$69,332,000,000	$15,634
Cuba	Havana	Cuban peso	–	–
Cyprus	Nicosia	Euro	$24,943,000,000	$32,745
Czech Republic	Prague	Czech koruna	$216,354,000,000	$20,760
Denmark	Copenhagen	Danish krone	$340,029,000,000	$62,097
Djibouti	Djibouti	Djiboutian franc	$982,000,000	$1,252
Dominica	Roseau	East Caribbean dollar	$364,000,000	$5,082
Dominican Republic	Santo Domingo	Dominican Republic peso	$45,597,000,000	$4,992

LAND AREA	POPULATION	LIFE EXPECTANCY	LITERACY RATE
42,810 sq. miles (110,879 sq. km)	7,590,000	73	98.3%
105,869 sq. miles (274,200 sq. km)	15,757,000	51	23.6%
10,745 sq. miles (27,830 sq. km)	8,303,000	49	59.3%
69,898 sq. miles (181,035 sq. km)	14,805,000	62	73.6%
183,568 sq. miles (475,440 sq. km)	18,879,000	52	67.9%
3,855,102 sq. miles (9,984,670 sq. km)	33,707,000	80	99.0%
1,557 sq. miles (4,033 sq. km)	509,000	71	81.2%
240,535 sq. miles (622,984 sq. km)	4,511,000	47	48.6%
495,755 sq. miles (1,284,000 sq. km)	10,329,000	78	25.7%
291,932 sq. miles (756,102 sq. km)	16,970,000	78	96.5%
3,705,407 sq. miles (9,596,961 sq. km)	1,331,398,000	73	93.3%
439,737 sq. miles (1,138,914 sq. km)	45,065,000	72	92.7%
862 sq. miles (2,235 sq. km)	676,000	64	56.8%
132,046 sq. miles (342,000 sq. km)	3,683,000	53	84.7%
124,503 sq. miles (322,463 sq. km)	21,395,000	52	48.7%
905,350 sq. miles (2,344,858 sq. km)	68,693,000	53	67.2%
19,729 sq. miles (51,100 sq. km)	4,509,000	78	95.9%
21,851 sq. miles (56,594 sq. km)	4,433,000	76	98.7%
42,803 sq. miles (110,860 sq. km)	11,225,000	77	99.8%
3,571 sq. miles (9,251 sq. km)	1,072,000	78	97.7%
30,450 sq. miles (78,867 sq. km)	10,511,000	77	99.0%
16,638 sq. miles (43,094 sq. km)	5,529,000	78	99.0%
8,957 sq. miles (23,200 sq. km)	864,000	54	70.3%
289 sq. miles (751 sq. km)	72,000	75	88.0%
18,791 sq. miles (48,670 sq. km)	10,090,000	72	89.1%

COUNTRY	CAPITAL CITY	CURRENCY	GDP	GDP PER CAPITA
East Timor	Dili	U.S. dollar	$499,000,000	$469
Ecuador	Quito	U.S. dollar	$52,572,000,000	$3,928
Egypt	Cairo	Egytian pound	$162,617,000,000	$2,162
El Salvador	San Salvador	U.S. dollar	$22,115,000,000	$3,824
Equatorial Guinea	Malabo	CFA franc	$18,525,000,000	$14,941
Eritrea	Asmara	Eritreian nakfa; Ethiopian birr	$1,476,000,000	$295
Estonia	Tallinn	Kroon	$23,232,000,000	$17,532
Ethiopia	Addis Ababa	Birr	$25,658,000,000	$333
Fiji	Suva	Fijian dollar	$3,590,000,000	$4,094
Finland	Helsinki	Euro	$271,867,000,000	$51,588
France	Paris	Euro	$2,866,951,000,000	$46,037
Gabon	Libreville	CFA franc	$14,519,000,000	$9,998
Gambia	Banjul	Dalasi	$808,000,000	$497
Georgia	Tbilisi	Lari	$12,870,000,000	$2,924
Germany	Berlin	Euro	$3,673,105,000,000	$44,729
Ghana	Accra	Cedi	$16,124,000,000	$739
Greece	Athens	Euro	$357,548,000,000	$32,105
Grenada	Saint George's	East Caribbean dollar	$639,000,000	$6,587
Guatemala	Guatemala City	Quetzal	$38,956,000,000	$2,850
Guinea	Conakry	Guinean franc	$4,542,000,000	$439
Guinea-Bissau	Bissau	CFA franc	$461,000,000	$264
Guyana	Georgetown	Guyanese dollar	$1,130,000,000	$1,509
Haiti	Port-au-Prince	Gourde	$6,952,000,000	$790
Honduras	Tegucigalpa	Lempira	$14,126,000,000	$1,826
Hungary	Budapest	Forint	$155,930,000,000	$15,523

LAND AREA	POPULATION	LIFE EXPECTANCY	LITERACY RATE
5,742 sq. miles (14,874 sq. km)	1,154,000	60	50.1%
109,483 sq. miles (283,561 sq. km)	13,625,000	75	91.0%
386,662 sq. miles (1,001,450 sq. km)	78,629,000	72	71.4%
8,123 sq. miles (21,041 sq. km)	7,339,000	71	80.5%
10,830 sq. miles (28,051 sq. km)	676,000	59	87.0%
45,405 sq. miles (117,600 sq. km)	5,073,000	57	60.5%
17,462 sq. miles (45,228 sq. km)	1,340,000	73	99.8%
426,372 sq. miles (1,104,300 sq. km)	82,825,000	49	35.9%
7,055 sq. miles (18,274 sq. km)	844,000	68	94.4%
130,558 sq. miles (338,145 sq. km)	5,339,000	79	99.0%
248,428 sq. miles (643,427 sq. km)	62,621,000	81	99.0%
103,346 sq. miles (267,667 sq. km)	1,475,000	57	84.0%
4,361 sq. miles (11,295 sq. km)	1,609,000	58	42.5%
26,911 sq. miles (69,700 sq. km)	4,611,000	74	–
137,846 sq. miles (357,022 sq. km)	81,980,000	79	99.0%
92,098 sq. miles (238,533 sq. km)	23,837,000	59	57.9%
50,948 sq. miles (131,957 sq. km)	11,277,000	79	97.1%
132 sq. miles (344 sq. km)	106,000	79	96.0%
42,042 sq. miles (108,889 sq. km)	14,027,000	78	69.1%
94,925 sq. miles (245,857 sq. km)	10,058,000	54	29.5%
13,947 sq. miles (36,125 sq. km)	1,611,000	45	44.8%
82,999 sq. miles (214,969 sq. km)	773,000	65	99.0%
10,714 sq. miles (27,750 sq. km)	9,242,000	58	54.8%
43,278 sq. miles (112,090 sq. km)	7,466,000	72	80.0%
35,918 sq. miles (93,028 sq. km)	10,024,000	73	99.4%

COUNTRY	CAPITAL CITY	CURRENCY	GDP	GDP PER CAPITA
Iceland	Reykjavik	Icelandic króna	$17,549,000,000	$53,058
India	New Delhi	Indian rupee	$1,206,684,000,000	$1,017
Indonesia	Jakarta	Rupiah	$511,765,000,000	$2,239
Iran	Tehran	Iranian rial	$335,233,000,000	$4,600
Iraq	Baghdad	Iraqi dinar	$91,453,000,000	$3,007
Ireland	Dublin	Euro	$267,579,000,000	$60,510
Israel	Tel-Aviv	Israeli new shekel	$202,101,000,000	$28,409
Italy	Rome	Euro	$2,313,893,000,000	$38,996
Jamaica	Kingston	Jamaican dollar	$14,397,000,000	$5,199
Japan	Tokyo	Yen	$4,910,692,000,000	$38,457
Jordan	Amman	Jordanian dinar	$20,030,000,000	$3,626
Kazakhstan	Astana	Tenge	$135,601,000,000	$8,719
Kenya	Nairobi	Kenyan shilling	$30,236,000,000	$838
Kiribati	Tarawa Atoll	Australian dollar	$137,000,000	$1,372
Kosovo	Pristina	Euro	–	–
Kuwait	Kuwait City	Kuwaiti dinar	$158,089,000,000	$45,920
Kyrgyzstan	Bishkek	Kyrgyzstani som	$5,049,000,000	$951
Laos	Vientiane	Kip	$5,260,000,000	$859
Latvia	Riga	Lats	$34,054,000,000	$14,964
Lebanon	Beirut	Lebanese pound	$28,939,000,000	$7,708
Lesotho	Maseru	Loti, maloti; South African rand	$1,620,000,000	$660
Liberia	Monrovia	Liberian dollar	$836,000,000	$216
Libya	Tripoli	Libyan dinar	$89,916,000,000	$14,479
Liechtenstein	Vaduz	Swiss franc	–	–
Lithuania	Vilnius	Litas	$47,304,000,000	$14,086

LAND AREA	POPULATION	LIFE EXPECTANCY	LITERACY RATE
39,768 sq. miles (103,000 sq. km)	321,000	81	99.0%
1,269,219 sq. miles (3,287,263 sq. km)	1,171,029,000	65	61.0%
735,358 sq. miles (1,904,569 sq. km)	243,306,000	70	92.0%
636,371 sq. miles (1,648,195 sq. km)	73,244,000	71	82.4%
169,235 sq. miles (438,317 sq. km)	30,047,000	58	–
27,132 sq. miles (70,273 sq. km)	4,528,000	79	99.0%
8,522 sq. miles (22,072 sq. km)	7,634,000	80	97.1%
116,348 sq. miles (301,340 sq. km)	60,274,000	81	98.9%
4,243 sq. miles (10,991 sq. km)	2,702,000	72	79.9%
145,913 sq. miles (377,915 sq. km)	127,568,000	82	99.0%
34,495 sq. miles (89,342 sq. km)	5,915,000	72	91.1%
1,052,089 sq. miles (2,724,900 sq. km)	15,880,000	66	99.6%
224,080 sq. miles (580,367 sq. km)	39,070,000	53	73.6%
313 sq. miles (811 sq. km)	99,000	61	–
4,203 sq. miles (10,887 sq. km)	2,222,000	69	–
6,879 sq. miles (17,818 sq. km)	2,985,000	78	94.5%
77,201 sq. miles (199,951 sq. km)	5,304,000	66	99.3%
91,428 sq. miles (236,800 sq. km)	6,320,000	61	68.7%
24,937 sq. miles (64,589 sq. km)	2,256,000	72	99.8%
4,015 sq. miles (10,400 sq. km)	3,876,000	72	89.6%
11,720 sq. miles (30,355 sq. km)	2,135,000	36	82.2%
42,999 sq. miles (111,369 sq. km)	3,955,000	46	–
679,362 sq. miles (1,759,540 sq. km)	6,283,000	73	84.2%
61 sq. miles (160 sq. km)	36,000	80	–
25,212 sq. miles (65,300 sq. km)	3,339,000	71	99.7%

COUNTRY	CAPITAL CITY	CURRENCY	GDP	GDP PER CAPITA
Luxembourg	Luxembourg	Euro	$54,973,000,000	$113,044
Macedonia	Skopje	Macedonian denars	$9,569,000,000	$4,657
Madagascar	Antananarivo	Malagasy ariary	$9,254,000,000	$468
Malawi	Lilongwe	Malawian kwacha	$4,268,000,000	$313
Malaysia	Kuala Lumpur	Ringgit	$221,606,000,000	$8,118
Maldives	Male	Rufiyaa	$1,259,000,000	$3,654
Mali	Bamako	CFA franc	$8,783,000,000	$657
Malta	Valletta	Euro	$8,338,000,000	$20,281
Marshall Islands	Majuro	U.S. dollar	—	—
Mauritania	Nouakchott	Ouguiya	$3,161,000,000	$1,042
Mauritius	Port Louis	Mauritian rupee	$8,738,000,000	$6,872
Mexico	Mexico City	Mexican peso	$1,088,128,000,000	$10,200
Micronesia	Palikir	U.S. dollar	—	—
Moldova	Chisinau	Moldovian leu	$6,124,000,000	$1,693
Monaco	Monaco	Euro	—	—
Mongolia	Ulaanbaatar	Tugrik	$5,258,000,000	$1,975
Montenegro	Podgorica	Euro	$4,822,000,000	—
Morocco	Rabat	Moroccan dirham	$88,879,000,000	$2,827
Mozambique	Maputo	Metical	$9,654,000,000	$477
Myanmar (Burma)	Rangoon	Kyat	$27,182,000,000	$446
Namibia	Windhoek	Namibia dollar; South African rand	$8,456,000,000	$4,278
Nauru	No official capital	Australian dollar	—	—
Nepal	Kathmandu	Nepalese rupee	$12,698,000,000	$444
Netherlands	Amsterdam	Euro	$876,970,000,000	$52,500
New Zealand	Wellington	New Zealand dollar	$128,409,000,000	$30,030

LAND AREA	POPULATION	LIFE EXPECTANCY	LITERACY RATE
998 sq. miles (2,586 sq. km)	498,000	80	99.0%
9,927 sq. miles (25,713 sq. km)	2,049,000	74	97.0%
226,657 sq. miles (587,041 sq. km)	19,464,000	58	70.7%
45,746 sq. miles (118,484 sq. km)	14,214,000	46	64.1%
127,354 sq. miles (329,847 sq. km)	28,295,000	74	91.9%
115 sq. miles (298 sq. km)	315,000	73	97.0%
478,840 sq. miles (1,240,192 sq. km)	13,010,000	56	24.0%
122 sq. miles (316 sq. km)	414,000	79	92.4%
69 sq. miles (181 sq. km)	54,000	66	—
397,955 sq. miles (1,030,700 sq. km)	3,291,000	60	51.2%
787 sq. miles (2,040 sq. km)	1,276,000	72	84.3%
758,449 sq. miles (1,964,375 sq. km)	109,610,000	75	92.8%
271 sq. miles (702 sq. km)	111,000	67	—
13,069 sq. miles (33,851 sq. km)	4,133,000	69	99.2%
0.7 sq. miles (2 sq. km)	35,000	—	—
603,908 sq. miles (1,564,116 sq. km)	2,708,000	64	97.3%
5,332 sq. miles (13,812 sq. km)	628,000	73	—
172,413 sq. miles (446,550 sq. km)	31,495,000	70	52.3%
308,642 sq. miles (799,380 sq. km)	21,971,000	43	38.7%
261,228 sq. miles (676,578 sq. km)	50,020,000	61	89.9%
318,260 sq. miles (824,292 sq. km)	2,171,000	47	85.0%
8 sq. miles (21 sq. km)	10,000	55	—
56,826 sq. miles (147,181 sq. km)	27,504,000	64	48.6%
16,039 sq. miles (41,543 sq. km)	16,527,000	80	99.0%
103,363 sq. miles (267,710 sq. km)	4,317,000	80	99.0%

COUNTRY	CAPITAL CITY	CURRENCY	GDP	GDP PER CAPITA
Nicaragua	Managua	Córdoba	$6,350,000,000	$1,028
Niger	Niamey	CFA franc	$5,379,000,000	$391
Nigeria	Abuja	Naira	$207,116,000,000	$1,401
North Korea	Pyongyang	North Korean won	–	–
Norway	Oslo	Norwegian krone	$451,830,000,000	$94,387
Oman	Muscat	Omani rial	$52,584,000,000	$21,646
Pakistan	Islamabad	Pakistani rupee	$164,557,000,000	$1,022
Palau	Melekeok	U.S.dollar	–	–
Panama	Panama City	Panamanian balboa	$23,088,000,000	$6,784
Papua New Guinea	Port Moresby	Kina	$8,092,000,000	$1,306
Paraguay	Asuncion	Guarani	$16,006,000,000	$2,601
Peru	Lima	Peruvian nuevo sol	$127,462,000,000	$4,448
Philippines	Manila	Philippine peso	$166,909,000,000	$1,845
Poland	Warsaw	Zloty	$527,866,000,000	$13,846
Portugal	Lisbon	Euro	$244,640,000,000	$23,041
Qatar	Doha	Qatari riyal	$102,302,000,000	$93,204
Romania	Bucharest	Romanian leu	$200,074,000,000	$9,310
Russia	Moscow	Rouble	$1,676,586,000,000	$11,807
Rwanda	Kigali	Rwandan franc	$4,459,000,000	$465
Saint Kitts and Nevis	Basseterre	East Caribbean dollar	$555,000,000	$10,310
Saint Lucia	Castries	East Caribbean dollar	$1,025,000,000	$5,806
Saint Vincent and the Grenadines	Kingstown	East Caribbean dollar	$601,000,000	$5,615
Samoa	Apia	Tala	$537,000,000	$2,608
San Marino	San Marino	Euro	–	–
São Tomé and Príncipe	São Tomé	Dobra	$176,000,000	$1,094

LAND AREA	POPULATION	LIFE EXPECTANCY	LITERACY RATE
50,336 sq. miles (130,370 sq. km)	5,669,000	71	76.7%
489,191 sq. miles (1,267,000 sq. km)	15,290,000	57	28.7%
356,668 sq. miles (923,768 sq. km)	152,616,000	47	69.1%
46,539 sq. miles (120,538 sq. km)	22,665,000	71	99.0%
125,020 sq. miles (323,802 sq. km)	4,827,000	80	99.0%
119,498 sq. miles (309,500 sq. km)	3,108,000	74	81.4%
307,373 sq. miles (796,095 sq. km)	180,808,000	63	49.9%
177 sq. miles (459 sq. km)	21,000	71	–
29,119 sq. miles (75,420 sq. km)	3,454,000	75	93.4%
178,703 sq. miles (462,840 sq. km)	6,610,000	57	57.3%
157,047 sq. miles (406,752 sq. km)	6,349,000	71	94.6%
496,224 sq. miles (1,285,216 sq. km)	29,165,000	71	89.6%
115,830 sq. miles (300,000 sq. km)	92,227,000	69	93.4%
120,728 sq. miles (312,685 sq. km)	38,146,000	75	99.3%
35,556 sq. miles (92,090 sq. km)	10,639,000	79	94.9%
4,473 sq. miles (11,586 sq. km)	1,409,000	75	93.1%
92,043 sq. miles (238,391 sq. km)	21,474,000	71	97.6%
6,601,668 sq. miles (17,098,242 sq. km)	141,839,000	67	99.5%
10,169 sq. miles (26,338 sq. km)	9,877,000	47	64.9%
100 sq. miles (261 sq. km)	50,000	70	97.8%
237 sq. miles (616 sq. km)	172,000	73	94.8%
150 sq. miles (389 sq. km)	110,000	72	88.1%
1,093 sq. miles (2,831 sq. km)	190,000	73	98.7%
23 sq. miles (61 sq. km)	31,000	82	–
374 sq. miles (964 sq. km)	163,000	64	84.9%

COUNTRY	CAPITAL CITY	CURRENCY	GDP	GDP PER CAPITA
Saudi Arabia	Riyadh	Saudi riyal	$469,462,000,000	$18,855
Senegal	Dakar	West African franc; CFA franc	$13,350,000,000	$1,066
Serbia	Belgrade	Serbian dinar	$50,061,000,000	$6,782
Seychelles	Victoria	Seychelles rupee	$834,000,000	$9,640
Sierra Leone	Freetown	Leone	$1,955,000,000	$332
Singapore	Singapore	Singapore dollar	$181,939,000,000	$38,972
Slovakia	Bratislava	Euro	$95,404,000,000	$17,646
Slovenia	Lkubljana	Euro	$54,639,000,000	$27,149
Solomon Islands	Honiara	Solomon Islands dollar	$473,000,000	$1,228
Somalia	Mogadishu	Somali shilling	—	—
South Africa	Cape Town	Rand	$276,764,000,000	$5,685
South Korea	Seoul	South Korean won	$929,124,000,000	$19,136
Spain	Madrid	Euro	$1,601,964,000,000	$35,117
Sri Lanka	Colombo	Sri Lankan rupee	$39,604,000,000	$1,972
Sudan	Khartoum	Sudanese pound	$57,911,000,000	$1,522
Suriname	Paramaribo	Surinamese dollar	$2,415,000,000	$5,504
Swaziland	Mbabane	Lilangeni	$2,843,000,000	$2,778
Sweden	Stockholm	Swedish krona	$478,961,000,000	$52,181
Switzerland	Bern	Swiss franc	$500,260,000,000	$68,433
Syria	Damascus	Syrian pound	$54,803,000,000	$2,768
Taiwan	Taipei	New Taiwan dollar	$391,351,000,000	$16,987
Tajikistan	Dushanbe	Tajikistani somoni	$5,135,000,000	$795
Tanzania	Dodoma	Tanzanian shilling	$20,721,000,000	$520
Thailand	Bangkok	Baht	$273,313,000,000	$4,116
Togo	Lome	CFA franc	$2,890,000,000	$436

LAND AREA	POPULATION	LIFE EXPECTANCY	LITERACY RATE
829,999 sq. miles (2,149,690 sq. km)	28,687,000	76	82.9%
75,954 sq. miles (196,722 sq. km)	12,534,000	62	39.3%
29,912 sq. miles (77,474 sq. km)	7,322,000	73	96.4%
175 sq. miles (455 sq. km)	87,000	72	91.8%
27,698 sq. miles (71,740 sq. km)	5,696,000	48	34.8%
269 sq. miles (697 sq. km)	5,113,000	81	94.4%
18,932 sq. miles (49,035 sq. km)	5,417,000	74	99.0%
7,827 sq. miles (20,273 sq. km)	2,043,000	78	99.7%
11,156 sq. miles (28,895 sq. km)	519,000	62	76.6%
246,200 sq. miles (637,657 sq. km)	9,133,000	48	–
468,376 sq. miles (1,219,090 sq. km)	50,674,000	50	82.4%
38,502 sq. miles (99,720 sq. km)	48,747,000	79	99.0%
195,124 sq. miles (505,370 sq. km)	46,916,000	80	97.9%
24,173 sq. miles (65,610 sq. km)	20,502,000	71	90.8%
967,499 sq. miles (2,505,813 sq. km)	42,272,000	58	60.9%
63,251 sq. miles (163,820 sq. km)	502,000	69	90.4%
6,704 sq. miles (17,364 sq. km)	1,185,000	33	79.6%
173,859 sq. miles (450,295 sq. km)	9,288,000	81	99.0%
15,937 sq. miles (41,277 sq. km)	7,754,000	82	99.0%
71,498 sq. miles (185,180 sq. km)	21,906,000	73	80.8%
13,891 sq. miles (35,980 sq. km)	23,079,000	78	–
55,251 sq. miles (143,100 sq. km)	7,450,000	67	99.6%
365,754 sq. miles (947,300 sq. km)	43,739,000	51	69.4%
198,116 sq. miles (513,120 sq. km)	67,764,000	72	94.1%
21,924 sq. miles (56,785 sq. km)	6,619,000	58	53.2%

COUNTRY	CAPITAL CITY	CURRENCY	GDP	GDP PER CAPITA
Tonga	Nuku'alofa	Pa'anga	$258,000,000	$2,510
Trinidad and Tobago	Port-of-Spain	Trinidad; Tobago dollar	$24,806,000,000	$19,870
Tunisia	Tunis	Tunisian dinar	$40,348,000,000	$3,955
Turkey	Ankara	New Turkish lira	$729,983,000,000	$10,479
Turkmenistan	Ashgabat	Turkmen manat	—	$3,606
Tuvalu	Funafuti	Australian dollar	—	–
Uganda	Kampala	Ugandan shilling	$14,529,000,000	$455
Ukraine	Kyiv	Hyrvnia	$179,604,000,000	$3,910
United Arab Emirates	Abu Dhabi	UAE dirham	$262,150,000,000	$55,028
United Kingdom	London	Pound sterling	$2,680,000,000,000	$43,734
United States of America	Washington, D.C.	U.S. dollar	$14,441,425,000,000	$47,440
Uruguay	Montevideo	Uruguayan peso	$32,262,000,000	$9,654
Uzbekistan	Tashkent	Uzbekistani som	$27,918,000,000	$1,027
Vanuatu	Port-Vila	Vatu	$573,000,000	$2,442
Vatican City	Vatican City	Euro	—	–
Venezuela	Caracas	Bolivar	$319,443,000,000	$11,388
Vietnam	Hanoi	Dong	$89,829,000,000	$1,042
Yemen	Sanaa	Yemeni rial	$27,151,000,000	$1,171
Zambia	Lusaka	Zambian kwacha	$14,323,000,000	$1,248
Zimbabwe	Harare	Zimbabwe dollar	$3,145,000,000	$268

LAND AREA	POPULATION	LIFE EXPECTANCY	LITERACY RATE
288 sq. miles (747 sq. km)	103,000	71	99.2%
1,979 sq. miles (5,128 sq. km)	1,333,000	69	98.7%
63,170 sq. miles (163,610 sq. km)	10,429,000	74	74.3%
302,534 sq. miles (783,562 sq. km)	74,816,000	72	88.7%
188,456 sq. miles (488,100 sq. km)	5,110,000	62	99.5%
10 sq. miles (26 sq. km)	11,000	64	–
93,065 sq. miles (241,038 sq. km)	30,700,000	48	66.8%
233,031 sq. miles (603,550 sq. km)	46,030,000	68	99.7%
32,278 sq. miles (83,600 sq. km)	5,066,000	78	90.0%
94,058 sq. miles (243,610 sq. km)	61,823,000	79	99.0%
3,794,100 sq. miles (9,826,675 sq. km)	306,805,000	78	99.0%
68,036 sq. miles (176,215 sq. km)	3,364,000	76	97.9%
172,742 sq. miles (447,400 sq. km)	27,562,000	67	96.9%
4,706 sq. miles (12,189 sq. km)	239,000	67	74.0%
0.16 sq. miles (0.44 sq. km)	826	77	100.0%
352,144 sq. miles (912,050 sq. km)	28,368,000	73	95.2%
127,996 sq. miles (331,210 sq. km)	87,263,000	73	90.3%
203,849 sq. miles (527,968 sq. km)	22,880,000	61	54.1%
290,587 sq. miles (752,618 sq. km)	12,555,000	38	68.0%
150,872 sq. miles (390,757 sq. km)	12,523,000	40	91.2%

Data sources

The statistical information throughout the book has been taken from the following sources:

Earth

18–19 Quakes and Shakes
Earthquake frequency: British Columbia Institute of Technology *Measuring Earthquakes: Magnitude and Intensity* http://www.bcit.ca

30–31 Island Formation
Islands types: United Nations Environment Programme Islands directory www.islands.unep.ch

36–37 Life on the Land
Earth's terrestrial biomes: Bradshaw, M., Weaver, R. *Physical Geography* (Mosby, 1992)

42–43 Under Threat
Total number of species and number of threatened species figures: International Union for Conservation of Nature Redlist www.iucnredlist.com

44–45 Six Degrees of Change
Rising sea levels and global warming figures: *IPCC Fourth Assessment Report: Climate Change 2007* www.ipcc.ch

Information on degree-by-degree temperature rises: *What will climate change do to our planet?* http://www.timesonline.co.uk

People

50–51 How many People on the Planet?
Population figures: *PRB Datafinder*, Population Reference Bureau www.prb.org

Population growth: *The World at Six Billion*, United Nations Population Division www.un.org/esa/population

52–53 City Populations
World's most populous urban areas (agglomerations): *The Principal Agglomerations of the World* www.citypopulation.de

The rise of city living: *United Nations World Urbanization Prospects* (New York, 2007)

54–55 Changing Populations
Fertility, birth, and death rates: *World Population prospects: The 2008 revision* www.data.un.com

56–57 How Long do you Have?
Population pyramids: *Midyear Population, by Age and Sex* www.census.gov

Life expectancy figures: *PRB Datafinder*, Population Reference Bureau www.prb.org

58–59 Ways to Go
What are the chances?: *The global burden of disease: 2004 update*, World Health Organization www.who.int

Different ways to die: Roper, M., *101 Crazy Ways to Die* (Penguin, 2008)

60–61 Diseases and Health Care
Across continents: *The global burden of disease: 2004 update*, World Health Organization www.who.int

Doctors and patients and Cost of care figures: *Population, Health and Well-Being database*, Earthtrends www.wri.org

62–63 Water
Global usage: *SIWI Statistics*,

Stockholm International Water Institute www.siwi.org

Domestic usage: *Facts and Figures.* World Water Council, www.worldwatercouncil.org

Stressed resources: *AQUASTAT main country database*, AQUASTAT www.fao.org

Water for the people: *AQUASTAT main country database*, AQUASTAT www.fao.org;

PRB Datafinder, Population Reference Bureau www.prb.org

64–65 Hunger
Where hunger hits the hardest: *The State of Food Insecurity in the World 2008*, Food and Agriculture Organization;

The United Nations World Food Programme www.wfp.org

Food aid: *Aid targets slipping out of reach?* (OECD, 2008)

66–67 Food Waste
Worst offenders: Quested, T., Johnson, H., *Household Food and Drink Waste in the UK* (WRAP, 2009)

What's in the garbage can?: Quested, T., Johnson, H., *Household Food and Drink Waste in the UK* (WRAP, 2009)

Rotten refuse: Quested, T., Johnson, H., *Household Food and Drink Waste in the UK* (WRAP, 2009)

Waste at every stage: Stuart, T., *Waste* (Penguin, 2009)

68–69 Globesity
Portion sizes: *Portion Distortion Interactive Quiz*, National

Institutes of Health www.nih.gov

Weight across the nations: *BMI adults % obese*, World Health Organization www.apps.who.int/bmi

Health issues: *WHO Global Infobase*, World Health Organization www.who.int

Diabetes Atlas 2006, International Diabetes Federation www.diabetesatlas.org

70–71 Daily Diets
What's in the fridge?: *FAOSTAT: Food consumption pattern of main food groups*, Food and Agriculture Organization www.fao.org

Cost of consumption: *International Food Consumption Patterns*, United States Department of Agriculture www.ers.usda.gov

Counting the calories: *FAOSTAT: Kcals per day*, Food and Agriculture Organization www.fao.org

72–73 Look who's Talking
Top 25 languages: *Summary by language size*, Ethnologue www.ethnologue.com

76–77 Tribal Peoples
Indigenous inhabitants: *Tribes & campaigns*, Survival International www.survivalinternational.org

78–79 Beliefs and Believers
Religions of the world: *Major Religions of the World* www.adherents.com

80–81 The Big Six
Figures on faiths and adherents: *Major Religions*

of the World
www.adherents.com

82–83 The Gender Gap
Heads of state:
CIA Chiefs of
State & Cabinet
Members directory
www.cia.gov

Mapping inequality:
Hausmann, R., Tyson,
L. & Zahidi, S., The Global
Gender Gap Report
(World Economic
Forum, 2007)

Nobel Prize winners:
Nobel Laureates Facts
www.nobelprize.org

Percentage of females enrolled in
primary education: The State of
the World's Children 2009
www.unicef.org

84–85 Happy Families
Family statistics:
UNECE Statistical
Division Database
www.unece.org;

Brown, S. et al.,
Economist Pocket World in
Figures, (Profile Books Ltd,
2009); UNESCO Insitute
for Statistics
www.uis.unesco.org;

86–87 Childhood
Figures from: The State of
the World's Children 2009
www.unicef.org

88–89 School Days
UNESCO Insitute for Statistics
www.uis.unesco.org;

The State of the
World's Children 2009
www.unicef.org

90–91 Work
Annual hours at work:
OECD Employment Outlook
(OECD, 2008)

Size of workforces:
CIA World Factbook
www.cia.gov

iPod index: Ranking: The richest
cities in the world
www.citymayors.com;

Prices and Earnings
www.ubs.com

92–93 The Teenage Day
Figures on time spent on various
activities: How high school
students use time: a visual essay
www.bls.gov

Teen TV viewing around the
world: How Teens Use Media
www.nielsen.com

96–97 Who's Happiest?
Life satisfaction chart:
Gallup Well-Being Index
www.worldview.gallup.com

GNI Per capita figures:
CIA World Factbook
www.cia.gov

98–99 People and their Pets
Pets in the U.S.A.: The American
Pet Product Association
www.americanpetproducts.org

Pet ownership figures:
American Society for the
Prevention of Cruelty to Animals
www.aspca.org;

The Humane Society of the
United States
www.humanesociety.org;

The American Pet
Product Association
www.americanpetproducts.org

Power

104–105 Countries and Flags
Population figures:
PRB Datafinder,
Population Reference Bureau
www.prb.org

116–117 International Alliances
Organizations information:
North Atlantic Treaty
Organization
www.nato.int;

Organization for
Economic Development
www.oecd.org;

Organization of
American States
www.oas.org;
Association of Southeast

Asian Nations
www.aseansec.org;

Organisation of the Islamic
Conference
www.oic-oci.org;

African Union
www.africa-union.org;

League of Arab States
www.arableagueonline.org;

Organization of Petroleum
Exporting Countries
www.opec.org;

Gulf Cooperation Council
www.gcc-sg.org/eng

118–119 European Union
EU Parliment:
The European Parliament
www.europa.eu

Money matters: The 2008
EU budget Financial Report
www.europa.eu

120–121 United Nations
Information from:
The United Nations
www.un.org

122–123 War and Terrorism
Definition of conflicts
and other information:
Uppsala Conflict Data Program
www.pcr.uu.se

124–125 Explosive Budgets
SIPRI Yearbook. Armaments,
Disarmament and International
Security. (SIPRI, 2009)

126–127 Far From Home
Refugees and asylum seeker
numbers: UNHCR. Refugees,
Asylum-seekers, Returnees,
Internally Displaced and
Stateless Persons
(United Nations, 2008)

128–129 Human Rights
Child labor: Child labour
www.childinfo.org

Press freedom: Press Freedom
In the World 2009
www.freedomhouse.org

Freedom of religion:
Global Restrictions on Religion
www.pewforum.org

130–131 Crime
Crime and police figures:
The Tenth United Nations Survey
of Crime Trends and Operations
of Criminal Justice Systems
(United Nations, 2006)

132–133 Punishment
Under lock and key and Prison
population rate: Walmsley, R.,
World Prison Population List
(Kings College London, 2008)

134–135 Surveillance
Smart cards: Prime Numbers:
The Plastic Revolution
www.foreignpolicy.com

136–137 Big Business
Powerhouses: List of the top
100 multinational corporations
www.money.cnn.com;

Wal-mart
www.walmartstores.com

Biggest employers:
Biggest employers
www.money.cnn.com

Investment in developing
countries figures: Miroux, et al.,
World Investment Report 2008.

Transnational Corporations and
the Infrastructure Challenge
(United Nations, 2008)

138–139 Making Money
Global currencies:
Currency in Circulation
www.dollardaze.org

Who's has the gold?: Who Owns
Most of the World's Gold?
www.goldworld.com

140–141 Wealth of Nations
Figures from: World Economic
Outlook Database: 2008
International Monetary Fund
www.imf.org

142–143 Inequality
Less than $1.25 a day:
Population living on less
than $1.25 a day
www.unicef.org

Haves and have-nots: The World
Distribution of Household
Wealth. World Institute for
Development Economics
Research of the United

Nations University
www.wider.unu.edu

Who wants to be a billionaire?:
Billionaires by country of origin.
www.forbes.com

World's richest people:
Forbes Billionaire list 2009
www.forbes.com

Wealth within countries: *World
Development Indicators 2007*
www.web.worldbank.org

144–145 Balancing the Books
A helping hand: *UNDP Human
Development Report 2007-2008*
(Palgrave Macmillan, 2007)

Indebted countries: *Total debt
service as a percent of export
earnings: Economics, Business
and the Environment
database*, Earthtrends
www.wri.org

Aid as a percentage of income:
*Aid as a percent of GNI:
Economics, Business and the
Environment database*,
Earthtrends
www.wri.org

Top recipients:
Top Ten Recipients of Gross ODA
www.oecd.org

Industry

150–151 World Market
Imported commodities and
Balancing the scales:
*International Trade Centre
statistics*
www.trademap.org

Balance of trade figures:
Trading Economics
www.tradingeconomics.com/

Raw materials and finished
goods *Nigerian National
Petroleum Corporation 2008
ASB 1st Edition Web*
www.nnpcgroup.com/

152–153 Japanomics
GDP and Economy figures:
CIA World Factbook
www.cia.gov

154–155 Energy Resources
Different sources: International
Energy Agency. *Key World
Energy Statistics* (OECD, 2009)

Energy use by sector:
*International Energy
Agency data services*
www.iea.org

Per capita energy consumption:
International Energy Agency.
Key World Energy Statistics.
(OECD, 2009)

Increase in energy consumption:
*International Energy
Outlook 2009*
www.eia.doe.gov

How long will supplies last?:
BP: *World oil and gas reserves
still growing at healthy pace*
www.energybulletin.net;

Supply of Uranium
www.world-nuclear.org;

*International Energy
Outlook 2009*
www.eia.doe.gov

156–157 Fossil Fuels
Oil, gas, and coal reserves
figures:
*International Energy
Outlook 2009*
www.eia.doe.gov

Coal consumption:
*British Petroleum Statistical
Review of World Energy*
(BP, 2009)

158–159 Renewable Energy
Power for the people:
International Energy Agency.
World Energy Outlook.
(OECD, 2004)

160–161 Nuclear Energy
Energy equivalents:
Mitchell, M., *A prospector's
guide to uranium deposits in
Newfoundland and Labrador*
(Prospectors Resource
Room, 2007)

Hazardous waste:
*Waste Management
in the Nuclear Fuel Cycle*
www.world-nuclear.org

Relying on nuclear power:
Nuclear share of generation
www.world-nuclear.org

Clean and green: *Risks and
Benefits of Nuclear Energy*
(OECD, 2007)

168–169 Forestry
Figures from:
*Global Forest Resources
Assessment* (FAO, 2005)

170–171 Farming
Rice and wheat figures:
FAOSTAT: Food and Agricultural
commodities production, Food
and Agriculture Organization
www.fao.org

Key crops: Williams, et al.,
World Agricultural Production
(USDA, 2009)

Livestock populations:
FAOSTAT: *Selected Indicators
of Food and Agriculture
Development*, Food and
Agriculture Organization
www.fao.org

Organic farming:
Willer, et al., *The World of
Organic Agriculture. Statistics
and Emerging Trends.* FiBL-
IFOAM Report (ITC, 2009)

172–173 Cocoa and chocolate
Cocoa consumption:
*Cocoa: actual and projected
consumption* www.fao.org

Who profits?:
*All children have the
right to nutritious food*
www.unicef.org.uk/teacherzone

Cocoa production information:
FAOSTAT: Major Food and
Agricultural Commodities
and Producers, Food and
Agriculture Organization
www.fao.org

174–175 Fishy business
Fish production:
*World Fisheries production,
by capture and country*
www.fao.org

Fish species: *The State of
World Fisheries and
Aquaculture* (FAO, 2009)

176–177 Mining
Metal ore, precious metals,
and gem figures: Brown, T. J. et
al., *World Mineral Production
2003–07* (British Geological
Survey, 2009)

178–179 Diamonds
Diamond production figures:
Brown, T. J. et al., *World Mineral
Production 2003–07* (British
Geological Survey, 2009)

180–181 Making the Modern World
The leaders of tomorrow:
*Manufacturng output as a
percent of world manufacturing
output* www.bls.gov

A cast of millions:
Employment in manufacturing
www.bls.gov

Auto increase:
2008 production statistics
www.oica.net

Toy exports: *Top 20 Exporter
Activity Statistics*
www.exportbureau.com

182–183 Robots
Robot density:
*Top 10 Countries
by Robot Density*
www.asia.cnet.com

Robots by industry and service
figures: *World Robotics 2009*
www.ifr.org

186–187 Shop 'til you drop
Big spenders:
World Federation of Direct
Selling Associations
www.wfdsa.org

The world's biggest
shopping malls:
The World's Largest Malls
www.forbes.com

Biggest retailers:
*Global Powers
of Retailing*
www.deloitte.com
Shopping online:
Trends in online shopping
www.nielsen.com

188–189 Advertising
Global advertising budget
figures: *Global advertising*

expenditure by medium
www.zenithoptimedia.com

Most advertised figures:
Advertising Age
www.adage.com

190–191 Human Impact
Oil spills:
Case histories.
The International
Tanker Owners
Pollution Federation
www.itopf.com

Sulphur dioxide and carbon
emissions figures:
*Sulfur dioxide emissions.
Energy and Resources
database*, Earthtrends
www.wri.org

Waste per capita:
*Municipal waste generation
per capita* (OECD, 2009)

Connections

196–197 On the Move
Car ownership:
Brown, S. et al., *Economist
Pocket World in Figures*
(Profile Books Ltd, 2009)

Emissions from transportation:
*World Greenhouse Gas
Emissions. Energy and
Resources database*,
Earthtrends
www.wri.org

Distance travelled by rail:
*Economist Pocket World in
Figures* (Profile Books Ltd,
2009)

198–199 Up and Away!
Aircraft sizes and speeds figures:
Aircraft Data
www.airliners.net;

Commercial Airplanes
www.boeing.com;
Aircraft families
www.airbus.com

Priciest planes:
www.forbes.com

Busiest routes by
passenger numbers:

Why the plane in Spain
continues to reign
www.oag.com

Busiest airports by
passenger numbers:
*The ACI World Airport
Traffic Report 2008*
www.aci.aero

200–201 Shipping and Ports
Busiest ports:
Port of Rotterdam Authority.
Port Statistics. Rotterdam
(Port of Rotterdam
Authority, 2009)

202–203 Tourism
Top destinations:
*World's Top 10 Tourism
Destinations, 2007*
www.unwto.org

On the rise:
*International tourism,
expenditures (current US$)*,
World Development Indicators
Database
www.web.worldbank.org

The biggest earners:
*World's Top 10 Tourism
Earners 2007*, World
Tourism Organization
www.unwto.org

Travel bug:
*International tourism,
receipts (current US$)*,
World Development I
ndicators Database
www.web.worldbank.org

204–205 In the Mail
Mail figures:
The Universal Postal Union
www.upu.int

206–207 Internet
Online access:
World Internet Users
www.internetworldstats.com

Internet speed: *The 2008 ITIF
Broadband Rankings*
www.itif.org

208–209 Online Crime
Confidence tricks
and Online fraud:
the culprits: *Internet
Crime Complaint Center*
www.consumerfraudreporting.org

Who sends the spam?:
*McAfee Threats Report: Second
Quarter 2009*
www.mcafee.com

210–211 Sports Watch
Worldwide TV viewing figures:
Alavy, K., Mison, S. & Salazar,
V., *Viewer Track. The most
watched TV sporting events
of 2008*
(Futures sport +
entertainment, 2009)

Show me the money!:
The World's Highest-Paid Athletes
www.forbes.com

212–213 Movie Magic
Production costs per movie:
Bollywood vs. Hollywood
www.mpaa.com;

*Outlook for the Chinese
Film Industry*
www.midlinc.net

Movies produced:
*Number of feature
films produced*
www.data.un.org

Marketing costs per movie:
*Entertainment Industry Market
Statistics 2007*
www.mpaa.com;

Bollywood vs. Hollywood
www.mpaa.com

Top moviegoing nations:
Brown, S. et al., *Economist
Pocket World in Figures*
(Profile Books Ltd, 2009)

214–215 Media
Biggest media organizations:
Global 500 by sector
www.ft.com

Magazines:
National Geographic
www.ngm.nationalgeographic.
com;

TIME
www.timemediakit.com;
Newsweek
www.magazine.org;

U.S. News & World Report
www.magazine.org;

The Economist
www.economist-circulation.com;

India Today
www.indiatodaygroup.com;

Veja
www.publicidade.abril.com.br;

New Yorker
www.magazine.org;

Der Spiegel
www.media.spiegel.de

Online:
Largest Online News
Websites Globally
www.techcrunchies.com

Television:
CNN25
www.edition.cnn.com;

BBC Press Office
www.bbc.co.uk/pressoffice;

*al-Jazeera Reaches
100m English-Speaking Homes*
www.warc.com

218–219 Satellites
Launch cost figures:
*Big Growth in World Satellite
Market Over The Next Ten Years*
www.spacemart.com

220–221 International
Space Station
Space station, NASA
www.nasa.gov

226–227 Our World
in the Future
Largest economies in 2050:
Hawksworth, J,. Cookson, G.
The World in 2050.
(PricewaterhouseCoopers
LLP, 2008)

Largest populations in 2050:
PRB Datafinder,
Population Reference Bureau
www.prb.org

Acknowledgments

DK would like to thank:
Additional designers: Spencer Holbrook, Johnny Pau, Owen Peyton Jones, Smiljka Surla, and Jacqui Swan.
Additonal editors: Carron Brown and Caitlin Doyle.
Additional writing: Philip Steele.
Proofreading and Americanization: Caitlin Doyle.
Indexer: Jackie Brind.

Happiness data p96: copyright © 2010 Gallup, Inc.
Viewing figures p210: thanks to futures sport + entertainment.

The publisher would like to thank the following for their kind permission to reproduce their photographs:

Key: a-above; b-below/bottom; c-center; f-far; l-left; r-right; t-top

21 Corbis: Arctic-Images (tr); Roger Ressmeyer (cra); Jim Sugar (crb); Tony Waltham / Robert Harding World Imagery (br). Getty Images: Arlan Naeg / AFP (cr/ Mount Pinatubo). Photolibrary: Dani / Jeske N/A (cr/Krakatau). **27** Corbis: (cra) (br); Hervé Collart (crb); Ilya Naymushin / Reuters (tr); Wen Zhenxiao / XinHua / Xinhua Press (cr). **28** Corbis: Stuart Westmorland / Science Faction (bl). FLPA: Norbert Wu / Minden Pictures (br). **29** Corbis: Bettmann (br). Science Photo Library: Dr Ken Macdonald (bl). **38** iStockphoto.com: Laurence Dean (cra) (cr) (crb); Paul Pantazescu (tr); Clee Villasor (br). **39** iStockphoto.com: Laurence Dean (tl); Cihan Demirok (r); fajean (fbr); Jamie Farrant (bc); grimgram (tc); Paul Pantazescu (br); penfold (c); Yevgeniy Il\'yin (cb). **40** iStockphoto.com: Oscar Fernandez Chuyn (crb); Josef Prchal (cr) (cb); Panagiota Vorgia (br). **40-41** iStockphoto.com: Mark Stay (t). **41** iStockphoto.com: David Crooks (br/bee); cyfrogclone (bl); Jim Snyder (cl); Michael Travers (br/fly); Yevgeniy Il\'yin (br/ant). **42** Getty Images: AFP (br). iStockphoto. com: Laurent Renault (tl). **43** Alamy Images: blickwinkel (tl). Corbis: Alberto Aparicio/Xinhua Press (bc); Keren Su (bl).

iStockphoto.com: Tanveer Ali (clb); alle12 (cla); Ivan Bajic (cb); Ermin Gutenberger (cra); Jun Yan Loke (tr); Carlos Santa Maria (crb); John Woodworth (tc). NHPA / Photoshot: Joe Blossom (br). **44** iStockphoto. com: creatingmore (r). **57** Corbis: Jean Pierre Fizet / Sygma (tc). **62** iStockphoto. com: Gürsel Devrim Çelik (br/footprints); Igor Djurovic (cr); fckuen (tl); Dave Stevens (c/house & factory). **63** iStockphoto.com: breckeni (br/microchips); julichka (bc/ paper); Leontura (tr); Spauln (br/gun). **64** iStockphoto.com: song_mi (bl). **66** iStockphoto.com: Stephen Dumayne (tc); Julien Grondin (b); Alison Hess (c) (bc); sorbetto (cb). **67** iStockphoto.com: Roman Dekan (bc); Paul Fleet (fbl); grimgram (fcla); Alison Hess (c); Giovanni Meroni (fbr); Mark Stay (cl); Hogne Botnen Totland (cla). **68** iStockphoto.com: (fbr); Dmitriy Osminskiy (br); Edyta Pawłowska (c); Stockphoto4u (cr); Kristina Velickovic (bc). **69** Corbis: E.M.Pasieka / Science Photo Library (bc). **80** Alamy Images: JTB Photo Communications, Inc. (br). Getty Images: Paul Beinssen (bl); Richard Nowitz (bc). **81** Corbis: Herbert Spichtinger (bl). Getty Images: Martin Gray (br); Nabeel Turner (bc). **86** iStockphoto.com: song_mi (bl). **91** iStockphoto.com: Brendon De Suza (br); Kathy Konkle (cra). **93** iStockphoto.com: bubaone (ca); Qizhi He (cla); Paul Pantazescu (tr). **98** Corbis: DLILLC (cra); Pat Doyle (cl); Martin Harvey (fcra) (cr/rabbit); Jakob Helbig / cultura (c); Mark Mawson / Robert Harding World Imagery (ca); Hans Reinhard (cla). **99** Getty Images: John W Banagan (c). **110** iStockphoto.com: James Steidl (br). **114-115** iStockphoto.com: Illustrious (b). **116** NATO: (tl). OAS: (bl). OECD: (l). **117** OPEC: (clb). **118** iStockphoto.com: Brandon Laufenberg (tr). **119** iStockphoto. com: Brandon Laufenberg (tl). **120** UN/DPI Photo: (cla). **121** UN/DPI Photo: (br). USPS: (tr). **122** iStockphoto.com: creatingmore (cl); Karlkotas Inc (cla); Karl Kotas (clb). **125** iStockphoto.com: 4x6 (cr); apatrimonio (tr). **134** iStockphoto.com: Marc Brown (cla) (br) (c); Sander Kamp (tr); Frank Ramspott (ca). **135** iStockphoto.com: Marc Brown (tl); bubaone (bl); David Foreman (cr). **138** iStockphoto.com: Er Ten Hong (cla);

-Mosquito- (ca). **138-139** iStockphoto.com: imgendesign (banks / wallet). **139** Getty Images: Thomas Northcut (tr). iStockphoto. com: Er Ten Hong (ca/bank note); -Mosquito- (br) (ca/cakes); roccomontoya (br/ wheelbarrow). **143** Corbis: Peter Turnley (tr). **151** The Fairtrade Foundation: (crb/ logo). **155** iStockphoto.com: Peter Garbet (br); Nicky Laatz (t/lightbulbs); pialhovik (bl); Russell Tate (c). **156** iStockphoto. com: andres (tr/flames); Goce Risteski (tr/ oil rigs). **157** iStockphoto.com: (tr/power stations); Pavel Khorenyan (tl/oil rig). **160** iStockphoto.com: Todd Harrison (bc/ oil) (bc); Aleksandr Volodin (br). **166** Getty Images: gulfimages (tr). **166-167** iStockphoto.com: Teun van den Dries (b). **167** Getty Images: (tr). **174** Alamy Images: Markus Redmann / imagebroker (c). **175** Corbis: Bloomimage (br); Image Source (cra). **178** Corbis: Reuters (tl); Tugela Ridley/epa (cl). Getty Images: Richard du Toit (bl). **178-179** Science Photo Library: Christophe Vander Eecken / Reporters (b). **182** Corbis: James Leynse (bc); Julian Martin/epa (bl). **183** iStockphoto. com: AtomA (br). **190** iStockphoto.com: Christopher Hudson (bl). **191** iStockphoto. com: Giovanni Banfi (tr); Philip Barker (cr); Bob Vidler (br). **202** iStockphoto.com: Albert Campbell (bc) (cl) (clb) (crb). **203** iStockphoto.com: renatorena (tl); Jeffrey Thompson (cb). **206** iStockphoto.com: _zak (tr). **207** iStockphoto.com: Dave Hopkins (bc); _zak (tr). **208** Science Photo Library: Laguna Design (br). **210** iStockphoto.com: Nicolas Hansen (fbl) (bc) (bl) (br) (fbr). **212** iStockphoto.com: addan (clb); Petr Stepanov (cl). **213** iStockphoto.com: Petr Stepanov (b); _zak (tc). **218** iStockphoto. com: rdiraimo (cb). **220** Science Photo Library: Friedrich Saurer (tl). **221** Corbis: NASA/Reuters (tr). NASA: (tl) (ftl). Science Photo Library: NASA (ftr)

All other images © Dorling Kindersley
For further information see:
www.dkimages.com